D0398475

Building a Winning Sales Force

Powerful Strategies for Driving High Performance

Andris A. Zoltners
Prabhakant Sinha
Sally E. Lorimer

AMACOM

American Management Association

NEW YORK ▲ ATLANTA ▲ BRUSSELS ▲ CHICAGO ▲ MEXICO CITY ▲

SAN FRANCISCO ▲ SHANGHAI ▲ TOKYO ▲ TORONTO ▲ WASHINGTON, D.C.

Special discounts on bulk quantities of AMACOM books are available to corporations, professional associations, and other organizations. For details, contact Special Sales Department, AMACOM, a division of American Management Association, 1601 Broadway, New York, NY 10019.
Tel.: 212-903-8316. Fax: 212-903-8083.
Web site: www.amacombooks.org

This publication is designed to provide accurate and authoritative information in regard to the subject matter covered. It is sold with the understanding that the publisher is not engaged in rendering legal, accounting, or other professional service. If legal advice or other expert assistance is required, the services of a competent professional person should be sought.

Library of Congress Cataloging-in-Publication Data

Zoltners, Andris A.
  Building a winning sales force : powerful strategies for driving high performance / Andris A. Zoltners, Prabhakant Sinha, Sally E. Lorimer.
     p. cm.
  Includes index.
  ISBN-13: 978-0-8144-1040-0
  ISBN-10: 0-8144-1040-5
  1. Sales management. 2. Sales personnel. I. Sinha, Prabhakant. II. Lorimer, Sally E. III. Title.

  HF5438.4.Z648 2009
  658.8'102—dc22
                                                                2008049520

Printing number

10 9 8 7 6 5 4 3 2 1

Contents

Preface

The sales function is front and center in the challenge to meet or exceed business growth objectives. Sales force effectiveness is a critical success factor, as sales leaders are challenged to respond to events within their companies, their markets, and their environment, while at the same time, striving to continuously improve sales force performance.

We wrote *Building a Winning Sales Force: Powerful Strategies for Driving High Performance* to provide current and aspiring sales leaders with innovative yet practical strategies for dealing with their most critical and frequently faced sales force challenges and opportunities. The book lays out an actionable and relevant blueprint for building and sustaining sales force success in any business environment. It is designed to help you assess how good your sales organization really is, identify current and future sales force improvement opportunities that have large bottom-line impact, and implement tools and processes that immediately enhance sales effectiveness. Drawing on our experience consulting with companies all over the world, we strive to make complex and elusive concepts easy to understand and to provide ideas that can be implemented right away to address challenges and opportunities such as:

- Creating a winning sales organization by aligning the sales system around company goals and strategies to drive results.
- Developing sales strategies that demonstrate value to customers and create competitive advantage.

- Sizing, structuring, and aligning the sales organization to effectively and efficiently realize market opportunity and drive long-term success.

- Attracting and retaining talented salespeople by developing world-class recruiting processes and building a sales culture that nurtures learning and development.

- Arming salespeople with the tools and information they need to meet customer needs and achieve company sales goals.

- Developing sales compensation programs that motivate high levels of sales effort.

- Setting territory-level goals that are fair, realistic, and motivational and managing sales force performance so that goals are consistently achieved.

- Preventing sales force complacency – a silent killer of sales effectiveness.

- Implementing sales strategy changes as markets and company strategies evolve.

- Ensuring that sales resources are deployed to the right customers, products, and selling activities.

- Integrating sales and marketing strategies to create a successful customer-facing organization.

- Using analytic tools and structured processes to constantly identify sales force improvement opportunities and enhance sales effectiveness.

Kash Rangan, our colleague and friend at the Harvard Business School, sums up the book's contribution when he writes:

This terrific book achieves the rare feat of providing robust frameworks for addressing the most important problems facing the sales forces of today. It has rigor and relevance rolled into one. The book brings a masterful combination of highly practical insights gained from hundreds of industry applications with the sophistication of decades of academic thinking and writing. It lays out the blueprint for achieving excellence, presents lucid frameworks for tackling the core issues of how to size and structure a sales force, provides deep insights on how to manage the human side (sales force recruiting, motivating, and compensating), and provides advice on how to mold the sales force organization into a dynamic customer-centric unit. Underpinning the key ideas is breakthrough thinking on some of the most difficult issues facing the $800 billion industry.

We have written several books before this one, including *The Complete Guide to Accelerating Sales Force Performance* (Amacom Books, 2001), *Sales Force Design for Strategic Advantage* (Palgrave / Macmillan, 2004), and *The Complete Guide to Sales Force Incentive Compensation: How to Design and Implement Plans that Work* (Amacom Books, 2006). These books have been mostly reference books. Bestselling author Neil Rackham shared with us: "They are the best sales management books out there, but they are a serious read." With *Building a Winning Sales Force: Powerful Strategies for Driving High Performance,* we aim to capture the attention of sales leaders, engaging them through an array of deep yet practical insights on what works when running a selling organization. Kash Rangan observes, "The book is organized into short, crisp chapters and concepts are illustrated clearly through stories and a broad range of examples." For readers who desire greater detail, our reference books are a complement to this book.

How the Book is Organized

Building a Winning Sales Force: Powerful Strategies for Driving High Performance includes twenty chapters organized into three major parts.

- Part 1 – A Blueprint for Sales Force Excellence – organizes the components and complexities of the Sales System into a framework that shows sales leaders how the decisions, processes, systems, and programs that they are accountable for (called the sales effectiveness drivers) influence salespeople, their activities, and ultimately customer and company results. By managing the sales effectiveness drivers well, sales leaders can build a high-quality sales force that engages in the right selling activities to meet customer needs and achieve company financial goals.

- Part 2 – Improving the Top Sales Effectiveness Drivers – presents strategic frameworks, case studies, and real-world analyses showing sales leaders how to get maximum impact from the top 12 sales effectiveness drivers — sales strategy, sales force sizing, sales force structure and roles, sales territory design, recruiting, learning and development, culture, the sales manager, leveraging information, compensation and incentives, territory-level goal setting, and performance management.

- Part 3 – Addressing Common and Challenging Sales Management Issues – helps sales leaders use the sales effectiveness drivers to create solutions for important sales force issues. The issues include those that we hear about frequently and consistently from sales leaders — preventing sales force complacency, changing the sales strategy, allocating sales resources profitably across customers, products, and selling activities, retaining successful salespeople, managing tensions between sales and marketing, and establishing successful programs for continuously enhancing sales effectiveness.

Readers who desire a complete look at how to build and sustain a winning sales force can read all the chapters sequentially. Other readers who are looking to solve a particular issue or concern can start by reading Part I. Then, they can jump directly to the chapters most relevant to their needs, guided by the diagnostic process suggested in Chapter 2.

Acknowledgments

This book is a collaborative effort between numerous individuals, including our university colleagues and students, our consulting clients, and the talented staff at ZS Associates.

We are grateful to Northwestern University's Kellogg School of Management for providing a fertile environment for ideas to flourish. Thousands of executives have participated in our Executive Education and MBA Programs at Kellogg and more recently, at the Indian School of Business. Our classroom interactions with these individuals have been invaluable for turning our theories and frameworks into practical sales force management tools. We would like to thank all our colleagues at Northwestern and elsewhere who have supported us academically and as friends.

As consultants, we have worked personally with executives, sales managers, and salespeople at over 400 companies all over the world. The clients of ZS Associates have helped us discover, develop, test, and refine many of the concepts described in the book. Because of confidentiality, many of the people and companies must remain anonymous, but we owe a great deal of gratitude to all those who have used their experience, creativity, judgment, and guidance to help us develop and enhance our ideas. Special contributions from ZS clients came from Jeff Foland (United Airlines), Jay Graf (Guidant), Chris Hartman (Boston Scientific Corporation), Quinton Oswald (Genentech), and Gregory Schofield (Novartis). In addition, we are grateful for the input of a first-class sales effectiveness team at GE led by Kevin Decker (GE Corporate) and including Trish Anderson (GE Commercial Finance Enterprise Client Group), Dean DeStazio (GE Healthcare Financial Services), Yvan Giroud (GE Trailer Fleet Services), Michael Pindell (GE Capital Solutions), and Aileen Sheppard (GE Trailer Fleet Services).

We would also like to thank the people of ZS Associates, the consulting firm that we founded in 1983. ZS Associates today has more than 1,000 employees with 17 offices in 9 countries. ZS employs some of the finest consultants and businesspeople in the world, and those people have contributed to the book immensely by contributing ideas and evaluating our frameworks based on their creativity and practical knowledge of what works in the real world. Special contributions came from the following people: Chad Albrecht, Angela Bakker-Lee, Julie Billingsley, Jason Brown, Sandra Forero, Shelley Gabel, Kevin Josephson, Pratap Khedkar, Mike Moorman, Marissa Paine Saluja, Stephen Redden, Ladd Ruddell, Braden Rudolph, Arun Shastri, Scott Shimamoto, Scott Sims, Nancy Smith, Marshall Solem, and Kelly Tousi.

We were very fortunate to have several research and editorial assistants working with us on this project. Mary Henske (ZS Associates) helped us gather information and reviewed every chapter for clarity and content, suggesting revisions based on her extensive business knowledge. Linda Kluver (ZS Associates) applied her careful attention to detail to review the entire manuscript for consistency and clarity and to develop the book's more than 175 illustrations. Ramya Balasubramanian, Sugandha Khandelwal, Pria Sinha, and Krupali Thapar were our outstanding research team. Through their dedication and creativity, they uncovered many of the examples used throughout the book. Greg Zoltners researched and developed content as a coauthor of one of our earlier books. Thank you to all of these fine collaborators who helped to improve the quality of this book substantially.

P A R T **1**

A Blueprint for Sales Force Excellence

CHAPTER 1

The Dimensions and Drivers of a Winning Sales Force

The sales force is a powerful driver of revenues, and because sales-people are entrusted with a company's most important asset—its relationship with its customers—they have a significant and often determining impact on an organization's success.

Cisco, Microsoft, IBM, and Oracle each have over 11,000 sales-people in the United States. Pfizer, Johnson & Johnson, and Glaxo-SmithKline each have more than 7,000. These seven companies spend a total of over $20 billion a year on their sales forces. The amount invested across all U.S. companies exceeds $800 billion, close to three times the amount of money spent on advertising. On average, companies invest about 10 percent of their annual revenues in their sales forces.

Because of the high cost of maintaining a sales force and because sales are directly linked to profitability, most companies take an active interest in maximizing sales force effectiveness, setting up initiatives with titles like "Sales Force Effectiveness Review—Winning for the Customer," "Global Sales Force Effectiveness Benchmarking," and "Sales Effectiveness and Growth Initiative." In many companies, a full-time employee with a title like "Director of Sales Effectiveness" manages a team responsible for improving the competence and productivity of the company's salespeople.

Practically every company can dramatically improve its sales revenues by implementing the right effectiveness initiatives. In our interactions with corporate sales leaders and executives, we often see revenue increases of at least 10 percent.

But discovering the best way to enhance the workings of the sales force is not easy. "Increasing sales force effectiveness" has different meanings for different stakeholders. A vice president of sales might see it as "providing value to the customer beyond the product itself by changing the sales process from transactional to consultative." A sales compensation analyst might view it as "increasing sales force morale and motivation through better incentive compensation programs." A sales training manager might see increased effectiveness as involving "increasing salesperson competency through innovative training programs." A finance manager might view it as "increasing sales per salesperson" or "holding sales force costs below a benchmark percentage of sales."

Individual sales leaders typically struggle to define what sales force effectiveness means for their companies, and to determine how to make improvements that will have a substantial positive bottom-line impact. With this book, we hope to make that struggle a little easier as we lay out—with in-depth discussion, real-world examples, and graphics—the basic principles of how to build a winning sales force.

The Sales System: Dimensions of a Winning Sales Force

At the beginning of the course we teach at Northwestern University's Kellogg School and other venues, called "Accelerating Sales Force Performance," we ask the sales leaders in attendance a simple question: "How do you know when you have a successful sales organization?" Their answers, both spontaneous and reflective, span a wide range of topics but generally fall into five dimensions of sales effectiveness.

The Five Dimensions of Sales Organization Success

Company Results The first responses are usually predictable and focus on company results. Examples include:

- Our sales, market share, and profitability targets are achieved.
- We are growing faster than our competition.
- Our sales are growing, and our costs are in line with industry averages.

Sales leaders are interested in results. After all, they are evaluated on and rewarded for goal achievement, and results are the most visible and objective indicator of success. Company results are the organization's financial outcomes, in which the efforts of the sales force play a major role. Such results can be measured using sales, profits, market share, return on investment, or some other metric, and they can be expressed as absolute levels, percentages of goal attainment, or growth over last year. It's useful to evaluate results from both short-term and long-term perspectives, because decisions involving the sales force affect both.

Customer Results Other responses revolve around customers. A successful sales organization has:

- Deep customer relationships and customer trust
- High customer retention and low defection
- A loyal customer base

Customer results affect company results, which is why companies frequently use customer satisfaction scores and customer retention rates or repeat sales to assess how customers view the sales organization. Customers will not buy from people they do not like.

Activities Sales leaders say that a successful sales organization allocates its time effectively and ensures that every activity is of high quality and delivers value. Their comments include statements like:

- Products that have strategic importance get appropriate attention.
- The sales force serves our best customers well.
- We participate in new business development, balancing hunting and farming.

- We spend a lot of time with customers and keep administrative work to a minimum.
- The quality of our activity is as important as the quantity.

Salespeople's activities are typically organized in a multistep process that includes steps such as lead generation, needs analysis, solution development, proposal presentation, negotiation, installation, customer service, and account maintenance and expansion. Sales force activities drive customer results.

Salespeople The fourth group of responses describing a successful sales organization focuses on the salespeople. Sales leaders say:

- Ultimately, it is our salespeople who make us successful.
- Our salespeople know our products, customers, and competitors really well.
- Our people have the right values, attitudes, and capabilities.
- They are constantly learning and developing new skills.
- They adapt as new selling processes emerge.
- The turnover of high performers is very low.

Successful sales organizations seek to employ competent, motivated salespeople and establish a "success" culture to lead them to demonstrate effective behaviors and engage in effective activities.

Sales Effectiveness Drivers The fifth group of responses focuses on the decisions, processes, systems, and programs that sales leaders are responsible for—the sales effectiveness drivers. People who take our course tell us that successful sales organizations must make the right decisions in areas such as:

- Sales strategy (market segmentation, value proposition, and selling process)
- Sales force size
- Sales force structure and roles

- Sales territory design
- Recruiting
- Learning and development
- Culture
- The sales management team
- Leveraging information (customer research and targeting; data, tools, and CRM)
- Compensation and incentives
- Goal setting and forecasting
- Performance management

There are many sales effectiveness drivers; which ones are most important depend on the sales force's situation. The 12 drivers listed here are the ones that sales leaders suggest to us most consistently. A chapter in this book is dedicated to each of these top 12 sales effectiveness drivers.

The Chain of Outcomes

The diverse responses of sales leaders have taught us that it's not easy to describe success in a system as complex as a sales organization. Doing so requires acknowledging all of the multiple components and how they are linked.

Figure 1-1 lays out the basic relationship of the five dimensions of sales organization success. At the "Results" end of the chart, sales force activities affect customer results, and customer results affect company results. That's the easy part to comprehend.

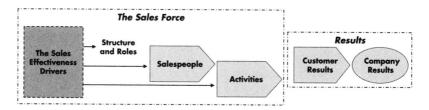

Figure 1-1. Relationships among the dimensions of sales organization success

Meanwhile, salespeople have complex sets of skills, capabilities, values, and motivations that influence their behavior and activities. The basic decisions, processes, systems, and programs that we call the sales effectiveness drivers are at the root of the entire system. Some of these drivers have a direct impact on salespeople's skills, capabilities, values, and motivations. Others affect what activities salespeople engage in, and still others define the sales force structure and roles.

The sales leadership team is responsible for managing all the sales effectiveness drivers as effectively as possible.

The Sales System and the Sales Effectiveness Drivers

Sales effectiveness drivers fall into five categories, each with a specific impact on the sales organization. *Definer* drivers set up the organizational structure and salesperson roles. *Shaper* drivers—hiring, training, and coaching practices—affect salespeople directly. *Enlightener, exciter,* and *controller* drivers affect the activities performed by the sales force. Figure 1-2 shows where each driver category comes into play in the overall Sales System.

Figure 1-3 lays out the impacts of the sales effectiveness drivers on the sales force and provides examples of drivers in each category.

Some sales effectiveness drivers appear in more than one category. For example, compensation and incentives shows up in three:

- It is a *shaper* because an effective compensation and incentive plan helps attract the right type of person to the sales job.

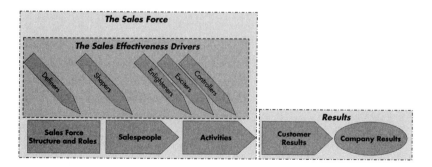

Figure 1-2. The Sales System

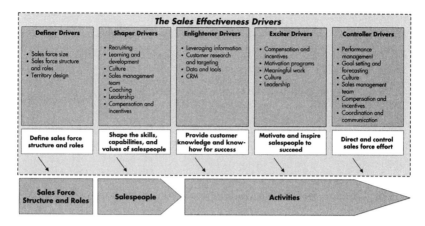

Figure 1-3. The five categories of sales effectiveness drivers and their impacts

- It is an *exciter* because the right compensation and incentive plan motivates salespeople to work hard to achieve challenging goals.
- It is a *controller* because by aligning incentives with the right products or customers, the company communicates to salespeople what it wants them to do.

The reality is that most drivers—defined in the section that follows, with examples—have influence across multiple categories. For simplicity, the figure shows them only in those categories in which they have the most significant impact.

Definers: A Successful Sales Organization Has Clearly Defined Sales Roles, Giving Salespeople a Straight Line of Vision *Definer* decisions define the sales job by clarifying roles and territories. Does the sales force need to increase in scale in order to go after additional markets or give more time to new products? Will specialization increase its effectiveness with important, large customers? Should it be redeployed to reflect changing marketplace demographics? Successful definer decisions are consistent with and reinforce company marketing and sales strategies. Generally, making definer decisions before addressing the other four categories of sales effectiveness drivers helps ensure that the decisions you make concerning the other driver categories will be compatible with and reinforce the definer decisions.

Sun Microsystems Adjusts Sales Force Definers to Increase Customer Focus

---

Before 2006, large customers of Sun Microsystems dealt haphazardly with a dozen or more different Sun salespeople from seven different business units. To reduce customer frustration and confusion and improve profitability, Sun redefined its sales roles so that each major account was assigned to one main salesperson who understood the account's overall business needs and could coordinate the activities of product experts.

Shapers: A Successful Sales Organization Has Excellent Hiring, Training, and Coaching Programs That Are Aligned to Encourage the Right Values, Attitudes, and Capabilities in Its People Sales leaders hear it often enough: "People are our most important asset," or "In the twenty-first century, companies will win in the marketplace because they are winning the war for talent." If you believe these statements, as we do, then the *shaper* category of sales effectiveness drivers is critical, as these drivers influence the skills, capabilities, and values of the sales team.

Marriott Vacation Club Adjusts Sales Force Shapers to Improve Sales Force Talent and Become an Industry Leader

---

Leaders at Marriott Vacation Club (MVCI), a seller of time-share vacation ownerships, realized that if the company was to achieve its aggressive growth goals, it needed to improve its sales force hiring process. Sales leaders identified 125 of MVCI's top-performing salespeople and put them through intensive interviews and psychological testing to tease out the unique traits that led to their success. Among the traits identified were competitiveness, high levels of motivation, strong interpersonal skills, integrity, and a desire to constantly improve. MVCI added these traits to the recruiting profile and adopted a new selection process that screened candidates for them. The change helped a company that had been a small player in the vacation-ownership market become the industry leader.

Enlighteners: A Successful Sales Organization Has Good Information and Uses It Effectively to Help Salespeople Understand Customers and Be Successful How well do salespeople know their customers' buying processes, attitudes, and needs? How do salespeople decide who to spend time with and what to do for each prospect or customer? *Enlightener* drivers include processes and systems that provide salespeople with customer knowledge, enabling them to understand the marketplace, prioritize opportunities, solve customer problems, and use their time more effectively. Enlightener drivers often use information technology (IT) to capture knowledge and thus increase sales impact. The use of IT in sales is constantly evolving. The heavy, complex, and rigid systems that burdened rather than assisted sales forces in the past are giving way to lighter, nimbler, and more flexible solutions.

AlliedSignal Adjusts Sales Force Enlighteners to Improve Customer Focus

By the mid-1990s, the sales organization at airplane parts supplier AlliedSignal had become very large and complex. Because of the company's broad and technical product line, major customers had as many as 50 different contact points within the AlliedSignal sales force. Lack of coordination among salespeople who called on the same accounts frustrated customers, many of whom were turning to lower-cost suppliers. To improve the coordination of sales efforts, AlliedSignal developed a companywide customer relationship management (CRM) system that provided a single source of customer information for sales reps, field service engineers, product-line personnel, and response center agents across three business units. This system allowed quick access to customer information so that sales activities could be coordinated at the customer level more easily.

Exciters: A Successful Sales Organization Has Inspiring Sales Leaders and Motivating Incentive Programs That Encourage Salespeople to Work Hard and Achieve *Exciter* drivers inspire and motivate the sales force.

Courier Company Adjusts Sales Force Exciters to Improve Sales Force Retention and Grow Sales

A small local courier service was not achieving its aggressive sales growth goals. Salespeople earned a salary, and many of them were not motivated to work hard to grow their business. Those who were successful would demand raises as their business grew, threatening to jump ship to a competitor that paid on commission if their demands were not met. The company revised its pay plan, replacing salaries with a commission structure. Retention of the company's best performers improved, and sales grew 130 percent within a year.

Controllers: A Successful Sales Organization Has Effective Processes to Ensure that the Entire Sales System Stays on Course Every organization needs a control system. In addition to the firm's overall culture, such control is what ensures that salespeople, working largely unsupervised, continue to do what they are supposed to do over time. *Controller* drivers direct sales force activities and behavior, which, in turn, determine performance.

Rapid Coat Tightens Up Its Management System

Rapid Coat is a small manufacturer of powder chemistries used in place of conventional paint to create a hard finish on numerous household and industrial items, including steel furniture, fans, air conditioners, washing machines, and automobile parts. Founded in India in 1974, the company was focused largely on production and product quality. Its sales force had grown to 10 salespeople in an ad hoc manner over a 25-year period, with all salespeople reporting directly to the company's founder. The mandate was simple: "Go get orders." Orders came in and products were shipped, but collections lagged. Eventually, Rapid Coat was in dire straits, with a severe cash crunch. There had been inadequate control of the quality of orders, and insufficient attention had been paid to customers' ability to pay promptly. In 1999, as part of a revamping of its sales function, the company hired a professional sales manager and segmented its customers into three groups—small job coaters, medium-size coaters, and large original equipment manufacturers (OEMs) and multinational users. Segment-specific and sometimes customer-specific product, sales process, pricing, placement, and credit policies were implemented. An ISO 9001:2000 system was installed in 2001 to continually improve customer satisfaction and meet other quality objectives. The company put in place a performance management system for salespeople, along with a training and coaching program. Collections improved dramatically, and the company came out of the red and set forth on a healthy growth path. Between 2001 and 2006, the company grew to three times its former size.

A Successful Sales System Has Excellent Sales Effectiveness Drivers That Produce Results

Of course, customer and company results are not determined by the sales force alone. Environmental and company factors contribute as well. Figure 1-4 expands the Sales System to include these forces (see the top right corner). This figure elaborates on how a successful Sales System functions as it creates customer and company results.

The World of Sales

Understanding the effectiveness of your Sales System requires looking at your sales organization within the context of your overall company, industry, and business environment. To begin with, the Sales System is affected by forces and decisions that originate in other parts of the company and in the marketplace. These forces help shape company strategies, which in turn affect marketing and sales strategies and decisions regarding the sales force. At the same time, sales leaders are constantly hunting for opportunities to improve the effectiveness of their sales organizations. Together, these external and internal forces and decisions

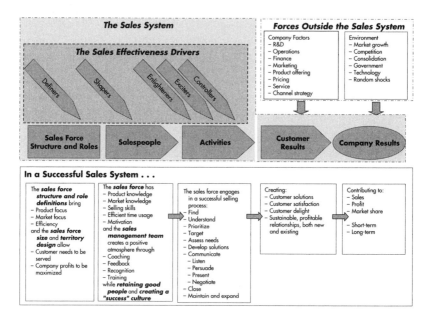

Figure 1-4. How a successful Sales System functions

influence customer and company results. Figure 1-5 provides a broad view of the Sales System and its relationship to these forces and decisions.

How Selling Partners Affect the World of Sales

Some companies have a sales force that includes two types of salespeople: those employed by the firm and external selling partners. Depending on the industry, a selling partner can be an agent, a broker, a distributor, a manufacturers' representative, an independent contractor, a wholesaler, a dealer, a value-added reseller, or another type of independent selling organization. Some selling partners sell a single company's products and services exclusively. Others also sell complementary or competitive products from different manufacturers, making the dynamics of the company's World of Sales more complex. Partner sales organizations make sales effectiveness driver decisions that enhance the performance of their entire product and service portfolio. Companies that want to influence those decisions and affect the way in which their partners use sales time and other assets to support their

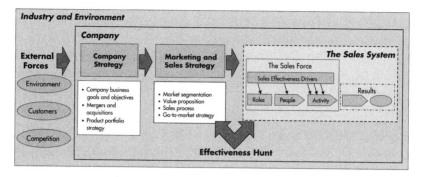

Figure 1-5. The World of Sales

products and services can use partner incentive programs, marketing pro-grams, partner managers, sales process assistance, sales analytics, and end-user pull-through as levers if not to control, at least to influence how selling partners operate.

The Forces Behind the Sales System

Forces and decisions within your World of Sales will influence your Sales System. *External forces* include customers, competitors, and the environment. External events create both opportunities and threats. Opportunities can arise, for example, when new customer segments emerge, competitors go out of business, helpful technologies appear, or a booming economy creates new possibilities. On the other hand, com-panies can be threatened when sales strategies become dated as cus-tomers change their buying processes, competitors attack profitable market segments, or an economic downturn reduces customer demand.

Adapting to a Changing World

- Beginning in the early 1990s, retail giants like Wal-Mart and Target began to dominate the industry, forcing many smaller, independent retailers out of business. Consumer products firms, like Procter & Gamble, that sold to these retailers restructured their sales organiza-tions around the new and evolving needs of national and large regional chains. Sales forces that had formerly been organized by product category were reorganized into vertical selling teams focused on the needs of a single major customer.

- In 2002, several of AT&T's competitors—including Global Crossing, Qwest, and WorldCom—were either facing bankruptcy or dealing with financial scandals. AT&T took advantage of its prime position in the industry to steal market share from these struggling companies. AT&T hired more than 600 salespeople from other telecom companies and asked them to talk to every customer of the distressed companies about AT&T's reliability, financial stability, and professionalism.

- When the U.S. economy began to weaken in 2001 after a 10-year boom, the phones stopped ringing at Laird Plastics, a distributor to businesses. After years of reactive selling, the company's sales force took a much more proactive approach, including cold calling on customers, creating new applications for the company's products, asking for orders, and offering better deals.

Company strategy also affects the Sales System. Company strategies include setting corporate business goals and objectives, launching new products, redesigning and relaunching existing products, entering new markets, and merging with or acquiring other companies.

Marketing and sales strategies also influence your Sales System. These strategies define whom the company sells to, what the customer offering is, and how the selling is to be done. Sales and marketing teams are primarily accountable for these decisions, developing and continually fine-tuning them through market segmentation, product and service offerings and value propositions, sales process design, and go-to-market strategy development.

Adapting to Company, Marketing, and Sales Strategy Change

- In 2000, records management firm Iron Mountain launched a new document-shredding service to augment its traditional services of corporate records storage and off-site data protection. The traditional services required a consultative, long-term sales approach; the new service required a transactional, high-volume approach that was incompatible with the skills of the existing salespeople. The company created a new, separate sales force and hired candidates with the right skills from outside the company.

- During the late 1990s, United Parcel Service had a strategic objective of penetrating the rapidly growing dot-com business segment. The company established a dedicated e-commerce sales force of about 140 people.

- Iowa-based Brenton Banks wanted to encourage cross-selling of products and services across its banking and brokerage divisions. The divisions were restructured so that bankers and brokers no longer operated in "silos," but instead shared a single income goal. All bankers and brokers were trained to sell the full product offering, the incentive plan was restructured so that everyone could receive commissions for all products, and bankers and brokers began meeting twice weekly to share leads and plan joint sales calls.

- Medical equipment maker SonoSite had been using a national medical products distributor to sell its new handheld ultrasound device in the United States. Disappointed with its sales results, the company dropped the distributor and hired its own salespeople so that it had more control over the amount and quality of the selling effort.

There's an additional force originating within the company that affects the Sales System: the *effectiveness hunt*. The best sales organizations use it for constant performance improvement. Many familiar performance challenges—high turnover of top salespeople, slow sales growth, the need to develop more new accounts, a sales force that is complacent—if left unaddressed, can escalate into bigger problems. In addition, opportunities to become more effective may arise—for example, newly discovered sources of customer value may be incorporated into the sales process, or sales leaders may learn that upgrading sales force quality has a substantial positive impact on performance. Companies that are always on the hunt for effectiveness will respond to these challenges and take advantage of these opportunities.

How the Effectiveness Hunt Helps Sales Forces

- When a newspaper company surveyed its advertising sales force to find out how its salespeople were spending their time, it learned that only one-third of the sales force's time was spent selling. Much more time was spent servicing existing accounts and performing administrative tasks—activities that did not require the skills of an expensive salesperson. The company hired lower-paid sales assistants to take over many of these activities, and efficiency improved dramatically.

- Too many new salespeople were leaving a direct-marketing company within their first six months. Through exit interviews, the company learned that a lack of training and attention from first-line district sales managers was the leading cause. The company invested in programs to train and develop its managers; it also changed the managers' compensation plan, tying more incentive money to metrics reflecting managerial responsibilities, such as goal achievement by new employees.

What Is on the Minds of Sales Leaders?

At the start of our "Accelerating Sales Force Performance" executive education programs, in addition to asking sales leaders how they know when they have a successful sales organization, we also pose an open-ended question: "What sales productivity issues are you currently faced with?" While our primary goal in asking this question is to tailor the course content to student needs, the information we've gathered over the past 10 years is useful for illustrating and understanding the Sales System and the World of Sales from a sales leadership viewpoint. Based on responses from more than 700 sales and marketing executives—representing 400 different companies in more than 20 countries, from a wide range of industries, and with varying sales force sizes—we have developed an inventory of more than 2,000 sales force productivity issues.

The issues that sales leaders face originate in every part of the World of Sales and the Sales System. Figure 1-6 shows the percentage of responders who mentioned issues related to each section of the World of Sales and provides examples of their responses. Since most of the

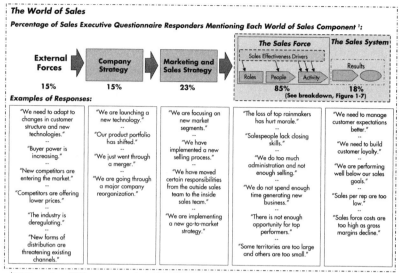

Figure 1-6. Sales executives' responses and the World of Sales

executives who attend our courses have primary accountability for the Sales System, the majority of the responses fall within that area. These responses are further broken down in Figures 1-7 and 1-8.

Diagnosing and Addressing Sales Force Issues and Concerns

By organizing the components and linkages that exist within sales organizations, our Sales System and World of Sales concepts help sales leaders successfully diagnose problems, recognize opportunities, and adapt their sales forces as needed. The Sales System chain of outcomes shown in Figure 1-1 highlights two useful observations about sales force effectiveness. First, sales force effectiveness issues, challenges, and concerns will always lie in one of the five dimensions of sales organization success. For example:

- Company results: "We are not making our goal."
- Customer results: "Customers are not happy with the service they are getting."

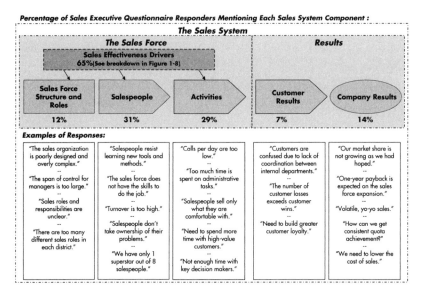

Figure 1-7. Sales executives' responses and the Sales System

		% of Responders[1]	Example Response
Definers	Sales Force Structure and Roles	12%	"Should we have product specialists?" "We have changed our structure 5 times in 2 years."
	Sales Force Size	8%	"I suspect our team is not large enough." "We need to reduce headcount."
	Territory Design	8%	"Large differences in territory potential create unfairness."
Shapers	Recruiting	5%	"How to recruit top sales talent." "Ensuring that we hire the 'right' person."
	Learning and Development	6%	"How to train the sales force over time." "Need better training for sales managers."
	Culture	3%	"Blending two cultures after a merger." "How to create a success culture."
Enlighteners	Customer Research/Targeting	9%	"Better target certain customer segments." "Need to improve ability to qualify leads."
	Data, Tools, and CRM	14%	"Need better information on competitor's offers." "Informational gaps due to IT problems."
Exciters	Sales Management Team and Leadership	5%	"Inexperienced first-level sales management." "Company leaders need to reinforce sales force focus."
	Compensation and Incentives/ Motivation Programs	18%	"The comp plan doesn't reflect our business priorities." "Not enough opportunities for top performers."
	Meaningful Work	2%	"Sales force turnover is high because salespeople face considerable customer rejection."
Controllers	Performance Management and Measurement	13%	"How to fix underperformers." "Can't measure sales performance accurately."
	Goal Setting and Forecasting	6%	"Low morale due to targets that are too high." "Hard to forecast sales of new products."
	Coordination and Communication	5%	"Poor sales and marketing coordination." "Need to improve communication with technical staff."

[1] 65% of responders mentioned at least one sales effectiveness driver. Many responders provided multiple driver responses.

Figure 1-8. Sales executives' responses and the sales effectiveness drivers

- Activities: "Our sales force is spending too much time on administrative tasks and not enough developing new accounts."
- Salespeople: "Our senior people are too complacent."
- Sales effectiveness drivers: "We need to restructure because of a selling process change."

Frequently, sales leaders have a good sense of their major concerns, but because the Sales System is complex, they can easily overlook important considerations. To conduct a comprehensive assessment of sales effectiveness in your organization, use our Sales System framework to ask yourself questions that focus on the five dimensions of sales organization success. For example:

- Are our goals being achieved across product lines? (Company results)
- Are our customers' needs being met? (Customer results)
- Are our salespeople engaged in the right activities? (Activities)
- How good are our salespeople? (Salespeople)
- Are we implementing best practices with each of the sales effectiveness drivers? (Sales effectiveness drivers)

The second useful observation is that true effectiveness stems from the sales effectiveness drivers that are at the root of the Sales System. Excellence in the drivers creates strong salespeople, encourages quality sales activity, and generates strong results.

When a division president asked a sales leader, "How good is the sales force?" the leader replied, "It is excellent." When asked "Why?" the leader replied, "Because the sales force has achieved its goal seven years in a row." But goal achievement is only a partial indicator of how good a sales force is. Another sales executive who worked in an industry that was becoming increasingly competitive told us, "Last year, the fish were jumping into our boat; this year, we have to learn how to fish." When the going is good, even a mediocre sales organization looks good.

Making the numbers is a sign of success, but it can also be a sign of luck. Understanding sales effectiveness requires looking beyond the achievement of sales goals. To get a complete sales effectiveness perspective, one needs to look at all the sales effectiveness drivers. Only when all the drivers are excellent is the sales force excellent. To achieve excellence in your sales force, you must optimize your use of sales effectiveness drivers.

The World of Sales shown in Figure 1-5 highlights the need for sales organizations to continuously adapt. The roots of change lie in two places. First, change can be external to the sales organization. Markets shift, new products are launched, and companies change their strategies. Such events can affect what the sales force needs to do to be successful.

Second, the best companies never stop identifying opportunities and concerns. Sales forces that continually change to realize opportunities and correct concerns are better positioned to grow faster than their competitors. Chapter 2 further develops these two change paradigms.

Achieving Sales Force Excellence

The Two Types of Sales Force Effectiveness Opportunities

Each sales organization faces unique sales force opportunities and challenges, which fall into two categories. First, sales leaders need to focus
on sales force effectiveness when *events* originating outside the Sales System require quick and appropriate action. Some examples:

- The company launches a significant new product line.
- An economic boom creates new opportunities for sales.
- The company has acquired a firm with a sales force that covers
  many of its current customers.
- Because customers are consolidating, the current selling process is
  no longer effective.
- Competitors have increased their investment in their sales force and
  are attacking the most profitable market segments.
- As increasing numbers of similar products and services come into
  the marketplace, the sales force needs to provide unique value.

Second, sales leaders are constantly looking for ways to make their organizations better. They are engaged in *ongoing effectiveness hunts* designed to improve aspects of the Sales System by responding quickly to signs of trouble, such as:

- The best salespeople are leaving the company, and sales management is ineffective at dealing with salespeople who are not performing well.
- Salespeople are spending too much time calling on friends and too little time with strategically important accounts.
- Profitability has declined because the sales force is cutting prices to meet its sales targets.
- The sales force has missed its goal for several quarters.

The best sales leaders are constantly seeking opportunities to improve their Sales System, even before signs of trouble appear. For example:

- Following several years of strong sales growth, the best sales leaders keep salespeople motivated to seek out new sales opportunities.
- When internal projects demand more time, smart sales leaders maintain a focus on the customer and minimize the time salespeople spend on nonselling activities.
- The best sales leaders understand that building a stronger interface between sales and marketing creates a more powerful bond between the company and its customers.

The Sales System and World of Sales frameworks, introduced in Chapter 1, provide structured approaches for diagnosing problems, recognizing opportunities, and developing effective solutions.

Responding Successfully to Events

Major events compel companies to react quickly. If, say, your company launches an important new product, the government enacts a new regulation, or your company is involved in a merger or acquisition, the sales force must respond immediately. Other events happen over time and cause a more gradual change—customers may begin to consolidate and alter their buying processes, or the economy may slow down or pick up. In such cases, the status quo can continue for a while, but eventually the Sales System will begin to break down and major changes will be needed to align the sales force with evolving customer needs and company strategies.

Consider two events that created a need for sales force response, analyzed using the World of Sales and Sales System concepts.

Shell Energy Responds to Government Deregulation

Deregulation of the U.S. utility industry has had dramatic implications for the industry's sales forces. Utility companies—once regulated monopolies with captive customers—now have to actively sell to customers in a competitive marketplace. Sales organizations that, in the monopoly environment, were activity-oriented, risk-averse, reactive, and technical have had to become sales-oriented, risk-taking, proactive, and relationship-focused. Figure 2-1 uses the framework of the World of Sales and the Sales System to show how, in 1999, Shell Energy responded to the deregulation of the natural gas industry in the state of Georgia by establishing a new sales organization.

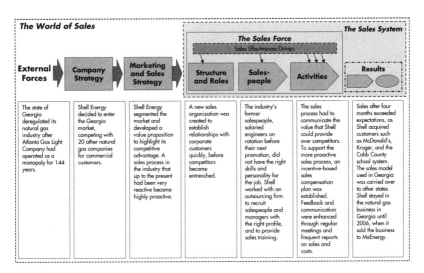

Figure 2-1. Shell Energy's response to government deregulation of the natural gas industry in Georgia

Kinko's Enters New Markets

In the late 1990s, management at Kinko's, a provider of document solutions and business services, made a strategic decision to proactively seek out larger corporate customers. Historically, most of Kinko's customers had been business travelers, college students, or employees of small businesses who periodically visited the company's 24-hour copy and business service centers. With the new strategy, Kinko's hoped to establish longer-term, profitable partnerships with large corporations by providing comprehensive printing and copy services. Figure 2-2 shows how the Kinko's sales organization responded to this change in corporate strategy.

How to Respond to Events

When an external event occurs or when your company changes its strategy, start by looking at the logical flow of the World of Sales (Figure 2-3). First, evaluate the impact of the event on your marketing and sales strategies, particularly potential changes in the selling process. Then assess the impact on the sales force itself—its structure and roles, the skills and capabilities of your salespeople, and the drivers of sales force activity.

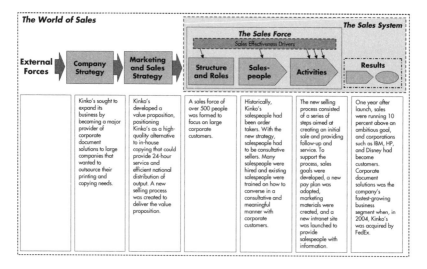

Figure 2-2. Kinko's enters new markets

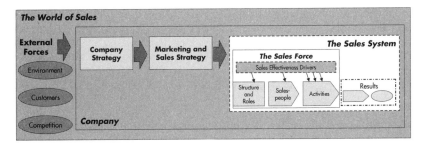

Figure 2-3. The World of Sales

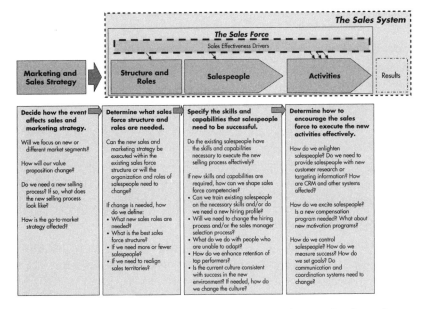

Figure 2-4. A decision-making process for adapting a sales force to major events

Figure 2-4 suggests a series of questions to ask when your sales force needs to adapt and you need to develop an action plan for success.

The Sales Force Merger Challenge

When two companies merge, there is often strong pressure to implement changes in the sales force very quickly in order to minimize negative effects on customer perception, employee morale, and company profits. If the two merging companies already have sales forces in place, there are usually redundancies in coverage. The newly formed company will be seeking cost reductions, and downsizing is likely. However, the need for speed may not allow enough time to reevaluate sales and marketing strategies properly, to find the best sales force design, or to update all the necessary sales effectiveness drivers. The focus of decision making quickly shifts from structure and roles (how much do we downsize?) to the salespeople (who stays and who goes?). Often insufficient attention is paid to developing and aligning all of the sales effectiveness drivers after a merger.

Solutions Frequently Involve Multiple Sales Effectiveness Drivers

A productive response to most events involves adjusting multiple sales effectiveness drivers. Because Shell Energy and Kinko's were establishing brand-new sales organizations, their solutions focused on drivers in all five categories:

- Definers. Both companies had to define sales roles, establish territories, and create a managerial structure for the new sales organization.
- Shapers. Both had to establish sales force hiring profiles and recruit and train salespeople.
- Enlighteners. Both Shell Energy and Kinko's had to provide salespeople with the customer information that they needed if they were to be successful.
- Exciters. Both companies had to create sales compensation plans that would motivate salespeople.
- Controllers. Both had to set goals for salespeople and establish ongoing feedback systems.

Companies that respond to events by changing existing sales forces, rather than creating new ones, may not need to implement changes in every category of sales effectiveness drives, but the best solutions usually involve adjustments to more than one. When sales forces fail to adapt successfully to events, it is often because the scope of the changes in sales effectiveness drivers is too narrow.

Dropping an Incentive Plan Is Not Enough to
Transform a Selling Process

A maker of preprinted business forms wanted to transform its sales approach as demand for electronic forms that customers could design and modify themselves replaced the demand for preprinted paper forms. As the company's offering evolved to meet this demand, a less aggressive and more consultative sales approach was needed. To encourage salespeople to refocus their efforts on solving customers' long-term needs (rather than going for short-term sales), the company eliminated its sales incentive plan; salespeople who had once earned a significant portion of their earnings through incentives began to be paid a salary exclusively. The sales force was not happy about the change. Most of the company's salespeople were aggressive risk takers who had thrived in the previous sales-oriented, "eat what you kill" environment. The company's sales force culture was totally incompatible with the new approach, the change was too sudden, and many of the best salespeople left the company, which hurt financial results. A broader solution was needed to successfully transform the sales force to fit the new market realities.

The Sales System and the World of Sales concepts highlight the critical need for sales leaders to focus on integrating their decisions and making them mutually compatible as they respond to external events.

The Effectiveness Hunt

Smart sales leaders do not wait to fine-tune their efforts until events in the marketplace or changes in corporate strategy take place. Progressive sales executives make constant improvements and take steps to enhance the performance of the sales force. If sales leaders do not adapt the sales effectiveness drivers continuously, the sales force's strength will slowly erode over time.

Selling processes can become dated. Sales managers' skills can atrophy. Recruitment processes can fail to produce consistently high-quality hires. If sales compensation plans become misaligned with company priorities, strategic products or valuable customers may receive too little sales effort. And if sales force issues that appear minor are ignored, they can escalate into bigger problems.

Most sales force issues, concerns, challenges, and opportunities can be addressed by adapting one or more of the sales effectiveness drivers. This may involve implementing new sales force decisions, processes, systems, or programs; redesigning current ones; and/or executing them more effectively.

Most companies instinctively make some improvements to their sales effectiveness drivers every year. The best companies use a structured approach to continually assess sales force effectiveness and enhance the drivers. The process begins with diagnosis to identify the drivers that may be at the root of a problem or issue. Since the resulting list of candidates can be quite large, the next step is to prioritize the drivers based on their likely impact on sales effectiveness.

As you identify the highest-priority drivers, it's vital that you check for compatibility and consistency with company goals and strategies. Figure 2-5 lays out suggested steps for a sales force effectiveness improvement process that will support the desired outcome.

Step 1: Diagnose

Just as physicians perform diagnostic tests to determine the cause of a patient's symptoms, sales leaders must diagnose the problem to identify any sales effectiveness drivers that might be a source of concern.

Three situations provide opportunities to enhance sales effectiveness. First, experienced sales leaders may pinpoint specific sales effectiveness drivers that need improving (for example, "The hiring process is not producing quality candidates" or "The incentive plan does not pay for performance"). Second, leaders may identify specific issues relating to structure, people, activities, or results that need to be addressed (for example, "Salespeople are not spending enough time with strategic accounts" or "Sales goals are not being achieved"). Finally, sales leaders may simply want to enhance overall sales effectiveness, feeling that "the organization needs to get better," or they may want to "invest in sales force projects that have high impact."

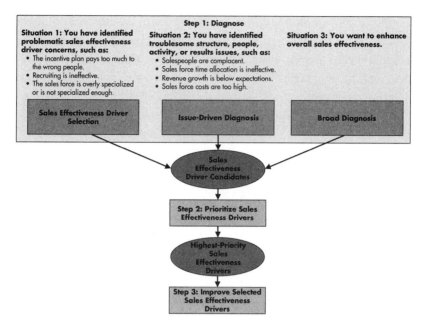

Figure 2-5. A process for making constant sales force effectiveness improvements

Situation 1: Sales Leaders Have Identified Specific Sales Effectiveness Driver Concerns Often sales leaders know which sales effectiveness drivers need to be changed in order to address their concerns. Of the more than 700 executives who have responded to our sales force issues questionnaire, 65 percent attributed effectiveness concerns to a specific driver (see Chapter 1).

However, sales leaders who look for sales effectiveness driver solutions too quickly often focus on those that are highly visible (such as compensation), that are nonthreatening (such as training), or that offer new hope (such as customer relationship management [CRM]) rather than looking for the drivers that are the true source of the problem. Certainly in many situations, compensation, training, and CRM are linked to effectiveness and can be key parts of the solution. But solutions very often lie in sales effectiveness drivers that are less obvious and more difficult to change, such as culture, leadership, sales force structure, or recruiting—areas that are easily overlooked by sales leaders who are looking for quick solutions.

A word of caution for sales leaders who feel that they have identi-fied troublesome sales effectiveness drivers through intuition alone: Double-check your assumptions and challenge the validity and com-pleteness of your explanations before you draw definite conclusions. The issue-driven diagnosis and broad diagnosis techniques described here for Situations 2 and 3 usually point to multiple sales effectiveness driver solutions to the most difficult sales challenges.

Training Alone Cannot Make Cross-Selling Successful at a Bank

A bank saw an opportunity to increase its revenues by making its branch per-sonnel more sales-oriented. The human resources and marketing directors agreed that sales training was the answer, and a major effort to train all branch managers, new account representatives, and tellers in effective sales techniques was implemented. While most of the employees said that they found the training useful, one year later there was no evidence that referrals and sales had increased. No system existed to track referrals and sales within the branches accurately. Job descriptions and hiring profiles that reflected the increased emphasis on sales and customer service had yet to be defined, and since the branch managers had no sales goals, they quickly lost interest in the project. By limiting the scope of its solution to training, while ignoring other important sales effectiveness drivers, the bank failed to capitalize on the cross-selling opportunity.

Part 2 of this book (Chapters 3 through 14) is designed to help sales leaders who know which sales effectiveness drivers need to be adjusted, either through their own insights or because they have used the issue-driven or broad diagnostic processes suggested for Situations 2 and 3 to identify problematic drivers.

Situation 2: Sales Leaders Have Identified Structure, People, Activity, or Results Issues Sales leaders regularly receive signals from customers, salespeople, sales managers, and other executives about potential con-cerns within the Sales System. A customer may ask, "There are so many different salespeople from your company who call on our account. Why can't I just talk to a single salesperson who understands all my needs?" A salesperson might say, "I don't understand the new incentive plan, so I ignore it and just do my job." A sales manager may lament, "The Omaha territory is vacant again for the third time this year. We can't seem to find the right person for that job." The sales leaders who answered our questionnaire revealed numerous issues originating within their Sales Systems, including concerns with salespeople (for example, "Turnover is too high"), sales force activities ("Not enough time is spent with key decision makers"), customers ("We need to build customer loyalty"), and company results ("Our market share is not growing"). In fact, 93 percent of the responders mentioned issues in these four categories.

As sales leaders identify Sales System issues, the process of issue-driven diagnosis described here can reveal which sales effectiveness drivers should be modified to remedy each issue. The diagnosis uses the Sales System to trace the cause of an issue back to the root drivers. For example, a concern about not developing enough new business can be addressed by adjusting multiple sales effectiveness drivers. Figure 2-6

Sales Effectiveness Drivers		Questions
Definers	Sales Force Size	Is the sales force large enough to provide time for prospecting?
	Structure and Roles	Do we need some salespeople to specialize in new account development?
Shapers	Recruiting	Are we hiring hunters?
	Learning and Development	Are we equipping them to succeed?
	Culture	Do we celebrate new customer development?
Enlighteners	Leveraging Information	Does the sales force have sufficient information about potential accounts and about the sales process for new accounts?
Exciters	Compensation and Incentives	Are we providing sufficient incentives to reward new business development?
	Leadership	Do sales leaders communicate a compelling vision for new customer development?
Controllers	Goal Setting	Are motivating goals set for new business development?
	Performance Management	Is new business development a metric in the performance management system?

Figure 2-6. Some questions for identifying sales effectiveness driver solutions to a concern about not developing enough new business

suggests some questions that can help identify the drivers that might be responsible for the issue.

Figure 2-7 shows, step by step, how one company diagnosed the reason for a specific sales force problem—"Sales growth is below expectations"—by tracing the cause of the problem through the Sales System. While causality flows from left to right in the Sales System, diagnosis proceeds from right to left as answers to the "why" questions lead upstream to the sales effectiveness drivers.

Solutions to the most difficult sales force challenges typically involve adjustments to multiple sales effectiveness drivers.

Hewlett-Packard Transforms Its Sales Force Culture by Enhancing Multiple Sales Effectiveness Drivers

---

When Mark Hurd took the helm as CEO and president of Hewlett-Packard (HP) in March 2005, sales were flat, customers were unhappy, and the sales force was demoralized. HP implemented numerous changes to the sales effectiveness drivers, including:

- *Sales force structure.* Salespeople had been selling the entire line of HP products, yet fully understanding the company's broad and complex product line was virtually impossible for most salespeople. Hurd decentralized and specialized the sales force around three business divisions: the IT needs of large enterprises, printers and printing, and personal computers. This specialized structure increased the sales force's customer and product knowledge and improved the product divisions' ability to control the sales process. At the same time, several administrative layers within the sales organization were eliminated, increasing the responsiveness of the sales force to customer needs.

- *Sales force systems.* Since HP was a mature company that had grown in part through acquisitions (including Compaq), its sales forces had been using more than 30 different sales automation systems. Now the sales force adopted a single companywide system, giving it better analytic control of its sales pipeline and making management of the sales compensation system easier.

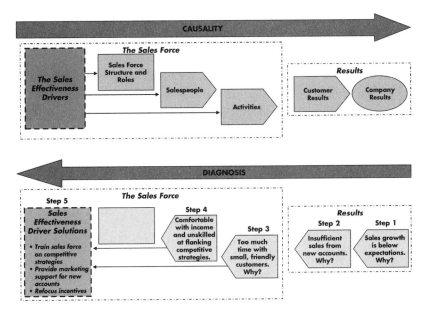

Figure 2-7. Diagnosing problems in a Sales System

- *Performance measures.* HP's Total Customer Experience Program— which measures sales force promise fulfillment, adequate follow-up, and customer support—placed new emphasis on becoming more customer-centric.
- *Sales training.* HP made significant investments to improve sales force training. A program called Sales Excellence includes individual development and gap and skill analysis targeted to each salesperson's role.
- *Other sales effectiveness drivers.* The company made significant investments to improve sales force hiring programs and sales compensation systems.

These changes in sales effectiveness drivers are credited with boosting income, driving revenues, and improving the company's reputation with customers and on Wall Street.

Part 3 of the book (Chapters 15 through 20) shows how issue-driven diagnosis can reveal sales effectiveness driver solutions for several of the most common and important Sales System issues.

Situation 3: Sales Leaders Want to Enhance Sales Effectiveness Diagnostic tools—some utilizing internal company data, and others relying on external sources of information—are available to sales leaders who know that their sales forces can be more effective and who want to determine areas for improvement. Performance Frontier Analysis and sales effectiveness driver Health Checks can identify opportunities to improve effectiveness through the analysis of internal company data. But also look outside the company. Benchmarking your organization against others and studying best practices are also productive ways to gauge improvement opportunities.

Performance Frontier Analysis Performance Frontier Analysis enables sales leaders to discover who their best salespeople are. By observing the personal traits and activities of those people, the leaders gain a better understanding of the factors that contribute to sales success and can adapt the sales effectiveness drivers to encourage development of those characteristics across the entire sales force. Many sales organizations have used Performance Frontier Analysis to discover and capitalize on opportunities to improve sales effectiveness.

Of course, how to identify the best performers is not always obvious. Sales leaders get a sense of who their good salespeople are from sales manager input, performance rankings, and territory metrics such as sales, market share, and quota attainment. Yet evidence suggests that these traditional ways of identifying strong performers do not always provide a complete picture, since they may not separate the sales impact of territory factors (market potential, competitive intensity) from the sales impact of the salesperson's ability and hard work.

Performance Frontier Analysis enhances traditional methods of identifying a sales force's top performers by using historical territory-level data to evaluate salespeople's performance. The analysis isolates the impact of the salesperson on territory performance by controlling for territory differences—say, in market potential, prior sales, or market share.

This approach can include multiple dimensions of territory differences, but it is most intuitive when it is viewed in two dimensions, as in the packaging company example in Figure 2-8. Each dot in the plot represents a sales territory. Territory sales are thought to be influenced by territory potential. In this example, territory potential is expressed as an

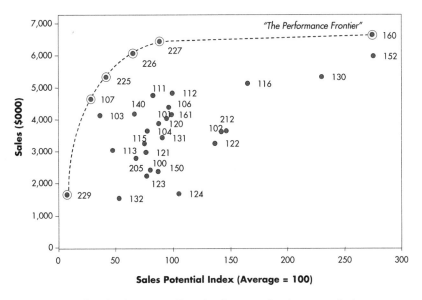

Figure 2-8. The Performance Frontier for a packaging manufacturer

index (100 represents the average territory) and is based on a combination of account-specific estimates provided by salespeople and business demographic data. The best-performing territories are those with the highest sales relative to their potential.

The dotted curve connecting the best-performing territories at the top of the plot represents the Performance Frontier, which predicts the sales that are possible for territories with different amounts of potential. Why? Because someone in the sales force has demonstrated that it is possible to achieve this level of performance. For example, by looking at the range of sales between territories 225 and 226 (between $5.2 and $6 million), it is possible to forecast how much a salesperson with similar territory potential (45 percent of average to 70 percent of average) should be able to sell.

Performance Frontier salespeople are those who are close to the Performance Frontier curve. Many companies use a range, such as 10 percent, to define this group.

Once the Performance Frontier salespeople have been identified, sales leaders need to understand the reasons for their strong performance. The answers are sometimes evident from the numbers. A high performer may work more days, make more calls, or allocate effort in a smarter way than an average performer. However, the reasons for performance differences are frequently qualitative. A high performer may be more motivated, have stronger selling skills, or engage in behaviors that are particularly effective with customers.

Observation and understanding of the traits and behaviors of both Performance Frontier salespeople and those who fall short of the frontier are required to discover the characteristics, skills, and behaviors that lead to sales success. Based on the analysis, sales leaders can identify a set of success principles that differentiates Performance Frontier salespeople.

To bridge the gap between the best salespeople and average ones, sales leaders must determine the adjustments to sales effectiveness drivers that are needed. If the entire sales force is to benefit from the success principles employed by Performance Frontier salespeople, multiple driver adjustments are often required. For example:

- Changing hiring profiles so that job candidates are screened for characteristics and skills discovered among Performance Frontier salespeople.
- Enhancing training programs to emphasize the skills used by Performance Frontier salespeople.
- Reinforcing the Performance Frontier success principles through sales manager coaching and performance management processes.
- Sharing data and tools developed by Performance Frontier salespeople throughout the sales force.
- Setting territory goals to challenge salespeople to move closer to the Performance Frontier. Challenging salespeople who are already on the frontier can shift the entire frontier upward.

Successful implementation of Performance Frontier Analysis has helped numerous companies move many salespeople closer to the Performance Frontier and raise the performance level of the entire selling organization.

Sales Effectiveness Driver Health Checks Sales effectiveness driver Health Checks can reveal whether specific drivers need improvement.

Most companies can conduct these checks, which provide insights through analysis of cross-sectional, territory-level data and compare how different salespeople are performing, fairly rapidly and easily.

The activities and successes of individual members of the sales force provide valuable information about how well the sales effectiveness drivers are working. In a sense, each salesperson is an experiment, so there are experiments going on all the time within every sales force.

Health Checks can be either one- or two-dimensional. One-dimensional checks examine the pattern of a specific sales force measure to see if it is within normal limits. Two-dimensional checks examine the relationship between two measures. The presence or absence of a relationship between two measures can point to either a problem or an opportunity. Some sales effectiveness driver Health Checks are described briefly here. Later chapters provide more detail and use specific examples to explain how to perform these Health Checks.

- A sizing Health Check (Chapter 4). A quick calculation provides insight concerning the size of the current sales force: Divide an estimate of the incremental first-year sales that an additional salesperson can generate by the break-even sales (the cost of a salesperson divided by the gross contribution margin rate) for that incremental salesperson. The higher the number, the greater the chance that the sales force is undersized. By incorporating estimates of the multiyear impact of this year's sales effort, a multiyear return on investment (ROI) can be computed.

- A territory alignment Health Check (Chapter 6). Evaluate the account workload of each sales territory and compare it to the capacity of the salesperson or sales team assigned to cover the territory. When a mismatch between the amount of work to be done and the capacity of salespeople is identified, the smart sales leader will enhance sales effectiveness by redistributing accounts across sales territories.

- A recruiting Health Check (Chapter 7). Look at the performance of salespeople who have been with the company for one to three years and compare it to the ratings (e.g., interviewer ratings or psychological test scores) these salespeople received when they were candidates for the job. If the salespeople who received the highest ratings do not consistently turn out to be top performers, you may need to improve your recruiting processes. Studying the traits of those who received high ratings in the recruiting process but did not turn out to be successful makes it possible to uncover specific characteristics that are over- or underemphasized by recruiters. For example, past experience is often stressed during recruiting, but is not always linked to ultimate success. At the same time, integrity is often closely linked to ultimate success, yet it may not be screened for effectively during the recruiting process.

- A sales manager Health Check (Chapter 10). Ask salespeople to anonymously evaluate their immediate manager on important competencies, such as leadership, communication, and coaching. Poor scores can reveal a weak sales manager team.

- An incentive compensation Health Check (Chapter 12). Look at the best measures of salespeople's performance (using a tool such as Performance Frontier Analysis) and compare them to the salespeople's incentive earnings during the last incentive period. If strong performers did not earn appreciably more incentive pay than average or weak performers, the sales compensation plan is not paying for performance.

- A goal-setting Health Check (Chapter 13). Look at the goal attainment of salespeople who have territories with high, medium, and low market size, market share, and/or market growth rate. If goals are systematically harder to achieve in those territories that fall into any of these categories, then there may be a bias in the goal-setting method.

- A culture Health Check (Chapter 9). Ask salespeople and their managers to respond to questionnaires that establish how they would make important work style choices. For example, is it best to work for short-term results or long-term customer relationships? Is it more important to adhere to company guidelines or to be empowered to make situation-appropriate decisions? Cultural norms and values, as well as culture consensus, can be estimated after analyzing the questionnaire responses.

- Resource allocation Health Check (Chapter 17). Analyze how sales force time is allocated across customers, products, or sales activities. Are important strategic priorities getting enough attention? Is too much time being spent on low-value customers, products, or activities?

Benchmarking and Best Practice Assessment Many industries capture and make available data that are useful for benchmarking sales effectiveness drivers. Here we briefly describe some ways to use external benchmarks.

- Sales force size benchmarking (Chapter 4). Compare the size of your sales force with that of your competitors. Is your sales force being outshouted in the market?
- Incentive compensation benchmarking (Chapter 12). Compare your salespeople's earnings to industry benchmarks to ensure that your pay levels are competitive, particularly for top performers.
- Sales force turnover benchmarking (Chapter 18). Compare sales force turnover to industry benchmarks. How much turnover is an expected part of your business model, and by how much can undesirable turnover be reduced?

Keeping up with industry best practices can also help you discover opportunities to enhance effectiveness. Books like this one, executive-level courses, industry conferences, and trade publications are all good sources of ideas for innovative and practical ways of enhancing sales effectiveness.

Step 2: Prioritize the Sales Effectiveness Drivers

Diagnosis of sales force issues can lead to a long list of sales effectiveness drivers that are candidates for improvement. If your analysis yields a long list, you may get the best results by prioritizing the drivers and focusing your improvement efforts on a small number of the most important ones first. The performance scorecard described here is useful in assessing sales force effectiveness and prioritizing initiatives based on their likely impact. The Sales Force Performance Scorecard profiles each sales effectiveness driver in terms of two measures: *performance* and *strategic impact.* A performance score reflects how competent or capable a selling organization is at maximizing each sales effectiveness driver. Effective methods of deriving performance scores include the following:

- Quantitative approaches. Companies can use data analysis to measure the performance of sales effectiveness drivers—for example, assessing territory alignment by evaluating territory workloads and comparing them with each salesperson's capacity.

- Qualitative approaches. Sales leaders can conduct a thorough and consistent evaluation of each driver's performance by using a questionnaire to assess current practices within the context of best practices.

Strategic impact reflects the importance of a particular driver for an organization's ability to succeed. Most companies rely on management judgment and/or outside experts to derive strategic impact scores.

The Sales Force Performance Scorecard provides a snapshot of an organization's performance and the strategic impact of the sales effectiveness drivers at a particular point in time. Figure 2-9 shows a scorecard

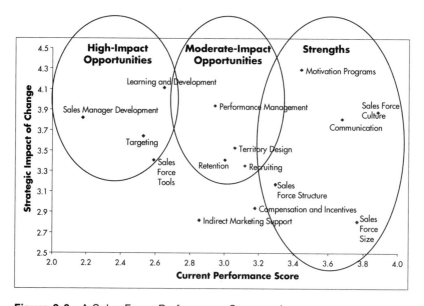

Figure 2-9. A Sales Force Performance Scorecard

that one company developed to assess the effectiveness and impact of several important sales effectiveness drivers.

The position of each driver on the scorecard suggests an action. A driver with low strategic impact but high performance, such as sales force size in the example, can be maintained at current levels. Sales effectiveness drivers with high strategic impact and high performance, such as motivation programs, need to be monitored closely to ensure that their performance remains high. Drivers with low strategic impact and low performance, such as indirect marketing support, can be monitored to see whether their impact increases over time.

Sales effectiveness drivers with low performance and high strategic impact, such as learning and development, sales manager development, targeting, and sales force tools, present the greatest opportunity for effectiveness gains and thus are top priorities for sales leaders.

The Sales Force Performance Scorecard is very specific to a company and its condition at the time the assessment is conducted. Sales effectiveness drivers move to the right as the sales force's performance improves and to the left if performance slips because changes in the environment render current practices less effective or because sales leaders and individual salespeople fail to maintain high performance standards. Drivers move up or down when their strategic impact changes as a result of modifications in environmental conditions and company strategy.

Sales leaders gain particular insight when they conduct assessments on a regular basis and track changes over time. Figure 2-10 compares the performance scores in Figure 2-9 to scores gathered a year later. The company has improved its performance on several sales effectiveness drivers, including learning and development and performance management, but performance has slipped on a few others, including motivation programs and compensation.

Step 3: Improve the Sales Effectiveness Drivers

Once sales leaders identify high-impact improvement opportunities, they can begin to implement appropriate changes in the sales effectiveness drivers involved. Part 2 of the book (Chapters 3 through 14) provides numerous insights concerning how to enhance many of the drivers for maximum impact.

Figure 2-10. Change in sales effectiveness driver performance year over year

To help avoid the common problem of management introducing incompatibilities into the Sales System when it implements changes to the sales effectiveness drivers, we've formulated what we call the compatibility check.

The Compatibility Check Sales force effectiveness is enhanced by a consistent and compatible Sales System. When sales leaders conduct periodic compatibility checks of the sales effectiveness drivers, they ensure that the Sales System operates as a cohesive, well-aligned force that works to accomplish company goals. The compatibility check is mainly a qualitative assessment using the "3 Cs" guidelines given in Figure 2-11. The examples of problems in the figure illustrate how easy it is for incompatibility or inconsistency to creep into the Sales System. Misalignments between the various sales effectiveness drivers and with sales and marketing strategies can inhibit the accomplishment of company goals.

The Novartis Approach to Constant Improvement
Novartis, a leading multinational manufacturer of pharmaceutical products, uses a structured process supported by analytic tools to enhance

The 3 Cs Guidelines

Sales effectiveness drivers have Consistency with . . .	Compatibility across the sales effectiveness drivers . . .	Appropriate Consequences for . . .
• Company strategies • Marketing strategies • Sales strategies	• Definers • Shapers • Enlighteners • Exciters • Controllers	• Company results • Customer results • Sales force activities • Salespeople

The Alignment Check Process

Consistency check	Compatibility check	Consequence check
Check the sales effectiveness drivers one by one, looking for inconsistencies with company, marketing, and sales strategies.	Look for sales effectiveness drivers that are incompatible with one another.	Look for sales effectiveness drivers that are producing unintended consequences for people, activities, or customer and company financial results.

Examples of Problems That Could Be Revealed

Inconsistency	Incompatibility	Unintended consequences
• The selling process includes a large service component, but the sales force earns incentives on quarterly sales, so salespeople who sell rather than service earn more. • Salespeople are asked to focus on new customer development, but the company provides no prospect lists, nor does it provide training on new business development strategies.	• Sales territories have unequal potential, yet salespeople are stack ranked on sales volume and are recognized publicly for where they rank. • The hiring profile calls for assertive, highly motivated salespeople, yet salespeople are paid a straight salary that is at the industry average. • Salespeople are evaluated based on sales goal attainment, yet territory sales goals are routinely inaccurate and unfair.	• SPIFFs on nonstrategic products are diverting sales force attention, causing the company to miss its sales goal. • The sales force is too small, and the needs of many customers are unmet. • The CRM system is too complex, and sales force administrative time has increased. • Training programs are dated, and salespeople lack critical new skills.

Figure 2-11. Using the 3 Cs guidelines to check for inconsistencies and incompatibilities in the Sales System

global sales effectiveness. As of year-end 2006, the process had helped drive six consecutive years of double-digit top-line growth in the United States, well ahead of the industry average. The company conducts an annual sales force effectiveness review to identify high-priority sales effectiveness drivers. After building an annual improvement plan around the highest-priority drivers, management executes the plan and measures progress year over year. Several resulting initiatives have significantly enhanced sales force effectiveness. In the first year, an analysis of customer targeting revealed that sales force time was scattered across too many physicians. By strategically concentrating sales activity on approximately 35 percent of the highest-valued physicians, the company realized a significant sales increase and a large improvement in sales productivity.

In the second year, high-performing salespeople (identified using Performance Frontier Analysis) were observed on typical sales calls in order to identify how they influenced the customer buying process. Average performers were also observed, and their behavior was compared with that of the high performers. Sales leadership identified a set of success principles that differentiated top-performing salespeople and incorporated those principles into a training program for the sales organization.

At a presentation to analysts in September 2003, the company showcased the fact that the salespeople who had been trained to emulate the behaviors of top performers were chosen by physicians as the best salesperson they see 46 percent of the time, compared to only 22 percent of the time for salespeople who did not complete the training. The physicians' preference was also linked to better sales results. Novartis continued to conduct annual effectiveness reviews, revealing new opportunities for sales effectiveness driver enhancement.

Now Go for It

Your company will be more successful at enhancing sales force effectiveness when you use a systematic and comprehensive approach, whether you are responding to *events* originating outside the Sales System or engaging in ongoing *effectiveness hunts* to create constant improvement within your Sales System. The World of Sales and the Sales System together provide a structured framework that you can use to diagnose sales effectiveness problems, recognize opportunities, and develop successful solutions.

P A R T **2**

Improving the Top Sales Effectiveness Drivers

CHAPTER 3

Sales Strategies That Win with Customers

C ompanies have very different sales strategies. Here are some examples:

- A pharmaceutical company's sales force represents a line of prescription medications and calls on physicians. The salesperson's role is to educate physicians about patient profiles and the benefits and side effects of the company's drugs for treating different diseases. Because salespeople typically have only a few minutes with each physician, the company's marketing group—basing its recommendations on an analysis of a physician's prescribing behavior and call history—tells the salespeople whom to call on and how often, which products to discuss, and in what order. Carefully scripted sales messages encourage salespeople to be consistent in their communication with physicians and help ensure that the information that they deliver is accurate and within FDA guidelines.

- A confectionary company sells a large and diverse line of candy and gum products through food, drug, mass merchandise, and convenience stores. The sales force works directly with retailers, but the selling process differs depending on the size and needs of each account. For retail chains, salespeople work with buyers at the retailer's headquarters to ensure that stores are selling the appropriate products, priced correctly, with optimal shelf placement, prominent displays, and effective promotional support. Chain retailers range in size from the very large, such as Wal-Mart, to chains with a dozen or so stores. The largest national chains require sizable teams of dedicated salespeople who meet with the retailer's decision makers at least weekly to review selling strategies; discuss in-depth, account-specific market analysis (for example, scanner data results); review product-line performance at the account; and develop innovative and highly customized solutions for expanding sales. Smaller regional chains are handled by customer business managers (CBMs), who visit the retailer's headquarters at least quarterly to discuss distribution, shelf placement, and display strategies, and to share general market analysis and growth strategies. Independent retail stores and small chains (those with fewer than 10 stores) are covered by territory sales managers (TSMs). Since each TSM covers as many as 1,000 stores, he can spend only a limited amount of time at each account. The confectionary company provides TSMs with detailed instructions concerning which accounts to call on, how frequently to visit them, and how much time to spend on particular high-priority activities designed to drive distribution and volume. TSMs also cover individual stores of some national accounts, such as Wal-Mart, that need direct in-store coverage.

- A semiconductor company develops microprocessors that are embedded in a number of electronic products. Its customers are manufacturers of computers, industrial equipment, telecommunications products, automobiles, information and entertainment systems, and medical equipment. Acquiring new business takes many months of work by a sales team that includes individuals with both business and engineering skills. The multistage, highly consultative sales process involves extensive collaboration between the members of the sales team, the semiconductor company's design engineers, and engineers at the prospective customer's site. When a high-potential prospect is identified, sales team leaders make initial contact with the prospect's CEO or general manager and present a strategic vision of how the company's products can help the prospect gain competitive advantage. After the team leaders win high-level approval from the customer, the sales effort shifts to technology stakeholders within the organization. The sales team assesses the prospect's technological needs and communicates specific requirements to the company's design engineers. Over a period of several months, the sales team coordinates the efforts of its design engineers and those at the prospective customer in order to develop a competitively superior functional prototype. Then the sales team works out the commercial details of a relationship, including supply chain logistics, legal contracts, volume requirements, and price. Members of the sales team work with customers on an ongoing basis, supporting their needs and looking for opportunities to expand the relationship.

Defining Sales Strategy

A sales strategy defines *who* a company's customers and prospects are, *what* the value proposition is, and *how* the selling is done. It articulates the communication and the activities that need to take place between the company and its customers and prospects with the goal of understanding customer needs and demonstrating how the company's products and services create value by meeting those needs. Figure 3-1 compares the sales strategies of the three companies in the examples just given.

A successful sales strategy:

- Focuses sales force attention on attractive market segments that value the company's offering.

- Tailors the value proposition and the sales process to each market segment's specific needs.

- Defines cost-efficient sales processes that communicate the value that the offering creates for customers.

Industry	Who is sold to	What value proposition is sold	How the selling is done
Pharmaceuticals	Physicians	Patients with the right profile benefit by using the company's drugs.	"Detail" physicians by delivering short and carefully scripted sales messages that highlight product benefits and risks.
Confectionaries	Retail buyers and store managers	Store volume increases when the company's line of confectionaries is sold and backed by strong merchandising support.	Work with buyers at retail chain headquarters to develop strategies and programs for increasing in-store volume. Provide merchandising support as needed at local stores.
Semiconductors	Business and technical teams at electronics manufacturers	Competitive advantage is gained when the company's high-quality, custom-designed microprocessors are embedded in the customer's electronics.	Sell a strategic vision to the highest-level management. Over a period of many months, collaborate with the customer's technical teams to develop and refine a functional prototype. If successful, work with the customer's business teams to work out legal, distribution, and pricing details.

Figure 3-1. A comparison of sales strategies at companies in three different industries

- Helps salespeople develop business relationships that benefit both the company and the customer.
- Shifts the selling emphasis away from price and toward business value.
- Increases sales relative to the competition.

Marketing and sales leaders are jointly responsible for developing a sales strategy, which must constantly evolve in response to shifting circumstances in the marketplace—including changes in customer needs and buying processes, the competitive landscape, the economy, and the overall industry—as well as changes in the company's strategy as it enters new markets and launches new products. Even when circumstances within the company and at the customer remain stable, the best sales and marketing leaders continually fine-tune their sales strategy as they strive to increase their effectiveness and beat their competitors.

Developing a Sales Strategy

Figure 3-2 shows three activities that are essential in developing a sales strategy. First, the company must understand its customers' needs. Because most companies have many customers and prospects with many different needs, developing a sales strategy often involves segmenting the market in a way that allows sales leaders to draw up a plan of action. Next, the company must articulate a value proposition for

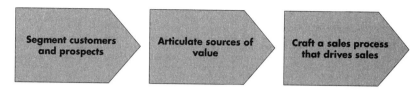

Figure 3-2. The sales strategy development process

each customer segment. Finally, sales leaders need to craft a way to communicate the value of the company's product or service for each market segment. Careful execution of the sales strategy development activities enables customer success and enhances company sales.

Segmenting Customers and Prospects

A company with a limited number of large potential customers, such as a first-tier supplier of gaskets to automobile manufacturers, can develop a sales strategy for each customer individually. However, for companies that have many possible customers (in other words, most companies), it is more practical to begin by organizing customers and prospects into market segments in which customers or prospects value similar product or service offerings and respond to the same sales process.

Markets can be segmented using many different criteria, as shown in Figure 3-3. Sales leaders often look first at customer *profile* characteristics that indicate the type of sales effort that is needed. For example, a large customer has different needs from a small customer and often requires more sales effort. Sales leaders can improve their profile-based segmentation by incorporating *behavioral* criteria that reflect what a customer does. For example, how loyal a customer has been to the company will influence the design of a selling process intended to generate repeat purchases. And the most sophisticated customer segmentation schemes incorporate customer *needs* explicitly. For example, a customer's buying process can help determine what activities are needed to sell to that customer successfully.

In business-to-business markets, many companies use *industry* as a segmentation criterion, since it is often a good indicator of the products and services that a customer or prospect will value and the type of sales process that will be successful. And almost every company considers

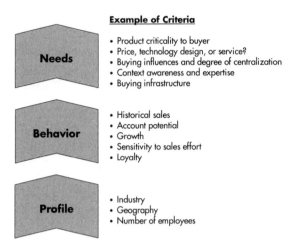

Figure 3-3. Examples of market segmentation criteria

account size when segmenting accounts. Large (key, national, enterprise, global) accounts demand special attention.

Companies can make their customer segmentation more powerful by investing in ways to measure account potential, in addition to looking at historical sales. If direct measures of account potential are not available, companies can develop surrogate measures using *firmographics* (like the number of employees) combined with input from the sales force.

Estimates of account potential allow salespeople to see the extent to which accounts have been penetrated, help them determine how much effort to apply with various accounts, and suggest an appropriate value proposition and sales process. Solid, long-term customers may need value-added programs that enhance loyalty, while newer accounts may require salespeople to evaluate the needs of the customer and assess the strength of the competition. The best segmentation schemes are often based on creative combinations of multiple criteria.

Articulating Sources of Value

Different market segments are likely to value a company's offering in different ways or for different reasons. Customers tend to perceive proposed offerings that are tailored to their specific needs as having greater value. And perceived value is greater when it is effectively communicated, proven, and continuously reinforced.

The major source of value for customers is usually derived from the product itself. Yet selling teams can extend the value of a product beyond its tangible characteristics by developing value propositions that emphasize services, programs, or systems that help customers address specific business needs. Value enhancers, such as those shown in Figure 3-4, can be a source of considerable competitive advantage, particularly in markets where there is little differentiation among products offered by competing companies.

Value-Enhancing Services
- Delivery—short customer lead times, low variation from promised delivery dates, good condition of the product on arrival, just-in-time delivery, willingness to hold inventory for customer
- In-person sales calls providing valuable expertise
- Installation, after-sale support, and maintenance services
- Customer training
- Assistance with resolution of quality control and production issues
- Assistance with integrating the firm's products with the customer's products
- Ways to get help with troubleshooting—toll-free help lines, user manuals, Internet sites

Value-Enhancing Programs
- Custom sizes and mix variety
- Long-term contracts that avoid price fluctuations
- Financing options—deals, terms, conditions, rebates or guarantees
- Partnering—co-design, joint marketing research, or co-promotion
- Programs that provide advice and consulting, specification, process engineering, or redesign

Value-Enhancing Systems
- Ordering systems—computer-to-computer ordering, shared material resource planning, electronic information exchange, order tracking
- Credit, billing, and collection procedures and systems
- Systems that improve responsiveness, such as databases that log complaints or monitor actual delivery dates against promised dates
- Supply chain management systems

Figure 3-4. Services, programs, and systems that create customer value

---

Sources of Customer Value at GE Healthcare

GE Healthcare has a diagnostic imaging business that provides hospitals with major medical imaging systems, including MRI, CT, and x-ray machines.

While the products themselves are the primary source of value for GE's customers, the company offers a number of programs and services that increase the value of the offering for some customers. GE offers an array of financing programs, including one in which units can be purchased on a shared-risk basis, with GE taking a fraction of the revenue generated by the units. GE also offers services to customers who need help designing space for the units, training or hiring personnel, and/or managing the units on an ongoing basis. GE even provides continuing education programs to its customers to help the leaders of diagnostic imaging departments address the challenging issues confronting them. The array of offerings is tailored to the specific needs of each hospital or health-care network.

Value can also be delivered through the sales process itself. Anyone who is dealing with a damaged automobile appreciates an insurance agent who processes the claim expeditiously and quickly authorizes repairs. A software buyer may value the experience and perspective of a salesperson who has dealt with similar customers. A purchasing agent who is responsible for buying hundreds of replacement parts may value a computerized inventory management and ordering system that eliminates the need to contact a salesperson for routine purchases.

Crafting a Sales Process

In order to deliver the right value proposition to the right customers, salespeople must engage in particular activities. And connections between customers and salespeople are more effective when these activities are organized into a defined sales process for each market segment. The sales process is an important way for companies to deliver value to their customers.

The specific steps involved in the sales process depend on a variety of factors, including customer needs, product and market characteristics, the industry and economic environment, and company strategies and culture. Figure 3-5 shows some typical steps required for a company to attract and retain customers.

Figure 3-6 shows the sales process that United Airlines uses to sell business travel services to corporations and travel agents. The company's salespeople use this process to deliver and reinforce a value

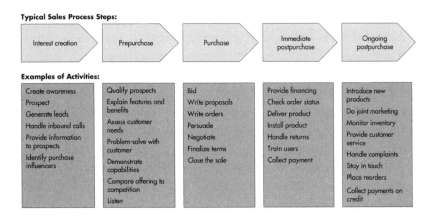

Figure 3-5. A typical sales process and examples of the activities involved

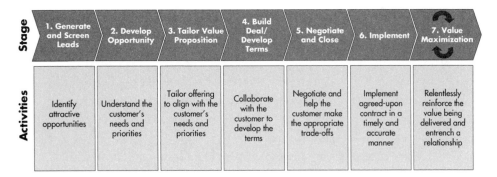

Figure 3-6. Example of the sales process that United Airlines uses to sell business travel services

proposition that includes flight services, easy travel booking, travel expense control, and travel management support. An important last step in the process is ongoing—salespeople are asked to continually reinforce the value that the company delivers in order to strengthen relationships with customers.

An effective sales process communicates the value proposition, gets the appropriate price, and results in a transaction.

Different Customers Require Different Sales Processes

Two different customers want to buy computer hardware and software for their businesses. The first customer is the owner of a small business who knows very little about computers. He needs a lot of advice and support, including consulting to decide which products to buy, training to learn how to use them, and ongoing access to support services. The second customer is a computer specialist at a large company who has consulted with experts within her company and knows what she wants to buy. She needs minimal ongoing advice and support—these services are provided by other people within her company. It is important to this buyer that she get a good price and that the buying process is efficient, with all the needed products conveniently bundled together. Computer hardware and software companies that want to be successful at selling to both types of customers must create two different value propositions and sales processes.

Implementing a Sales Strategy

Members of the sales force are key implementers of a company's sales strategy. The best salespeople are highly effective at customizing a sales strategy for each customer. Successful salespeople are flexible. As they listen to their customers, assess their needs, provide tailored solutions, reduce complexity, and handle objections, they create value with every customer interaction.

A few companies empower salespeople to develop their own sales strategy for each customer. In most cases, however, it is too much to expect a diverse sales force whose members have different experience and performance levels to consistently develop effective sales strategies without some guidance. Sales leaders who direct their salespeople effectively—providing guidance about whom to call on, what value proposition to sell, and how to make the customer connection— enhance the ability of their sales organizations to achieve strong results.

As shown in Figure 3-7, a cohesive sales strategy includes how much time salespeople spend on individual accounts or groups of accounts, the products that they focus on, and the selling activities that they engage in.

When the sales strategy is implemented effectively, the sales force carries out the right activities to create customer and company results. Successful implementation of a sales strategy requires aligning the sales effectiveness drivers in every category (discussed in Chapter 1) to support and reinforce that strategy. The right sales force activities are more likely to be carried out when:

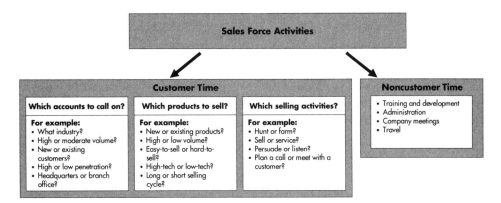

Figure 3-7. Sales strategy communicates the best sales force activities

- The sales force is sized and structured appropriately. A sales force needs adequate capacity and "bandwidth" to undertake all of the responsibilities required by the sales strategy (the *definer* drivers).

- Salespeople have the necessary skills and capabilities. Companies that hire people with the right capabilities and then develop their skills and knowledge through training and coaching have a much better chance of implementing the sales strategy successfully (the *shaper* drivers).

- The company provides salespeople with data and tools that enable them to execute the strategy knowledgeably (the *enlightener* drivers).

- Salespeople are motivated to do what the company asks them to do. Incentive compensation and motivational programs—and, of course, strong leadership—inspire salespeople to implement the sales strategy (the *exciter* drivers).

- Salespeople know what is expected of them. Performance management processes and goals reinforce the behaviors and results that the strategy requires (the *controller* drivers).

By successfully aligning the sales effectiveness drivers to reinforce the sales strategy, companies encourage their salespeople to engage in the kinds of sales activities that drive results.

CHAPTER 4

Sizing Your Sales Force for Long-Term Success

A vice president of sales wonders if her sales force is too small. Several years ago, when the sales force was established, she decided that each salesperson could handle a $2 million sales territory. Now that sales have grown to more than $3.5 million per territory, she senses that there is significant unrealized opportunity in many territories and wonders if the size of the current sales force is restricting the company's continued growth.

The president of a business unit suspects that his sales force has grown too large. Two years ago, business was so brisk that the attitude throughout the industry was that sales forces should be bigger, always bigger. But the economy is now persistently sluggish, and the president feels pressure to cut costs, trim fat, and increase the productivity of salespeople.

The size of the sales force affects customers, salespeople, and the overall company. If the sales force is too small, it cannot serve the needs of customers effectively; salespeople are likely to be overworked, and the company will miss key sales opportunities. If the sales force is too large, salespeople can become an annoyance to customers; salespeople probably are not challenged, the costs of maintaining the sales force will be too high, and productivity will be low.

A sales force that is the right size connects with customers effectively. Salespeople are challenged, but not overworked. Sales are high, costs are reasonable, and profitability is strong.

Matching Sales Force Size to the Business Life Cycle

The size of the sales force needs to change as a company progresses through its life cycle. Over time, companies evolve their products and adapt to changing market conditions. A sizing strategy that works well for a new and growing business is different from one that works well for a mature business. Insights that help new and growing companies size their sales forces for maximum impact differ from those that help mature businesses.

Sizing Strategies for New and Growing Businesses

Having a sales force of the right size is critical for new and growing businesses. Aggressive investment in sales force resources during the start-up and growth stages allows companies to capitalize on early opportunities, increase sales and profits quickly, preempt competitors, and build a strong base of loyal customers who will buy for years into the future. However, because they are uncertain about what the future holds, many new and growing businesses are too conservative in staffing their sales forces. As a result, they leave significant amounts of money on the table.

Here are several guidelines for sales leaders in new and growing businesses to consider as they build a sales force.

Do Not Undersize When Uncertainty Is Low. A small U.S. company and a Japanese company entered into an agreement in which the U.S. company would sell the Japanese company's product in the U.S. market. Everyone agreed that the product—which was patent-protected and had been launched successfully in other countries—was going to be a blockbuster. Yet the U.S. company's cautious leadership team was unwilling to expand the sales force to support the launch. The U.S. company used the "earn-your-way" sizing strategy, shown in Part C of Figure 4-1, waiting to see how the product sold before adding salespeople over a three-year period. Hindsight analysis revealed that if the company had pursued the "quick-build" sizing strategy (Part A of the figure) and added all the salespeople before the U.S. launch, profits would have been about $50 million higher over the three-year period.

We looked at data from 11 recent sales force sizing studies that our consulting firm, ZS Associates, conducted for start-up businesses. Each study determined an optimal sales force size based on data-driven analysis that projected the three- to five-year profit consequences of different levels of investment in the sales force. In 10 of the 11 studies, sales leaders launched their sales force at a size that averaged just 60 percent of the optimal size. The one company that sized its sales force at the optimal size went on to become the leader in a highly competitive market.

We do not fault organizations for investing cautiously when they have significant financial constraints, when the future is highly uncertain, or when the best selling process has yet to be discovered. But we often see companies using a cautious earn-your-way approach even when they are getting clear signals that a new product or venture will be a success.

Sales leaders typically view the consequences of hiring too many salespeople as being more serious than those of hiring too few. If they hire too many salespeople and the sales forecast is not realized, then at some point they must take the unpleasant step of reducing the size of the

	+1 Year	3-Year Total
Strategy	Contribution	Contribution
A: "Quick build"	$83	$351
B: "Play it safe"	$84	$321
C: "Earn your way"	$87	$301

Note: Contribution is in millions.

Figure 4-1. Comparing the profit consequences of alternative sales force sizing strategies

sales force, perhaps leading to a loss of faith in the leadership team and a lowering of morale. If, on the other hand, they hire too few salespeople, sales leaders rarely recognize their failure to make the most of a significant opportunity. The business achieves its conservative sales and profit targets, sales force pay and morale are high, and the sales leaders walk around with smiles on their faces, giving little thought to what might have happened if the sales force had been larger. Yet sizing too conservatively can result in significant lost opportunity, a substantial forfeiture of sales and profits, and, in the long term, reduced business strength.

In the words of one sales leader, "You live with what you launch with." The sales gap created when a company initially undersizes its sales force has a permanent impact on its ability to grow its sales and reach peak market share. Smart sales leaders escalate sales force investment as early success signals emerge.

Size More Cautiously When Uncertainty Is High.

Software Developer Evolves Its Sales Strategy as It Learns From Early Customers

In 2003, software developer Scalix launched a new e-mail software product that was designed to cut the cost of e-mail administration in large corporations by at least 50 percent. Hosted on the Linux operating system, the program had several unique advantages over traditional Windows-based e-mail programs, including superior reliability, security, scalability, and cost-effectiveness. Early market research had revealed a very positive response from CIOs to the software's value proposition, so the company decided to expand its sales force quickly, hiring a number of people with enterprise experience to sell directly to CIOs at large companies. Unfortunately, after the product's launch, the company encountered a serious problem with its marketing strategy. Many of the operations people one level down from the CIO, who were influential in the purchasing decision, were not comfortable with a Linux-based system, and so they were not receptive to the company's value proposition. As a result, the sales strategy had to be revised. Sales efforts were redirected to a more focused audience of education and public-sector organizations, where acceptance of Linux was strong. Because much of the work required to sell to this audience could be handled by two in-house telesales people, a large field sales organization was not needed. This new, more focused and cost-effective sales strategy worked well for Scalix. Yet the company could have saved a lot of money and gotten on the right track more quickly if it had delayed hiring a big sales force and instead hired a small number of sales-people to focus on learning about customer needs and refining the market-ing strategy prior to a full-scale launch.

When a high level of uncertainty surrounds the launch of a new prod-uct or service, it's prudent for sales leaders to act conservatively as they size their sales force.

Companies that launch new products into markets that are new to them learn a lot as they acquire their first customers. Early sales experi-ences often reveal that some of the product features do not work exactly as described or that selling strategies are not as effective as market research may have predicted. As the sales force learns more about how customers acquire, use, and value the product, sales processes evolve, the value proposition is fine-tuned, and sales effort is refocused on the most valuable customer segments.

Smaller sales forces are more flexible than larger ones. When a sales force is small, salespeople can share the knowledge they acquire more readily and adapt to shifts in sales strategy more quickly. The faster the sales force learns and adapts, the sooner it becomes effective and efficient at selling, and the more rapidly a stable model of sales success will emerge. And, of course, in highly uncertain situations, a conservative approach to expanding a sales force puts the company's finances at less risk.

In new and growing companies, it makes good sense to expand the sales force aggressively to capture early market opportunity when uncertainty is low, but to be conservative in order to provide flexibility when uncertainty is high.

The Sales Force Is a Long-Term Investment

New and growing businesses should size their sales forces based on at least a three-year time horizon of future sales aspirations. If sales are expected to rise quickly, but company leaders focus only on current-year sales when deciding how many salespeople to hire, they are likely to undersize the force. Sales forces are not variable resources that can be switched off and on quickly, like an advertising budget. It takes many months to hire and train good salespeople, and it takes time for salespeople to build relationships with customers.

Sizing Strategies for Mature Businesses

Typically, as a business matures, there is less focus on the size of the sales force. However, there are situations in which modest upsizing is appropriate, especially if the sales leaders were conservative during the growth stage. Other businesses may need to downsize slightly as pressure to deliver profitable sales intensifies, products mature, and markets become increasingly competitive.

In some cases, the current size of a sales force may be appropriate. Later in the chapter, we will describe several tests to help you determine if this is true for your company. First, though, we offer some background discussion and a series of observations about the dynamics of sizing a sales force.

Gains from Working Smarter Can Exceed Gains from Increasing Size. For mature businesses, smart sales effort allocation is actually a more significant profit enhancer than sales force sizing. Financially, it may make sense to improve the *quality* of the sales effort, not to increase the *quantity* of effort. When we analyzed a sample of data-driven, analytical sales force sizing studies that ZS Associates conducted for 50 companies, we discovered that, for mature businesses, smarter allocation of sales time across customers, products, and selling activities has an almost 2.5 times greater profit impact than an increase in the size of the sales force. You can improve the allocation of effort across the sales force by enhancing several sales effectiveness drivers—for example, by providing the sales force with better targeting information, coaching salespeople to perform critical sales activities more effectively, or adjusting the compensation plan to encourage sales of the most profitable product lines.

Downsize Strategically. As a business moves from maturity into decline, downsizing of the sales force is inevitable. As the size of the sales force is reduced, it is most effective to deploy direct salespeople to perform the most critical, high-value selling activities with the most profitable, retainable, and strategically important customers and product lines. Sales leaders can use more efficient sales resources, such as sales assistants, a telesales group, Internet channel partners, or other lower-cost selling partners, to reach other customer segments, sell less strategic product lines, and perform some selling activities.

Lubricants Manufacturer Increases Reliance on Selling Partners as It Downsizes

A lubricants manufacturer that was facing declining sales, with no turnaround in sight, needed to make cost reductions to preserve its profitability. The company revised its worldwide selling channel strategy, moving hundreds of thousands of customers that had formerly been covered by the company's own direct sales force into coverage by lower-cost partner sales organizations. The partners were able to spread their overhead (such as office space and employee benefits) across a wider array of products than the manufacturer could and therefore were able to conduct the selling process much less expensively. The size of the manufacturer's direct sales force was reduced substantially, and the much smaller group of direct salespeople that remained began to focus exclusively on value-based selling to large, strategically important customers.

Activity Specialization Improves Efficiency for Grainger

W. W. Grainger, a maintenance, repair, and operational (MRO) supply company, achieved efficiency gains by reassigning some selling tasks from expensive salespeople to a cheaper resource. Once a sale is made, the sales force turns many accounts over to an inside telesales group that handles postsales support, such as order placement and delivery.

Sales Force Sizing Dynamics

Smart sales leaders understand several dynamics about sales force size and its impact on performance. Figure 4-2 shows the relationship between sales force size and some commonly used performance metrics. The metrics represent activities and results over a year's time. Following the three graphs, we offer several observations about the relationships they describe.

Observation 1: There Are Diminishing Returns to Sales Force Effort

The relationship between sales force size and either sales or gross contribution margin (sales less variable product costs) yields diminishing returns, as shown in Figure 4-2, Graph A. A division president overlooked this fact when he negotiated with his vice president of sales, who wanted to add 10 salespeople. The president asserted that in order to add headcount, the VP had to promise to deliver more sales. Since the average salesperson was generating $2 million in sales per year, the president proposed adding $20 million to the VP's sales goal for next year.

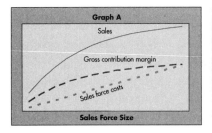
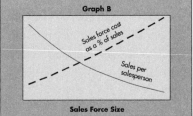
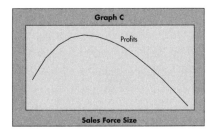

Figure 4-2. The relationship between sales force size and several sales force performance metrics

The president was partly right—more salespeople should be expected to generate more sales. However, his assumption that additional salespeople could deliver the same average sales as existing salespeople was flawed. First, new salespeople need time to learn the company's products, markets, and selling process and to establish effective customer relationships; thus, their effectiveness during the first year may be only 50 to 60 percent of that of a veteran.

Second, even after they have become fully effective, additional salespeople tend to bring down the average sales per salesperson. The existing sales force has gathered the low-hanging fruit; when the sales force expands, all the salespeople will have to dig deeper into the universe of customers and work harder to earn their sales. Only in very rapidly growing markets or when a sales force is significantly undersized is it reasonable to expect additional salespeople to match the average sales of current salespeople.

Observation 2: Sales Force Size Affects Financial Ratios

The relationships between sales force size, sales, and sales force costs have implications for the financial ratios that many companies use to manage their sales force investment. Graph B shows the relationship between sales force size and two commonly used financial ratios: sales per salesperson and sales force costs as a percentage of sales. Sales leaders like to have high sales per salesperson and a low sales force cost as a percentage of sales; they feel that these relationships imply high sales force effectiveness and productivity. Yet high sales per salesperson or low sales force cost as a percentage of sales can also be a sign that the sales force is undersized. Think about it this way: The best way to maximize sales per salesperson and minimize sales force cost as a percentage of sales would be to fire all but one salesperson!

Observation 3: There Is a Sales Force Size That Maximizes Profits

Graph C shows the relationship between sales force size and profits (gross contribution margin less sales force costs). Profits are highest when the size of the sales force is such that the incremental contribution of the last salesperson added is equal to the incremental cost of that salesperson. Compare Graphs B and C, and note that even when the sales force is smaller than the profit-maximizing size, adding salespeople to increase profitability reduces sales per salesperson and increases sales force costs as a percentage of sales. These relationships tend to be a little counterintuitive, since many sales leaders view high sales per salesperson and low sales force cost ratios as surrogates for profitability.

Consider Carryover When Sizing the Sales Force

Changes in the size of a sales force have both short-term and long-term impacts on costs and sales. As salespeople are added, incremental sales increase slowly at first and accelerate over time as the new salespeople become acclimated to their jobs and the new customers that they acquire make repeat purchases. Sales increases appear more slowly in companies with long selling cycles—that is, when many months of selling effort are needed to close a sale.

On the other hand, when sales force size decreases, sales may not decline immediately, as repeat purchases by loyal customers continue to contribute to sales for a period of time despite reduced sales force coverage. Only over time does the impact of the size reduction become apparent as this repeat business gradually dwindles.

The long-term impact of changes in sales force sizing is clearer when sales leaders take into account *carryover sales*—sales that are attributable to this year's effort and will continue in the future without further sales force effort. Carryover sales occur when a product meets the needs of a customer, and that customer continues to buy it even if a salesperson is no longer promoting it. Carryover is especially likely when switching products is costly. The impact of carryover increases as products mature. In some markets, carryover sales represent a large portion of total sales.

Because of carryover, the multiyear sales impact of adding or reducing salespeople is much larger than the one-year impact. Upsizing a sales force can result in an incremental profit reduction in the first year because sales force costs increase immediately, whereas sales increase slowly, but a significant profit improvement can be attained as the impact of carryover sales is fully realized over three, four, and five years. Similarly, reducing sales force size can have an immediate and positive profit impact because costs are reduced right away, but the positive profit impact will dwindle over time as carryover sales are lost.

When we analyzed a sample of sales force sizing studies that ZS Associates conducted for 50 sales forces, we discovered that the sales force size that maximizes one-year profits is 18 percent smaller, on average, than the size that maximizes three-year profits (see Figure 4-3). The considerable difference between the one-year and three-year profit-maximizing size creates a dilemma for sales leaders who recognize that three-year revenue streams are less predictable than one-year streams, and at the same time are under pressure to deliver short-term results.

Figure 4-3. Carryover and sales force sizing

Risk Aversion and Sales Force Size Changes

The uncertain and long-term sales impact of a sales force size change tends to make sales leaders cautious about making such changes. During periods of growth, leaders look for about a 50 percent incremental return on their investment when adding salespeople, and risk aversion causes them to stop adding people before they reach the long-term profit-maximizing size. Yet when they are downsizing, sales leaders require only a positive incremental return; they stop cutting when they reach the long-term profit-maximizing size. If sales leaders were to use consistent sales force sizing criteria when upsizing and downsizing, they would expand more in favorable circumstances and cut more in unfavorable circumstances. By using one of the market-based approaches we describe later in this chapter, companies can overcome the conservatism that leads to a sales force size that fails to maximize profits.

How to Size Your Sales Force for Success

Figure 4-4 shows the steps involved in a systematic process for sizing your sales force.

Figure 4-4. A sales force sizing process

Assess the Current Size of Your Sales Force

You can quickly and easily perform five tests to help you decide whether your sales force is the right size. The different tests provide insights to different company stakeholders. Sales management is likely to care most about the results of the customer, sales force morale, and selling activity tests. Marketing leaders will be most interested in the competitive position test results, and finance leaders are likely to focus on the findings of the financial test.

Customer Test

Customer Reaction Plays a Role in Sales Force Reductions in the Pharmaceutical Industry

Physicians increasingly say that they are annoyed by the large number of pharmaceutical salespeople. In 2007, over 90 percent of physicians and other health-care professionals felt that drug companies spent too much money promoting their products. Some doctors are visited by more than 20 different pharmaceutical salespeople every day, many of whom sell the same products and provide only one-way communication. In other words, because of the high profit margins and aggressive competition in the industry, pharmaceutical sales forces have increased in size beyond what customers say they want or need. Between 2004 and 2007, Pfizer, Bristol-Myers Squibb, and Eli Lilly all cut the size of their field sales forces and sought better ways to leverage the smaller sales forces for improved interaction with physicians.

Because customers' comments can provide important signals, consider using customer surveys to assess the size of your sales force. Figure 4-5 depicts customers' reactions to a sales force that is either too large or too small.

If your company collects data that measure customer-level market sales and potential, you can complement qualitative input from customers with a quantitative look at your market coverage. You can gain insights about sales force size by comparing the percentage of your customers that contributes 80 percent of company sales to the percentage that accounts for 80 percent of the market's sales (or potential). Company sales that are far more concentrated than the market's may be an indication that your company is focusing on a small number of customers and leaving money on the table; you may need more salespeople to go after more customers. Company sales that are less concentrated than the market's may indicate that too many salespeople are going after lower-potential customers; you can afford to reduce sales force size and focus more on valuable customers.

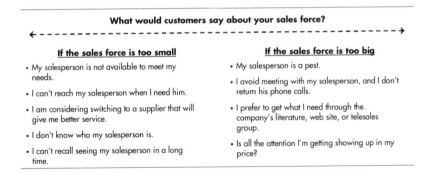

Figure 4-5. The customer test of sales force size

Sales Force Morale Test

Too Much Sales Force Travel Causes Morale Problems and Turnover

A company had 28 salespeople covering the United States. Some territories encompassed several large states; the salespeople in these territories were almost never home and consequently suffered a great deal of stress. The sales force had a high turnover rate (40 percent per year), which the company attributed to the heavy travel requirements. Because the company's products were very complex and specialized, the cost of hiring and training new salespeople was significant. The company increased the number of salespeople and thus reduced each individual's need to travel, funding the expansion in part through the reduced hiring and training costs as turnover decreased. Also, a reduction in territory vacancies translated into fewer lost sales.

The morale of your sales force can be linked to its size. When there are either too many or too few salespeople, morale suffers. While many salespeople have complaints whenever they speak to their managers, the frequency and strength of their complaints intensify when a sales force is not the right size, and high sales force turnover can be a signal that a sales force is not sized correctly. Effective sales leaders listen closely to the complaints of good salespeople.

If good salespeople are leaving your company, you must find out why. Figure 4-6 lays out some typical comments from salespeople that may be important indicators about the size of a sales force.

Selling Activities Test. To help determine if your sales force is the right size, use sales force surveys, call reporting data, and observations by sales managers to study how your salespeople are spending their time. Figure 4-7 provides some signs that the sales force is either too large or too small.

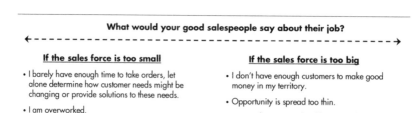

Figure 4-6. The sales force morale test of sales force size

Competitive Position Test. Another way to judge the size of your sales force is to compare your company's investment in its sales force with that of your competitors. Market share often depends more on "share of voice" with customers than on the absolute amount of time the sales force spends with those customers. If your major competitors are reducing their sales staffs, you may be able to downsize your sales force as well without losing market share. Sales may decline if the entire market is declining, but a company often maintains or strengthens its competitive position by maintaining or increasing its share of voice. Similarly, if competitors are increasing their sales staff, your company's sales force also needs to expand in order to maintain share of voice and thus preserve market share.

A competitive benchmarking analysis like the one shown in Figure 4-8 can help you determine a sales force size that ensures that you are not outshouted by your competitors. The analysis compares the estimated number of offices and salespeople that major competitors in the insurance industry have in the western region of the United States. The company that did the analysis has 14 salespeople in this region—more than Competitors A, B, and C, but less than half as many as Competitor D. If the company hopes to take market share from Competitor D, it needs to increase the size of its sales force.

Financial Test. A breakeven analysis can help determine whether your

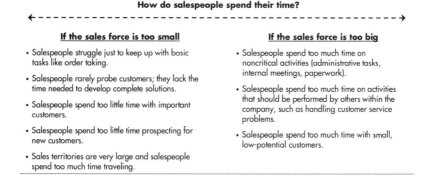

Figure 4-7. The selling activities test of sales force size

sales force is too large, too small, or about the right size. Use the following seven steps to conduct this analysis.

1. **Estimate the annual cost of a salesperson.** Include all costs that vary with the number of salespeople, including salary, benefits, taxes, bonuses, automobiles, travel expenses, computers, call reporting, administrative support, and field support.

2. **Estimate the gross contribution margin rate.** This is the percentage of sales that the business keeps, after taking out variable product costs. Variable product costs include raw materials, manufacturing, royalties, freight to factory, and shipping to customers. Variable costs do not include allocations of fixed costs, such as factory overhead and R&D.

3. **Calculate breakeven sales.** This is the amount that a salesperson must sell in a year to cover his cost. Divide the annual cost of a salesperson by the gross contribution margin rate.

4. **Estimate the incremental sales that an additional salesperson could generate in a year.** The current average annual sales per salesperson provides a reference point for what this level of sales might be. Incremental annual sales per additional salesperson will be less than the average annual sales per current salesperson because of the diminishing returns on additional sales force effort and because of the lower effectiveness of new salespeople.

5. **Divide incremental annual sales per additional salesperson by breakeven sales to get the breakeven ratio.** This ratio reflects the

State	Our Company (Offices, Salespeople)		Competitor A		Competitor B		Competitor C		Competitor D	
California	Los Angeles	5	Los Angeles	4	Los Angeles	3	Orange County	4	Los Angeles	13
	Orange County	3			Santa Ana	1			San Diego	3
	Sacramento	2	San Francisco	4					Sacramento	2
	San Francisco	2			San Francisco	4	San Francisco	5	San Francisco	7
Hawaii			Portland, OR	1						
Oregon	Seattle	2			Portland, OR	3	Seattle	2	Seattle	4
Washington			Seattle	2						
Alaska										
Totals	**5 offices**	**14**	**4 offices**	**11**	**4 offices**	**11**	**3 offices**	**11**	**5 offices**	**29**

Figure 4-8. Competitive benchmarking of sales force size at an insurance company

extent to which the sales generated by an additional salesperson will cover her costs. For example, a ratio of 2.00 implies that on average, a new salesperson will generate gross margin equal to twice her cost within a year.

6. Estimate the percentage of this year's sales that will be maintained next year without any sales force effort next year. This is the carry-over rate.

7. Use the table in Figure 4-9 to find out what the breakeven ratio and the carryover rate imply about sales force size. The numbers in each cell of the table represent a three-year ROI on incremental sales force investment. The sizing recommendations are based on the following ROI targets:

- ROI of less than 50 percent: The sales force is too large.

- ROI of 50 to 150 percent: The sales force is the right size.

- ROI of more than 150 percent: The sales force is too small.

These ROI targets are consistent with those commonly used by the sales organizations we have worked with; however, the ROI targets can be adjusted to a specific situation and the sizing recommendation adjusted accordingly.

For a given breakeven ratio, the ROI (and therefore the sales force sizing recommendation) varies depending on the carryover rate. For example, a ratio of 1.00 implies that in a low-carryover environment (that is, less than 40 percent of sales would be maintained next year without effort), the sales force may be too large. In a moderate-carryover environment (more than 40 percent but less than 90 percent of sales maintained next year without effort), the sales force is about the right size. In a high-carryover environment (90 percent or more of sales would be retained next year without effort), the sales force may be too small.

Figure 4-10 shows an example of the financial test calculations for one sales organization.

Assessment Summary. The analysis in Figure 4-11 summarizes the results of the five sales force sizing tests for one company. Notice that the tests produce conflicting conclusions. The sales force morale test suggests that

New Salesperson Sales/ Breakeven Sales	Carryover									
	0%	10.0%	20.0%	30.0%	40.0%	50.0%	60.0%	70.0%	80.0%	90.0%
0.25	−75%	−72%	−69%	−65%	−61%	−56%	−51%	−45%	−39%	−32%
0.50	−50%	−45%	−38%	−31%	−22%	−13%	−2%	10%	22%	36%
0.75	−25%	−17%	−7%	4%	17%	31%	47%	64%	83%	103%
1.00	0%	11%	24%	39%	56%	75%	96%	119%	144%	171%
1.25	25%	39%	55%	74%	95%	119%	145%	174%	205%	239%
1.50	50%	67%	86%	109%	134%	163%	194%	229%	266%	307%
1.75	75%	94%	117%	143%	173%	206%	243%	283%	327%	374%
2.00	100%	122%	148%	178%	212%	250%	292%	338%	388%	442%
2.25	125%	150%	179%	213%	251%	294%	341%	393%	449%	510%
2.50	150%	178%	210%	248%	290%	338%	390%	448%	510%	578%
2.75	175%	205%	241%	282%	329%	381%	439%	502%	571%	645%
3.00	200%	233%	272%	317%	368%	425%	488%	557%	632%	713%
3.25	225%	261%	303%	352%	407%	469%	537%	612%	693%	781%
3.50	250%	289%	334%	387%	446%	513%	586%	667%	754%	849%
3.75	275%	316%	365%	421%	485%	556%	635%	721%	815%	916%
4.00	300%	344%	396%	456%	524%	600%	684%	776%	876%	984%
4.25	325%	372%	427%	491%	563%	644%	733%	831%	937%	1052%
4.50	350%	400%	458%	526%	602%	688%	782%	886%	998%	1120%

Matrix contains the 3-year sales force ROI.

☐ = Oversized   ☐ = Right-sized   ■ = Undersized

Figure 4-9. Implications of the incremental sales per additional salesperson/breakeven sales ratio and carryover for sales force size

the sales force size should be reduced, while the competitive position and financial tests suggest that it should be maintained or increased. The customer and selling activities tests reveal more effective ways for salespeople to spend their time; further evaluation is needed to determine the impact of this reallocation of effort on sales force size. A synthesis of all the tests is required in order to make a final sales force sizing assessment.

Determine a Better, New Size

If the five quick tests suggest that your sales force size needs to change, you can examine several possible approaches for determining the best size.

Several Common Sales Force Sizing Decision Rules Can Sacrifice Profitability. Companies frequently employ one or more of the following six decision rules to size their sales forces. However, because these rules ignore market needs, they can lead to poor decisions. The first three are cost-focused decision processes that emphasize affordability.

Test Step	Example Calculation
1. Estimate the annual cost of a salesperson.	$75,000 salary and bonus (total compensation) + 22,500 benefits (30% of total compensation) + 11,250 field support (15% of total compensation) + 9,250 T&E, automobile, computer, phone, etc. $118,000 total annual cost of a salesperson
2. Estimate gross contribution margin rate.	($900 MM sales –$300 MM variable product costs)/ ($900 MM annual sales) = 66.7% gross contribution margin rate.
3. Calculate breakeven sales.	$118,000 cost of a salesperson/0.667 gross contribution margin rate = $176,912 breakeven sales.
4. Estimate annual incremental sales revenue that an additional salesperson could generate.	$525,000 incremental sales revenue per year per salesperson, according to management estimate.
5. Calculate the breakeven ratio.	$525,000 incremental sales/$176,912 breakeven sales = 2.97 breakeven ratio.
6. Estimate the carryover rate.	60% carryover according to management estimate.
7. Use the table in Figure 4–9 to find out what the estimates imply about sales force size.	The three-year ROI on incremental sales force investment is about 488%. According to the criteria used in most sales organizations, the sales force is undersized.

Figure 4-10. Financial test calculation example

	Main Findings	Implications for Sales Force Size
Customer test	• Customers want less frequent but more in-depth interactions with salespeople.	• Reevaluate sales force size assuming that salespeople make longer but less frequent calls on customers.
Selling activities test	• Salespeople spend similar amounts of time with all customers, even though business is fairly concentrated.	• Reevaluate sales force size assuming that salespeople reallocate some time from small customers to large customers.
Sales force morale test	• Salespeople are frustrated that many customers will not see them as often as they'd like.	• Reduce sales force size to reflect customer restrictions on salespeople's face time.
Competitive position test	• Main competitors show no sign of pulling back effort.	• Maintain or grow sales force size to maintain or grow share of voice.
Financial test	• Current sales force size is producing a 50 percent marginal ROI, but new products are coming.	• Grow sales force size to support the new products, but continue to size to 50 percent marginal ROI, reflecting the moderately aggressive company stance on investment.

Figure 4-11. Results of the five sales force sizing tests at one company

If a company follows any of these practices, its sales force may not be sized correctly to maximize profit.

Decision Rule #1: Maintain a sales force size that keeps sales force costs at a constant percentage of sales. At an international sales force productivity workshop, a country general manager asserts that he maximizes profits. When asked how he does this, he responds that he "keeps sales force costs at 11 percent of sales." Since sales are down this year, he'll have to cut the sales force in order to contain costs, an approach that focuses on affordability, not profitability. This decision rule is based on logic that is backward thinking; it implies that sales should drive sales force effort. But the cause and effect are in the other direction—sales force effort drives sales. Maintaining the sales force cost-to-sales ratio is not the same thing as maximizing profits. While it may seem counterintuitive, when the sales force is undersized, adding salespeople increases the sales force cost-to-sales ratio, but at the same time increases profitability. The dynamics are more intuitive when the sales force is oversized—cutting headcount reduces the sales force cost-to-sales ratio and also increases profitability. It is always possible to reduce the sales force cost-to-sales ratio by cutting headcount, yet the impact on profitability can be either positive or negative. Figure 4-2 shows how this can happen. While companies sometimes strive to maintain an industry average cost-to-sales ratio, this practice can hurt small-share companies, which may need to maintain a higher sales force cost-to-sales ratio than that of their larger-share competitors in order to get an adequate share of voice with customers.

Decision Rule #2: Split a territory as soon as its sales hit a certain threshold level. At one company, as soon as a territory hits $3 million in sales, the sales leadership feels that it can afford another salesperson and gives part of the territory to the new salesperson. The veteran salesperson's "reward" for working hard to build business is to have his territory reduced. As a result, over time, too many salespeople are placed in geographies where salespeople were successful initially and too few salespeople are placed in other geographies. The company does not consider how much sales potential there is in a given territory or how much of that potential remains untapped. Another downside to this decision rule: It gives salespeople who have a territory with sales that are approaching the threshold level an incentive to stop selling in order to keep their territory intact.

Decision Rule #3: Add salespeople when the current sales force generates enough sales to afford an increased investment. This rule is an "earn-your-way," risk-averse strategy, once again focusing on affordability rather than profitability. Many growing companies that follow this very conservative approach to managing sales force growth leave millions of dollars on the table. The approach may be necessary in markets with very high uncertainty or when a company is cash-strapped; however, when there is reasonable certainty of success and available financing, companies that take this risk-averse approach to sales force growth undersize their sales forces and miss out on considerable opportunity. The sales force should be viewed as an investment that drives sales, not as a cost item that needs to be justified by sales.

Three additional decision rules for sales force sizing reflect common thinking patterns. Many companies follow these practices and as a result may miss out on growth opportunities, give effectiveness priority over investment, or allow complacency to creep into their sales forces.

Decision Rule #4: It's not necessary to increase sales force size to pursue new opportunities. A company plans to launch an exciting new product in the coming year. Since the product will be sold to many existing customers and requires selling skills that are similar to those for other company products, the vice president of sales decides to add the new product to the sales force's portfolio. "This will be an exciting new challenge for the sales force and will give us something new to talk about with our customers," she reasons. However, she downplays the fact that the new product will consume 50 to 60 percent of the sales force's time during the launch phase, drastically curtailing the time available to sell other products. It's dangerous to assume that existing products will maintain their rate of sales in the absence of sales force effort. Often companies pursue new opportunities that require considerable attention from the sales force, while still maintaining aggressive, history-based sales goals for existing products. But when new opportunities consume significant amounts of sales force time, existing products often fail to make their goals. Adding sales force capacity is the only way to give a significant new opportunity the attention it needs if it is to be successful and at the same time protect existing products and customers.

Decision Rule #5: Get more effective and reduce headcount. A company installs a new customer relationship management (CRM) system and implements an expensive new training program. The sales leaders' reasoning goes like this: "These initiatives will increase sales force effectiveness by 10 percent. Therefore, we can reduce our sales force from 100 to 90, and the reduction will pay for the initiatives." This reasoning fails to take into account that the effectiveness initiatives reduce selling costs and at the same time increase the effectiveness of each sales call by allowing salespeople to accomplish more in less time. A lower selling cost and higher sales per call enable the company to call on more accounts and prospects profitably. Customers who were too expensive to call on before are now profitable to visit. Hence, expanding the sales force upon the implementation of the new effectiveness-enhancing programs may actually increase profitability. In some cases, effectiveness enhancement means doing more with less, but at other times, the sales force actually becomes more effective when the company invests to do more with more.

Decision Rule #6: If the current sales force size worked last year, avoid disruption and keep the size the same this year. A vice president of sales is preparing his budget for the upcoming year. He reasons, "We had a sales force of 90 last year, and we made our numbers. Next year's goal is a stretch, but why change anything? It's working!" The vice president is satisfied because by staying at the same size, he doesn't incur any reorganization costs and avoids disrupting customer relationships. However, the "same as last year" rule may have failed to consider that during the past year, the economy slowed down, the company canceled the launch of a new product, and major competitors decreased their sales force sizes by 30 percent. All these changes suggest that perhaps last year's sales force size is too large for this year. While it's tempting to avoid rocking the boat when things are working, most markets are fairly dynamic, and sales force size needs to be reevaluated annually. A nondecision to keep sales force size the same is in fact a decision that may not be the best option.

Market-Based Approaches: A Better Way to Make Sales Force Sizing Decisions. These six decision rules, which sales leaders commonly rely on when considering whether to resize a sales force, can lead to nonproductive outcomes. The reason? They do not pay enough attention to market dynamics. Market-based approaches acknowledge that the size of the sales force determines how many customers the company can cover, how much time is spent with those customers, and how much sales effort various products can receive. Therefore, sales force size drives company sales and profits. Market-based approaches combine analysis with management input to create good, data-driven recommendations for sizing a sales force.

A market-based approach to sizing a sales force begins with a focus on the customer. Figure 4-12 outlines two necessary basic steps.

Step 1: Understand and segment customers. To identify meaningful customer segments, study the customer universe; understand the product, service, and support needs of different customer types; and cluster customers with similar needs into market segments in order to tailor sales strategies to the needs of each segment. Approaches for segmenting customers and prospects are described in more detail in Chapter 3.

Customers differ in many ways. Some are large and some are small. Some want the best price; others want the best service. Some are early adopters, eager to try the latest innovation, while others prefer well-tested solutions. Some customers are interested in many of the products and services that the company has to offer, whereas others want only a select few of them. Customers also vary in their buying processes. Some make purchasing decisions centrally, while others delegate purchasing to individual departments or locations. Some have a single point of control for purchases, while for others, many people influence buying decisions.

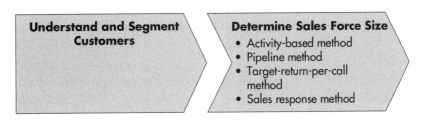

Figure 4-12. A market-based process for sizing the sales force

Customer segmentation organizes a large universe of current and potential customers into groups with common characteristics so that companies can prioritize accounts and customize value propositions and sales processes. A company with a limited number of potential customers (for example, a first-tier supplier of gaskets to automobile manufacturers) is likely to develop a unique value proposition and sales process for each individual customer. However, if there are many possible customers with diverse needs, it is more practical to prioritize and plan at the segment level.

The best segment selling processes acknowledge the value that each segment can generate for the company. Companies typically use financial measures such as sales, unit volume, and profits to determine a segment's value.

Step 2: Determine sales force size. Determine the number of salespeople needed to implement the desired sales strategy for each market segment. Market-based sizing methodologies vary in terms of their sophistication in measuring the link between the number of salespeople, their coverage of customers, and the value (such as sales or profits) that coverage generates.

Sales force size is determined by aggregating the coverage plans—in other words, the sales force time required to execute the sales process—for each customer segment. Increasing the size of the sales force increases costs, but also allows greater coverage of customers, which in turn creates more sales. Similarly, reducing the size of the sales force lowers costs but reduces customer coverage and results in lower sales. Determining the right sales force size and level of coverage is critical to maximizing profits.

Measuring the link between sales force size, segment coverage, and segment financial value is not easy. With the right data and analytical capabilities, some companies can measure the link directly; however, many rely on management input to develop estimates of these relationships.

Four market-based sizing methodologies, listed in increasing order of sophistication, are described in Figure 4-13. The *activity-based* and *pipeline* approaches rely on structured management input about the coverage needed in order to be successful with different market segments. The *target-return-per-call* approach builds on these methods by adding management estimates of financial value to the calculations so that return on investment (ROI) can be used to evaluate sales force coverage options.

The *sales response* method relies on a combination of management input and analysis of historical data to measure the link between sales force size and financial value explicitly. The most sophisticated of the four approaches, sales response analysis suggests a sales force size that maximizes profit. Companies have successfully used all four of these approaches.

As shown in Figure 4-14, the four effective market-based approaches to sales force sizing vary in terms of their complexity, cost, and probability of determining the best size.

These four market-based sizing methodologies are examples from several frameworks and analytic approaches that exist to help sales leaders determine the right size for their sales force. A useful reference for anyone who wants to determine the most profitable sales force size is *Sales Force Design for Strategic Advantage* by Zoltners, Sinha, and Lorimer (Palgrave Macmillan, 2004).

Is It Better to Be Vaguely Right or Precisely Wrong?

The affordable approaches to sales force sizing described earlier (Decision Rules 1, 2, and 3) typically employ a precise logic in their calculus—for example, sales force expenditures will be 3 percent of sales. The market-based approaches are not as precise. They require an understanding of the marketplace and estimates of good coverage strategies and the financial value they will bring. Because sales force sizing decisions drive market outcomes, we believe that the affordable approaches are precise but invoke a wrong logic, while the market-based approaches are vague but use a compelling logic. As Len Lodish of Wharton Business School once said, "I would rather be vaguely right than precisely wrong."

Implement the New Size
Growing Your Sales Force. You may face several challenges when you increase the size of your sales force. Two of the most significant are

Sizing method	Steps required for each customer segment	Simplified example for one customer segment
Activity-based	• Develop a list of sales activities to be performed at accounts. • Estimate the time it takes to complete those activities (can be expressed as calls per year and time per call). • Calculate the total hours required to cover accounts in the segment. • Estimate the call capacity of a salesperson and calculate the number of salespeople required to cover the segment.	In a retail merchandising sales force: **Segment: Direct Retail Stores / # of Accounts / Calls per Year / Hours per Call / Total Hours / Salespeople Needed** | Segment: Direct Retail Stores	# of Accounts	Calls / Year	Hours / Call	Total Hours	Sales-people Needed | |---|---|---|---|---|---| | Over $25K | 112 | 12 | 2.0 | 2,688 | 2.0 | | $12 – 25K | 784 | 6 | 2.0 | 9,408 | 7.1 | | $5 – 12K | 2,543 | 4 | 2.0 | 20,344 | 15.4 | | Under $5K | 6,559 | 3 | 1.0 | 19,677 | 14.9 | | Total Direct Retail | 9,998 | — | — | 52,117 | 39.4 | Hours per salesperson per year: 1,325
Pipeline	• Map the sales process stages. • Estimate the number of prospects entering the sales pipeline. • Estimate the sales time required at each stage and the success rate resulting from that effort. • Estimate the total sales time required and the number of accounts successfully sold. • Estimate the call capacity of a salesperson and calculate the number of salespeople required to cover the segment.	In a medical device sales force: Leads entering pipeline: 1240 Qualify lead: .5 hr x 90% success rate Educate customer: 7.5 hrs. x 35% success rate Sell value proposition: 3.75 hrs. x 70% success rate Service and support: 10 hrs. Sales time required: 13,192 hours to get 273 accounts Hours per salesperson per year = 1,250 Salespeople required: 10.6 for one year
Target-return-per-call	• Estimate the number of salespeople needed to cover the segment (could use the activity-based or pipeline method). • Estimate the cost of coverage (salespeople required x cost per salesperson). • Estimate the value of coverage (contribution generated). • Calculate a segment ROI. • Compare to a target ROI to determine if the segment should be covered.	In a not-for-profit sales force: | | Segment 1 | Segment 2 | |---|---|---| | Salespeople needed to cover | 4.2 | 1.5 | | Cost to cover | $1,050K | $375K | | Value of sales force coverage | $8,423K | $832K | | Segment ROI | 702% | 122% | | Target ROI | 200% | 200% | | Cover segment? | Yes | No |
Sales response method	• Measure the relationship between sales force effort and sales for each product, market, or product/market combination directly using historical and judgmental data. • Use the relationship to evaluate the short- and long-term sales and profit consequences of alternative sales force sizes.	A pharmaceutical sales force used data to derive the following response curves:

Figure 4-13. Four market-based methods of sales force sizing

Approach	Understand-ability	Data	Analysis	Cost	Probability of Getting a Good Answer
Activity-based	Simple, easy to explain	Relatively easy to obtain	Straightforward	Low to moderate	Moderate
Pipeline	Moderate	Relatively easy to obtain	Straightforward	Low to moderate	Moderate to high
Target-return-per-call	Complicated	Easy to obtain	Straightforward	Low	Moderate
Sales-response	Complicated	Requires sales and activity data	Requires statistics	Moderate to high	Very high

Figure 4-14. Comparing the market-based approaches to sales force sizing

addressing the resistance of the sales force to expansion and establishing effective processes for assimilating new salespeople.

Salespeople Often Fight Sales Force Expansion

At a medical devices company, when sales leaders set out to implement an expansion plan involving 25 additional sales territories, the salespeople and sales managers strongly resisted. The salespeople, who were paid on commission, feared that the change would have an adverse impact on their earnings. They had worked hard to develop their "book of business," and they felt that they deserved to reap the benefits of their past efforts by earning commissions on easy repeat sales to current customers. They argued that the new territories were not justified, and they did whatever they could to make sure that their will prevailed, including threatening to resign and go to work for competitors (taking their accounts with them) if their account base was reduced. Salespeople put so much pressure on management that only 12 of the 25 proposed new territories were ultimately implemented.

For sales forces that are paid largely on commission, several incentive compensation plan strategies can reduce the resistance to expansion. These strategies include establishing a precedent for change early in the life of an incentive compensation plan, designing a goal-based plan that does not penalize salespeople who give up accounts to expansion territories, and establishing temporary transition compensation plans that keep salespeople's compensation "whole" for a period following expansion. Sales leadership can reduce the sales force's resistance to expansion by managing the expansion carefully—for example, establishing objective and quantifiable business criteria for territory size, such as an ideal level of untapped market potential or a maximum number of key accounts per territory. Expansion decisions that are based on consistent criteria are more likely to be perceived as uniformly fair. If expansion decisions are based primarily on executive opinions rather than on data, salespeople will come up with countless reasons why new territories are not needed.

When the size of a sales force increases, recruiting and training new salespeople adds significantly to the workload of sales managers. Managers in rapidly growing businesses often struggle to keep up with their day-to-day coaching and selling responsibilities, and they may not have sufficient time to hire and train large numbers of new salespeople. One way to ease this stress is to keep the sales force span of control (the average number of people that report to each sales manager) at a reasonable level while the sales force is growing. This will ensure that managers have enough time to manage their people well and, at the same time, recruit and train effectively. Also, leverage external resources and build strong support programs to assist sales managers with their hiring and training responsibilities. One company hired a recruiting/training manager and paid him incentives based on the second-year performance of all new hires.

Downsizing a Sales Force

Multiple Waves of Downsizing Affect Sales Force Morale and Motivation

During the downsizing of the sales force for a telecommunications company, managers attended a one-day workshop on how to fire salespeople. Since this was the third (and they knew not the last) downsizing at the company, managers wondered, "Is someone being trained on how to fire me?" Morale and motivation were at new lows and had not hit bottom yet.

During downsizing—a painful process that can be devastating for sales force morale—sales leaders are challenged to reduce the sales force headcount strategically while minimizing the pain to the organization and keeping a core group of salespeople who will retain key customers.

Sometimes it is possible to avoid massive layoffs by anticipating a need for future downsizing and using attrition to slowly reduce the sales force to the desirable size. To be successful, attrition management programs need to be systematic. Too often, companies implement across-the-board hiring freezes that result in insufficient coverage of important customers when top salespeople in high-potential territories leave the company. Intelligent attrition management programs consider "territory opportunity," closing down vacant territories in low-potential areas but retaining those in high-opportunity areas. When the smartest companies implement hiring freezes, they evaluate the potential of every territory that becomes vacant and will transfer current salespeople or allow selective hiring to fill important vacancies.

A Canadian Company Uses Systematic Attrition Management to Downsize Its Sales Force

A company in Canada was selling a mature product line and had no major new products in the pipeline. Since sales leaders knew that the decline stage was imminent and that sales force layoffs were coming soon, they created a plan to make the impending downsizing less painful. The company had 100 salespeople and expected a reduction to 70 salespeople in about a year. Sales leaders laid out 70 sales territories for the downsized sales force, and the top 70 salespeople, based on performance rank, were each given a territory in the new configuration. Those who were ranked below the top 70 were put into "overlay" territories and were asked to assist the 70 salespeople by co-selling at important accounts. The salespeople in the overlay territories were told that as attrition among the top 70 salespeople occurred over the next year, they would be offered a territory based on their performance rank and location. Planning ahead helped the company retain the best salespeople and make the transition to the new, smaller organization successfully.

When a significant decline in sales opportunities is not anticipated far enough in advance, the only viable strategy is to reduce the sales force rapidly. Survivors will know quickly that they have a job and some reasonable level of job security, customers will have greater confidence about what the future holds, and sales leaders can begin to rebuild a new, smaller, and more focused sales organization.

Protecting the company's top customers and best salespeople should be the highest priorities when a sales force must be downsized.

CHAPTER 5

Structuring Your Sales Force for Efficiency and Effectiveness

Sales forces can be structured in a variety of ways. Here are a few examples:

- Salespeople at Avon, a beauty products company, are generalists. The company has more than five million independent sales representatives who sell not only Avon's extensive line of beauty products, but also fashion jewelry and accessories, apparel, gifts, and collectibles. There are no defined sales territories; Avon salespeople can sell to any customer with whom they develop a relationship. Sales leadership at Avon allows salespeople to decide how to spend their time and encourages independence and entrepreneurship.

- At Roche Diagnostics, a major supplier of medical diagnostics products, salespeople specialize by product. The company has a broad, complex product portfolio that includes four major product lines: research equipment and its reagents, analyzers and their reagents, glucose meters and strips, and diagnostic tests. The sales force is organized as four separate product-specialty teams that share hospitals as major customers. Functioning as product specialists allows the sales force to be very knowledgeable and effective at selling a large and complex product line.

- W. W. Grainger, a maintenance, repair, and operational (MRO) supply company, improves efficiency through activity specialization. It assigns routine, administrative selling tasks, such as postsales support, order placement, and delivery, to a less expensive inside telesales group, with field salespeople performing activities that require more detailed knowledge of the company's products and services.

- Nextel salespeople are industry specialists. Salespeople who sell to this wireless telecommunications company's large corporate customers specialize by industry segment—for example, construction, financial services, health care, manufacturing, or government. Specialization allows salespeople to become experts in a particular industry so that they can provide more value to customers.

- Television network ABC uses a hybrid selling model. Client specialists focus on selling advertising time to a particular advertising agency or directly to a major client. In addition, product specialists, called daypart specialists, focus on selling ads that run during a particular part of the day, such as daytime, prime time, or late night. A client specialist is responsible for developing a partnership, executing buying and planning goals, and finalizing deals with a particular major client or agency. The client specialist engages the daypart specialists to help with pricing and with the specific details of the deal for the various dayparts.

Having the right sales force structure allows companies to conduct effective sales processes with every targeted customer segment, directing the selling effort to the right products, markets, and activities, while utilizing sales resources efficiently. The structure of your sales force can have a significant impact on your customer and company results.

Structuring the Sales Force for Results
How Specialized Should a Sales Force Be?

Should your salespeople be *generalists*, selling all products and performing all selling tasks for all types of customers (as salespeople do at Avon)?

Or should they be *specialists*, focusing on a particular product (as at Roche Diagnostics), market (as at Nextel), and/or selling activity (as at Grainger)? Or are multiple types of specialists needed to serve customers effectively (as they are at ABC)?

Two primary factors influence the ideal degree of specialization, as shown in Figure 5-1. The first factor is the sales process. A sales process that is complex and diverse relative to the bandwidth, skills, or capacity of the salespeople who perform it requires specialization, while a sales process that is straightforward can be accomplished more efficiently with generalists.

The second factor that plays a role in determining how specialized the sales force should be is company objectives and strategy. Such goals and strategies as "increase customer focus," "reduce selling costs," "increase organizational flexibility," and "encourage cross-selling" affect the type of sales force structure that is best.

Sales Processes That Require Complex and Diverse Skills Lead to Sales Force Specialization

Members of a single generalist sales force are *efficient*—they will have smaller sales territories and less travel time, and thus they can spend more time with customers.

Figure 5-2 shows the efficiency that a generalist sales force offers as compared with that of a specialized sales force.

However, while a generalist sales force is efficient, it may not be very *effective*—in other words, salespeople may have a low impact per call. A company's sales process can be quite complex if it requires

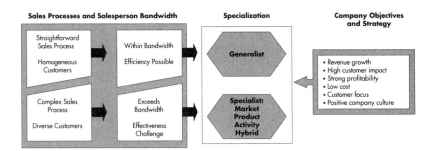

Figure 5-1. Should salespeople be specialists or generalists?

	Scenario I	**Scenario II**
Sales force organization	A single geographic team	Two specialty teams
Number of salespeople	100	70 and 30
Sales territory description	Each sales territory has roughly 1% of the country	Overlapping territories: The 70-person team has territories that are on average 43% larger in size than the geographic team. The 30-person team has territories that are on average 3.3 times as large as those for the geographic team.

Figure 5-2. A comparison of efficiency for a generalist versus a specialized sales organization

diverse skills, if it needs to be adapted significantly for different types of customers, and/or if it requires knowledge of a broad and complex product line. One salesperson may not be able to acquire the skills and knowledge required to execute a complex sales process effectively.

What Is the Bandwidth of the Sales Force? In the world of telecommunications, bandwidth refers to the amount of information that can be carried through a communication channel, such as a phone line, cable, fiber, or satellite connection. The bandwidth concept can also be applied to salespeople. There is a limit to how much an individual salesperson can understand and be effective at selling. At some point, a salesperson who is responsible for selling a large, complex, or hard-to-sell product and service portfolio, or who is expected to perform many different selling tasks for several different customer segments with complex and diverse needs, will not be able to perform the job effectively. The job will exceed the salesperson's bandwidth.

When this happens, salespeople are likely to ignore those customers, products, or selling activities that are most difficult or unpleasant for them. Unfortunately, these customers, products, or activities may have strategic importance for the company or represent a large profit opportunity, so a salesperson who is trying to do a job that exceeds his bandwidth may not be able to produce the results the company wants.

Companies that sell many complex products to multiple diverse markets require a sales bandwidth that is much greater than the capacity of a single salesperson. For example, IBM sells hundreds of different hardware and software products, as well as professional services. It sells to numerous industries in more than 90 countries and to customers of all sizes, from huge multinational corporations to small "mom-and-pop" businesses. Figure 5-3 lists the major categories of products, services, and markets sold by IBM in 2007, according to the company's web site. The bandwidth required for a salesperson to understand all of these would be enormous. No single salesperson, no matter how intelligent or hardworking, could ever do this job.

IBM's Sales Force Structure

To bring its customers the needed expertise, IBM has created a highly specialized sales force structure. More than 40,000 people are organized into many different sales divisions with dozens of different types of sales specialists, structured around markets, products, and activities. In addition, the company relies on thousands of business partners—distributors, value-added resellers, and software vendors, among others—to sell many of its products in many markets. IBM has restructured its sales organization many times to address bandwidth concerns. For example, a major sales force restructuring in 2001 organized the sales force into teams based on customer size and industry. Before the restructuring, many of IBM's customers felt that IBM salespeople knew a little about a wide variety of topics but lacked the in-depth industry knowledge that they needed. With the new market-based structure, salespeople were trained as industry experts and became able to respond to specific customer needs more quickly. IBM industry teams included product experts, whose detailed knowledge of specific products and services allowed them to solve customers' problems quickly without help from other sales organizations.

The number of products and markets that a salesperson can handle increases if the products are simple, the target markets are homogeneous, and the selling processes across products and markets are similar or require similar skills.

Services Sold	Products Sold	Markets Sold To
IT Services • Applications on demand • Business continuity and resiliency • End user services • Integrated communications • IT strategy and architecture • Maintenance and technical support • Middleware services • Outsourcing/hosting • Security and privacy • Server services • Service-oriented architecture • Services for mid-market business • Site and facilities • Storage and data **Application Services** • Application management services • Application integration services • Services-oriented architecture/web services **Business Consulting** • Financial management • Human capital management • Customer relationship management • Strategy and change • Supply chain management **Business Process Outsourcing** • Training • Classroom training • Onsite training • E-learning • Certifications • Strategy and design **Note:** This list includes just the major service categories. The "Services A to Z" listing on the company website lists more than 500 different IBM service offerings.	**Systems and Servers** • System i (iSeries) • System p5 (pSeries) • System z (Mainframe) • System x (xSeries) • BladeCenter • Cluster servers • UNIX servers • Linux servers • POWER processor-based servers • Intel processor-based servers • AMD processor-based servers **Software** • Application servers • Applications—desktop and enterprise • Business integration • Commerce • Data and information management • Host transaction processing • Learning software • Messaging applications • Mobile, speech, and enterprise access • Networking • Operating systems • Organizational productivity, portals and collaboration • Security • Software development • Storage management • Systems management **Storage** • Disk systems • Tape systems • Storage area networks • Network attached storage • Storage software • Hard drives/microdrives **Semiconductors** **Upgrades, Accessories, and Parts** **Printing Systems** **Point-of-Sales and Self-Service Offerings** **Workstations** • IntelliStation Pro • IntelliStation POWER • Workstation accessories **IBM Certified Used Equipment** **PC Recycling and Buyback Programs** **PC Products from Levono**	**By Size** • Multinational corporations • Large business • Medium-sized business • Small business • Home and home office **By Industry** • Aerospace and defense • Automotive • Banking • Chemicals and petroleum • Consumer products • Education • Electronics • Energy and utilities • Financial markets • Government • Health care • Insurance • Life sciences • Media and entertainment • Retail • Telecommunications • Travel and transportation • Wholesale distribution **By Geography** • Africa • Asia • Australia • Europe • North America • South America • 90+ countries • 30+ languages

Figure 5-3. Sales bandwidth required for IBM

Specializing for Strategy

Sales force specialization can reinforce company strategies and make it easier to accomplish important objectives. Following are several examples that show how changes in sales force structures have helped companies achieve specific objectives for revenue growth, profitability, customer focus, and company culture.

Microsoft's Strategy: Grow Revenues Through Increased Emphasis on Solution Selling. In 2002, Microsoft's sales strategy was aimed at growing revenues and income through increased emphasis on selling customers not just software, but also business solutions. "Solution selling" required greater industry expertise, so Microsoft expanded its sales force by 20 percent and established seven new vertical selling teams to serve the needs of large customers in the retail, health-care, automotive manufacturing, high-tech manufacturing, oil and gas, media and entertainment, and professional services industries. These industry-specific vertical teams were added to five vertical teams that had been established two years earlier for the financial services, telecommunications, state and local government, federal government, and education sectors. The new sales teams ranged in size from 90 to 300 people and included industry specialists in sales, service and support, partnering, and marketing. The vertical teams allowed Microsoft to get closer to the business challenges faced by its customers within each industry, enabling the sales force to sell more complete solutions that addressed specific business needs. Industry sales teams were sometimes located near the headquarters of key customers—for example, the oil and gas industry team was located in Houston, Texas, and its salespeople were proficient at selling highly specialized and integrated geological and geophysical applications as part of the total Microsoft solution. In short, the new structure encouraged Microsoft salespeople to be more effective sellers and helped the company grow revenues.

SAP's Strategy: Improve Profitability Through Cost Reductions. At SAP, one of the world's largest providers of business software, bleak economic conditions in 2002 led to a sharp decline in revenue. In order to improve profitability, the company focused its strategies on cost reduction. In addition to eliminating 132 sales positions in the United States (a 3 percent reduction in its total sales force), SAP restructured its sales force. Instead of each salesperson specializing in a particular industry, sales territories were reorganized geographically so that each salesperson sold a wider array of products to a more local group of customers. The new geographic sales territories allowed salespeople to be more efficient in covering their customers and helped the company reduce costs.

Procter & Gamble's Strategy: Grow Sales and Profits by Focusing on Key Customers. When Procter & Gamble (P&G) wanted to improve its relationships with its most important national and regional chain customers in the United States, it established vertical selling teams dedicated to serving their needs. The teams were organized around individual accounts or types of accounts. For example, P&G had approximately 300 people dedicated to serving the needs of its largest customer, Wal-Mart, at its headquarters in Bentonville, Arkansas. P&G's Wal-Mart team consisted of people from sales, marketing, distribution, supply chain management, IT, and finance. Its goal was to enhance Wal-Mart's profitability from P&G products while increasing revenues and profits for P&G.

W. L. Gore's Strategy: Create Success Through a Culture of Innovation and Teamwork. At W. L. Gore, the maker of Gore-Tex weatherproof fabric and other innovative products, a unique culture has been built around innovation, empowerment, and teamwork, and the company's sales force structure is designed to encourage that culture. The sales force is organized into what Gore calls a lattice structure—there are no titles and no official lines of reporting. Every salesperson has a sponsor, who functions as a mentor, not a boss, and sales leaders function like coaches and help salespeople set their own sales goals. Salespeople work together on teams to meet the needs of their customers. This structure helps perpetuate the company's entrepreneurial culture. Salespeople stay focused on long-term customer success and are willing to help one another out as needed to respond effectively to customer needs.

Choosing the Right Sales Force Structure and Managing its Stresses

In many ways, the structure of a sales force is like the skeleton of a building—it supports certain parts of the building, but causes stresses in others. Success requires finding an excellent sales force structure, one that allows salespeople to be effective within their bandwidth and helps the company accomplish its objectives. At the same time, it is important to create effective mechanisms for dealing with the stresses that the structure creates. In this section we describe the advantages of different types of sales force structures and ideas for addressing the stresses they cause.

Generalist Sales Forces Are Efficient but Not Always Effective

Generalists in the Bottled-Water Industry

A company that sells bottled water to residential and commercial accounts uses generalist salespeople to sell water coolers and bottled-water delivery contracts. The salespeople are also responsible for installing the coolers and making bottled-water deliveries on a regular basis. Territories are determined by geography, so that every salesperson covers both the residential and commercial accounts that fall within a compact geographical area.

A sales force of generalists provides several benefits:

- There's no duplication of effort, since just one salesperson calls on each customer.
- Salespeople can live close to their accounts, minimizing travel time and costs and maximizing the time devoted to face-to-face selling.
- There's no confusion regarding who is responsible and accountable for each customer; customers always know whom to talk to.
- The generalist approach encourages entrepreneurship among salespeople, as they "own" their customers and have the freedom to make decisions about how to spend their time.
- It's a flexible structure, allowing quick reallocation of sales effort to different customers or product lines as company priorities change, and it can evolve to become more specialized fairly easily, if necessary.

The primary disadvantage of generalist salespeople is that they are typically not as effective as specialists. Many start-up companies launch their first products using generalist salespeople but have to shift to a more specialized structure as salespeople come to need more product expertise and deeper customer knowledge in order to win at competitive accounts.

Other disadvantages of having a sales force of generalists are:

- Generalists are single individuals who have to do everything, including administrative tasks that take time that might otherwise be spent making sales calls.
- Generalists who are asked to sell many products to many diverse customers often choose to work within their comfort zone and may tend to ignore some strategically important products, customers, or selling activities.

Sales Assistants Enhance Productivity at International Paper

A number of generalist salespeople in the xpedx distribution division of International Paper hire their own sales assistants to help with administrative tasks, freeing time for selling. The commissions that the salespeople receive from their incremental sales more than cover the cost of paying a sales assistant's salary.

If your company fields generalist salespeople, you can employ a number of sales effectiveness drivers to ease the stresses associated with the generalist approach and to direct the efforts of salespeople toward important customers, products, and activities. For example:

- Exciters. You can use incentives to direct the sales force's attention to key customers, products, or selling activities. For example, a medical instruments company encourages salespeople to focus on the right products by paying a 6 percent commission on sales of strategic products, 4 percent on growth products, and 2 percent on core products.
- Enlighteners. Providing salespeople with information can help them make good decisions about how to spend their time. For example, an automobile tire manufacturer gives salespeople lists of accounts in their territories that have high potential but low penetration.
- Shapers and controllers. You can train salespeople in effective time-allocation strategies and challenge them to achieve specific customer, product, or activity goals. For example, an executive search

firm encourages new salespeople to engage in activities that drive success (like calling potential job candidates and making company visits) by developing skills that help them excel at such activities during training and giving new salespeople daily and weekly goals for the activities.

There's no guarantee that you will be successful in using exciters, enlighteners, shapers, and controllers to influence the allocation of selling effort in a generalist sales force. The best way to ensure that a strategically important product, customer, or activity attains a specific level of selling effort is to set up a dedicated sales force that sells that product or focuses on that customer or activity. This important point deserves repeating:

> The best way to ensure that a strategically important product, customer, or activity attains a specific level of selling effort is to set up a dedicated sales force that sells that product or focuses on that customer or activity.

Specializing in Particular Products and Selling Activities Enhances Expertise in Those Areas, but Can Compromise Customer Focus

Product Line Expansion Drives New Sales Roles at Hollister

Hollister, a health-care products manufacturer, broadened its product line over many years through a mix of new product development and acquisitions. By 2000, Hollister's single generalist sales team was selling five different product lines. Each line had its own set of customers and decision makers, with little overlap, and the products were at very different points in their life cycles. Each product line had a very distinct value proposition and faced a different set of competitors, requiring the sales force to master multiple positioning messages. In order to increase the effectiveness of its salespeople and drive revenue growth, Hollister split the product portfolio between two separate sales teams. Selling a smaller number of products to a more focused audience allowed each salesperson to be more knowledgeable and thus more effective.

Product specialization gives a sales force several advantages:

- When a product line is broad or complex, a specialized sales force has better product knowledge and thus is more effective.
- Sales leaders can intensify and direct the sales effort toward strategically important products more easily.
- The sales force becomes more accountable to product-based business units.

Activity Specialization Enhances Effectiveness in the Computer Industry

Some firms in the computer industry organize their sales forces into a "hunter/farmer" structure. "Hunter" salespeople specialize in finding business at new accounts. Once a sale is made, a "farmer" salesperson takes over the account to cultivate the relationship and generate repeat business. Companies that use these two sales roles can better match salespeople's personalities and skills to the tasks at hand and thus increase overall effectiveness.

Activity specialization has several advantages:

- The sales force has better knowledge of and effectiveness in sales activities that require diverse skills and knowledge.
- If some tasks can be assigned to cheaper selling resources, such as sales assistants or telesales, the company may be able to improve its efficiency.

Field and Telesales Teams Improve Efficiency at Oracle

At software maker Oracle, inside and outside salespeople are matched up in teams that work together to meet customer needs and achieve territory sales goals. Some of the inside salespeople who are assigned to teams that cover U.S. customers are located in India. These team members handle telephone prospecting, online product demonstrations, and other selling tasks that can be done remotely.

Companies that structure the sales force to specialize by product or selling activity will have to deal with a few challenges:

- Lack of customer focus. Customers may dislike dealing with several salespeople from the same company, preferring the convenience of working with one salesperson who is responsible for all products and all activities.
- Duplication of effort. More time and money is expended when several salespeople must travel to the same customer.
- Increased coordination requirements. Salespeople may spend a considerable amount of time documenting customer information or communicating internally with colleagues who also call on the shared customer—activities that reduce the amount of time spent with the customer.
- Missed opportunities for cross-selling. Salespeople are focused on their own products and may miss opportunities to sell other products in the company's portfolio that can meet customer needs.

Customers of a Medical Systems Company Want to See Fewer Salespeople

A medical systems company sold hospitals and other medical facilities a broad line of products ranging from large capital equipment and software systems to smaller machines and reagent chemicals. Because the company's products were diverse and technically complex, the company assigned each customer several specialist salespeople who had deep technical expertise. But feedback from customers, most of whom saw five, six, or seven different salespeople from the company, indicated that they preferred to deal with just one or two company salespeople.

If your company structures the sales force as product and activity specialists, there are several sales effectiveness drivers that you can use to minimize these disadvantages:

- Exciters. You can use team-based incentives to encourage specialists who call on common customers to share leads and coordinate their efforts in the customer's best interest.

- Enlighteners. Utilizing CRM systems that provide a centralized source of customer information will allow sales specialists to easily obtain information about companywide contacts with their customers.

- Controllers. Consider establishing customer-centric goals that are shared by salespeople who call on common customers.

- Shapers. Focused training can help sales team members communicate with one another efficiently.

AlliedSignal Adjusts Its Sales Force Structure and Systems to Improve Its Customer Focus

As described in Chapter 1, the sales organization at airplane parts supplier AlliedSignal (which merged with Honeywell in 1999) was very large and specialized. The company had a broad and technical product line, and major customers had as many as 50 different contact points within the sales force. Lack of coordination among the salespeople who called on the same accounts frustrated customers, many of whom were turning to lower-cost suppliers. To improve the coordination of its sales efforts, AlliedSignal developed a companywide CRM system that provided a single source of customer information for sales reps, field service engineers, product-line personnel, and response center agents across three business units. Quick access to customer information meant that sales efforts could be easily coordinated at the customer level.

Exploiting Cross-Selling Opportunities in Product-Based Structures

A sales force that has more than one product specialist covering a customer contact can use cross-selling to leverage key customer relationships and enhance sales force effectiveness. For example, a bank encouraged cross-selling between bankers (who sold deposits, loans, and trust services) and brokers (who sold investment products) by leveraging several sales force effectiveness drivers to create a cross-selling culture. Bankers and brokers were given a single net income goal. Bankers could earn commissions for selling brokers' products, and brokers could earn commissions for selling bankers' products. Bankers and brokers with common clients met weekly to discuss plans and share client names, and the bank encouraged joint sales calls that crossed traditional banking and brokerage boundaries. The approach helped the entire sales force become more sales-oriented and proactive in developing and sharing leads.

A company that sold specialized software to banks encouraged successful cross-selling of its various software products to major banks by enhancing its product-based sales force structure. Each major bank was assigned to an account manager, who played the role of "quarterback," bringing in product specialists at the right time to meet customer needs. Medium-sized community banks that did not justify an extra selling face were covered by multiple product-line salespeople, who communicated with one another to identify cross-selling opportunities. The smallest banks were covered by telesales people who sold the entire product line.

Market Specialists Enhance the Company's Understanding of Customer Needs, but Their Product and Selling Activity Expertise and Focus Can Be Compromised

Market Diversity Drives Specialization in a Networking Equipment Sales Force

A networking equipment manufacturer uses sales force specialization based on customer size and industry. There are three main sales groups, organized around customers of different sizes: The *enterprise account group* covers the firm's largest, most strategically important accounts; a *mid-market account group* covers moderately large accounts; and a *geographic account team* calls on smaller accounts. To enhance the effectiveness of its sales efforts at enterprise accounts, salespeople in that group are assigned to different industry teams. One team focuses on carriers and service providers (such as AT&T and Sprint); another calls on government, education, and utility accounts; a third calls on finance and retail accounts; and a fourth calls on health-care and high-tech accounts.

Market Focus Enhances Sales Force Effectiveness

A company that sells airport parking services targets two separate markets: travel agents who influence leisure travelers, and corporations who influence business travelers. Even though salespeople have enough bandwidth to cover both markets, the company's sales force is specialized by market, as this increases the effectiveness of sales calls. Each salesperson becomes more focused on the needs of her assigned market segment (either travel agents or corporations), making the sales force more knowledgeable and valuable to customers and thus able to generate higher sales.

Market specialization has several advantages:

- It increases salespeople's knowledge of customers and enhances their ability to meet the complex needs of a diverse customer base.
- Salespeople become highly adaptable to changes in customer needs and buying processes.
- Sales leaders can intensify and direct sales efforts toward strategically important customers more easily.
- It creates clear accountability for sales that meet the customer's overall needs.
- Assigning smaller or geographically remote customers to cheaper selling resources, such as telesales, creates opportunities to improve efficiency.

The major disadvantage of specializing by market is the potential for compromising a focus on products or selling activities. When their attention is centered on markets and customers, salespeople may not have complete knowledge of the company's products, and their focus on particular brands may be diminished. A market-focused sales structure can also make it hard for sales leaders to properly allocate effort to strategically important products or selling activities. Market-based specialization can be difficult to implement at companies with product-based business units, where unit leaders want control of their own sales force resource.

If your company structures its sales force using market specialists, you can use the sales effectiveness drivers to minimize these disadvantages:

- Shapers. You can provide training that increases the sales force's knowledge of important products or selling activities.
- Enlighteners. Innovative systems can give salespeople access to detailed product information or provide "how to" guidance for critical selling activities.
- Exciters. Incentives—for example, paying a higher commission rate on sales of strategic products—will direct the sales force's attention to key products.
- Controllers. You can establish product-based or selling activity goals for salespeople (in addition to customer-based goals).

Achieving Both Customer and Brand Focus at Procter & Gamble

When P&G restructured its sales organization from product-based to market-based specialization during the early 1990s, the sales force became more responsive to the needs of major customers. However, the company did not want to take focus away from the performance of individual brands. In an effort to keep the strength of the P&G brands, major accounts were serviced by account teams that included salespeople who focused on particular product lines—for example, laundry detergent, health and beauty aids, or diapers. Team members worked together to coordinate efforts within the account.

In Complex Selling Environments, Hybrid Structures Enhance Efficiency and Effectiveness

As we noted earlier in this chapter, IBM's sales force has dozens of different types of sales specialists and business partners, organized around markets, products, and activities. Complex hybrid structures like this one frequently evolve when the bandwidth of a generalist sales force is challenged by product-line growth and market expansion.

Hybrid sales force structures include teams of salespeople with different expertise working together to serve the needs of customers. Teams can include a mix of generalists and product, market, and activity specialists.

A Hybrid Sales Structure Enhances Effectiveness with Customers at a Tire Manufacturer

A tire manufacturer meets the diverse needs of its customers with a hybrid sales force structure. The company sells several brands of tires into two major markets with very different needs. The first market, original equipment manufacturers (OEMs), includes automobile and truck makers and farm equipment manufacturers that use the tires on new vehicles. The second market includes mass merchandisers, retailers, automobile repair chains, and small tire retailers that sell replacement tires. In the OEM market, each tire is custom designed for a particular vehicle. Success in this market requires a highly specialized sales force. For every OEM account, each type and brand of tire has an account team of sales, engineering/R&D, and customer service personnel who collaborate to create products that best fit the customer's needs and provide adequate returns to the company. For the replacement market, there is virtually no product customization, and salespeople who sell to this market sell all types and brands of tires. Major accounts—Wal-Mart, Sears, and national auto parts chains—are covered by dedicated vertical sales teams. Smaller accounts—independent auto parts chains and small retailers—are covered by generalist salespeople assigned to geographic sales territories. A hybrid sales structure enables the company to be effective and efficient at selling its broad product line to customers with diverse needs.

Hybrid specialization allows sales forces that face diversity and complexity in their products, markets, and/or selling activities to deliver value to customers more effectively. The customer intimacy that hybrid specialization can create for a company can be a significant source of competitive advantage.

The major disadvantage of hybrid sales force specialization is that it is often very complex and challenging to implement successfully, for several reasons:

- It requires a high degree of internal coordination, which means that more sales managers or salespeople have to spend more time coordinating their activities and less time selling.

- Salespeople need to learn not only their customers' organizations and buying processes, but also the complexities of their own sales organization in order to assemble the right resources to address each customer's needs.

- Individual accountability is diminished, since several people work together to sell to each customer.

- Flexibility is limited when a sales organization has many interdependent parts and overlapping responsibilities and when salespeople are so specialized that it takes a lot of effort to retrain them when customer or company needs change.

Companies can use the sales effectiveness drivers to minimize these disadvantages. The methods suggested in this chapter for addressing the stresses that arise with generalist, product and activity specialist, and market specialist structures can be leveraged jointly to create a hybrid structure that enhances sales effectiveness.

Insights for Better Sales Force Structures
Match the Sales Force Structure to the Company's Business Life Cycle

Company strategies change as businesses move through their life cycles, and good sales force structures adapt accordingly. A structure that works well during the start-up phase is often different from what works when the business is growing, during its maturity, and through its eventual decline. Figure 5-4 suggests a classic evolution of sales force structure across a business life cycle.

During start-up, companies use selling partners or create a small sales force of generalists to sell a narrow product line to a limited number of market segments. As the business ramps up and the company enters the growth stage, the complexity of the sales job increases: The company launches new products and/or targets new markets that require salespeople to engage in new selling activities. Smart sales leaders establish more specialized sales roles to expand the sales force bandwidth to meet an increasingly diverse set of customer needs effectively.

As growth slows and the company enters maturity, maintaining the specialized sales force structures that evolved during the growth stage often becomes too expensive as the company becomes more focused on costs and profitability. At this point, sales leaders need to create more efficient sales force structures (for example, replacing some of the specialists with generalists) and leverage lower-cost sales resources like telesales to reduce costs. They will need to utilize even more cost-efficient resources during the decline stage, reducing the size of the sales force and redirecting the attention of the direct sales force to the most strate-

Decision	Business Life Cycle Stage			
	Start-up	Growth	Maturity	Decline
Customer strategy	Create awareness and generate quick uptake in high-potential market segments that are responsive to selling effort.	Penetrate initial market segments while developing new segments.	Focus on customer retention and serving existing market segments more efficiently.	Continue efficiency focus, protect key customer relationships, and exit unprofitable segments.
Sales force structures	Use selling partners or create a small sales force of generalists.	Grow the sales force and create specialized sales roles as job complexity starts to challenge sales force bandwidth.	Cut costs by reducing the number of specialist teams and leveraging lower-cost resources, like telesales.	Reduce sales force size and refocus effort on strategically important customers and products; continue to leverage lower-cost selling resources.

Figure 5-4. Customer strategy and sales force structure throughout the business life cycle

gically important customers and products. A sales culture that encourages a flexible, change-friendly sales force makes it possible to redesign the structure of the force as business needs change.

Focus on Implementation

Changing the structure of a sales force is not easy. Sometimes it creates so much chaos and disruption for customers and salespeople that the benefits of a theoretically better design are never realized because there is no practical way to make the transition from the current to the new design. In many companies, the sales force has been unable to successfully shift from product-based specialization to market-based specialization because the accounting system measures profit and loss by product and not by market, making it very difficult to hold a market-based sales force accountable for results.

Even the best sales force structures will fail if they are not implemented effectively, so paying careful attention to customer transition strategies during a sales force restructuring is critical. When a sales force restructures, customers may see more or fewer of the company's salespeople and may need to establish relationships with different salespeople. An effective transition from one sales force structure to another enhances the company's relationship with its customers and adds customer value. An ineffective transition can reduce service levels for the customer, disrupt important relationships, and result in lost sales and market share.

What Xerox Customers Said About the Firm's Reorganization

Xerox implemented a two-phase reorganization of its sales force in 1999, in an effort to shift more direct selling effort toward its largest global customers while creating industry-specific selling teams. The restructuring effort was not initially successful: Performance fell well short of company goals, and many salespeople left the company. Customers complained of neglect by Xerox salespeople after the restructuring and cited a lack of willingness to negotiate price even when sales were being lost. One commercial printing customer, whose long-time Xerox service rep was reassigned during the restructuring, reported seeing 11 different service reps over a five-month period, none of whom knew how to service his machines. As a result, the customer replaced his Xerox machines with those of a competitor.

Any change in the structure of a sales force obviously affects salespeople. When a restructuring is done right, sales force morale and motivation improve, or at least remain constant. Good sales leaders anticipate problems and deal with them effectively. But poor implementation of a new sales force structure can damage the motivation that drives the sales force. Salespeople may not work at peak performance and may spend too much time on nonproductive tasks. Good salespeople may leave the company. Sales force reorganizations can also create considerable stress for sales managers and other employees who support the sales force, including human resources, systems, and training personnel.

Change typically creates anxiety, but it also creates excitement. Reorganization gives a sales force new opportunities. A star performer picks up a major new account with big earnings potential. A salesperson is reassigned to a new industry team, giving her an opportunity to learn and expand her experience. A district sales manager must hire several new salespeople, allowing him to upgrade the existing skill sets of his team and improve sales in his region. Successful sales force restructuring initiatives emphasize the positive aspects of change, leverage the excitement it creates, and use it to build new and revitalized energy within the sales force.

Strategies for Implementing Successful Change in Sales Force Structure

- Protect the best customers. Understand which customers contribute the most to company profits, and make sure that they are well taken care of during the transition.
- Protect the best salespeople. Know who the top producers are, understand how the change affects their responsibilities and opportunities to earn incentives, and ensure that they are on board with the change.

- Avoid structures that are highly complex. The more complex a sales force structure is, the harder it will be to implement well. Think long and hard before making changes that severely disrupt customers, the sales force, and sales support structures.

- Begin implementation planning as you design the restructuring. Develop a plan for making the transition to a new structure when the process of designing the new structure begins. Involve key stakeholders—customers, salespeople, sales managers, and other company departments—appropriately in the process, and keep the channels of communication open.

- Stress the positive. Set a good example for the rest of the sales force by embracing change. Create an atmosphere of excitement about what lies ahead.

A Useful Reference

Numerous frameworks and analytic approaches can help sales leaders create sales force structures that will have maximum impact. A useful reference for anyone who is planning to restructure a sales organization is *Sales Force Design for Strategic Advantage* by Zoltners, Sinha, and Lorimer (Palgrave Macmillan, 2004).

Designing Sales Territories for Maximum Success

Sales Leaders Often Overlook Sales Territory Design

Sales leaders assign responsibility for customers and prospects, along with the associated selling activities, to salespeople and teams when they design sales territories. When these territories are well designed, the workload and opportunity in every territory are well matched to the capacity of the salesperson or team assigned to cover that territory.

But sales leaders can overlook the power of sales territory design as a sales effectiveness tool, and they often misdiagnose symptoms of poor territory design, focusing instead on other sales effectiveness concerns. Here are six examples:

Example 1: Targeting Problem?

"Why can't our sales force learn to target more effectively?" wonders a marketing manager. "The salespeople in Dallas have visited only 10 percent of the good leads that we passed on. No wonder our market share in Dallas is

115

so low! And in Atlanta, salespeople are spending too much time with low-potential prospects that aren't even on the target list."

Example 2: Hiring and Retention Problem?

"The Detroit territory is vacant again," says a frustrated Midwest regional director. "This is the fifth vacancy in just two years. In their exit interviews, the people who left implied that they were not given enough opportunity to succeed."

Example 3: Compensation Problem?

"I can't make any money with this incentive compensation program," complains an office products salesperson who has just completed his first year on the job. "I'm working twice as hard as veteran salespeople who are milking their well-established books of business, yet I earned just a small fraction of what they made this year."

Example 4: Award Trip Criteria Problem?

"This is the same group of salespeople who went on the award trip last year," observes a vice president of sales. "I wonder why several of the salespeople who I thought worked really hard this year didn't make the cut."

Example 5: Rank-Ordering Problem?

"Why do they insist on publishing these district market share rankings?" complains a pharmaceutical district sales manager in Denver. "My district has so much potential spread out across a huge geography, and I don't have enough salespeople to possibly cover it all. The rankings are unfair."

Example 6: Quota-Setting Problem?

"I had a good year, and now I'm rewarded with a huge quota for next year," complains a medical supply sales rep. "I'll never achieve that quota. Why can't my manager understand that the potential in my territory has been maxed out?"

A smart sales leader can at least partially remedy all of these situations through better territory design. In Example 1, targeting may improve if salespeople are redeployed from Atlanta (where low-potential prospects are being overcovered) to Dallas (where good leads are being neglected because the salespeople are too busy to follow up). In Example 2, the Detroit salesperson may stay on the job if her territory is enlarged so that she has more opportunity to generate sales. In the other examples, better territory design can lead to fairer recognition and rewards for the salespeople.

If sales leaders have not evaluated the territory design and adapted it to current business needs within the last year or two, it is likely that sales territory misalignments are keeping the sales force from achieving its maximum effectiveness. Poor territory design makes it impossible for the sales force to give all valuable customers the attention they deserve and, at the same time, underutilizes many talented salespeople. Poor territory design also makes it extremely difficult to identify and reward the true top performers and thus affects sales force morale and motivation. Poor territory design can also result in high travel costs.

Good Sales Territory Design Encourages Sales Success
Well-Designed Sales Territories Enhance Customer Coverage
Well-designed territories lead to increased sales because they allow salespeople to improve their customer and prospect coverage. A

salesperson in a territory with too much work or travel cannot possibly cover all the customers and prospects assigned to him. He probably spends his time traveling to and calling on accounts he's comfortable with, ignoring other, more challenging, but potentially more profitable, accounts. As a result, the company misses out on important sales opportunities. Likewise, a salesperson in a territory with too little work will spend a disproportionate amount of time on nonproductive activities, such as calls on low-potential customers, despite the fact that the sales generated from those customers are likely to be much less than the potential sales from the accounts that are not covered in high-workload territories. When sales leaders redesign territories, they can assign undercovered profitable accounts from high-workload territories to salespeople who have time to call on them; this increases sales force effectiveness, which leads directly to higher sales and profits—without increasing sales force headcount.

Figure 6-1 charts the results of a sales territory design assessment that shows the extent to which customer coverage needs and sales force capacity can be mismatched. The cosmetics company sales force in the example performs merchandising duties at retail stores—stocking shelves, setting up displays, and taking inventory. The company's intention was to design each territory's store workload to approximately match the capacity of a full-time salesperson.

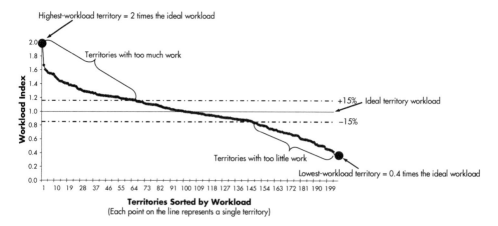

Figure 6-1. Sales territory design assessment: mismatches in sales force capacity and customer coverage needs for a cosmetics sales force

For the assessment, actual territory workloads were calculated by estimating how long merchandising tasks should take at the different types and sizes of stores in each territory. The territory workloads were indexed on the vertical axis, and the territories were sorted from highest to lowest workload and plotted as points along the curved line on the graph. An "ideal territory workload" range was determined (sales leaders felt that it was reasonable to expect almost all sales territory workloads to fall within 15 percent of the annual capacity of a salesperson). A comparison of the points along the curved line representing actual territory workloads with the horizontal band representing the ideal workload reveals the extent to which customer needs and sales force capacity were misaligned. Approximately 60 percent of the territories had either too much work or too little work for a full-time salesperson.

The extent of misalignment shown in Figure 6-1 is quite typical. Data for a convenience sample of over 4,800 territories from 18 sales territory redesigns that ZS Associates conducted in four industries in the United States and Canada showed that the majority of sales territories either had too much work for a salesperson to handle effectively (25 percent of territories) or had too little work to keep a salesperson fully busy (31 percent). Because of these mismatches, those businesses missed opportunities to add 2 to 7 percent to their revenues every year.

Well-Designed Sales Territories Improve Morale and Enhance the Power of Reward Systems

There is a high correlation between territory potential and territory sales. Across companies and industries, territory potential is often a better predictor of territory sales than any other factor, including the salesperson's experience, ability, and effort. Territories with high market potential often have high sales regardless of sales force effort. In fact, in environments with significant carryover, it is not uncommon for a vacant sales territory with high sales potential to have higher sales than a fully staffed territory with low sales potential. Similarly, territories with low potential tend to have low sales, but high market share.

Frequently, sales leaders do not place enough emphasis on differences in territory potential when they evaluate, compensate, reward, and acknowledge salespeople. When leaders underestimate the importance of these differences and treat salespeople as if their territories were identical, sales force morale suffers. Few salespeople will be content with what they consider to be inferior account assignments while their colleagues are making more money and getting more recognition with less effort because they have superior territories. Territories with low potential, intense competition, or too many small accounts, but a high quota, lead to low job satisfaction and low motivation for salespeople. For this reason, unfair sales territories often lead to salesperson turnover.

The link between territory design and sales force morale is especially strong when a large proportion of salespeople's pay and rewards is tied to their level of sales. For example, most of the salespeople's earnings at a medical device company came from incentives paid as a commission on sales. Morale was quite low because the sales force did not feel that the wide range of incentive pay across salespeople, shown in Figure 6-2, accurately reflected true performance differences. For example, the skills, capabilities, and motivation of the bottom 10 salespeople, who earned an average of just $28,500 in incentive pay, did not appear to be substantially different from those of the top 10, who earned an average of $116,000 in incentive pay—more than four times as much. Sales leaders assumed that something was wrong with the incentive plan. However, analysis revealed that poor territory design was the major cause of the variation in payout, and that the incentive plan could work quite well if territories were redesigned so that potential was distributed more equitably across the sales force.

The link between territory design and sales force morale is also strong when nonmonetary recognition—plaques, award trips, or invitations to join select groups such as the President's Club—is tied to territory sales. And territory balance is a *must* for those companies that publicly publish a forced ranking of all salespeople on any sales metric.

Well-Designed Sales Territories Keep Travel Time and Costs Under Control

Sales territories that minimize sales force travel allow more face time with customers and have a positive impact on sales force morale, especially when sales leaders distribute travel requirements fairly. As the cost of gasoline and other travel expenses rises, travel-efficient territories are increasingly important for managing sales force costs. More and more companies are discovering that the time and cost required for a

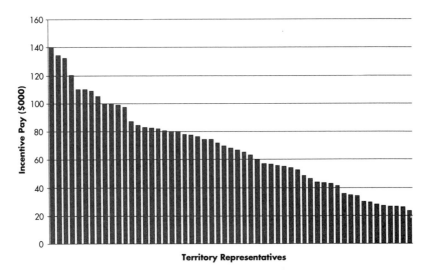

Figure 6-2. Range of incentive pay by salesperson at a medical device company

salesperson to travel a great distance to reach one potentially large customer cannot be justified; they find that they get a greater return from calls on several midsize customers closer to home.

Less Travel Allows More Selling Time for an Industrial Distribution Sales Force

The realignment of a large industrial distribution sales force resulted in a 13.7 percent reduction in salesperson travel time. That reduction translated into an almost $1 million savings in travel expenses in the mid-1990s, when gasoline cost about $1 a gallon; the savings would be considerably greater today. In addition, reducing travel time enabled the sales force to increase its selling time by 2.7 percent. The company estimated that this increase in coverage resulted in over $15 million in additional sales and over $3 million in additional profits.

Differences in travel requirements sometimes create a need for different sales force structures in remote and urban areas. Companies that use industry or product specialists in compact urban areas will often choose to place generalists in remote areas in order to minimize travel. Companies can also reduce sales force travel time and costs by using less expensive selling channels, such as telemarketing, direct mail, and Internet selling, to reach low-potential accounts in remote locations.

Insights for Overcoming Implementation Challenges

When companies take an "update as needed" and decentralized approach to territory design, the inevitable consequence is territories that do not effectively match sales force effort to customer needs, that compromise methods for evaluating and rewarding sales force performance, and that require excessive travel time and costs.

Companies can create and maintain well-designed territories by developing accurate measures of account workload and potential, auditing sales territory design at least every one or two years, and using well-thought-out, structured processes and efficient tools to change territories as necessary to support the needs of the business. In the sections that follow, we describe several components of a successful structured approach to sales territory redesign.

Evaluate Territory Design Decisions Using Defined Business Objectives

A structured territory redesign process begins with stated objectives that reinforce sales force strategy. Sales leaders can then evaluate proposed territory changes based on these unbiased business objectives, which might include:

Match territory workload to salesperson capacity. Having the right workload distribution across the sales force improves responsiveness to customers, ensures that salespeople are challenged but not overworked, and improves sales force morale.

Distribute sales potential fairly to salespeople. Equitable distribution of potential to salespeople improves sales results and morale. Depending on the compensation plan, the right distribution of sales potential can be critical to providing all salespeople with a fair opportunity to earn money.

Develop compact, travel-efficient territories. Territories that are geographically compact and efficient to reach make it easier for salespeople to be responsive to customer needs. Compact territories also reduce the need for overnight trips and keep travel costs down.

Unfortunately, these business objectives cannot always be achieved simultaneously. For example, it may be necessary to build territories with lighter workloads or lower potential in sparsely populated areas in order to make them geographically compact or to compensate for a large travel requirement. Often it is not possible to achieve equitable workload distribution and equitable sales potential distribution simultaneously. While workload and potential are closely correlated, territories with a greater proportion of large accounts will have a higher potential-to-workload ratio, whereas those with a greater proportion of small accounts will have a lower potential-to-workload ratio. The importance of each objective depends upon the mission of the sales force, the compensation plan, and the nature of the sales force's relationship with customers.

A Comparison of Territory Redesign Objectives

Part-Time Merchandising Sales Force	The primary business objective for a part-time merchandising organization in the consumer products industry was to build compact territories with manageable workloads. This would enable salespeople to perform their required duties at stores (stocking shelves, setting up displays, and taking inventories) without exceeding the weekly hour limit for part-time personnel.
High-Commission Chemicals Sales Force	The primary business objective for a highly commissioned chemical sales force was to distribute sales potential fairly. An equitable distribution of potential across sales territories provided the salespeople with fair

earnings opportunities. In addition, minimizing disruption between customers and salespeople was very important for this sales force because the sales process was complex and customer knowledge was a significant source of competitive advantage.

Companies frequently make the mistake of designing sales territories around the needs and desires of individual salespeople. While this strategy may keep a few salespeople happy in the short term, it can result in gerrymandered sales territories that do not make good business sense and that are likely to outlast the tenure of the people they were designed for. Sales territories are best designed from a customer and company perspective first; then the salespeople can be wisely matched with jobs that are consistent with long-term business needs.

Manage Disruption of Account-Salesperson Relationships

Sometimes companies are reluctant to redesign sales territories because they don't want to disrupt the continuity of salespeople's relationships with customers. Particularly in industries where the salespeople's customer knowledge is a source of competitive advantage, an ineffective transition from one salesperson to another could result in inadequate servicing of the customer and ultimately loss of business.

The good news is that a well-thought-out, comprehensive transition plan can make it less likely that the company will lose sales because of the territory redesign. For example, an industrial distribution company implemented a major redesign that resulted in many accounts being assigned to a different salesperson. To measure the sales impact of this disruption, the company tracked monthly sales prior to and following the redesign, comparing sales performance in accounts that had been reassigned to sales performance in accounts that had maintained a relationship with the same salesperson throughout. The sales impact of the disruption varied across three volume-based account segments, as shown in Figure 6-3. With small- and medium-volume accounts, salespeople generally did not have strong relationships with customers prior to the redesign, so the change in relationship had little or no impact on sales. At larger accounts, however, sales force relationships before the redesign were much stronger, and the change did have an impact. Large-volume accounts that had been reassigned purchased 20 percent less than those that kept the same salesperson throughout.

For its extra-large-volume accounts, the company took the relationship transition very seriously. The former salesperson introduced each affected customer to the new salesperson, the company encouraged teamwork between the former and the new salespeople, and the two shared commissions for a brief period. Because of the special attention the company gave to reassigned accounts in this segment, there was no falloff in sales. Had a similar transition program been implemented in the large-volume account segment, it's likely that the 20 percent sales loss would not have occurred.

Pay Attention to the Sales Compensation in Making the Transition

Sales force incentive compensation plans can create major obstacles when companies redesign their sales territories. Incentive compensation plans influence sales force behavior, and unfortunately this behavior is not always consistent with what is best for the organization as a whole. For example, incentive plans based on sales volume encourage salespeople to

	Small- and Medium-Volume Accounts	Large-Volume Accounts	Extra-Large-Volume Accounts
Annual purchasing volume ($000)	$2–50	$50–100	$100+
Purchasing affected by change in salesperson relationship?	No	Yes	No
Did strong salesperson relationships exist before realignment?	No	Yes	Yes
Was relationship transition program implemented?	No	Somewhat	Yes

Figure 6-3. Disruption impact from an industrial distribution sales force realignment—results summary

want more accounts than they can cover effectively, since having more accounts means having more opportunities to build sales. Incentive plans based on market share encourage salespeople to want fewer accounts than they can manage so that they can penetrate their accounts more deeply and drive out the competition. A salesperson whose territory is targeted for change may fight the change, stating: "I have done a good job for you. I built this territory. It is unfair that my 'reward' is to have my territory disrupted." Managers who get complaints from their best performers may relent in their effort to redesign territories.

Salespeople's resistance to changes in sales territories increases as the proportion of pay based on incentives (as opposed to salary) increases—the higher the incentive component of compensation, the more likely it is that a change in territory boundaries will affect a salesperson's income. The table in Figure 6-4 compares the percentage of territories that were properly sized before and after a territory redesign. The study was based on data from approximately 2,800 territories at eight companies, of which five paid mostly salary and three paid mostly incentives. The percentage of properly sized territories improved significantly after the redesign for both the salary and the incentives companies. However, a higher percentage of salary territories were the right size both before and after the territory design change. Fear of the possible impact on salespeople's earnings prevented the management of the companies with incentive territories from achieving better territory design.

If your company expects to change territories frequently—for example, if you are planning substantial sales force growth—you should consider a change-friendly incentive plan. For example, a quota-bonus plan that pays incentives for achieving a territory-specific quota allows greater flexibility in changing territories than does a plan that pays a commission on total territory sales. With the commission plan, territory earnings opportunity is affected with every account reassignment; opportunity decreases for the salesperson who gives up an account and increases for the salesperson who gains the account. With the quota-bonus plan, however, you can make quota adjustments when accounts are reassigned to ensure that the territory earnings opportunity remains constant for each salesperson affected by the change. You can also address concerns over the possible reduction of a salesperson's income resulting from territory changes by phasing in compensation changes

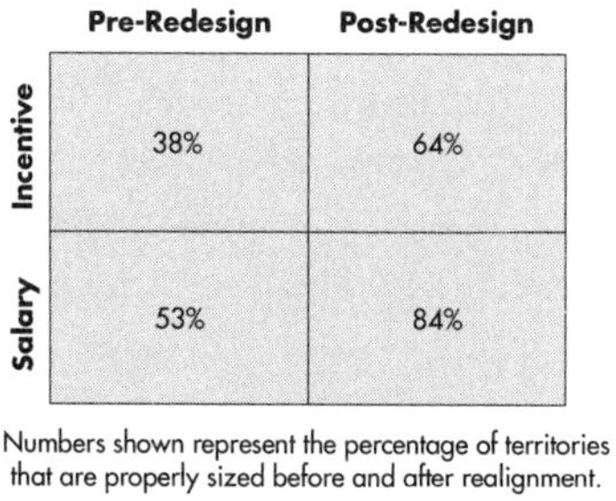

	Pre-Redesign	Post-Redesign
Incentive	38%	64%
Salary	53%	84%

Numbers shown represent the percentage of territories
that are properly sized before and after realignment.

Figure 6-4. Comparison of territory design quality: mostly incentive versus mostly salary territories

over time. For example, each salesperson could be guaranteed at least 80 percent of last year's earnings in the first year following a territory change, with the percentage diminishing over time.

Alternatively, for a period of time, salespeople could continue to earn some fraction of the incentive payout on their accounts that are reassigned to another salesperson. This approach can work well at companies with longer selling cycles, where it is important for the old salesperson and the new salesperson to work together to ensure a smooth transition for accounts with potential sales in the pipeline. A phased-in compensation plan may cost more money in the short term. However, the incremental sales created by more equitable sales territories can more than fund this temporary cost.

Use Structured Processes and Efficient Tools

Companies should view sales territory redesign as a significant change management effort. A successful redesign is one that is handled carefully and intentionally using a well-thought-out process. The best processes start with a centrally developed territory design proposal based on objective business criteria and consistent logic for determining staffing needs. The proposal acts as a benchmark, providing quantifiable criteria (such as territory workload, potential equity, and travel time) against which all territory design changes can be judged. By allowing field sales managers to make local adjustments to the centrally developed proposal, sales leaders ensure that the redesign takes local conditions into account. Incorporating local input also makes it easier for the entire sales organization to accept territory changes.

Fortunately, with today's technology, sales managers no longer have to spend days poring over maps and account-level reports to redesign sales territories. Computer-assisted analysis, when coupled with structured processes, makes it possible for sales managers to create good territories quickly without frustration and without losing significant time in the field. Software such as MAPS by ZS Associates (available for use on personal computers or via the Internet) allows sales managers to create their own "what-if" territory design scenarios using computerized maps and worksheets. Territory optimization software is also available that uses mathematical algorithms to evaluate millions of potential territory designs to find one that best meets a company's objectives for profitable territories, equitable workload and sales potential, and reasonable territory size and need for travel, as well as minimal disruption.

Assess Territory Design Every One to Two Years

Companies in which territory design has been neglected for long periods of time are usually seriously out of sync with current market needs and are leaving millions of dollars on the table. Many valuable customers are not getting the attention they deserve, and many talented salespeople are not being fully utilized. Smart sales leaders assess territory design on a regular basis to ensure that it keeps pace with ongoing market and product-line changes and that territory workload and opportunity are well matched to the talents and capacity of salespeople.

CHAPTER 7

Sales Force Recruiting: Winning the War for Talent

Recruiting the Highest-Quality Salespeople Leads to Success

We often ask the sales leaders who attend our executive-level courses to list (unaided and prior to attending the course) ways in which they can increase the effectiveness of their sales forces. Training, compensation, and CRM are always popular choices. It is not often that these leaders include recruiting on their initial lists, yet they usually quickly reprioritize the importance of effective recruiting when we ask them to contrast their top performers with their average performers.

Top performers have traits that allow them to be successful—traits that average performers often lack. Fortunately, companies can identify these success traits and screen for them in their recruiting process. Our experience suggests that, for most companies, recruiting is the most important sales force effectiveness driver, although it is also one of the most difficult to do well. In their initial responses, perhaps our sales leaders feel that their companies have mastered recruiting or that recruiting is just not as important as other sales force effectiveness drivers. On reflection, though, they concur with us.

A bad hiring decision can easily cost a company many times the salesperson's annual compensation, including salary, expenses, training costs, benefits, and incentive pay. It takes an average of two years to recover from the mistake of hiring the wrong person for a sales job: one year to discover that a performance problem exists and document that problem, six months to try to fix the problem through coaching and performance management, and another six months to replace a persistently poor performer. Meanwhile, the company loses opportunity in the territory, customers may turn to competitors, and the salesperson is unmotivated because she is not succeeding in her job.

It is impossible to select the right candidate every time. Sales success is a gestalt. Top producers are not all identical, and it is difficult to know the precise combination of characteristics that a person needs to have to become a top producer. Even the most experienced recruiters make mistakes—a 50 percent error rate in hiring salespeople is the norm. An additional challenge is that the responsibility for sales force recruiting is often shared by sales and human resources (HR) personnel: HR may do the initial screening of candidates, while sales makes the final selection. This division of labor works well when the sales and HR functions are aligned with each other and both are looking for the same characteristics in candidates. But when sales and HR have a dysfunctional relationship, it can be difficult to recruit effective salespeople.

Companies that utilize well-developed and tested recruiting processes can dramatically improve their chances of hiring successful salespeople. While most sales managers rely in part on their own experience and intuition in determining which candidates will be successful salespeople, intuition alone is not enough to ensure consistently strong recruiting results. Success in hiring is enhanced when a company employs a well-thought-out process for profiling successful salespeople, finding and selecting people who fit the profile, and attracting those people to the company. Well-defined processes for managing talent after salespeople join the organization can help companies spot hiring errors quickly so that they can deal with them early.

Processes for Better Recruitment

An effective recruiting process has four main steps, as shown in Figure 7-1. The first three steps occur sequentially, while the final step begins to ramp up during the earlier steps.

What actions can you take to perform these steps effectively? The following sections explain the process.

Design the Right Recruiting Profile

A recruiting profile defines the specific skills, qualifications, and personal characteristics needed for success in a job. Profiles are useful because what makes a candidate "good" needs to be specified before good candidates can be identified. Examples of recruiting profiles for sales jobs at Hewlett-Packard (HP) and GAINSCO Auto Insurance are shown in Figure 7-2. These two companies look for some of the same characteristics in the salespeople they hire—for example, both look for an appropriate degree or work experience, self-motivation, and presentation skills. But HP and GAINSCO each list characteristics that the other ignores. The HP job involves developing innovative technical solutions for customers; hence, creative ability, acuteness, and intellectual flexibility are important to job success there. An insurance sales position requires a great deal of persistence with prospective customers; hence, a high energy level and motivation for sales are important components of GAINSCO's success profile.

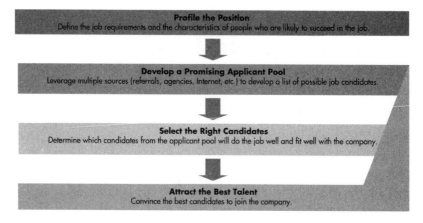

Figure 7-1. Steps in the recruiting process

Qualifications for a Sales Job

	GAINSCO Auto Insurance	Hewlett-Packard
Education or Work Experience	Bachelor's degree or equivalent work experience	Degree in business or relevant experience
Experience, Skills, and Knowledge	Marketing experience and auto insurance background a plus Excellent computer skills: MS Word, MS Excel, MS Outlook.	Experience with business plan development, account planning, selling complex products and solutions, and/or project management Sound knowledge of IT sales Customer and product knowledge
Motivation	Motivation for sales High energy level Ability to work independently and be a self starter in a fast-paced environment	A self-motivated, go-and-get approach and the will to win
Interpersonal Skills and Abilities	Excellent presentation skills Professionalism Excellent communication and interpersonal skills	Strong presentation, sales, negotiation and influencing skills Team player Self-confidence Leadership qualities, credibility
Intellectual Skills and Abilities		Creative ability Acuteness Intellectually flexible
Source	www.insurancesalesjobs.com (2/21/07)	www.hp.com (2/21/07)

Figure 7-2. A comparison of qualifications for sales jobs at GAINSCO Auto Insurance and Hewlett-Packard

Which Characteristics Do You Hire and Which Do You Train? The profile characteristics listed in the "Education or Work Experience" category in Figure 7-2 act as a screen for narrowing the pool of potential candidates to those whose backgrounds are most likely to lead to sales success in each company. The characteristics listed in the "Experience, Skills, and Knowledge" category can also be used as a screen for hiring, but it is possible to develop these traits in candidates by training them after they are hired. The majority of the characteristics in the two profiles—including all those that appear in the "Motivation," "Interpersonal Skills," and "Intellectual Skills" categories—are inherent in the candidate's personality, character, and aptitude. Training has limited ability to affect such characteristics as energy level, interpersonal skills, and intellect.

Breaking down characteristics in this way highlights the critical importance of strong and solid sales force recruiting. In the words of one sales leader, "You can't send a duck to eagle school." In the words of another, "You can teach a turkey to climb a tree, but it's easier to hire a squirrel." A manager at Nordstrom, the U.S. department store chain known for its impeccable service, once emphasized the importance of hiring the right salespeople by telling us, "Nordstrom doesn't train its salespeople to be customer-oriented—their families do."

Elements of the Profile Can Change Over Time. As the selling process changes, the qualities needed for sales success change. Sometimes the change is dramatic—for example, when an industry is deregulated and salespeople have to sell competitively for the first time. At other times, the change is more subtle—for example, when the sales process becomes more consultative and salespeople need to spend more time understanding customers' needs and developing solutions, in addition to providing product information and handling transactions.

United Airlines Transforms Its Sales Process and Its Sales Force Hiring Profile

The sales organization at United Airlines is responsible for building and managing relationships with corporate customers and travel agencies. Since 2005, the organization has completely transformed its sales process. Whereas sales success was previously driven by price and by personal relationships between salespeople and their customers, success today is built around a value-based selling model that focuses customers on the total business value that United creates. The new model requires salespeople to sell a mix of consultative services and travel management and support programs that create business value well beyond lower-price airline alternatives.

The new sales approach created a need for a new sales force hiring profile. In addition to traditional sales and relationship-building skills, the new profile calls for salespeople who can work closely with customers to understand their business needs and demonstrate how United can meet these needs. The change in hiring profile required United's sales leaders to make some difficult personnel decisions, and about 30 percent of the people in the sales organization were replaced. Performance management and compensation programs were also realigned to match the expectations of the new selling model.

Sales managers and HR screeners need to adapt hiring profiles as the selling space changes. If recruiters continue to use old profiles in their screening, it is likely that new hires will fail to succeed in the new selling environment.

No Profile Is Perfect. Profiles provide useful guidelines for hiring, but it is impossible to create a list of truly discriminating characteristics that can predict success accurately each and every time. There are bright people who are average salespeople and people with average intelligence who are great salespeople. There are experienced people who are good salespeople and experienced people who are poor salespeople. There are extroverted people who are good salespeople and introverted people who are good salespeople.

Usually, however, a significant lack of an important profile characteristic will lead to sales failure. Consequently, candidates who are significantly deficient in any single profile characteristic should be eliminated.

At the same time, candidates should not be selected simply because they are very strong in a single profile characteristic. For example, individuals who are not self-motivated are highly unlikely to be successful in sales at either HP or GAINSCO. However, not everyone who is self-motivated will succeed at these companies. The best candidates are self-motivated and also possess some level of competence on all of the other profile characteristics.

How to Determine the Right Profile Characteristics. A good starting point for determining what is required to be successful in a sales job is to examine the current sales force. Companies that analyze their top-performing salespeople can discover the skills and traits that contribute to these people's success, and these characteristics can be incorporated into the recruiting profile.

A productive analysis consists of three parts. First, the company must identify its highest-performing salespeople, using both recent performance rankings and historical data. Second, the company needs to understand the reasons behind the outstanding performance of these salespeople. These reasons may include high levels of motivation, strong selling skills, empathy, integrity, and intelligence, but observation and synthesis are required to identify the desirable characteristics, skills, and behaviors for a given company and sales job.

Finally, the company has to divide the traits that make for success into those that it will hire for and those that will become part of its learning and development efforts. For example, it might add traits like motivation, empathy, integrity, and intelligence to the recruiting profile, but it might decide to enhance a new hire's selling skills through training and coaching programs designed to impart specific skills and make salespeople throughout the entire sales organization into high performers.

Marriott Vacation Club Redefines Its Recruiting Profile and Achieves Aggressive Sales Growth Goals

---

As mentioned in Chapter 1, sales leaders at Marriott Vacation Club International (MVCI), a seller of time-share vacation ownerships, realized in 1995 that if the company hoped to meet and exceed its aggressive sales growth goals, hiring the best possible sales talent would be a top priority. Previously, the company had relied on a loosely defined system for selecting new salespeople that combined interviewing with gut feel; predictably, that system yielded mixed results. In order to improve sales force hiring, the company first identified 125 of MVCI's top-performing salespeople and interviewed and tested them to discover common traits leading to sales success. It added these traits to its recruiting profile and adopted a new selection process that screened candidates for them. MVCI also made improvements to its sales force training; established processes for sharing best practices; and enhanced its sales recognition, reward, and incentive programs. By 2003, the company had grown from a small player in the vacation-ownership market to the industry leader, and its sales force was recognized with an American Business Award for best U.S. sales organization.

Companies can use a mix of data analysis and input from sales managers to identify top-performing salespeople. One analytical technique that is useful for identifying the best performers is Performance Frontier Analysis, which uses historical territory-level data to determine the level of performance that is possible for each territory. Performance

Frontier Analysis is discussed in Chapter 2. By controlling for territory differences (for example, in market potential, prior sales, or market share), this method isolates the variation in performance that results from a salesperson's efforts.

Figure 7-3 shows each territory's sales relative to an index of territory potential. The sales of the top performers at each level of market potential create the performance frontier. Salespeople in territories that fall below the performance frontier are not performing up to their potential; other salespeople in territories with similar market potential have demonstrated that higher sales achievement is possible.

Sales leaders at this company observed the Performance Frontier salespeople on typical sales calls in order to identify the levers they used to successfully influence the customer buying process. Sales leaders also observed the calls of salespeople who fell short of the frontier in order to contrast their behavior with that of the high performers. The fruit of these observations was a set of success principles differentiating the Performance Frontier salespeople. The company's sales force hiring profile and sales training programs were updated to incorporate these principles.

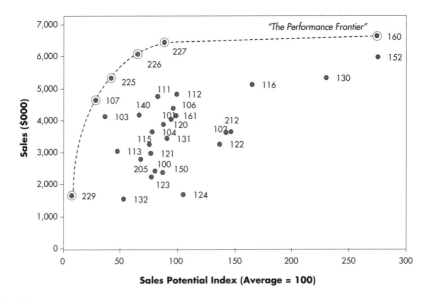

Figure 7-3. Performance Frontier method—example

Should You Hire Experienced Salespeople? Some companies hire only experienced salespeople who can contribute to the selling effort right away. Others like to groom their own salespeople and hire for talent rather than experience. Most companies use a mixture of the two models, hiring both experienced and inexperienced people. Candidates who have both relevant experience and strong talent (in other words, they possess the traits in the recruiting profile) are ideal; yet there usually are not enough of these candidates, and recruiters need to balance the importance of experience against their need for talent. Even though almost every company uses experience as a screen for sales candidates, evidence suggests that experience is not the best predictor of sales success. (See Figure 7-5 later in this chapter.)

How appropriate is it to use experience as a hiring profile dimension? It depends on the selling situation. Figure 7-4 summarizes the conditions in which it makes sense to use experience as a screen for sales candidates and those that favor talent over experience.

Develop a Strong Applicant Pool That Will Lead to Strong Hires

The quality of the candidates who are offered jobs depends upon the quality of the applicant pool. Companies use numerous sources for

Figure 7-4. Should experience or talent get top priority in hiring?

attracting applicants—referrals, campus recruiting, internal placements, agencies, company recruiting web sites, headhunter web sites, Internet job boards, unsolicited write-ins, job fairs, current and former employees, customers, competitors, advertisements, and trade shows. Referrals from current employees or customers and internal placements are consistently ranked by sales leaders as the best sources of new salespeople.

Numerous surveys (including several that we have conducted with sales leaders in our short courses at Kellogg) reveal that recruiters have the most success in developing a strong applicant pool when they favor trusted sources who can provide reliable information about a candidate and his likelihood of success. Such a referrer has observed the candidate's past behavior, is familiar with the job requirements, and is thus able to match the candidate's skills and experiences to the job requirements. There is also relationship risk for the referrer (and some career risk, in the case of current employees). Most companies offer prizes or cash awards to employees who provide referrals of candidates for sales positions who are hired and stay with the company for a predetermined period of time, usually at least six months. Companies can also encourage referrals by publicly recognizing employees who bring in candidates.

Select the Right Candidates

Selection is the process of gathering information about all of the candidates in the applicant pool and sifting through it to determine who is best.

What Are the Best Selection Techniques? Companies use a number of different selection techniques—résumé screens, interviews, tests to select the best candidates—that have varying degrees of effectiveness.

Figure 7-5 summarizes the results of a study conducted by American psychologists Frank L. Schmidt and John E. Hunter that measured the effectiveness of different employee selection techniques. While the study included data from many different research studies across a wide variety of jobs, we believe that the results are also appropriate for sales jobs. The validity figures reflect the correlation between various predictive techniques and ultimate job success. A 0.00 validity indicates that the technique has no predictive power—in other words, using the technique to predict job success is no better than flipping a coin. Age, for instance, is useless as a predictor of job success. A 1.00 validity indicates that the predictive technique is completely accurate. Work sample tests, including hands-on situations and case studies that simulate important parts of the job, have the highest predictive ability of all the techniques analyzed.

Structure Your Interviews. Most companies rely on interviewing as a primary means of screening sales candidates. Notice that in Figure 7-5, unstructured interviews (those in which the interviewer creates her own questions and evaluates candidates based on summary impressions and judgments) are only an average predictor of job success (a validity of 0.38). Selection processes that rely on this type of ad hoc interviewing alone to select candidates for sales positions are likely to produce only average results. Interview-based candidate selection can be improved significantly when structured interviewing approaches are used (a validity of 0.51).

Structured interviews use predetermined questions that are based on careful job analysis and employ a consistent method for scoring candidates. And combining structured interviewing with behavioral consistency techniques increases the validity of the interviewing for predicting sales success even further. Behavioral interviewing builds on the observation that a candidate's past behavior is a good predictor of his

Predictive Technique	Validity
Work sample tests	0.54
Employment interviews (structured)	0.51
Behavioral consistency methods	0.45
Job tryout procedures	0.44
Employment interviews (unstructured)	0.38
Assessment centers	0.37
Biographical data (data on resume and application)	0.35
Reference check	0.26
Job experience (years)	0.18
Graphology (handwriting analysis)	0.02
Coin flip	0.00
Age	-0.01

Figure 7-5. Results from the Schmidt and Hunter study of job success predictors

future behavior. Interviewers ask candidates to recount experiences in their lives in which they have demonstrated characteristics that are part of the hiring profile. For example, to assess a candidate's motivation level, a recruiter might ask the applicant to "talk about a project that you completed with little direction." To assess his persuasiveness, the recruiter might say, "Tell me about a situation in which you had to convince others that your position was right." Many interviewees are aware of behavioral interviewing techniques and arrive at the interview prepared to answer these types of questions. Interviewers must ask probing questions to ensure that candidates are not being superficial and that they are not misrepresenting their experience. Effective structured behavioral interviewing has significantly higher validity than informal, ad hoc interviewing.

Observe the Candidate's Behavior. Techniques that allow observation of the behaviors that lead to job success have good predictive validity. Work sample tests (a validity of 0.54) enable this type of observation. Effective tests include cases and role-playing exercises. For example, an interviewer might ask a candidate for a sales job to demonstrate her sales skills by "selling" something to the recruiter—"Sell me a corner of the room" or "Sell me yourself." Candidates with the strongest selling skills will begin by asking recruiters about their needs so that the candidate can emphasize the strengths and features that the interviewer values most highly. Job tryouts (a validity of 0.44) are another effective technique for observing candidates' behaviors. In Europe, it is common practice to hire employees for a short trial period. Some companies require candidates to undergo training before a final employment offer is extended.

Psychological Testing Is Controversial Psychological testing is another way to gain insight about a candidate's behavior, but the validity and legality of such tests is widely debated. Figure 7-6 shows the results of an analysis of the validity of one psychological test used by a company to screen candidates for sales positions. Each dot on the graph represents a salesperson who had been with the company for two to three years. The current-period goal attainment of each of these salespeople was plotted against the score that the salesperson

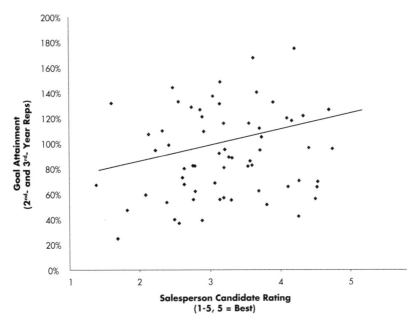

Figure 7-6. Validity check of a psychological test used to screen candidates for sales positions

received on the psychological test as a candidate in the recruiting process. These scores (the salesperson candidate rating) are on a 5-point scale that measures how compatible a candidate's psychological profile is with the job—a score of 5 indicates a profile that is highly compatible. Not all salespeople with high scores on the test turned out to be high performers. By studying the outliers, one can discover specific traits and characteristics that are being under- and overemphasized on the test. Companies that use psychological tests use them as one input among many in the selection process, not as the sole determinant of who should be hired. In some countries, psychological tests need to be linked to specific job qualifications in order to be legally used as a screening method.

Use Reference Checks with Caution. Many companies use reference checks to get insight about a candidate's past behavior. While the Schmidt and Hunter study found reference checks to be somewhat useful predictors of job success (a validity of 0.26), many sales leaders believe that reference checks are generally unreliable. People who act as references are often hesitant to share negative information, as doing so may expose them to legal liability; in fact, many organizations have policies stating that they will verify only dates of employment and titles for ex-employees. In addition, the results of reference checking may be misleading because applicants naturally provide references who will give positive feedback and may even coach them to say the right things. People who act as references may also have hidden agendas that compromise their objectivity. For example, a current manager might misrepresent a candidate's skills in an effort to either offload a weak employee or keep a good one.

While reference checks are not reliable for assessing how well a candidate did in past jobs, they can be quite useful for ensuring that candidates are representing the facts of their education and experience accurately. Since some staffing experts suggest that 30 percent of all job applicants lie on their résumés, résumé facts should always be confirmed, using either background checks or reference checks.

The Sales Manager's Role Is Critical. As the key decision makers in candidate selection, sales managers are vital in the recruiting process. People tend to hire individuals that they are comfortable with. Successful people will not be intimidated by successful job applicants—in fact, they look for people that they think will be successful. This brings up an important point: If you want excellent salespeople, make sure that the sales managers who make hiring decisions are excellent. If the sales management team is weak, it is highly likely that the candidates it selects to hire will be weak as well. A sales force that settles for average managers can never be excellent. It has been said, "First-rate people hire first-rate people. Second-rate people hire third-rate people."

Assess the Fit of a Candidate with the Organization. An important part of the selection process is determining the fit of the candidate with the organization's culture, work environment, and values. Since people are often more forthcoming in casual situations, a good way to assess fit is to go out to dinner with the candidate (and possibly a spouse or significant other). Another way to assess fit is to expose the candidate to the job, perhaps by arranging for him to spend a day in the field.

Such situations allow both the company and the candidate to make a more informed decision about mutual fit.

Use Multiple Predictive Techniques. No company's selection process is perfect. The most effective predictive technique, according to the Schmidt and Hunter study, is administering work sample tests, yet the validity rating of that predictor was only 0.54, so in many cases even the best predictor was wrong. Success is enhanced when companies use multiple predictive techniques as part of a thorough and cogent selection process. For example, companies are likely to be successful in hiring excellent people when they use a selection process that augments feedback from structured interviews with data obtained through work sample tests, behavioral consistency methods, and/or job tryout procedures.

Attract Strong Candidates to Your Company

Attraction is a key part of every step of the recruiting process. The job posting should describe the job in a way that attracts good candidates to the applicant pool, though it should not oversell the job. During the interview process, interviewers should provide candidates with a solid sense of the job and the company, in addition to assessing the applicants' skills. Part of every interviewer's task is to sell (but, again, not oversell) strong candidates on the employment opportunity, making sure that prospective employees develop an accurate picture of what the job is really like. Once applicants have passed the necessary hurdles for employment, the attraction process kicks into high gear with an employment offer and appropriate follow-up.

After doing so much hard work to find good candidates, it is frustrating to lose them after an offer has been made. Obviously a very attractive offer makes it more likely that the candidate will accept, but effective follow-up does not cost much and can also make a big difference. Let candidates know that you want them. Have several people call them to show interest, including the vice president of sales and possibly even the CEO.

The desire to attract job candidates needs to be balanced with the need to ensure that those candidates will be happy in the job. The best way to encourage high job satisfaction in new hires is to give them a realistic job preview before they accept an employment offer. If the job has been oversold or if its negative aspects have been downplayed, new hires are bound to be dissatisfied down the road.

Maximizing the Effectiveness of Your Recruiting Process
Avoid "Warm Body" Hiring

Salespeople tend to be self-directed and confident about trying new things. Consequently, in many sales forces, turnover is a regular occurrence. But vacant territories can create panic. Customers are not being served, new accounts are not being pursued, and the district or regional quota is in jeopardy. As a result, some managers rush to fill vacancies. This is a mistake. Rush to hire a star candidate, but never rush to fill a position. A vacant territory implies a temporary loss in sales, and, granted, this quarter's goal may be in jeopardy. But a poor "warm body" hire places sales in jeopardy for a much longer period of time. Alleviate the need for "warm body" hiring by always being on the lookout for new talent.

Recruit Constantly

The way to avoid vacant territory panic is to begin recruiting before a position becomes available. An empty position should be filled right away—with an excellent salesperson. Effective sales managers have a list of worthy candidates, so that when a vacancy occurs, they can check their list, make several calls, and hopefully staff the territory quickly.

Candidate lists can be composed of employee referrals, candidates who rejected offers in the past, candidates who were an excellent second choice on a prior recruiting foray, customer employees, former employees, employees in other functions, or even someone the manager met on an airplane who had just sealed a big deal. Keep a list—you never know when it can come in handy.

Don't Be Afraid to Challenge the Status Quo

As selling processes and sales jobs change, and as new assessment approaches are devised, the best sales forces reinvent their recruiting programs, continually adapting and improving their approach to recruiting the best salespeople.

Get New Salespeople Off to a Good Start

Bringing a new salesperson on board links recruiting to the learning and development sales effectiveness driver. The recruitment process is just the beginning of a new salesperson's experience with the company. As soon as new salespeople start to work, they need to be given the tools they need to do their job effectively and to connect with the people who can help them succeed.

New salespeople need to learn the company's selling process, as well as its products, markets, and customers. They need to get up to speed on corporate policies and culture to ensure that they become effective as quickly as possible. Careful attention to the process of bringing new employees on board helps new hires to rapidly become fully engaged and productive members of the sales organization.

CHAPTER 8

Developing More Effective Training Programs

The best sales force learning and development (L&D) programs make salespeople continually successful as they acquire and improve the skills and knowledge that they need. Top sales organizations view such programs as being broader than the structured, classroom-focused group sessions that were once the foundation of many sales training programs. Today, successful programs embrace a broader paradigm, in which *learning* means that salespeople improve their skills and deepen their knowledge, and *development* reflects the continuous accumulation of capabilities that increases a person's value to the organization and helps companies retain employees motivated by learning and growing.

In designing good L&D programs, sales leaders face three critical challenges. First, there are numerous choices about whom to train, what the training should impart, and how to train. How can a sales organization design a program that is *effective* and that really works? Second, in a rapidly changing world, there is a continuous need for learning. How can a sales organization design an *efficient* program that does not nibble away at the time salespeople spend taking care of customers? Third, the impact of training is enhanced through *reinforcement*. More than 80 percent of what salespeople learn in classroom training programs is soon forgotten. How can a sales organization link its L&D programs with complementary sales effectiveness drivers such as information support, coaching, and performance management? The sales manager plays an important role in this process, acting as a coach to reinforce the skills and knowledge that salespeople acquire and providing guidance concerning what L&D opportunities they should seek out.

An L&D Success Framework

What Should Influence the Design of Your L&D Program?

The competencies that your salespeople need if they are to execute your sales strategy and the degree to which these competencies are part of your company's sales force recruiting strategy should be the primary influences on the design of your L&D program. Design includes the content and the methods by which that content is delivered. Figure 8-1 illustrates the framework for such a design.

Competencies That Salespeople Need if They Are to Execute a Sales Strategy. Companies with complex and diverse product lines, customers, and/or sales processes need to invest more in L&D programs than companies for which selling is simpler. In addition, an environment in which customer needs, the offerings of competitors, and company sales strategies are evolving requires greater investment in sales force

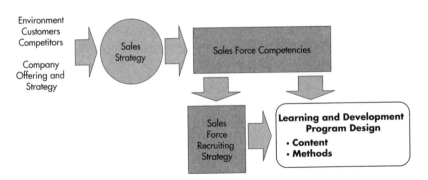

Figure 8-1. A framework for L&D program design

L&D programs than does a more stable environment. Major events like new product launches, environmental shifts, and mergers and acquisitions will often create a need for sales strategy changes that require the sales force to acquire new skills and knowledge. In addition, gradual changes in market consolidation, customer buying processes, or the economic outlook can also drive selling process changes that require this. In recent years, many companies have changed sales processes that were product- and relationship-based to processes that are focused on solutions and on providing more value to customers, and implementing those changes has required the rethinking of sales force L&D programs.

New Product Training at Cisco

At the height of the Internet boom, computer networking giant Cisco Systems acquired a new company roughly every three weeks. This meant that new products were constantly being added to the portfolio of Cisco's sales force—a difficult challenge in a complex industry where hundreds of new products are introduced every year. Cisco prided itself on having a well-trained sales force, but flying salespeople to a central location for training every time a new product was introduced soon became impractical. To help salespeople learn about newly acquired products quickly, the firm developed an online portal that gave salespeople access to thousands of training modules that they could view on screen, download to a computer, or print in magazine format. Salespeople could quickly familiarize themselves with new products without losing too much valuable time in the field. In addition to increasing selling effectiveness, the new system cut training-associated travel by 60 percent.

Making the Transition to Consultative Selling at Aetna

In the competitive insurance industry, health-care insurance provider Aetna recognized that strong customer relationships and ongoing customer loyalty were critical to its enduring success. In an effort to strengthen its relationships with corporate customers, Aetna developed an L&D program to help its salespeople who sell to businesses become more consultative in their sales approach. Since businesses with different profiles need different plans for the coverage they offer employees, Aetna salespeople could be more effective if they talked with customers about their specific health-care insurance needs instead of making product-based pitches. Aetna salespeople learned how to research and analyze each customer's business issues and how to develop and give a sales presentation that was customized to the client's needs and business style. They learned the value of focusing selling on "you" (the customer's needs) rather than on "me" (my products). While the consultative sales training did lead to some immediate bottom-line successes, the ultimate goal was to improve customer retention and long-term growth.

Sales Force Recruiting Strategies. Some established selling organizations—including Procter & Gamble, Johnson & Johnson, Coca-Cola, and Xerox—mainly hire recent college graduates for their sales positions. They invest heavily in L&D programs, which they view as a corporate asset that generates a competitive advantage. Other companies hire only people with sales experience who can hit the ground running. Most companies use some combination of these two approaches.

Larger companies are more likely to hire inexperienced salespeople, as they have the resources to build internal sales training departments and to provide the mentoring needed to develop new salespeople. Growing companies are more likely to rely on hiring experienced people. (See Chapter 7 for a discussion of the advantages and disadvantages of hiring experienced versus inexperienced salespeople in different sales environments.)

But L&D programs for newly hired salespeople are important for all sales organizations. As Figure 8-2 shows, all new hires, regardless of their experience, need to be educated about the company's products, processes, and culture. People with no prior experience require additional L&D programs covering a broad spectrum of customer and market knowledge, the sales process, and sales skills. The content of training can be customized to the specific needs of new hires who have some customer/market or selling experience.

Figure 8-2. L&D program content for newly hired salespeople

Selling Skills Training at Xerox

Xerox Corporation is widely recognized as a pioneer in sales training. During the 1960s, the company developed its Professional Selling Skills (PSS) sales training approach to educate its sales force. Soon it began packaging this approach and selling it to other companies, eventually spinning off the training unit into a separate company. The Xerox PSS approach included a five-step selling skills program that taught salespeople basic skills, such as how to open a sales call, listen effectively, handle objections, close sales, and follow up after a sale. Elements of the PSS approach are still used in many sales training programs, although there is usually less emphasis on persuasion and greater emphasis on listening and two-way communication.

A Biotechnology Firm's Hiring Strategy Influences Its L&D Program Design

---

When a biotechnology company was ready to launch its first product, the management team wanted to hire only the best pharmaceutical salespeople for its sales force. The company's profile of an ideal candidate was a pharmaceutical salesperson with five or more years of experience, a life science degree, in-depth territory knowledge, and a performance ranking in the top

20 percent in his current position. The company set its pay levels at 30 percent above the industry norm. Since all new hires were familiar with pharmaceutical sales processes and markets, the initial sales force training focused on the company's products and culture. In addition, salespeople were asked to join task forces charged with designing many of the sales effectiveness drivers, such as incentive compensation plans, performance management processes, and sales information systems. The combined prior experience of the task force members cut across many different pharmaceutical companies, enabling the firm to determine and adopt best practices for the sales effectiveness drivers.

What Content Should Your L&D Program Deliver?

Smart sales leaders build L&D program content around the skills and knowledge that salespeople need if they are to be successful with customers. In any sales organization, the best salespeople are skilled at developing an understanding of their customers' needs and creating customer value by customizing the company's offering to meet those needs.

The specific content of your L&D program will depend on the complexity of your sales process. If your process is relatively simple, your salespeople need product and customer knowledge and the basic selling skills necessary to be effective. If it is complex, your salespeople will also need highly developed consultative skills in order to be successful.

When the Sales Process Is Simple. In order to be effective with customers, salespeople need some basic skills and knowledge:

- An understanding of the selling process. Salespeople need proficiency in executing each step in the selling process effectively. The classic Xerox sales training approach breaks down selling skills into five parts: opening a call, listening, handling objections, closing, and following up after the sale.

- Product and company knowledge. Salespeople need to understand the features and benefits of the products and services that they sell. They must know their company's policies and resources for helping customers.

- Market and customer knowledge. Salespeople need to know the market and the nature of competitors' offerings. They must understand their customers, including how they will use the product or service, the value they perceive, and how their purchasing decisions are made.

- Territory management skills. Salespeople must learn how to manage their time and prioritize the customers to target, the products to sell, and the activities to engage in.

Figure 8-3 lists examples of the proficiencies needed for sales success. Sales leaders need to provide programs focused on these skills and knowledge whenever new salespeople join the company, or when changes in the environment or in company strategies require existing salespeople to expand their skill set and knowledge base.

Sales Training at Home Depot

Appliance salespeople at Home Depot go through extensive training to develop the competencies needed to be successful at selling all the major appliance categories. The training program combines self-paced materials, video-based courses, online assessments, and instructor-led training to help salespeople become familiar with all the products available in store showrooms. The courses also teach such important selling skills as:

- Following Home Depot selling strategies

- Recommending the right appliances based on the customers' needs

- Emphasizing the appropriate product features and benefits

- Addressing customers' questions

- Closing a sale

Knowledge	Sales Skills	Other
• Products	• Face-to-face selling	• Time and territory management
• Company	• Selling process execution	• Administrative procedures
• Customers		• Company culture
• Competition		

Figure 8-3. Examples of selling competencies needed for almost all sales processes

CIGNA Hires and Trains a New Sales Force to Pursue Middle-Market Accounts

In the late 1990s, CIGNA Group Insurance sold its products primarily to large companies with more than 10,000 employees. In 2001, CIGNA determined that the best opportunity for substantial, sustained growth was in middle-market accounts. Since the CIGNA sales force had few strong relationships with middle-market brokers and midsize companies, CIGNA set out to hire and develop a new sales force to seize a competitive share of this $9 billion market. Using a new hiring profile for salespeople who could be successful at selling in a fast-paced, high-volume environment, the company identified, screened, and hired a distinct group of successful sales professionals from outside the insurance industry who had diverse business experience and were comfortable selling high volumes of business to midsize companies. To develop the new salespeople, CIGNA created a program that it called Business Leadership and Sales Training (BLAST). Most of the new hires were competent salespeople but had little or no insurance industry experience, so the program emphasized product and industry information, in addition to selling skills. BLAST included classroom sessions that covered telephone prospecting, influencing skills, territory management, in-depth product information, and business and customer knowledge. Classroom learning was supplemented with structured field experience, self-study, and real-time case scenarios. Skills developed through BLAST were reinforced through dedicated, one-on-one coaching with sales managers.

When the Sales Process Is Complex. As product and service lines become complex and broad, or as companies seek ways to bring more value to customers, many sales organizations adopt a consultative model of value-based selling. A consultative selling model requires salespeople to have a range of skills and knowledge that goes beyond basic selling skills and strong product knowledge. Consultative salespeople also need to have an extensive understanding of a customer's business issues so that they can creatively develop value-based solutions. Companies need enhanced approaches to sales force L&D in order to impart such competencies, listed in Figure 8-4.

Knowledge	Sales Skills	Other
• Product offering and value proposition • Customer's industry/market (including business operations, industry drivers, and customers' strategic priorities and objectives) • Competitive value proposition	• How to identify the key players or key decision makers • How to assess needs • Customer's decision process map • How to tailor the offering and value proposition • How to pursue large deals • Negotiation	• How company resources can map to customer needs • Account management • How to prospect to build and maintain a good sales pipeline • Forecasting

Figure 8-4. Examples of selling competencies needed for complex sales processes

---

IBM Trains Sony on Consultative Selling

In response to massive changes in its markets, Sony Broadcast & Professional Europe wanted to strengthen its relationships with customers by becoming more than a supplier of products. The company's long-term vision was to be seen by its customers as a provider of strategic, complex communications solutions. To achieve this vision, Sony needed to adopt a more consultative sales approach. Enlisting the help of IBM sales trainers, Sony customized a consultative sales L&D program to teach salespeople how to build closer ties with clients by working jointly with them to solve problems. The program focused on specific competencies (such as communication skills), but its overall goal was to get Sony salespeople to think, act, and work as consultants with their customers. The training included many case studies and role-playing exercises centered on customers' business problems.

Comdata Uses a Creative Training Approach to Teach Salespeople to Sell Value

When the sales force at financial services company Comdata was asked to launch a new product into a market where it had little experience, sales leaders realized that the salespeople would be more effective if they could learn to think like the CEOs who were their potential buyers. Once they understood the strategies and situations that these CEOs face, salespeople would be able to better communicate how Comdata's products and services related to customer success and thus could sell more effectively. As part of its L&D program, Comdata used a board game called Zodiak, designed by Paradigm Learning, to teach its salespeople to think like CEOs. As they played the game, salespeople made decisions about strategic business investments across three years in the life of a customer's business, saw the impact of these decisions on the bottom line, and came to understand how the products they sold could solve the problems that CEOs encounter. This made them more effective at selling value.

Computer Companies Help Channel Partners' Transition to Solution Selling

Computer companies like Microsoft, Symantec, Cisco Systems, Veritas Software, and Intel rely on channel partners (such as value-added resellers) to sell to small and middle-market accounts. All these companies encourage their channel partners, which have traditionally sold individual technology products, to use a consultative approach that focuses on end-to-end solutions and business applications. Veritas reorganized the sales training it provides to channel partners by supplementing product-specific information with training organized around such business problems as regulatory compliance and disaster-recovery planning—key issues for small businesses. Microsoft has developed a Partner Learning Center web site where its partners can find unique training programs that help their salespeople understand the complexity and diverse nature of business software solutions.

The development of consultative selling competencies is particularly important for salespeople who are responsible for selling to large, complex "key" accounts that are of significant strategic importance to the company. Such accounts often have centralized purchasing, multilocation purchasing influences, a complex buying process, and a need for special services. L&D for sales success with key accounts typically focuses on developing competencies that allow salespeople to take a strategic approach to account management and customer relationships.

Training for Successful Key Account Selling

Many sales training companies offer courses in selling to key accounts. Examples of popular courses include Huthwaite's SPIN Selling, Miller-Heiman's Strategic Selling, the TAS Group's Target Account Selling, and Sales Performance International's Solution Selling. Many leading universities and professional associations offer similar courses. Some of the topics covered in a sample of key account development courses are:

- *Strategic Account Management, offered by University of Michigan Ross School of Business Executive Education.* "Develop and implement strategic account plans . . . understand key account business drivers . . . improve your firm's relationships, and therefore profitability, with strategic accounts . . . create and achieve cross functional support in acquiring and growing strategic accounts."

- *Selling to Major Accounts: A Strategic Approach, offered by the American Management Association.* "Learn to think strategically and differentiate between strategy and tactics . . . manage the selling process more effectively . . . define results indicators to improve the sales process . . . identify opportunities with high return for time, effort, and money invested . . . spread your risk by managing the pipeline . . . manage account performance strategically."

- *SAMA University: Critical Skills for the Strategic Account Manager, offered by the Strategic Account Management Association.* "Key learnings include competitive positioning . . . crafting opportunity value propositions . . . gaining entry . . . political alignment . . . relationship profiling . . . selecting account strategy . . . setting achievable revenue targets."

Developing Effective L&D Program Content.

Structure L&D program content around critical sales force competencies. Smart sales leaders use competency models, which define the skills, knowledge, and capabilities needed to be successful in a particular sales role, as blueprints for the design of sales force L&D content. Figure 8-5 describes a sales competency model used at a global computer

Needed Sales Competencies (Baseline and Advanced)		Courses Offered
Customer Orientation	**Baseline** • Understands customer needs • Focuses on quality	Sales Process Skills
	Advanced • Understands customer's business • Establishes business partnership	
Strategic Selling	**Baseline** • Drives for results • Knows products and services	Enterprise Selling Skills, Portfolio Management Skills, Territory Management Skills, Partner Planning, All Products and Services Training
	Advanced • Creates value-added solutions • Knows the market and the competition • Demonstrates entrepreneurial thinking	Account Planning/Opportunity Management
Organizational Leadership	**Baseline** • Acts with integrity • Develops and executes plans	Priority and Time Management, Enterprise Selling Skills, Portfolio Management Skills, Territory Management Skills, Partner Planning
	Advanced • Demonstrates organizational savvy • Exhibits business/financial acumen • Anticipates and adapts to change	Business Financials, Target Account Selling, Enterprise Selling Skills, Portfolio Management Skills, Territory Management Skills, Partner Planning
Collaborative Relationships	**Baseline** • Builds and maintains relationships • Communicates effectively	Sales Process Skills, Sales Presentations, Sales Negotiations, Business Writing
	Advanced • Builds global networks • Fosters teamwork and collaboration • Inspires trust	Solutions Sales Program

Figure 8-5. Map of critical sales competencies and courses offered at a global computer company

company that provides courses through its corporate sales training program or outside vendors to help salespeople develop a full range of selling competencies. The company in effect gives salespeople a map that shows the connections between the competencies they need and the courses offered, directing them to resources that can help them build the skills and knowledge needed for success. Such maps also help companies identify gaps in their L&D program content; in this example, courses need to be identified to help salespeople develop advanced customer orientation skills.

Learn from the best salespeople and focus L&D programs on the behaviors that drive their success. Study your salespeople to learn which behaviors drive sales success. Observing successful salespeople and average salespeople on sales calls and comparing their approaches with customers will allow you to discover the trainable behaviors that differentiate the best salespeople from average performers. Your L&D programs can then focus on these behaviors.

Novartis Learns From Its Best Salespeople

Chapter 2 describes how Novartis, a leading multinational manufacturer of pharmaceutical products, conducts an annual sales force effectiveness review to identify high-impact sales effectiveness initiatives. One of the initiatives to come out of this process was a training program based on observed characteristics of Novartis's best salespeople. High-performing salespeople (identified through a combination of data analysis and sales manager input) were observed on typical sales calls in order to identify the levers they used to influence the customer buying process. Average performers were observed on calls as well, and their behavior was compared with that of the high performers. The company then incorporated a set of success principles that differentiated top-performing salespeople into a training program for the sales organization. The salespeople who completed the new training were chosen by physicians as the best salesperson they see 46 percent of the time, compared to only 22 percent of the time for salespeople who did not complete the training, and the preference among physicians was linked to better sales results.

Keep learning focused. The time that salespeople spend attending classroom training, browsing e-training sites, and sharing ideas with colleagues is time that they are not spending with customers. As sales organizations add L&D programs, they must eliminate programs that have become less relevant. When organizations keep the number of "annual training days" to a reasonable level, salespeople can spend more time with customers and their learning stays focused on the most critical competencies.

An L&D capabilities/effectiveness matrix, like the one shown in Figure 8-6, is useful for prioritizing the critical competencies or "outputs" of L&D programs. The matrix helps sales leaders determine which outputs should be emphasized, which programs might need improvement, and which programs should be eliminated. Creating the matrix requires profiling sales force competencies based on how important they are for sales success and how effective the current L&D program is at delivering them. Companies rely on quantitative measures along with

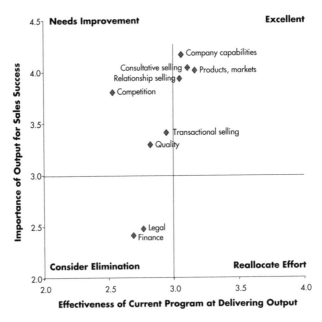

Figure 8-6. Example of an L&D capabilities/effectiveness matrix

qualitative inputs from internal and external experts to develop the importance and effectiveness scores.

For the company that created the matrix in Figure 8-6, the time devoted to learning about legal and finance matters should be limited, as this competency is considered to be relatively low in importance. The company should focus most of its L&D program time on more important outputs, including company capabilities, consultative selling, products and markets, and relationship selling. The company also should consider improving salespeople's knowledge about the competition, since the current programs are not considered very effective at delivering this important output.

L&D Methods

Blended Learning. As the examples used throughout this chapter illustrate, the L&D process in sales organizations takes place using multiple methods—training is not just about the classroom anymore. Successful L&D programs use a blended learning approach that relies on a planned combination of learning methods, including those listed in Figure 8-7.

Using Structured Learning Opportunities	Learning from Colleagues	Leveraging Learning Resources
• Corporate training courses • External classroom courses • Online courses • Self-paced courses • Video-based courses • University-sponsored courses • Case studies • Role-playing exercises • Board games • Structured field experience • Job shadowing • Seminars • Workshops	• Coaching by supervisors • Collaborating with peers • Informal chats with colleagues • Leveraging collegial relationships • Online communities • Best practices sharing sessions • Industry conferences	• Current business news • Business books • Reference manuals • Internet • Company web site • Company CRM system

Figure 8-7. Blended learning combines multiple methods of L&D

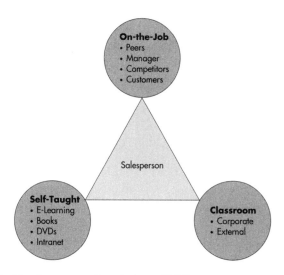

Figure 8-8. The learner-centered view of L&D

Effective blended learning focuses on the needs of the individual and acknowledges that people learn in many different ways. Figure 8-8 diagrams the important concept that the learner is at the center of blended learning, which allows salespeople to draw on multiple resources (including classroom training) to gain and reinforce their skills and knowledge.

Company	Situation	Learning and Development Program Methods Used to Enhance Classroom	Description of Blended Learning Approach
Cisco Systems	Frequent new product introductions create constant need for product-oriented sales training.	• Online	Salespeople can familiarize themselves with new products quickly without losing time in the field.
CIGNA	A new sales force is created; new hires have sales experience but lack industry experience.	• Self-study • Case studies • Field experience • Coaching	Product and industry knowledge gained in the classroom is supplemented through multiple learning methods and is reinforced by sales manager coaching.
Sony	The sales process is making the transition from consultative to transactional.	• Case studies • Role-playing exercises	Classroom selling-skill training is enriched by methods that develop think/solve competencies.
Comdata	A new product launch requires salespeople to sell to a new audience: CEOs.	• Simulation game	Classroom product-focused training is enhanced by a simulation game that teaches salespeople to think like CEOs.

Figure 8-9. Blended learning approaches used to accomplish different objectives in different situations

The best way to decide on the right combination of methods for encouraging L&D is to consider your objectives, your situation, the preferences of individual learners, and the information to be shared, in addition to your time and your budget. And the relevance of information to an individual's job is significantly more important to learning and retention than the method chosen to convey that information.

Figure 8-9 summarizes how several companies used as examples in this chapter have leveraged a blended learning approach, relying on a combination of methods to accomplish their L&D objectives in different situations.

A Blended Learning Process Gives a Financial Company Competitive Advantage

Sales leaders at Signature Resources, an independent office of the John Hancock Financial Network, rely heavily on L&D programs to encourage the continued success of their financial sales representatives as their customers become more affluent, sophisticated, and demanding. The company's L&D philosophy is summarized in three words: *capture, expand,* and *teach.* During the capture and expand phases, reps develop the expertise they need in order to be successful; during the teach phase, they share that expertise with newer reps.

New reps begin with a 15-month curriculum that allows them to *capture* essential skills and knowledge, like understanding of the product and how to communicate a value proposition. The course supplements concepts taught in the classroom with real-life exercises that allow reps to try out their new skills while actively seeking new prospects, which not only helps new reps learn concepts faster but also allows them to begin generating revenue sooner. All reps are required to develop a viable business plan for their practice that defines target markets in which they already have an interest or numerous contacts. The reps then work with their managers to customize their training and education to focus on what they need to know to be successful at executing their plan.

The second phase of training encourages the new reps to further develop their skills as they *expand* their knowledge in one of four areas of expertise: financial planning, estate planning, business planning, or wealth management. Reps select one area as a "major" and attend training boot camps that provide detailed product and marketing immersion in that area. During this phase, learning is supplemented with mentoring by an experienced rep, who helps the new rep develop important consultative selling skills and knowledge, such as deeply understanding a client's situation and leveraging the firm's resources to best meet client needs.

As reps develop strong experience and expertise in these areas, they in turn become mentors and can *teach* newer reps the skills and knowledge that they've gained. Teaching occurs not only through the formalized, one-on-one mentoring process, but also through weekly case studies, informal breakfast meetings, and formal seminars taught by experienced reps. Sales leaders feel that this unique and integrated approach to sales force L&D gives Signature Resources a competitive advantage and helps the firm attract the best talent.

Balancing Efficiency and Effectiveness. Time and budget are important considerations when selecting methods in a blended learning approach. Generally, the most effective learning methods (those that result in the highest levels of retention of skills and knowledge) are also the most time-intensive and costly. Figure 8-10 shows where several L&D program methods fall on an efficiency/effectiveness spectrum. Sales organizations that blend highly effective methods, such as on-the-job training, with more efficient methods, such as self-study, can accomplish their L&D objectives at a reasonable cost.

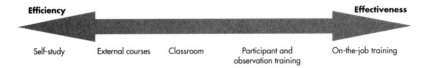

Figure 8-10. Trade-offs between effectiveness and efficiency of training methods

---

A Blended Sales Training Approach Increases Effectiveness at Saab Cars USA

The automobile industry is finding sales training to be increasingly important as easy access to information via the Internet makes potential car buyers increasingly savvy. Luxury automaker Saab Cars USA has a constant need for new sales training, as the company has dramatically increased its rate of new car development. Saab uses a blended sales training approach to educate approximately 1,800 salespeople throughout the United States every year. It offers a costly but highly effective 17-day "Ride and Drive" program, which allows salespeople to see how Saab vehicles perform compared to competing brands. A training web site includes "Saab Way" product training for Saab vehicles, checklists and guides designed to support salespeople while on the job, and customized training in the Saab selling process. By leveraging the Web, Saab gives its salespeople immediate access to training when they need it and can offer more sales courses at a lower cost.

Building Programs Around Adult Learning Models for Higher Impact. Research-based models of how adults learn can help you choose the most effective L&D program for your sales forces. American educator Malcolm Knowles, a pioneer in the development of adult learning models, observed that adults learn more when:

1. They are involved in the planning and evaluation of their instruction.
2. They engage in discussion and problem solving rather than just passive listening.

3. The learning has immediate relevance to their job or can be applied to their immediate circumstances.

4. Learning is problem-centered rather than content-oriented.

The most successful L&D programs build upon these four observations. Methods that acknowledge how adults learn—for example, case studies, role-playing exercises, on-the-job training experiences, and discussions—are often very effective.

Reinforcing Learning. People typically soon forget much of what they learn unless the learning is continuously reinforced. Linking L&D programs with complementary sales effectiveness drivers, such as information support, coaching, and performance management, lets companies significantly enhance the impact of L&D programs. Figure 8-11 shows a plan that one company used to reinforce classroom learning with other learning methods. This company had an eight- to ten-week training program for new hires to help them develop needed sales competencies. While it was primarily classroom-based, the program also included a field apprenticeship that allowed students to practice their newly acquired skills on the job.

During a new hire's first year on the job, the skills that she learned during the initial training were reinforced through coaching and case study exercises with first-line sales managers designed to strengthen

		Content: Needed Sales Competencies	• Core product knowledge • Selling skills • Territory management	• Targeting • Selling to groups • Building relationship versatility • Customer management	• Negotiation • Situational leadership
L&D Program		Period	Six to eight weeks	One week	One week
		Methods	• Classroom training • Field apprenticeship	• Classroom seminar	• External classroom seminar
Reinforcement		Period	Four months	Four months	Twelve months
		Method	Manager-Led • Coaching • Reinforcement of selling skills • Case studies Self-Managed • Product self-study guides • Intranet resources, tools, and tests	Manager-Led • Coaching • Reinforcement of group selling skills • Case studies Self-Managed • Targeting tools • Intranet resources, tools, and tests	Manager-Led • Coaching • Reinforcement of negotiating skills • Case studies Self-Managed • Intranet resources, tools, and tests

Figure 8-11. Example of an L&D program with reinforced learning

specific skills. The new salespeople were also expected to use self-study guides and intranet resources and tools to reinforce their learning.

L&D When the Sales Process Is Evolving: Creating a Learning Organization

When a sales environment is changing rapidly, there is continuous need for sales force L&D. A traditional model that relies on taking salespeople out of the field for classroom training probably cannot work by itself, as new learning needs to happen constantly. To be successful, salespeople must learn and adapt all the time, as they often must decide on the fly what it will take to be successful with customers as changes unfold.

Sales success in a rapidly changing environment requires that L&D become embedded in the culture of the sales organization. Two elements need to work in tandem. First, salespeople must be responsible for their own development and seek out ways to constantly improve their skills and knowledge. Second, sales leaders need to continuously encourage the sharing of knowledge, using both formal and informal means to capture and propagate learning throughout the sales force. The sales organization must become a "learning organization," in which the development and exchange of knowledge become inseparable from the work environment. These are culture-defining values.

Some major corporations have turned to organizational solutions as part of their conscious effort to build a learning organization. Such job titles as chief knowledge officer (CKO) and chief learning officer (CLO) have been created for the individuals charged with leading knowledge-management and learning efforts. An analogous trend within the sales organization is the transformation of the role of sales training director to a sales knowledge director or sales learning director responsible for initiating, driving, and integrating L&D programs across the sales force.

How Some Business Leaders Describe Their Learning Cultures

In a learning organization, L&D is an integral part of the company's culture. Here are some statements business leaders have used to describe the culture of their learning organizations.

- Ted Hoff, chief learning officer, IBM: "Learning is truly embedded in our work, truly pervasive day to day, not just courses."

- Dr. Ralph Shrader, CEO, Booz Allen Hamilton: "We view professional development as an invaluable opportunity and as a shared responsibility between staff members and the firm."

- Jack Welch, former chairman and CEO, GE: "The biggest competitive advantage that a company can have is creating an environment where people can learn from each other."

Self-Development

Sales organizations that are learning organizations view L&D as the collective responsibility of the company and of individual salespeople. The company makes numerous opportunities for learning and professional growth available, and the salespeople are expected to continuously seek out opportunities to improve their skills and knowledge.

Learning Is Part of Everyday Work at IBM

Recognizing that the most powerful learning occurs as part of an employee's experience on the job, IBM seeks to make learning a daily part of every salesperson's job. Consider the following story: An IBM salesperson assigned to the global account team that serves the airline industry is at his desktop reading a news article in which the CEO of one of his clients is interviewed about rising fuel costs. The salesperson wonders how the client's costs compare with the industry average. The news article guides him to a financial tool that lets him find out. He discovers that this client's costs are, in fact, higher than the industry average. He broadcasts worldwide to IBM's global airline sales team to see if anyone has relevant experience in helping a client deal with rising fuel costs and finds an in-house expert who has recently helped another airline in a similar situation. The salesperson collaborates with the in-house expert, working across time and distance, to develop a proposal for the client. The final proposal is posted so that all IBM salespeople on the global airline sales team have access to it, adding to the existing knowledge base and making the entire team more informed.

Making learning an everyday part of the sales job benefits both the company and individual salespeople. From a company perspective, a sales force that focuses on constant learning and improvement not only is more valuable to customers today, but can also adapt more readily in the future when competitive, environmental, and company strategy changes require changes in the selling process. From an individual salesperson's perspective, constant learning helps individuals grow in their current roles, enhances their success, and creates more career opportunities.

Knowledge Sharing

You can encourage the sharing of skills and knowledge across your sales force by leveraging information technologies, using nontechnological but formalized channels, and ensuring that your incentive plan encourages the sharing of knowledge. But perhaps the most powerful way to encourage the sharing of skills and knowledge is to build a culture that embraces informal knowledge sharing among salespeople.

Technology creates new opportunities to share knowledge across time and space. Chapter 11 provides many examples of ways in which you can use CRM and other systems to share customer knowledge across your sales organization.

Using Technology to Support the Sharing of Best Practices

Technology can allow sales teams to easily capture and share best sales practices and know-how for enhanced sales performance. E-mail, blogs, online forums and communities, and Web-based seminars let salespeople share insights across time and distance. Some examples of ways in which sales forces have benefited from technology-based sales collaboration are:

- A leading hotel site selection firm reduced the ramp-up time for new sales agents by encouraging them to post on a company blog questions for experienced agents around the world. The experienced agents, who themselves posted questions frequently, were eager to help.

- A salesperson for a software company e-mailed the rest of the sales force when he acquired valuable competitive intelligence from a customer. The information was of tremendous assistance in helping other salespeople sell against the competitor.

- Another software company captures the know-how of seasoned sales-people by posting their helpful materials and valuable tips on the company intranet, ensuring that their tremendous knowledge is not lost when they retire.

- ExactTarget has a web site that allows its 75 salespeople to post and answer questions for one another about the software company's products and procedures. The site has significantly reduced the workload for sales support staff and enables the sales force to get answers to customers' questions more quickly.

While technology clearly can play a role in enhancing information sharing in a sales force, companies also can be very successful at leveraging nontechnological but formalized channels to encourage their salespeople to share knowledge. Sales meetings and debriefings can provide a structured forum through which salespeople can share their experiences and brainstorm effective selling approaches. Many companies have formalized mentoring programs that allow newer salespeople to benefit from the experience and wisdom of veterans.

Perhaps the most powerful way in which knowledge is shared among salespeople is through informal means, such as chats during coffee breaks, sales meetings, or social outings. Since such talk is off the record, people generally share their personal knowledge more liberally than they do when they are using more formal modes of information exchange. Sales organizations can enhance L&D by encouraging their salespeople to share their knowledge informally and by providing opportunities for such exchanges.

Knowledge sharing is most successful in a sales force that has developed a culture of cooperation and teamwork. If a sales force's culture is highly competitive—for example, if individual success is valued over team success or if forced rankings of salespeople are published routinely—knowledge sharing probably won't work as well. To become a learning organization, a sales force must develop an externally competitive but internally cooperative culture.

Aligning L&D Efforts with Other Sales Effectiveness Drivers

Sales leaders often turn to L&D programs to cure many ills. If the sales of a new product are lagging, if salespeople are not spending enough time with large accounts, or if the competitive environment is changing, sales leaders frequently see a revamped L&D program as an answer that is easy to implement without much risk. Often L&D programs are part of a solution for changing sales force behavior. Consider the following statements by sales leaders:

- "Our salespeople like selling the easy, fun products that they know well. . . . We want to encourage them to spend more time selling our new, strategically important product. Additional new product training will help salespeople become more proficient and comfortable at selling the new product against entrenched competitors."

- "We want our salespeople to do more prospecting. They are spending too much time with familiar customers with whom they feel comfortable. A refresher course focused on how to effectively approach new potential customers will help salespeople improve their prospecting skills and confidence."

While training can be a good partial answer for many sales force issues, other solutions may also be part of the answer. For example:

- For a sales organization that spends too little time selling a new product, training alone is an insufficient solution if the salespeople do not have enough time to sell the new product and simultaneously support existing products. Addressing this problem requires increasing the size of the sales force, in addition to providing training.

- For a sales organization that spends too little time prospecting, training alone will have little impact if salespeople do not have the information they need to help them locate good prospects. Providing such information is necessary if training is to be fruitful.

L&D efforts are most powerful when they are reinforced by and aligned with the other sales effectiveness drivers.

CHAPTER 9

How to Create a Winning Sales Force Culture

Sales leaders often attribute their organizations' success to having a winning sales force culture. The world's largest package-delivery company, UPS, attributes its success in large part to the company's *customer service–focused* and *team-oriented* sales culture. To this day, the late Jim Casey, who founded the company in 1907, remains a powerful influence on the UPS culture. Jim had the ability to convey the core values of his company, including respect for the individual, a deep sense of honesty and integrity, a strong customer orientation, and the idea that the entire organization is greater than the sum of its parts. Every chairman since Casey has conveyed that same message through the people reporting to him—from the vice president of sales to the regional managers, to the district sales managers, and eventually down to the UPS people on the street who interact with customers on a day-to-day basis. In the words of former company CEO Jim Kelly, "We don't see ourselves as having a lot of superstars, but rather as being a lot of good people working together to accomplish the right objectives."

Company leaders at industrial products company W. L. Gore, best known for its Gore-Tex brand, have linked the company's success in part to its culture, which is built around *innovation, empowerment,* and *teamwork*. As discussed in Chapter 5, the Gore culture is encouraged through a lattice sales organization structure. Salespeople work together on teams to meet the needs of their customers. The teams decide who is hired and how much various team members should be paid. The most prestigious recognitions for salespeople are for their contributions to long-term company success—through such activities as helping out in other territories or coaching less experienced salespeople—not for achieving short-term sales goals. Sales forecasts are not dictated; they are generated by team members, who discuss their goals with sales leaders.

The American Family Life Assurance Company (Aflac) has been listed multiple times on *Fortune* magazine's lists of America's Most Admired Companies and Best Companies to Work For. Aflac's corporate culture is built around doing things "the Aflac Way," which means providing customer service that meets the principles passed down from one generation of employees to the next since 1955. The company's founders, brothers John, Paul, and Bill Amos, believed that if the company took care of its employees, then the employees would take care of the company. This philosophy applies both to corporate employees and to the 69,000 independent sales agents who sell Aflac life insurance and supplemental policies. Aflac takes care of its sales agents through a sales culture that appeals to their *competitive* nature and *entrepreneurial* spirit. The culture is reinforced through programs aimed at making agents successful and helping them grow their business. Recognition is an important element— there are literally thousands of sales contests and awards for agents and sales managers, including an annual convention trip for top-performing agents, special recognition for successful new agents, awards for the best sales managers, and membership in the prestigious President's Club, for which fewer than 1 percent of agents and managers qualify. Winners of all awards are publicized in the quarterly sales agent magazine. The sales agent web site has multiple pages devoted to recognizing successful agents and allows agents to see where they rank nationally.

Defining Sales Force Culture

Every sales force has a personality that is its culture. A sales force's history, its environment, and its people all help shape its culture. It can be thought of as the genetic makeup of the sales organization. Another way to think of "culture" is as the unwritten set of rules that guides the behavior of salespeople and sales managers as they encounter both familiar and new situations. It establishes a baseline for decision making and helps define acceptable and desirable activity.

While the organization's culture shapes the people, the people also shape the culture. It's helpful to consider cultures in terms of *choices* that are guided by the values of the organization and by the norms it maintains for appropriate behavior. Salespeople face numerous choices every day, For example:

- "Should I make quick hits in order to achieve a short-term sales goal, or should I try to penetrate a very large competitive account that requires a considerable investment of time and has an unknown likelihood of success?"
- "Should I take time away from selling to attend a professional development workshop?"
- "Should I visit a tough customer by myself, or should I ask my manager to join me?"
- "Should I compete with other salespeople so that I can get a top spot in the sales rankings and become part of the President's Club, or should I share my best ideas with others so that everyone benefits from my experience?"
- "Should I sell a high-margin product that is important to company success or a low-margin product that better meets the customer's basic needs?"

Salespeople look to their culture to suggest the best responses to these and other choices that they face every day. A strong culture provides guidance for salespeople so that they routinely make the appropriate choices.

You can shape the culture of your sales force by shaping its work style on six basic dimensions, as shown in Figure 9-1. There is no right or wrong way to direct a sales force on these dimensions; the choices you make are either appropriate or inappropriate depending on the selling environment and culture that you want to establish and maintain.

Long-Term	Short-Term
Decisions are made to increase the long-term welfare of the company.	Decisions are made to maximize short-term operating results.
Control	**Empowerment**
Management wishes to control the activity in the field.	Management wishes to empower the field to add value to customers and to select the most appropriate activity.
Activity	**Results**
Activity measurement is included in the performance management system and the incentive compensation plan.	The performance management system and the incentive compensation plan utilize financial measures, such as sales, profits, or market share, exclusively.
Cooperative	**Competitive**
Team success is valued over individual success. A cooperative environment enhances performance.	Individual success is valued over team success. A little competition gets the juices flowing.
Stable	**Adaptive**
Customer relationships are critical. Disruption should be minimized so that customers do not have to see new faces all the time.	Selling organizations need to adapt quickly to environmental changes. The sales force needs to be able and willing to change to conquer the competitive landscape.
Risk Averse	**Risk Taking**
The sales force needs to protect the company's strengths. Too much time spent pursuing unlikely prospects wastes valuable resources.	Salespeople need to take risks sometimes to be successful. Often persistence pays off, even with unlikely prospects.

Figure 9-1. Six dimensions that shape the sales force work style

What Makes a Sales Force Culture Successful?

While many different types of sales force culture can lead to sales success, the best of them share several characteristics. Effective sales force cultures not only embrace values and choices that are appropriate for the selling environment, but also create a strong consensus within the sales force and encourage salespeople to live the values with intensity.

A Winning Culture Embraces Appropriate Values and Choices

The right culture for your sales force respects the combined needs of three important constituents: your customers, your salespeople, and the company. It encourages decisions that align well with customer needs, and at the same time treats salespeople with respect and reinforces company objectives and strategies. While there are some cultures that are inappropriate for any sales force, other cultures may be appropriate in some situations but not in others.

Cultures That Are Always Inappropriate. No sales force should encourage a culture that mistreats customers, salespeople, or the company. "Live-for-today" and greedy cultures may create short-term gains, but they always fail in the long term. And victim cultures, unless they are changed, keep organizations mired in the quicksand of failure.

"Live-for-today" cultures mistreat customers and salespeople. In "live-for-today" cultures, excessive pressure to make short-term sales goals leads salespeople and sales managers to make choices that compromise long-term success. In such cultures, sales leaders allow and sometimes even encourage salespeople to act inappropriately with customers. For example, salespeople may mislead customers, make unrealistic promises, and sell products and services that customers do not need in order to maximize short-term sales.

Sears Modifies Its Pay Plan to Create Customer Focus

In the early 1990s, 3,500 employees of Sears Auto Center, the retail giant's very profitable automotive repair division, were paid straight commission on the parts and services they sold to customers who brought their cars in for repair. Not surprisingly, some employees were performing and charging customers for unnecessary work. In 1992, the company faced several lawsuits that were tied directly to its incentive pay plan. Sears had to pay out millions of dollars to consumers who felt that they had been enticed into authorizing and paying for needless repairs. In the wake of the scandal, Sears abolished commissions and sales goals in its automotive division, making customer satisfaction its number one priority.

In "live-for-today" cultures, sales leaders and managers can mistreat their salespeople. Obsession with making short-term revenue goals can dominate their actions, causing managers to put excessive pressure on salespeople to deliver immediate results. But in the long run, the company loses because salespeople—and customers—defect.

A Culture with an Excessive Short-Term Focus Hurts Company Performance

---

A company that sells a medical device to physicians (who can recommend the device to their patients) had a highly aggressive sales force culture that was hurting company performance. Interviews with salespeople revealed that the intense short-term focus of company leaders created an unsupportive, stressful work environment and an unsustainable pace of work for salespeople:

- "My manager is constantly demanding more output, yet he rarely coaches me on effective sales processes."
- "We are day trading our products rather than setting up the fundamentals for long-term growth."
- "Headquarters is constantly sending threatening messages, such as 'If you haven't met your sales goals, all Christmas vacations will be canceled.'"
- "People won't give honest answers because they feel that their jobs are in jeopardy on a daily basis."

At the same time, the physicians that the company's salespeople called on felt that the company's intense short-term focus was not in the best interests of their patients:

- "The company really pushes its salespeople to sell; they have quotas to meet, and everything is about money and not about what is best for the patient."
- "Top management is money-oriented; it has too much of a business culture and is not sensitive to patient needs."
- "I think the company will go under because of these heavy-handed marketing practices."

Change and improvement came only after the CEO resigned.

Greedy cultures overlook customer and company interests. In greedy cultures, the hunger for personal financial success on the part of salespeople, sales managers, and sales leaders prevails over their desire for customer and company success. People in the sales organization routinely make choices that put their own best interests first, even though those choices compromise customer and company interests. Salespeople may choose to manipulate the incentive plan by managing the timing of orders to maximize personal earnings or to sell customers the products that yield the highest commissions rather than the ones that best meet customer needs.

Greedy Cultures Can Encourage Salespeople to Deceive Customers

In 2004, the New York state attorney general investigated the world's largest insurance broker, Marsh Inc. (a unit of the Marsh & McLennan Companies), for allegedly cheating customers out of the best deals for insurance. Customers ranging from major corporations to small businesses hire insurance brokers like Marsh to find the proper insurance coverage at the best possible price. Brokers receive commissions from customers for arranging the coverage. The 2004 controversy stemmed from the fact that the brokers were also collecting commissions from the other side of the deal—the insurers. Insurance companies often paid brokers a commission for steering business to their company or for arranging a particularly profitable form of coverage. These payments, investigators claimed, enticed Marsh to choose insurers for customers based on the size of the fees the insurance companies would pay Marsh, not on the price and value of the policies offered to the customers. Marsh and the insurers were even accused of deceiving customers into believing that several bids were being competitively submitted for their business, when in fact Marsh had determined in advance which company would get the sale based on the size of the commission. As a result of the investigation, the largest insurance industry brokers stopped accepting commissions from insurance companies so that brokers' financial interests no longer conflicted with those of their customers.

Greedy Cultures Can Encourage Salespeople to Manage the Timing of Orders to Maximize Their Incentive Compensation

Salespeople at International Data Corporation (IDC), a publisher of market research for the technology industry, earned a percentage commission on every sale, but a very large portion of their incentive pay came in the form of a bonus for hitting a sales quota. Salespeople who achieved their quota before the end of an incentive period often chose to hold over subsequent deals until after the start of the next period, so that those deals could count toward the next period's quota. Sales leaders condoned this behavior, even though holding over sales was in neither the customer's nor the company's best interests. IDC's revenue stream would dry up at the end of each period, leaving the firm with a depleted cash flow and customers waiting too long for the product.

The problem of salespeople shifting sales forward or backward in time in order to increase personal earnings is common in sales forces that employ incentive plans with caps or with significant bonuses or accelerated commissions tied to short-term goals. To alleviate the problem, many companies have changed their incentive plans so that they align better with customer and company interests.

Victim cultures lack accountability and thwart customer and company success. In victim cultures, salespeople blame others for their failures, and no one feels accountable for results. Sales leaders allow a cynical attitude to pervade the sales force. Salespeople have very little confidence that positive change is possible. They are disengaged, and they constantly make excuses for their poor performance. Even the few salespeople who are successful show little loyalty to the company.

The Victim Culture at Guidant

When Jay Graf became president of the CRM division of medical device company Guidant in 1992, the company faced many challenges. Guidant's products were no longer competitive, and customers believed that the company was years behind in technology. The sales organization was not making its sales goals, and expenses were not under control. Unfortunately, an unhealthy victim corporate culture affected the sales force—and also R&D, manufacturing, and marketing—encouraging attitudes and behaviors among employees that Graf felt were destroying the company's future. After many years of failure, employees had no trust or confidence in the organization.

The attitude was, "We will never get out of this; things are not going to change; the company cannot design itself out of a paper bag." There was no accountability—no one could depend on anyone to do what he had promised to do. A large group of people sold virtually nothing and were satisfied with their low performance. Sales leaders gave credence to salespeople's constant excuses for not getting sales—they believed everything from "our products are no good" to "our price is too high" to "marketing isn't positioning us correctly." The small group of people who were successful at selling made lots of money and were arrogant about it, yet were not committed to the company. Sales leaders were intimidated when salespeople made such threats as, "If we don't get what we want, we will leave." Regional sales managers did not lead, and local sales managers did not train and coach their people. Graf realized that in order to get back on a success track, Guidant needed a major culture transformation. In just two years, he successfully changed the entire culture of his organization (see the conclusion to the Guidant story later in this chapter).

Cultural Values and Choices That Can Be Appropriate or Inappropriate, Depending on Conditions. The choices that define "live-for-today," greedy, and victim cultures are destructive in every selling environment. Yet most of the culture-defining choices that salespeople make are not clearly right or wrong; rather, they may be either appropriate or inappropriate, depending on the selling environment and the company situation. A culture that is successful in one sales environment can set up the conditions for failure in another context. For example, sales cultures can vary considerably across industries. Figure 9-2, using what we call the work style wheel, compares six work style choices that shape the sales culture in two industries with very different selling environments—insurance and pharmaceuticals.

The sales force at the insurance company sells a variety of types of insurance policies to individuals. Salespeople are expected to develop their own base of customers and are free to decide whom to call on and how to spend their time. Independence and entrepreneurship are encouraged. Since all sales force earnings come from a commission on sales, veterans who have built up a base of lucrative loyal accounts can

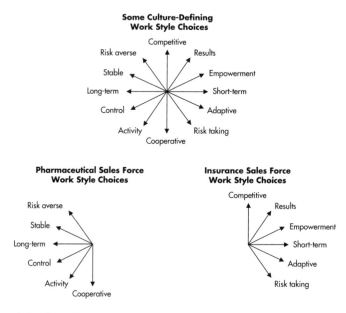

Figure 9-2. A work style wheel comparison of sales force cultures in two industries: insurance and pharmaceuticals

earn a lot of money. A newer salesperson must work hard to build an account base and often struggles to earn a good living in the early years.

At the pharmaceutical company, the salesperson's role is to educate physicians and other health-care professionals about the company's line of drugs. Salespeople work together in teams in assigned sales territories, with team members contributing different levels of expertise and knowledge of the science behind different types of drugs. Marketing provides the sales teams with detailed call plans and carefully scripted sales messages to ensure that the information delivered to physicians by the sales force is accurate and within FDA guidelines. Salespeople earn most of their pay through salary, but also earn bonuses for working together with team members to achieve sales goals for strategically important products.

Differences in the selling environments in these two industries create a need for very different sales force cultures. The culture at the insurance company (such as Aflac, mentioned earlier in this chapter) is characterized by empowerment, a focus on results, and competition.

Successful salespeople there are adaptive and risk taking. The sales culture at the pharmaceutical company is quite the opposite. Sales activity is carefully controlled, and successful salespeople cooperate with one another to ensure that a consistent sales message is delivered.

The culture of a sales force can evolve over time as the environment changes or as new management philosophies are adopted. Consider the case of an information technology company. In its early years, the company established a sales force culture that was competitive and focused on creating short-term results that would show immediate value to investors. Most earnings came from commissions, and salespeople were highly focused on making their quarterly sales goals. Since salespeople were competing for individual sales awards, they mostly worked alone and consulted with their colleagues only rarely. This culture worked well during the firm's early years, when sales cycles were short and selling was straightforward. However, as the industry evolved and the firm's product line broadened, the sales process became increasingly long, complex, and team-oriented. Sales success required salespeople to work together with systems engineers, service managers, technical consultants, and product specialists over a period of many months to provide business solutions for multiple decision makers. The importance of developing and maintaining long-term customer relationships increased considerably. The company was challenged to transform its sales culture to one that was more cooperative and focused on meeting the long-term needs of customers.

A Winning Culture Is Based on Consensus
Culture is a more effective driver of sales success when everyone is on board. In cultures that lack consensus, salespeople who face similar situations will make different choices about what to do. Inconsistent sales force choices can undermine business success.

Lack of Culture Consensus Creates Dissonance for an Office Equipment Sales Force

---

An office equipment maker sold products that were widely regarded as being of superior quality to those of its competitors. To preserve its premium image, the company built its sales culture around customer value, rather than low price. Salespeople were asked not to offer discounts to customers, although they were authorized to cut price by up to 10 percent if necessary to close a major deal. Most salespeople followed this guideline and routinely held the price. However, a few aggressive salespeople ignored the guideline and constantly pushed their managers to allow them to discount by more than 10 percent. Since the salespeople were ranked and paid commissions based on sales volume (and not margin), those who offered discounts consistently had higher sales, were ranked higher, and were paid more commission than those who did not. To further complicate the situation, some customers began sharing information about the prices they were getting from the company, and many became angry when they learned that they were not getting the best possible price.

Sales leaders tell us:

- "It's important to have the entire army marching in the same direction."
- "We want everybody in the sales force to be on board with our vision."
- "When everyone is passionate about the same values, the collective adrenaline makes the company unstoppable."

Culture consensus is driven by strong leadership. Leaders create consensus by establishing the desired values and norms and reinforcing them constantly.

Culture Consensus at GE Drives Company Success

In 1981, when Jack Welch became CEO of General Electric (GE), the company was a collection of businesses with vastly different cultures and varied expectations about the future. Welch used his powerful leadership skills to orient all of the businesses within GE around a single new mission: to be first or second in every business in which the company competed. Welch became well known for his aggressive management style as he worked to eradicate inefficiency by dismantling bureaucracy and systematically firing the bottom 10 percent of managers every year. Although he was initially disliked by many of those who worked for him, most employees eventually adapted to the culture he created and came to respect him. He achieved a fabled strong culture consensus within GE.

Many events can challenge a culture consensus. For example, new selling processes may need to be implemented as markets evolve and company strategies change. Some salespeople are unable to adapt. And new leadership can challenge a culture consensus.

Lack of Consensus Around Culture Change at Procter & Gamble Leads to CEO's Resignation

In 1999, the new CEO of Procter & Gamble (P&G), Durk Jager, announced a restructuring program that promised to make the company more responsive in a fast-moving, global marketplace. The program involved cutting worldwide headcount, reorganizing the corporate structure into global product category–based business units, and transforming the company's conservative culture into one that was faster-moving and more Internet-savvy. Analysts were initially enthusiastic about Jager's focus on innovation and his push to make the culture more entrepreneurial. However, not everyone at P&G agreed that the changes were necessary or that Jager's approach to implementing change was appropriate. The organization rebelled, and Jager was forced to resign after just 17 months. Alan G. Lafley, who took over as CEO, was committed to reestablishing P&G's traditional conservative culture, stating that Mr. Jager "tried to make changes too quickly."

Sales force mergers or acquisitions can create challenges to culture consensus. When the two companies that come together have divergent sales cultures, sales leaders need to create a consensus around a new blended culture, usually while facing the added pressure of cutting costs quickly.

P&G's Acquisition of Gillette Creates Challenges in Integrating Two Sales Force Cultures

P&G's 2005 acquisition of Gillette created some difficult challenges in integrating the two sales force cultures, which were dramatically different. P&G's culture focused on methodical consensus building, while Gillette's was built around relatively quick decision making. Prior to the merger, P&G and Gillette both had sales forces that were focused on getting the company's line of oral-care products into dentists' offices, and the two sales forces competed fiercely. P&G's major focus was on its leading toothpaste brand, Crest (with a secondary focus on SpinBrush toothbrushes), while Gillette's sales message was anchored by the world's number one toothbrush brand, Oral-B (with a secondary focus on its high-end Rembrandt toothpaste).

Recognizing the significant marketing power that would come from selling the Crest and Oral-B brands together, P&G decided to merge the Gillette and P&G sales organizations. Instead of subsuming the Gillette sales organization, as was P&G's usual practice with acquisitions, P&G gave the top job of merging the two sales forces to Gillette's oral-care president, Bruce Cleverly—a sign that P&G intended to retain some of Gillette's methods and talent. Yet Cleverly faced many challenges in achieving consensus around a consistent sales culture for the merged organization. He quickly discovered that he no longer had the free rein in decision making that he was used to having at Gillette. Instead, he had to contend with the lengthy consensus-seeking process that was part of the P&G culture. He also had the challenge of working with P&G's former oral-care president, Charlie Pierce, who, in an unusual structure, reported both to Cleverly and also directly to the CEO, creating some confusion about who was in charge. Instead of communicating through meetings, as was common practice at Gillette, the P&G culture favored communication through memos. Gillette people had to use glossaries to decipher the many acronyms that were part of the sales vernacular at P&G (for example, CIB for "customer is boss" and FMOT for "first moment of truth"). Tensions between the two organizations were high, as layoffs were imminent and both P&G and Gillette salespeople were competing for jobs. Eventually, Cleverly resigned his position, leaving Pierce in charge of a merged sales organization that would take on rival Colgate by promoting a combined Crest and Oral-B product line.

Pharmaceutical Company Mission Statements

Pharmaceutical Company #1
We will strive to achieve and sustain the leading place as the world's premier research-based pharmaceutical company. The company's continuing success benefits patients, customers, shareholders, business partners, families, and the communities in which they operate all around the world.

Pharmaceutical Company #2
Our mission is to provide society with superior products and services by developing innovations and solutions that improve the quality of life and satisfy customer needs, and to provide employees with meaningful work and advancement opportunities, and investors with a superior rate of return.

Computer Company Mission Statements

Computer Company #1
Our mission is to be the most successful computer company in the world at delivering the best customer experience in markets we serve.

Computer Company #2
As a global leader in the PC market, we develop, manufacture and market cutting-edge, reliable, high-quality PC products and value-added professional services that provide customers around the world with smarter ways to be productive and competitive.

Figure 9-3. The mission statements of several companies

A Winning Culture Lives Its Values with Intensity

Many companies attempt to influence their culture through corporate directives, slogans, or mission statements that characterize the values of the business. Such statements as "We take care of our customers," "Employees are our most important asset," and "We increase long-term shareholder value" can give employees inspiration and direction. However, it is not the words that are chosen for these directives that differentiate successful companies. Consider the mission statements of the two pharmaceutical and two computer companies shown in Figure 9-3. All four statements use powerful, success-oriented words, yet at one point in time, one of the companies in each industry had significantly higher market share than the other.

Enron Fails to Deliver on Its Mission

Following revalations in 2001 that energy company Enron's reported financial condition was sustained largely through accounting fraud, Enron has become a symbol of corporate corruption. Ironically, Enron's mission statement was built around admirable corporate values:

Enron's Mission Statement

Respect: We treat others as we would like to be treated ourselves. We do not tolerate abusive or disrespectful treatment. Ruthlessness, callousness, and arrogance do not belong here.

Integrity: We work with customers and prospects openly, honestly, and sincerely. When we say we will do something, we will do it; when we say we cannot or will not do something, then we will not do it.

Communication: We have an obligation to communicate. Here, we take the time to talk with one another . . . and to listen. We believe that information is meant to move and that information moves people.

Excellence: We are satisfied with nothing less than the very best in everything we do. We will continue to raise the bar for everyone. The great fun here will be for all of us to discover just how good we can really be.

Yet it is the intensity of belief in a corporate mission statement, more than the statement itself, that influences a company's culture. In successful cultures, directives, slogans, and statements are more than just words. Employees live the words with passion and use them every day to guide the choices that they make. Some well-known historical examples of high-intensity cultures include Nordstrom (a philosophy of doing what is right for the customer), 3M (a relentless focus on innovation), and Disney (a commitment to treating theme-park customers as guests). In each of these cases, the intensity of the corporate culture has played a major role in the company's success.

Physical Cues Encourage Strength of Culture

At networking company Cisco Systems, along with the usual security badge, employees wear two additional badges. The first presents the company's goals and objectives. The second displays Cisco's mission and lists the attributes of the company's culture, which is grounded in customer success. The badges are a constant reminder to employees that they are responsible for helping the company reach its goals and maintain its culture.

The distinctive corporate culture of the Ritz-Carlton Hotel Company is embedded in the company's "Gold Standards," which every employee carries on a laminated card. The card begins with a statement that forms the basis of the entire culture: "We are ladies and gentlemen serving ladies and gentlemen." It continues by enumerating several key service principles, including responsiveness to the expressed and unexpressed needs of guests, continuously seeking opportunities to innovate and improve the Ritz-Carlton experience, immediate resolution of guests' problems, and continuous learning and growing. Ritz-Carlton's values are not just printed on the cards. They are the basis for all employee training and rewards programs, and they are reinforced by managers in "lineup" sessions at the start of each employee shift.

SAP America Creates Success Through the Intensity of Its Sales Culture

In 2002, after a successful expansion that ended with the Internet bust of 2000, the future of SAP America, the largest subsidiary of German business software company SAP AG, appeared bleak. The company had had several years of disappointing revenue growth. With market buzz focused on the more exciting new dot-com businesses, SAP's mainstream software for accounting and manufacturing functions was not generating much interest.

Bill McDermott was brought on as the fifth CEO of SAP America in five years. In four years under his leadership, the company quadrupled its market value, tripled its market share, and generated record profits every year—a success attributable to the strong positive sales culture that he helped create. The SAP culture had all three characteristics of successful cultures:

- *Appropriateness.* SAP's technology-oriented sales culture was transformed into a "value-to-customer" culture that was significantly more effective at building long-term customer relationships and growing sales.

- *Consensus.* The leaders made sure that everyone in the company shared their vision for creating customer success.

- *Intensity.* The final ingredient, called the "Secret Sauce," was living the vision with passion.

Creating intensity around the new culture required constant communication with the sales force. The vision and the reasons behind the change were shared with the sales force at every possible opportunity. A newly developed advertising slogan reinforced the message: "The best run businesses run SAP." McDermott also reinforced the vision through his own actions—for example, he spent approximately 70 percent of his time with customers. SAP also achieved intensity by aligning all of the sales effectiveness drivers around the new customer-focused vision. (See, later in this chapter, "Sales Culture Transformation at SAP America Requires Changing the Sales Effectiveness Drivers.")

Implementing a Winning Sales Culture

Perhaps the most important job that sales leaders have is to shape, reinforce, and, if necessary, change the sales culture. Here we share some ideas on how to successfully assess an existing sales culture, sustain a winning culture, and transform a culture that is not working.

Leaders Create Culture at Microsoft

Operating on the belief that leadership is the most significant lever for influencing culture that companies have, software giant Microsoft has implemented a carefully engineered leadership development system that is designed to shape the company's future by developing leaders who are passionate about Microsoft's aspired-to culture of customer centricity and collaboration. Microsoft has conducted worldwide research to identify leadership competencies that are important at various career stages and to understand the types of experiences that aspiring leaders need to be successful during each stage. The competencies, career stages, and lists of experiences form a framework that affects numerous sales effectiveness drivers at Microsoft, including talent management programs, assessment techniques, training programs, succession planning, coaching, performance evaluation systems, and new manager orientation.

Assessing the Current Sales Culture

Smart companies continually assess their sales culture and constantly seek out ways to make improvements. Two useful assessment tools are the appropriateness-consensus-intensity decision framework and the work style wheel.

Using the Appropriateness-Consensus-Intensity Decision Framework. Think about the three critical elements of your sales culture—appropriateness, consensus, and intensity—as a hierarchy. An inappropriate culture cannot succeed in the long term, so give the highest importance to appropriateness. Once an appropriate culture has been established, work for consensus. Fragmented cultures, even if the salespeople mostly have the right values and mostly make the right choices, lead to a disruptive lack of internal harmony. Finally, encourage salespeople to intensively live, every day, the appropriate values and choices that everyone agrees to.

Leadership is critical to the success of your sales culture. Leaders who do not state and restate the right values at every opportunity and who do not live the values with intensity can see their cultures wither away. Figure 9-4 provides a thinking framework for assessing a sales force culture. The decision tree offers recommendations for improving cultures that are inappropriate or that lack consensus or intensity.

Using the Work Style Wheel. Sometimes a lack of consensus between sales leaders and salespeople, or between high-performing salespeople and average-performing salespeople, can point to ways in which a culture can be improved. Figure 9-5 shows the results of a questionnaire-based assessment that a health-care company conducted to determine the degree of consensus between sales leaders and high- and average-performing salespeople on five of the culture-defining dimensions we described earlier in the chapter as components of the work style wheel. (In this industry, the sixth dimension, risk orientation, was not considered to be relevant and so was not included in the analysis.)

Salespeople and sales leaders were asked for their opinions about appropriate work style choices in each dimension. One question for assessing the "competitive" dimension was, "Do you think it is more important for individual salespeople to strive to be number one (competitive) or to have a sharing spirit and offer advice to peers (cooperative)?" A question for assessing the "empowered" dimension was, "Do you think the company should tell salespeople which customers are best to call on (control), or should it provide salespeople with information so that they can decide which to call on (empowerment)?" Multiple questions were used to score each dimension on a scale of 1 to 5. The questionnaires did not suggest

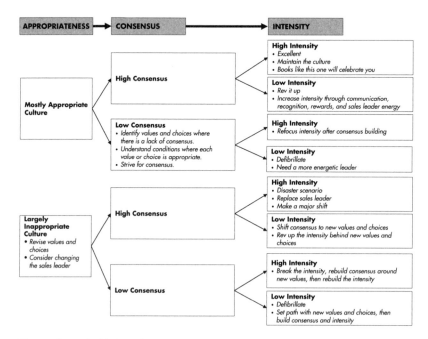

Figure 9-4. A thinking framework for sales force culture assessment: a decision tree for improving a culture that lacks appropriateness, consensus, or intensity

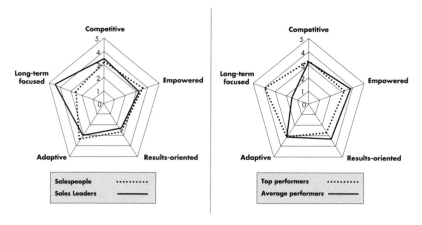

Figure 9-5. Results of a culture consensus assessment

right or wrong choices; they set up dilemmas. Both choices were desirable, and members of the sales force were asked to communicate their choices. Sales leaders were asked to respond to the questions in a way that reflected how they would want their salespeople to respond. The answers to the questionnaire provided a view of the sales force culture.

The assessment revealed that the opinions of sales leaders and salespeople were well aligned on four of the five culture-defining dimensions (see the left-hand graph). On the fifth dimension—"long-term focused"—sales leaders felt that the salespeople should be more focused on long-term success, whereas the salespeople felt that short-term success was more important. Interestingly, the opinions of top performers were more aligned with those of the sales leaders; it was the average performers who disagreed with the sales leaders on this dimension (see the right-hand graph). Assessments like this provide insights about what the leadership team can do to create a greater consensus around the long-term success culture that it hopes to create.

Sustaining a Winning Culture

As a strong sales leader, you must continuously reinforce appropriate culture choices. Here are some ways to do this:

- Communicate the preferred culture choices to the sales force continually. Use heroes, legends, myths, and parables to communicate these choices, since stories are remembered better than concepts. Begin employee indoctrination at the very first training session or orientation.
- Reward appropriate behaviors constantly.
- Celebrate the heroes who consistently make appropriate culture choices.
- "Walk the talk"—make sure that actions and words are compatible.

Use National Meetings to Reinforce the Right Culture Choices

National sales meetings are excellent occasions for reinforcing appropriate culture choices. We use the following technique at our consulting firm, ZS

Associates, to reinforce appropriate choices among our people. Several weeks prior to a companywide principals' meeting, we ask the attendees to provide a list of dilemmas they have faced when selling and delivering consulting work. The company leadership reviews the list of dilemmas, selects a few that are particularly relevant, and comes to an agreement about the best way to resolve each one. Through discussion at the meeting, the group shares experiences and ideas about how to handle each dilemma and comes to a consensus on the best choices for each situation. One of the dilemmas our principals face is what to do if an opportunity arises to sell work in another city and/or country where ZS has a local office. Should you pursue the opportunity yourself (and get credit for your office), or should you partner with the local office to sell the work? After much discussion, the group agreed that the right choice is to put the customer's needs first. Consequently, if involving the local office is in the customer's best interests, then that is the right choice to make. The discussion helped to reinforce the firm's customer-focused culture.

If you are a sales leader who wants to sustain a winning sales culture, you should be constantly on the lookout for culture breakers, which can include sales effectiveness drivers that do not reinforce the desired sales culture and people who are respected by the sales force but do not live the values that the culture tries to reinforce.

Culture Breaker: A Forced Ranking System Threatens the Collaborative Sales Culture

As a means of motivating the sales force through competitiveness, sales management at a bank started publishing a forced ranking of its salespeople and began to tie sales force incentive pay to the ranking. The new plan did spark a competitive fire among some of the company's salespeople. However, in time the ranking began to erode the supportive sales force culture that had contributed to the company's past success. Since the forced ranking plan meant that not everyone could win, internally focused competition increased. Salespeople who had once been quick to help each other out, share information, and collaborate became more concerned with how they compared to their peers than they were with serving customers and beating competitors. An "every man for himself" attitude developed. The forced ranking plan survived for just two years. Management replaced it with a goal-based incentive plan that allowed everyone to win, which helped to restore a more appropriate team-oriented sales culture.

Culture Breaker: A Sales Force Hero Becomes a Culture Rogue

Owen is a veteran salesman for the consumer division of a tool manufacturer. After many years of hard work developing a very lucrative territory for himself, he is ranked among the highest sellers in the company year after year. The sales force admires Owen for his obvious success, and for many years, sales leaders viewed Owen as a great role model for their salespeople. Recently, however, Owen's real estate investments have made him a lot of money. Consequently, he works when he wants to, usually three or four days a week, and takes long vacations. Many salespeople think, "Owen has got it made." Sales leaders are concerned that this one-time sales force hero now threatens the hard-working culture that drives the company's success. They must find ways to reduce Owen's influence and create new heroes who live the values that they want to reinforce.

Changing an Ineffective Culture

Cultures have inertia. Unless something specific is done to change an inappropriate culture or a culture that lacks consensus or intensity, the culture will just roll along. But as the marketplace and company strategies evolve, an outdated culture can become a liability for a sales force. For example, a culture that encourages stability rather than adaptability can get into trouble when markets evolve and customers begin to require a consultative rather than a transactional selling process; the culture of stability makes it difficult for salespeople to adapt as needed, yet change becomes necessary for continued success.

Culture change is hard work, and people are the change agents. Depending on the strength of a culture, it may take a very strong individual at the top of the organization to initiate change. Sometimes the best catalyst for change is a new sales leader from outside the company who brings a new perspective, can make objective choices, and is not responsible for the current culture. However, an outsider is an outsider. He needs to learn the organization and the nuances of the current culture quickly in order to be effective. A strong insider—one who knows the organization and its people, yet can separate herself from the current sales force culture—will have a very good chance of being successful. When salespeople view the change agent as "one of us," they often accept change more readily.

Figure 9-6 shows a process for changing an ineffective sales culture. Change begins with a vision of what having a "winning culture" means—a vision that needs to be communicated explicitly to the organization through mission statements, company presentations, sales meetings, and training programs. It also needs to be reinforced implicitly through stories and legends of company heroes who embody the values, norms, and work style desired in the new culture. As sales leaders take action to make the new culture a reality, highly visible rewards and recognitions help to reinforce the desired behaviors and make the new culture a reality.

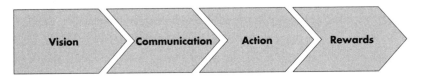

Figure 9-6. A process for changing an ineffective sales force culture

The Conclusion to the Guidant Story: From a Victim Culture to a Success Culture

As described earlier in this chapter, when Jay Graf became president of the CRM division of the medical device company Guidant in 1992, the company faced many challenges. A victim culture had developed over time, and Graf knew that a major transformation was necessary in order to get Guidant back on a success track. Over a period of two years, Graf successfully changed the entire culture of his organization. His process for effecting change incorporated the four steps of changing an ineffective sales force culture:

- *Vision.* Graf began by developing a vision for a success culture at Guidant—one in which employees had trust and confidence in the organization and people were held accountable for their results and could be expected to deliver on their commitments.

- *Communication.* He communicated this success culture to the organization at every possible opportunity. When he spoke at the annual national sales meeting, he shared his list of 10 measurable personal objectives. Throughout the year, he reported back to the group on his progress toward achieving those objectives.

- *Action.* Graf took several action steps to make the new culture a reality. He hired a new vice president of sales who had integrity, judgment, and the ability to make things stick. He gave the regional managers more responsibility and prominence and required them to manage their people. Those who could not adapt to the new culture left the company. Marketing support improved dramatically, as Graf worked to ensure that sales and marketing were on the same page.

- *Rewards.* Rewards and recognition were critical to the success of the new culture at Guidant. A new growth-oriented compensation plan and heightened recognition for good performance helped to reinforce the new culture of accountability. The new reward systems reflected Graf's belief that "you can't run an army without medals."

Shaping Sales Force Culture Through the Sales Effectiveness Drivers

As Figure 9-7 illustrates, the sales effectiveness drivers affect the culture of the sales force. Sustaining a winning culture involves constantly checking to ensure that the drivers are aligned with and reinforce the desired culture. At the same time, changing a sales force culture almost always involves changing the sales effectiveness drivers so that they align with and reinforce the new culture. Note that the culture changes that took place at Guidant and at SAP America required changes to multiple sales effectiveness drivers.

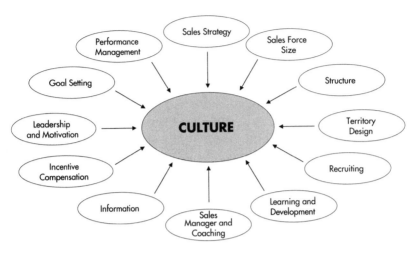

Figure 9-7. Culture change is initiated through the sales effectiveness drivers

---

Sales Culture Transformation at SAP America Requires Changing the Sales Effectiveness Drivers

---

Beginning in 2002, CEO Bill McDermott reignited success at the software company SAP America by transforming the company's formerly technology-oriented sales culture into a value-to-customer culture. (See, earlier in this chapter, "SAP America Creates Success Through the Intensity of Its Sales Culture.") A key part of this transformation was aligning the sales efffectiveness drivers around the new customer-focused vision. For example:

- *Definers.* Sales teams were restructured and regional sales operations were established so that salespeople were physically closer to customers.

- *Shapers.* Recruiting profiles were redefined, and salespeople who did not have the capabilities to implement the new customer-centered approach were let go. Those who remained at the company participated in aggressive training programs to develop the knowledge and skills required for success in the new culture.

- *Enlighteners.* A new sales intelligence center enabled salespeople to get up-to-date information about customers quickly.

- *Exciters.* High performers were rewarded generously, encouraging an intensity to win.

- *Controllers.* Salespeople were given challenging, customer-focused goals and were empowered to do whatever was right for the customer. To promote longer-term thinking, four-quarter rolling metrics replaced the quarterly metrics that had formerly been used to assess sales force performance.

CHAPTER 10

The Right Sales Manager: A Key to Sales Force Success

The Long-Term Impact of the Sales Manager

For many years we have been asking the sales leaders who attend our executive-level courses to answer the question posed as the title of Figure 10-1. The vote is nearly evenly divided.

In the short term, a team of excellent salespeople with an average manager easily outsells a team of average salespeople with an excellent manager. But over time, many excellent salespeople get promoted or retire, and others quit because their average manager is holding them back. And when they leave, they are usually replaced by average salespeople. An average manager rarely surrounds himself with excellent salespeople. He may be unable to recognize talent, or he may be intimidated by excellence. Remember: "First-rate people hire first-rate people; second-rate people hire third-rate people."

In the long run, an average manager brings all the territories in the district down to his level. On the other hand, an excellent manager brings excellence to all her territories. A great manager may inherit average salespeople, but in the long run she counsels, coaches, trains,

Figure 10-1. Which situation do sales leaders prefer?

and replaces those salespeople until the entire team is excellent. The sales manager's job is important because of this long-term effect.

When companies assess their sales management teams, they often discover serious deficiencies in the competencies of some sales managers. One company did an assessment in which salespeople were asked to complete 360-degree evaluations of their managers on important competencies, including leadership, communication, and coaching. The evaluations were done anonymously, and the results were not identified by individual manager, but rather were used to produce an overall assessment of the quality of the management team. Figure 10-2 shows how salespeople felt about their managers' leadership ability. While more than 40 percent of managers were rated "above average" or "excellent" on leadership, another 40 percent were rated "below average" or "poor." The distribution of scores on all the important managerial competencies followed a similar bimodal pattern. Sales leaders were concerned by these results and began a serious effort to upgrade the quality of the sales management team.

The Sales Manager's Role

The job of the first-line sales manager is arguably the most important job in the entire sales force. Top sales leaders determine the direction for the organization, but it is the first-line sales managers who ensure that the strategy is executed.

A Sales Manager Is Not a Salesperson

Most first-line sales managers are former salespeople. They know what it takes to succeed as a salesperson, and therefore they are capable of earning the respect of those who report to them. However, a salesperson who has been promoted quickly discovers that the role of sales manager is very different from that of salesperson.

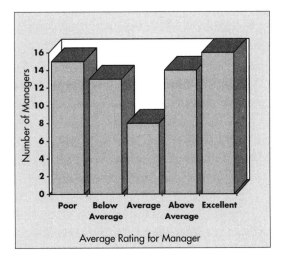

Figure 10-2. How salespeople rated their managers' leadership ability

Salespeople serve two constituencies: the customer and the company. They are successful when they meet the customers' needs and at the same time help the company achieve its objectives. Sales managers, on the other hand, serve the customer, the company, and a third constituent: the salespeople.

Like a salesperson, a sales manager succeeds by meeting customers' needs and achieving company goals. But the manager is not the hunter, the playmaker, or the center of action. Managers contribute to customer and company success when their people are successful. The fact that sales managers have that third constituency—salespeople—distinguishes their role. Managers are coaches, not players; they achieve their objectives through others.

As Figure 10-3 shows, managers are a critical link between the company and its customers. Sales managers are the voice of the company to the salespeople they manage. Salespeople, in turn, convey that voice to their customers. At the same time, when salespeople need something from the company for themselves or their customers, they usually go through their sales manager. Thus, sales managers are also the voice of salespeople and customers to the company. Not surprisingly, it is frequently said that salespeople take a job because of the company but leave or stay because of their sales manager.

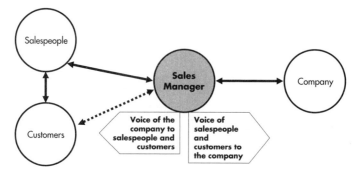

Figure 10-3. The role of the sales manager

A Key Implementer of the Sales Effectiveness Drivers

As Figure 10-4 shows, sales managers play a key role in the sales system as implementers of most of the sales effectiveness drivers. In terms of the drivers, sales managers are responsible for:

- Defining salespeople's responsibilities by creating territory alignments that enable them to succeed
- Shaping the sales team by recruiting, training, and coaching their people
- Enlightening the team by helping salespeople make the most effective use of customer research, data and tools, and targeting information
- Creating excitement among team members by promoting a culture of success, providing leadership, and implementing motivation programs
- Controlling sales activity through performance management processes, goal setting, and communication that keeps the team aligned with company goals and strategies.

The critical role of sales managers in keeping the sales system aligned and functioning prompted the following observation by Andy Anderson of Searle U.S.—former sales representative, district sales manager, regional sales manager, vice president of sales, and finally president of operations: "In any sales force, you can get along without the vice president of sales, regional sales directors, and the training manager, but you cannot get along without the district [first-line] sales manager."

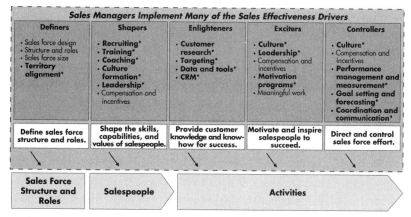

Figure 10-4. The role of sales managers in the sales system

A Manager of People

Sales managers are responsible for selecting, building, leading, managing, and rewarding their team.

Selecting the Team. Sales managers succeed through their people. Consequently, the best managers create a team of winners. The process starts with selecting the right people for the team. Typically, first-line sales managers have substantial input into who gets hired and who gets fired.

Team selection is an ongoing process. The best sales managers actively encourage, coach, and counsel their strong performers in order to retain them. If sales managers are doing their job well, they will advise poor performers that they would be more successful in another job. Because a certain amount of turnover is inevitable in any sales organization, effective sales managers anticipate territory vacancies and recruit continuously. Maintaining an active list of potential applicants so that they never get caught in a situation where they need to hire a "warm body" just to fill an opening, they focus on filling future spots rather than open spots. Effective sales managers understand that half of all recruiting can be accomplished before a job is posted.

Building the Team. Once the salespeople have been selected, the first-line sales manager focuses on how to build and develop the team for success. When new salespeople are hired, they usually do not arrive at the company highly skilled and completely aware of the firm's culture. When an inexperienced person is hired, the manager has to coach him as he climbs the learning curve. When an experienced person is hired, the manager has to focus on instilling company values.

Salespeople who have been in their jobs for some time also benefit from a sales manager's coaching and guidance. Managers are critical implementers of learning and development and performance management processes that help every salesperson on the team gain and refine the knowledge, skills, and capabilities needed to carry out the most appropriate selling process for each customer and prospect effectively.

Selling processes change over time, especially when markets are in transition. A successful manager detects the essential process modifications, identifies best practices, and then shares them with the entire sales team.

The sales manager is an important training partner—in effect, a personal trainer. Action learning occurs when the manager and the salesperson complete a customer visit, and the manager asks the salesperson what he was trying to achieve and then shares with the salesperson what she observed.

For many salespeople, the time spent on the job on any given day is part of a broader professional development experience. When a salesperson has ambitions beyond her current sales position, the sales manager's role expands to include career counseling and development. An excellent manager always works for the success of his people, even if it means that they are promoted or leave for other positions.

An old joke suggests that the two greatest sales force lies are:

Lie 1: When greeting a salesperson on his quarterly visit to the field, the sales manager says, "I am from headquarters, and I am here to help you."

Lie 2: The salesperson replies, "I am glad to see you."

The successful manager, in her role as a professional development facilitator and coach, converts the two lies into truths.

Leading the Team. As a leader, a sales manager can influence his team to share a common vision and to work to achieve common goals. Several leadership models are relevant for sales managers. One, developed by researchers and authors Jim Kouzes and Barry Posner, has been used successfully by many organizations. This model suggests that successful leaders:

- **Challenge the process** by searching for opportunities, experimenting, and taking risks.
- **Inspire a shared vision** by envisioning the future and enlisting the help of others.
- **Enable others to act** by fostering collaboration and strengthening others.
- **Model the way forward** by setting a good example and planning small wins.
- **Encourage the heart** by recognizing individual contributions and celebrating accomplishments.

Successful managers use their leadership skills to help the team succeed.

Managing the Team. A good first-line sales manager is a good human resources manager. Sales managers play an essential role in the performance management process. They work with their people to set goals and develop plans for meeting those goals. They guide salespeople's actions and measure their results, working with salespeople to evaluate whether they have achieved their goals, then supporting their perceived strengths and correcting their weaknesses. Through their role in the performance management process (see Chapter 14), sales managers help sustain sales force performance and continuously enhance it.

A good sales manager is a situational manager and leader, adapting her style to the person and the circumstances. She focuses on skills for those whose skills need enhancement and on motivation for those who have the skills. She focuses on skills and activities for the inexperienced salesperson and on activities and results for the veteran. The best managers communicate frequently and not just formally with their salespeople. More than being just cheerleaders, they constantly provide individualized support and feedback.

In the past, managers were heavy-hitting salespeople, and sales management was an extension of the sales job. But selling has become more complex, sophisticated, diverse, and fast-paced, and sales managers at many companies have had to become good general managers as well as good human resources managers. Sales managers today are often responsible for managing many company resources, including expenses and a local sales budget; physical assets, such as cars, computers, and demonstrator equipment; and informational assets, such as databases and insight into company strategy.

Rewarding the Team. A sales manager is responsible for rewarding the members of his team for their commitment, hard work, and results. A source of direction and motivation for salespeople, rewards can be a very effective means of aligning salespeople's motivators with the needs of the sales district.

Rewards can be extrinsic (bonuses, commissions, or salary increases) or intrinsic (appreciation and recognition). Companies usually centralize their extrinsic reward programs, but sales managers typically have some input into which extrinsic rewards are appropriate for their people and may have the authority to give out some such rewards directly. Intrinsic rewards, such as appreciation and recognition, are largely the responsibility of the sales manager.

Knowing what and when to reward is not always easy. Rewards should be deserved. Rewards "for breathing" have little impact. And rewards should not be casual. They should be associated with significant, tangible outcomes—increased sales, outstanding customer satisfaction, productive prospecting. Rewards should be sincere and meaningful. Constantly saying, "You are great" loses credibility over time.

Establishing and Sustaining a Vigorous Sales Management Team

The sales management team can be considered a critical sales effectiveness driver. It differs from the other drivers (see Figure 10-4) in that it is a collection of people rather than a decision, process, system,

Figure 10-5. A process for building and sustaining sales manager effectiveness

or program. This collection of people has a significant impact on many of the other sales effectiveness drivers. Figure 10-5 suggests a process for building and sustaining an effective sales management team.

The Role of the Sales Manager and the Team Structure

The Role of the Sales Manager. A first step in developing an effective sales management team is to define the role of the sales manager. In most sales organizations, the sales manager's most important responsibilities are to select, build, lead, manage, and reward a team of salespeople. But the best companies break down these responsibilities into a detailed job description so that managers know exactly what they are expected to do. Figure 10-6 is the sales manager job description at a medical instruments company.

In addition to their management responsibilities, some sales managers have responsibility for selling. They may assist salespeople on sales to large accounts or in difficult selling situations, or they may retain the responsibility for selling to important customers with whom they have strong relationships.

Sales managers who have many responsibilities need guidance from the company on how to spend their time. For example, it is common for sales managers who have selling responsibility to spend too much time selling and not enough time coaching their team. By aligning expectations, evaluation systems, and rewards for the sales managers appropriately, the company provides a consistent message to sales managers about how their time should be spent.

A Direct-Marketing Company Changes the Sales Managers' Pay Plan to Encourage More Coaching of New Salespeople

At a direct-marketing company, many new salespeople left the firm within the first six months. Through exit interviews, the company learned that lack of

RECRUITING
• Sourcing candidates (internal versus external)
• Formulating hiring criteria
• Interviewing

SETTING AND ACHIEVING SALES GOALS
• Regional
• Territory

MANAGING COMPANY ASSETS
• Cars, computers, telephones, fax machines
• Demonstrator equipment
• Office space

MANAGING OPERATING EXPENSES
• Salaries
• Relocation
• Automobile expense
• Regional overhead
• Samples
• Office supplies
• Recruiting fees
• Travel
• Telephone
• Meetings/Exhibits
• Training
• Postage/Freight

HUMAN RESOURCE MANAGEMENT
• Recruiting
• Career counseling
• Core competencies
• Selling skills
• Performance appraisals/rating
• Promotions
• Demotions
• Coaching
• Territory management
• Resolving conflicts
• Training

GENERAL MANAGEMENT
• Administrative reports and duties
• Marketing feedback
• Account records and strategies
• Forecast
• Itineraries planned
• Maintains customer satisfaction
• Territory alignment

TOTAL COMPENSATION MANAGEMENT
• Salaries (skills/experience)
• Bonus or commissions
• Rewards

Figure 10-6. The job description for a sales manager at a medical instruments company

coaching and attention from first-line district sales managers was the leading cause. The sales managers' primary responsibility was to train and guide new salespeople, but they also retained some selling responsibility, and a substantial portion of their incentive pay was based on their individual sales performance. Thus, sales managers' pay did not align well with their job responsibilities. The company changed the sales manager incentive program, reducing the amount of money that was tied to individual sales and increasing the amount that was tied to metrics that reflected sales managers' success in managing their people: Achievement of sales goals by new employees and year-to-year district revenue growth were added to the manager incentive pay formula. Turnover of new salespeople declined dramatically, and this ultimately helped to drive sales growth.

Sales Management Team Structure. The number of salespeople who report to a sales manager (the span of control) varies across companies. Sales managers can oversee as few as three or as many as thirty salespeople; however, seven to twelve is the most common range. The number of levels of management also varies from organization to organization.

The number of management levels and the span of control affect both the costs of maintaining the sales force and the revenues it generates. A flat sales organization—one with a high management span of control—creates efficiency. On the other hand, a multilevel organization with a lower span of control allows managers to spend more time with each of their people. If this time is used well, the sales organization becomes more effective. In any situation, there is an optimal span of control. Figure 10-7 illustrates the impact of having too small or too large a span of control.

In general, having fewer management levels with a higher span of control is appropriate when managerial tasks are not time-consuming. A lower span of control is appropriate when managerial tasks require more time. Several factors increase the amount of time that managers need to spend both with the people who report to them and on administrative managerial tasks and therefore suggest a smaller span of control:

- Dissimilarity of work across salespeople (more time is required to manage different types of people).

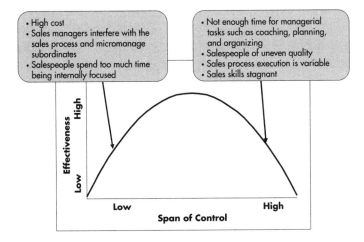

Figure 10-7. What is the right span of control?

- Geographic dispersion of salespeople (more travel time is required).
- Many inexperienced salespeople (they may need more coaching).
- A need to control sales force activity closely (this requires more management direction).
- A need for extensive coordination across salespeople or with others in the organization.
- A need for the manager to spend a significant amount of time with customers, to perform parts or all of some sales activities.
- A need for a significant amount of administrative time for tasks such as planning and expense management.

Smart sales leaders can take several approaches to determine the proper span of control. They can:

- Look at industry surveys for benchmarks and decide how the span of control should compare to industry norms.
- Ask the company's most successful managers to reflect on their personal experience and estimate an ideal span of control based on what has worked best for them.
- Look at sales force costs to determine how many levels and managers the company can afford while still keeping costs in line with the sales budget.
- Use a workload buildup approach. First, specify the activities that an effective sales manager should perform for each of her salespeople and estimate the average amount of time these activities require. Second, determine how much time managers have available for people management by subtracting the amount of time they need for "non-people-focused" tasks (administration, selling, and personal development) from the total work time. Third, determine the span of control by dividing the manager's time available for people management by the average time required to manage each salesperson.

The data required to implement this approach can be based upon both field input and external benchmarks.

Companies that are creating a sales force from scratch or that plan to expand a sales organization gradually sometimes begin with a lower span of control, with the intention of increasing it over time. This allows more sales management time for recruiting and training new salespeople while the organization is growing. As the team gets larger and more experienced, the proportion of newly hired salespeople naturally declines, and the span of control can increase.

The challenges of the sales management job vary with the size of the sales organization. In small sales forces, sales managers often have a general management role, with many varied responsibilities. There are few layers of management above them and limited headquarters resources available to help them do their jobs. In these situations, it can be difficult to find sales managers who have both the capability and the bandwidth needed to handle all of their various responsibilities well. On the other hand, in large sales forces, there are often many sales management levels, and there are teams and task forces at headquarters that take on specific responsibilities. First-line sales managers can become very focused on a single objective: making their numbers by making the people who report to them successful. It is important for every sales organization to consider the value of multiple management levels relative to their cost.

The Key Competencies of Sales Managers

The next step in developing an effective sales management team is to determine the key competencies that are required for success in the sales manager role. The company in Figure 10-8 used Performance Frontier Analysis (see Chapters 2 and 7) to identify top-performing sales managers. An observer watched these top sales managers interacting with their people in order to identify the capabilities and behaviors that contributed to their success. The observer also watched sales managers who fell short of the frontier in order to contrast their capabilities and behaviors with those of the high-performing managers. Based on these observations, a set of success principles was identified, differentiating the Performance Frontier sales managers and providing a list of key competencies for the sales management team. These key competencies were incorporated into the sales manager hiring profile, sales manager learning and development programs, and sales manager performance

Figure 10-8. Competencies of high-performing managers

management processes. The profiling discussion in the next section contains additional detail on sales management competencies.

Selecting a Sales Manager

The success of the first-line sales management team depends on effective selection of the sales managers. Too frequently, sales management teams suffer from the Peter Principle: Many managers rise to their level of incompetence and retire in this position. Selection errors are very expensive—it can take years to recover from selecting a poor sales manager.

The recruiting process for first-line sales managers follows the same major steps as the process for recruiting salespeople (see Chapter 7). The process is outlined again in Figure 10-9. The discussion focuses on the features of each step that are unique to the process of selecting a sales manager.

Profiling the Position of Sales Manager. Develop a hiring profile that includes the key competencies of the sales manager you need. Some of the characteristics that lead to success as a salesperson—ego, drive, empathy, motivation, integrity, communication skills, and versatility— also lead to success as a sales manager. However, an additional and very important characteristic needs to be added to the sales manager candidate profile; the acronym for this characteristic is TATATO, for "the ability to achieve through others." The importance of this ability is reflected in what one sales manager told us about how her job changed when she was promoted from salesperson to manager:

- "The day I became a manager, it became about them. My job is to walk around with a can of water in one hand and some fertilizer in the other hand."
- "I was used to winning through what I did. Now I win through what others do."

Sometimes good salespeople make bad managers. A player-star is different from a teacher-coach. Good coaches develop winning teams, but they do not score points themselves. Nor do they demand that everyone on the team play the same way that they played when they competed, or even as well as they played. They acknowledge that each member of the team does best when she uses her own natural skills.

Highly successful salespeople are often individualists who bask in the glory of their own results—they enjoy seeing their name at the top of the list. Great first-line sales managers must be willing to give up this type of credit and to achieve their objectives through other people. While they can receive credit for having the best district, they may find that their individual glory is diminished.

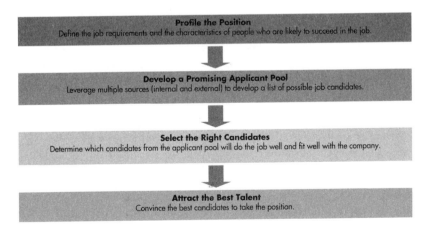

Figure 10-9. The manager selection process

Salespeople who work carefully to maintain accounts and develop relationships with customers are more likely to be good managers than salespeople who hunt down new accounts and convert them. The manager needs to develop working relationships with his salespeople, a process that is similar to fully developing a relationship with a customer.

Figure 10-10 summarizes some of the significant differences between good salespeople and good sales managers.

Developing an Applicant Pool. Good first-line sales managers have almost always had prior selling experience. It is very hard for a manager to gain the respect of her salespeople if she has not been a salesperson herself. In most situations, sales experience is a requirement for inclusion in the applicant pool.

When companies define the applicant pool for a first-line sales manager position, they usually focus on internal candidates who:

- Have a strong company identity and culture.
- Know the company's products, customers, culture, politics, procedures, and people.
- Have a proven track record. Generally their job performance with the company is a good predictor of their managerial capability.

Sometimes an unqualified internal candidate is placed in the applicant pool by a weak manager who does not have the fortitude to tell the

Good Salespeople	Good Sales Managers
Listen to customers	Listen to salespeople
Do it themselves	Allow others to step up
Strive for personal success	Strive for team success
Control	Motivate
Strive for strong quarterly performance	Strive for strong annual performance
Focus on customer needs	Focus on customer needs

Figure 10-10. The differences between good salespeople and good sales managers

candidate that he is not well suited for a sales management job. The weak manager chooses to let the recruiting system reject the candidate, rather than delivering the bad news herself. Because of this possibility, smart sales leaders always screen internal candidates carefully.

If no internal candidates have the necessary qualifications, the company needs to look at external candidates. The good news is that candidates from outside the company can bring a fresh perspective and may have new skills or knowledge that can help the company succeed in a rapidly changing marketplace.

Selecting the Right Candidates. Most of our recommendations for recruiting excellent salespeople (see Chapter 7) apply equally to selecting a first-line sales manager. The most important recommendations include:

- A job performance history is available for all internal candidates. Since past performance is a good predictor of future performance, you should give job performance history considerable weight in the selection process. Behavioral interviewing is useful for external candidates, but for internal candidates, past job performance is more useful.

- Do not select sales managers based upon sales results alone. As Figure 10-10 shows, the best salesperson is not necessarily the best sales manager.

- Test for the behaviors and skills that will lead to success in management. Business cases that focus on sales management issues are good assessment tools for first-line sales managers.

- Allow successful salespeople who are interested in becoming managers to take on responsibilities that help to prepare them for a managerial role. Roles such as local trainer, mentor, interviewer, or special projects participant can allow salespeople to demonstrate their capabilities, to assess whether they would like the manager's job, and to gain some initial on-the-job training.

- Consider putting sales management candidates through a sales manager training program before selecting them for the job. Their performance during training can be used as input for the selection process.

- Avoid the "warm body" approach. An effective sales leader is constantly assessing potential manager candidates and has a "bench" ready in case a manager position opens up.

Attracting the Best Sales Managers. It is usually easy to attract salespeople to the first-line sales manager's job. For many, this is their first potential career promotion, and the possibility is greeted with excitement. There are many rewards associated with the new job, including (usually) higher pay, management perks, greater power, and recognition of their achievement and success.

Two reasons that salespeople sometimes refuse a promotion to manager are an unwillingness to relocate and a reluctance to manage others. Attracting candidates to the sales manager position may require helping candidates to work through these issues. In some industries, salespeople who have responsibility for important accounts earn more than their managers, making it difficult for companies to attract competent sales managers.

Developing and Supporting the Sales Manager

Sales leaders often look at sales force training and coaching as a non-threatening and easy-to-implement means of enhancing effectiveness. When one salesperson's skills and knowledge are enhanced through training and coaching, performance improves in a single territory. When one sales manager's skills and knowledge are improved through training and development, performance improves in an entire district. Very often, the training and development of sales managers produces considerable gains in effectiveness for a relatively small investment, yet many companies do not have extensive or ongoing training programs for sales managers.

Most sales managers are former salespeople and do not come into their jobs knowing how to manage. Without training and support, they will have to improvise, and while the results that they achieve may be adequate, their performance is likely to fall short of what it could have been if the managers had been better prepared to take on their new responsibilities. Continuing success for the first-line sales management team requires a sales manager development program and ongoing support that enables the sales managers to do their job effectively.

We described a sales manager's responsibilities earlier in this chapter, and these responsibilities also appear in the first column of Figure 10-11. The sales effectiveness drivers in the second column directly affect these responsibilities. Sales managers are more likely to implement these sales effectiveness drivers well when they are provided with excellent development and support, using the mechanisms listed in the third column.

It can be challenging for sales managers to find the development and support that they need if they are to be successful in all of these areas, particularly when they are new to their job. A new salesperson almost always has a first-line sales manager that she can go to for advice and guidance—someone who has clear responsibility for coaching and developing her. Yet a new first-line sales manager probably reports to someone higher up in the organizational hierarchy whose main responsibility may be focused upward on strategy and high-level decision making, not downward on people development.

Rarely is there someone in a sales organization who has clear responsibility for coaching and developing first-line sales managers. Frequently, first-line sales managers are left on their own to incorporate the information provided into an effective work style.

Sales manager development programs vary greatly across companies. Much of the variance is explained by the size of the sales organization. Small sales forces do not have sufficient scale to run highly developed internal sales manager training programs. Since these sales forces typically have a limited number of sales manager vacancies in any one year, sales manager development tends to be ad hoc. New managers learn from other managers, through self-study, and by attending general enrollment programs offered by universities and sales training organizations. Larger sales organizations are more likely to have their own sales manager development programs. Typically, these programs do an effective job of training managers to execute some, but not all, of the sales effectiveness drivers successfully.

Some of the sales effectiveness drivers—coaching, performance management, and situational leadership—are emphasized in most corporate and general enrollment sales manager development programs.

Sales Manager Responsibility	Sales Effectiveness Driver	Ways that the Company Can Encourage Manager Development and Provide Support
Select the team	Recruiting	Provide a recruiting process and training for managers on how to recruit effectively.
Build the team	Training	Provide guidance on how to be an effective trainer. Provide a list of training resources that managers can recommend to their people.
	Coaching	Provide training on effective coaching.
Lead the team	Culture formation	Clearly communicate the sales culture to managers. Provide legends, heroes, stories, and metaphors that managers can easily share with their people.
	Leadership	Provide leadership training for managers.
Manage the team	Communication	Provide processes and technologies that encourage efficient and effective communication between managers and salespeople, and between managers and the leadership team.
	Territory alignment	Provide data and tools and guidance from the leadership team.
	Performance management	Provide processes and data and tools, and guidance from the leadership team.
	Goal setting	Provide processes, data and tools.
Reward the team	Motivation programs	Provide extrinsic and intrinsic recognition programs and spiffs.

Figure 10-11. The development and support that sales managers need if they are to carry out their responsibilities

Yet, as Figure 10-11 shows, many other sales effectiveness drivers are important for success as a sales manager. An excellent development program educates managers in all the critical sales effectiveness drivers, including topics that are outside the scope of traditional sales manager training courses, such as effective goal setting, recruiting, and territory alignment.

Medical device company Boston Scientific Corporation conducted a workshop for sales managers designed to improve the managers' skills in executing the sales effectiveness drivers that are most critical to their success. A summary of feedback about the success of the workshop appears after the course description.

An Enhancement Workshop for Sales Managers at Boston Scientific

A multiday development workshop to reinforce best practices for the most critical sales effectiveness drivers.

Purpose:

- This forum to develop first-line sales managers takes them out of the field, elevates their knowledge, and educates them in approaches to issues that are frequently left on the back burner as they deal with the day-to-day challenges of running their districts and hitting their revenue goals.

Topics:

(Groups choose a subset of the most critical issues to focus on.)

- Hiring
- Coaching
- Targeting
- Sales force sizing and territory alignment
- Helping salespeople prioritize their time across products, customers, and activities
- Manager effectiveness (including manager time and effort allocation)
- Sales force structure
- Incentive compensation
- Goal setting

Methodology:

- Workshop format
- Group size: 8 to 30 managers
- Topics are addressed in three ways:
  1. Sharing of best practices among participants, accomplished in subgroups of four to six people who then return to and share with the larger group.
  2. Moderator conducting a lecture/discussion of best practices. (The authors have moderated many of these sessions.)
  3. Discussion among participants—either in a single large group or in subgroups that then share with the large group—about how to adapt and apply the best practices in their districts.

- At the end of the workshop, participants are asked to write down one, two, or three ideas that they will implement as a result of the workshop.
- As a group, participants highlight the support that the company or region must provide to implement the best practices that were discussed, such as information, tools, or processes that are outside an individual manager's control.

Feedback:

Provided by course sponsor Chris Hartman, Vice President, Eastern Division, Boston Scientific Corporation—Cardiac Rhythm Management:

- "The course was excellent."
- "The program was designed by regional managers for regional managers. They chose the relevant effectiveness drivers."
- "Managers took ownership and developed action items that have been successfully implemented."
- "Sales manager and sales representative selection, recruiting, and talent management were improved significantly as a result of the workshop."

From course designer Marshall Solem, Office Managing Principal, ZS Associates, Evanston, Illinois:

- "Lots of ground was covered in two or three days—too many topics were discussed to expect change on every dimension, but the exposure provided good development for people."
- "Everyone took at least one idea (and often a few ideas) away from the workshop. A big takeaway for many was the value of using cases/selling vignettes rather than just behavioral interviews during the hiring process to test applicants' capabilities."
- "Managers appreciated the chance to share best practices among themselves as much as they valued learning best practices from the moderators."
- "Managers appreciated the time out of the field to focus on bigger issues and personal development."

The workshop helped sales managers at Boston Scientific identify and learn best practices for the sales effectiveness drivers that are critical to their job. The best sales managers constantly look for ways to improve and execute the sales effectiveness drivers to produce better results. The best companies help their sales managers develop and improve by creating training programs and other learning opportunities coupled with implementation support.

Several chapters in this book provide detailed guidance on sales effectiveness drivers that are relevant to the first-line sales manager's job, including recruiting, learning and development, culture, information, territory design, performance management, and goal setting.

CHAPTER **11**

Using Information Technology to Enhance Sales

The Changing World of Sales Information Technology

Sales forces are increasingly leveraging information technology (IT) to enhance accountability and fact-based decision making at many levels of their organizations. Throughout this book, we describe how *sales leaders* can use information to make better sales effectiveness driver decisions; in addition, *customers* can use IT to carry out parts of the buying process, such as ordering and order tracking. However, the focus of this chapter is on the use of IT by salespeople and sales managers:

- Salespeople can use IT, such as customer relationship management (CRM) systems, to assess their performance and to plan and enhance the sales process for more effective interaction with customers. Salespeople's use of information technology is the primary focus of this chapter.

- Sales managers can use IT to assess and improve the performance of their salespeople and to implement the sales effectiveness drivers more successfully. This is a secondary focus of this chapter.

Over the last two decades, companies and sales organizations have successfully used technology to automate such tasks as expense management, appointment scheduling, and territory routing. They have also had excellent success in leveraging technology to support naturally data-intensive tasks, such as product configuration, and communication-focused tasks, such as order placement, management, and tracking. These technologies have made sales forces more efficient. The automation of time-consuming tasks has enabled salespeople to complete their administrative work faster, leaving more time for high-value-added activities and face-to-face interaction with customers.

In recent years, much of the focus of and investment in sales information systems has shifted from technologies that increase the efficiency of the sales force to those that allow the sales force to be more effective. Such systems increase the value that salespeople can add through their interactions with customers. For example, sales information systems can help sales forces target more effectively, so that they spend their time with the right customers and prospects. These systems can be used to analyze customer needs and construct a basket of product and service offerings tailored to each customer's specific situation. The systems can also keep track of and strengthen complex sales processes by facilitating communication among multiple members of the sales team and helping to bring the right people and resources to each step of the customer buying process.

As the benefits of sales information systems shifted from enhancing efficiency to increasing effectiveness, the promise of gains outpaced the reality. Systems often became heavy, complex, and rigid, leaving sales organizations dissatisfied. But today an increasing number of sales forces are gaining enhanced sales effectiveness through technology, for several reasons:

- Companies and providers of sales systems are benefiting from the lessons they have learned from past failures and from their analysis of models of success.
- Early market leaders, such as Siebel Systems, and later entrants, such as salesforce.com, have developed lightweight systems that can be up and running in weeks instead of years.

- "Ecosystems" of organizations are working together to create and deliver IT products and services designed around the needs of particular industries. For example, salesforce.com partners with a large number of companies that provide "dashboard design" templates and tools for such industries as high technology, financial services, and pharmaceuticals.

How IT Enhances Sales Force Effectiveness

IT enhances the effectiveness of the sales force by helping salespeople and sales managers do their jobs better.

Giving Salespeople Insights

Information helps salespeople in two primary ways. First, it helps them understand their performance. Most companies provide salespeople with a sales report, or a sales "dashboard," to help them assess their current performance and figure out how to do better by analyzing data on activities, customers, market opportunities and potential, sales, expenses, and profitability. Second, information can help salespeople strengthen the sales process by assisting them with such activities as prospecting, qualifying, identifying customer needs, planning, designing the offering, creating value, tracking, targeting, and maintaining accounts.

The Role of Salesperson Dashboards. A sales force gains terrific value when IT systems give salespeople information that shows them how they are performing. Easy access to up-to-date performance data can make salespeople more informed and motivated, encouraging them to seek out ways to improve. The information does not have to be complicated to have significant impact. Figure 11-1 shows an example of a dashboard that one sales force uses to keep the salespeople informed about their performance relative to goal across products and market segments. Each salesperson has access to current information like this for her territory.

The data suggest ways in which the salesperson can improve. The salesperson whose performance is profiled in Figure 11-1 is doing well at selling Product 3, but her performance at selling Products 1 and 2 falls

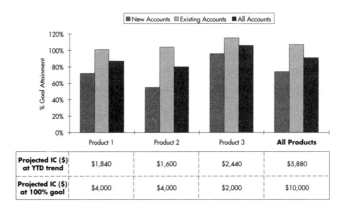

Figure 11-1. An example of a salesperson dashboard: goal attainment by product and market segment

short of expectations, particularly with new accounts. These data suggest areas where the salesperson needs to improve if she hopes to earn the target incentive compensation (IC) payout for achieving sales goals.

Figure 11-2 shows another example used by a sales force that has a multistage sales process. Salespeople can access an up-to-date dashboard showing them how many customers they currently have at each stage in the sales pipeline. They can compare their current customer conversion rate at each stage to a benchmark level established by the company's best salespeople. During the negotiation stage, the salesperson in Figure 11-2 is losing half the accounts that he has guided successfully through the solutions-development stage, an unfavorable conversion rate compared to the 75 percent rate for the company's best negotiators. These data might suggest that additional coaching or training in effective negotiation could help this salesperson improve his performance.

Figure 11-3 shows an interactive dashboard that allows salespeople to see a summary of their goal attainment for their territory as a whole and also to drill down to see goal attainment by specific customer so that they can determine the best way to spend their time. The territory summary information uses the familiar image of a speedometer dial and highlights performance ranges with the colors red, yellow, and green, as used in traffic signals, making the information visually meaningful and easily accessible.

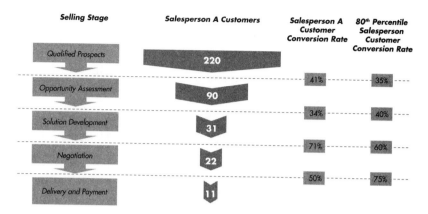

Figure 11-2. An example of a salesperson dashboard: sales pipeline with customer conversion statistics

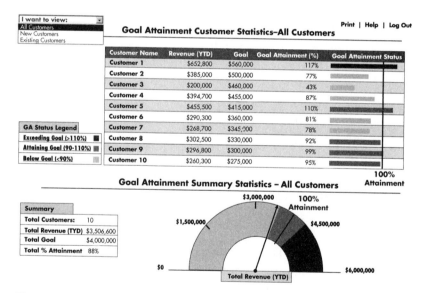

Figure 11-3. An example of an interactive salesperson dashboard: visual goal attainment summary with drill-down capability

A typical sales dashboard for a salesperson includes:

- A territory performance summary showing performance relative to territory objectives, compared either to peers or industry benchmarks or to past history

- Exceptions notifications showing business exceptions (such as geographies with a significant change in sales) and activity outliers (low or high call levels)
- Business development progress tracking sales in the pipeline or identifying new opportunities
- Synthesized information, such as reports reflecting the "issues of the month" or summaries of business analysis, that is separate from automated report generation

In most cases, providing feedback to salespeople on a particular performance metric (such as sales, profitability, or growth) improves sales force performance on that metric—whether or not the metric is tied to sales force incentive pay. The feedback is a signal to salespeople that the metric is important; they know that they are being measured, and hence they will work to improve. By the same token, a sales dashboard with too many metrics loses its punch because the salesperson cannot tell right away which areas are most important.

Strengthening the Sales Process. Providing salespeople with access to the right kind of information can make them more effective. Better planning of sales time and increased value within the sales process itself allows them to have increased impact with customers.

Improved planning. IT can enable salespeople to plan more effective customer visits. A salesperson can have more impact if, before a customer meeting, she has a complete, up-to-date understanding of the customer's situation. The account profile, records of historical purchases, status of outstanding service inquiries, and descriptions of previous contact with other company salespeople and departments all enable the salesperson to plan ways to strengthen her relationship with the customer, develop a more effective product positioning strategy, and be more successful at selling value to the customer and hence increasing sales.

The value derived from using IT for planning customer visits varies depending on the number of customers and prospects a salesperson is responsible for and on the complexity of the sales process. For salespeople with a straightforward sales process and large numbers of prospects and customers who buy repeatedly, IT helps with profiling and prioritizing the accounts to be covered, planning sales calls, and tracking sales activity. Figure 11-4 shows a system that a pharmaceutical sales force uses to profile and prioritize physicians, track call activity, and assist with call planning.

Companies that have straightforward sales processes and large numbers of customers should try to avoid two pitfalls in the use of technology to assist salespeople with territory planning. First, many companies mistakenly believe that they need an accurate and complete customer database before they can realize value from a customer information system. However, when companies wait until they have the perfect comprehensive database before implementing a system, they often either never implement a system or end up implementing one that is so complex and heavy that it does not work well. Even with simple and imperfect data, salespeople can realize value by using technology to help them segment customers and decide how to spend their time.

Wisconsin							Print | Help | Log Out	
Doctor Name	City	ST	Potential Segment	Sales Segment	Planned Visits	Completed Visits (YTD)	% Visits Completed	
Dr. Ramstein	Appleton	WI	Medium	Medium	18	7	39%	
Dr. Bildsten	Green Bay	WI	Low	Medium	12	5	42%	
Dr. Olive	Madison	WI	Medium	Low	18	7	39%	
Dr. Jewel	Madison	WI	High	High	24	7	29%	
Dr. Baghde	Milwaukee	WI	High	Medium	24	8	33%	
Dr. Stallworth	Milwaukee	WI	Low	Low	12	3	25%	
Dr. Franklin	Milwaukee	WI	Medium	High	18	4	22%	
Dr. Meyer	Milwaukee	WI	Low	Low	12	2	17%	
Dr. Mallik	Neenah	WI	Low	Medium	12	5	42%	
Dr. Engle	Oshkosh	WI	Medium	High	18	7	39%	
Dr. Shiner	Pulaski	WI	Low	Low	12	4	33%	

Dr. Baghde

Profile Information	Visit Information	Prescribing Information	Notes
First Name: Anand Last Name: Baghde Address: 201 North St City: Milwaukee ST: WI Phone: 414-492-3608	Completed Visits: 8 Planned Visits: 24 Last Visit: March 24 Next Visit: April 10 Samples Delivered: 120	YTD Product Rxs: 200 YTD Market Rxs: 500 Forecasted Product Rxs: 550	Dr. Baghde will be out of the office during the months of July and August.

Figure 11-4. A system that helps pharmaceutical salespeople plan physician calls

Second, having the right mindset about planning and prioritizing is much more important than having a complete and perfectly accurate customer database. Before codifying the customer data, sales leaders should ask salespeople whether they:

- Think about how their customers are different from one another.
- Consciously do different things with different customers.
- Spend more time where the opportunities are greater.
- Engage in different sales activities with prospects who have not bought before from those they use with loyal customers who buy regularly.

The fact that IT has been applied more successfully to well-structured, well-organized business processes than to those that are loosely defined and highly variable explains why most of the earliest IT successes were in the accounting area, where work procedures are highly structured and well documented. It also explains why CRM systems have high success rates in telesales but low success rates in field sales, where customer interactions are not scripted. A sales organization needs to develop a prioritizing-and-targeting mindset before it can benefit significantly from the use of technology for territory planning and customer targeting. If an organization starts with the right mindset and some reasonably correct data, information completeness and accuracy will follow and further enhance sales efforts.

For salespeople who execute a more complex, multistage sales process for a targeted number of customers and prospects, technology is useful for managing and strengthening the sales process itself. Most CRM systems today include modules for such popular sales process models as Strategic Selling, Target Account Selling, SPIN Selling, and Solution Selling. CRM systems can also be customized for a company-specified selling approach.

Systems can help salespeople profile customer organizations and their buying influences, and map stages of the sales process. The systems track important milestones with customers and prospects, such as lead qualification, initial communication, solution development, customer evaluation, proposal generation, negotiation, and delivery. Systematic tracking of the sales process helps salespeople mobilize the right resources at the right time.

Sales leaders can also use these systems for forecasting future sales levels in a complex environment. Figure 11-5 shows how IT can track the number of customers at each stage of the sales process, estimate the probability of advancing a customer to the next stage based on historical conversion rates, and thus come up with a reasonable prediction of future sales.

Value-added sales processes. For salespeople who have a few large key accounts that require a long and complex sales process, information systems can add value to the sales process itself by enhancing salespeople's interactions with customers. Salespeople can use technology during sales calls to demonstrate value to customers in two ways. First, systems can help the salesperson analyze a customer's unique needs and priorities in order to tailor solutions that align with those needs. Second, systems can reinforce the value that the company's product or service creates for an existing customer.

Figure 11-6 shows how systems add value to the sales process used by United Airlines. The United sales organization is responsible for building and managing relationships with corporate customers and

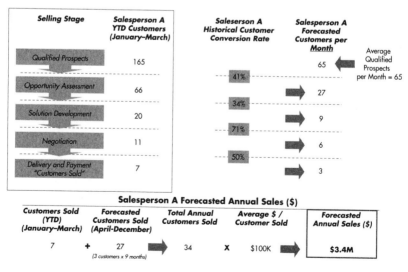

Figure 11-5. Example of using information from a CRM system to forecast future sales levels

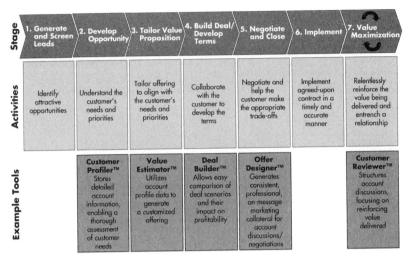

Figure 11-6. How systems add value to the sales process at United Airlines

travel agencies. Beginning in 2005, United adopted a value-based selling approach that focuses customers on the total business value that United creates, rather than on price. (See Chapter 16 for more information on how United has successfully made the transition to this new sales process.) United salespeople work closely with personnel at corporations and travel agencies to understand their needs and to show them how United can provide an appropriate mix of consultative services, travel management and support programs, and comfort and productivity for business travelers—all of which create business value well beyond best-price alternatives.

Sales systems have been an important part of United's implementation of the value-based sales approach. When salespeople work with customers, they rely on a suite of sales technology products that help them demonstrate the value that United offers. The technology facilitates a structured, menu-based discussion that helps salespeople to better understand the unique needs and priorities of each customer and to tailor solutions that best align with those needs. The technology also helps reinforce the total business value of United's solutions. The suite of IT products that United uses was developed based on input from more than 1,200 corporations and travel agencies.

Some of the most successful implementations of CRM applications that add value during the sales process are in telesales. During each call, a telesales representative sits in front of a computer screen while the system uses customer profile and purchasing-history data to determine the customer's likely needs and to script the sales process for maximum impact. The CRM system is an integral part of the sales call itself. In a more complex field sales environment, CRM systems have been used successfully for tasks that likewise are integral to the sales process, such as product configuration or the design of a unique customer offering (such as that at United Airlines).

CRM systems that are integral to the sales process are typically more successful than systems that add value only by helping salespeople plan better. Salespeople often see too little value relative to the effort it takes to use systems that solely aid with call planning. And they see more value in systems that enhance the sales process than in systems by which they report their activities to their managers. If a system's primary value is as a control device for managers, salespeople tend to see it as not adding enough value to motivate them to keep it up to date with accurate information.

Providing Insight to Sales Managers

If sales managers can access the latest performance data for the people they manage in a concise, actionable, and visually friendly format, they will become better coaches and will be better able to help their salespeople be more successful. Laptop computers and/or the company intranet can provide managers with performance dashboards that encourage more effective coaching of salespeople by focusing attention on common and consistent metrics. Figure 11-7 shows how integrating data from multiple sources into a single system makes the information more powerful and actionable for sales managers. By looking at the relationships between results, potential, and effort, sales managers can evaluate salespeople's performance against territory opportunity, identify possible improvements in customer targeting, and find ways to increase the effectiveness of sales force effort—all actions that enable the managers to be more effective coaches and performance managers.

Figure 11-8 shows a sales manager dashboard used at one company. Managers can use it to compare territories in their districts on multiple

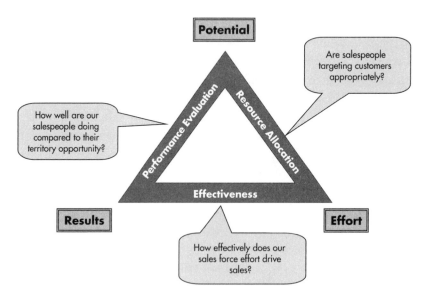

Figure 11-7. The power of integrating data from multiple sources on a performance dashboard for sales managers

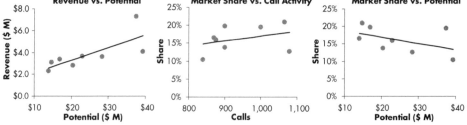

Figure 11-8. Example of a performance dashboard for sales managers

measures of effort, potential, and results. If a manager detects a problem or an opportunity, he can drill down to see more detail for a territory, and use that information to provide coaching and feedback to the salesperson. Several examples show how comparisons made possible by the dashboard help sales managers to be more effective.

- Comparing territory revenue to potential shows managers who their best performers are and where there is untapped opportunity.
- Comparing territory market shares and call activity lets managers see the effectiveness of their people and identify areas for improvement.
- Comparing market share with potential allows managers to identify opportunities to increase market penetration that they can share with salespeople.

While providing valuable information to sales managers is a powerful benefit of many sales information systems, salespeople need to benefit from the system as well. If the only reason for investing in an information system is to help sales managers control the salespeople, then the system is unlikely to work well for very long.

Effectiveness-Enhancing Sales IT Insights

We ask sales leaders who attend our executive-level courses two simple questions:

- How many of you have had a CRM system for two years or more?
- Of those who have, how many of you are satisfied with the system's performance?

While more than half of course participants have had systems for two years or more, fewer than a third of those are typically satisfied with their system's performance. Too many attempts to use IT to enhance the effectiveness of a sales force begin with hyped expectations and end in failure and dissatisfaction. Developing a system that will enhance effectiveness is not easy, and few organizations are satisfied with CRM or SFA (sales force automation) systems that overpromise.

There are three common sources of dissatisfaction with IT systems designed to increase the effectiveness of sales managers and salespeople.

- A system can become overly complex and hard for an average sales-person or manager to use effectively; when this happens, the system will quickly fall into disuse.

- It's possible for a system to introduce rigidity into the sales process, making it difficult for salespeople to adapt to individual customer situations and needs. Salespeople vary a great deal in their ability and desire to use technology during the sales process. In addition, customers have a wide range of different needs. Because it is hard to anticipate how every customer will make decisions, it can be diffi-cult to build a technology that can be used broadly, and a lack of flexibility can make a system inappropriate for many selling situa-tions. As a result, some sales managers and salespeople prefer low-tech solutions that they can adapt for individual situations.

- Too often systems are used as instruments of control by sales managers and leaders, not as value enhancers for salespeople and customers.

There are several ways in which companies can increase the odds of success when implementing sales information technologies aimed at enhancing the effectiveness of sales managers and salespeople.

Start Simple: Use an Evolving Design with Rapid Prototyping and Implementation

Design restraint is a characteristic of successful sales information sys-tems. Frequently, the design of such a system is controlled by a large committee that uses a democratic process to decide on the features of the system. The committee says yes to every whim of every person who suggests, "It would be great if the system could . . ." With this type of design process, the system rapidly becomes too complex, and its value diminishes. The best systems limit their functionality to relatively simple capabilities that can be performed quickly and that the sales force will use frequently. Other capabilities—those that are needed infrequently, that require significant effort and time to complete, and/or that require ad hoc diagnosis of special situations—are best performed by analysts at headquarters in response to requests from salespeople in the field.

When business needs are evolving rapidly, an overdesigned sales system can easily become obsolete. A comprehensive system that requires a long development cycle is likely to be out of sync with current business issues by the time it is ready for implementation. Rapid prototyping is essential, and that is possible only with systems that have limited scope. However, having too many small systems can create clutter and confusion, and maintaining them can become very expensive. Hence, sales leaders must achieve the right balance between comprehensiveness and flexibility in their IT systems.

Make Dashboards Visual, Useful, Customized, and Light

Effective performance dashboards provide information visually (as in Figure 11-3) so that salespeople can absorb it easily. But being visual is only the start. Dashboards also need to be useful. They need to highlight the information that the company feels is important and that will make the salesperson more successful. Individual managers and salespeople should have access to customized dashboards that provide only the data relevant to their own situation. Too much information can confuse or distract or can tempt people to micromanage and miss the big picture of what drives success in their job. The best dashboards are light and keep sales force attention focused on the company's priorities.

Make Sure That the System Adds Value to the People Who Keep the Information Current

Successful sales information systems allow the people who keep the data in the system current to derive a major portion of the system's benefit. When salespeople are asked to spend hours feeding data into a system so that management can track their activities, they have little incentive to provide high-quality data. On the other hand, if a system helps a salesperson target better or plan more effective sales calls (in addition to providing data to management), she is much more likely to learn the system and keep the information current. Likewise, if a customer derives value from an inventory management capability, he is more likely to refresh the data necessary to use it.

In Some Sales Information Systems, the Work Required Exceeds the Value to Salespeople

A company invested in a major project aimed at developing more focused and effective sales strategies. The marketing department conducted research on a sample of accounts to identify different customer segments and then developed customized selling strategies for each segment. The study revealed some valuable insights, and the company wanted to extrapolate the results across the universe of customers. The sales force was educated about the study results, and then each salesperson was asked to enter account profile data for hundreds of customers and prospects in her territory so that market segments (and hence effective selling strategies) for all accounts could be identified. The data were sent to headquarters, where they were entered into a national database and then sent back to the salespeople with a market segment designation for each account. This exercise was extremely frustrating for the sales force. Salespeople spent hours entering data and got back no new information in return. With the benefit of hindsight, the company realized that the value of the project to the sales force was in the education step; once the salespeople became aware of the insights gained through the market research, they began using those insights to be more effective sellers. Codifying the data was an unnecessary step that gave headquarters access to interesting data but did not benefit the sales force in any significant way.

Involve People Who Have Both IT and Sales Expertise
Creating a successful project team that includes people from both sales and IT is challenging. Employees in the two departments have very different mindsets, as summarized in Figure 11-9.

Often what looks easy and intuitive to a sales manager is an IT nightmare. At the same time, what seems logical to an IT manager may sound

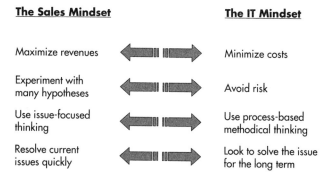

Figure 11-9. The sales and IT mindsets

irrational to a sales manager. Having team leaders who can successfully span the boundary between sales and IT is rare, but it is a key ingredient in the success of a sales IT project.

Conflicting Sales and IT Viewpoints: An Example

At a national district sales managers' meeting, the vice president of sales announced a sales force hiring freeze for the last quarter of the year. Several district managers who had current territory vacancies strongly objected, stating that this was unfair because a substantial portion of their bonus was tied to total district performance. The vice president agreed and promised that districts that had territory vacancies would have their goal adjusted so that managers would not be held accountable for fourth-quarter performance in vacant territories. This change appeared simple to the vice president, but it turned out to be virtually impossible to implement within the architecture of the current sales information system. A completely new and separate computer program had to be written to handle the special situation.

It Is Not Just About Tools

The success of a sales information system depends on its value to the sales force. Value is enhanced through usage when the system is integrated into the sales force work processes. If using the system entails a significant change in work processes or needed skills, then a focused change management effort is essential. Elements of this effort can include:

- Involving the sales force in system design to enhance its understanding of how the system will be embedded in work processes, and also to educate the sales force about system design challenges
- Clearly demonstrating the value of the new system—showing results, such as increases in call effectiveness, customer satisfaction, sales, and margin
- Creating excitement through newsletters and broadcasting the results achieved by champion users
- Addressing problems with current processes
- Providing excellent training and support
- Addressing sales force concerns, such as "Is the system going to create extra work for me?" or "Will it be used to spy on my activities?"

The successful implementation of sales IT requires a significant investment in support infrastructure—say, a help desk to assist users with problems, a facilities management group to keep the hardware working, a production support group to maintain the quality and timeliness of the data, and/or trainers who provide initial and ongoing educational programs. In addition, such an implementation requires a team that will orchestrate the continuous redesign and upgrading of the system, activities that are necessary to ensure that the system evolves as business needs change. Lack of experience with sales IT causes many companies to overestimate the benefits and underestimate the effort required for successful implementation. The most successful systems are those that:

- Limit functionality to the most valuable capabilities.
- Enlighten salespeople through dashboards that provide only essential information.
- Add value to those who keep the data current.
- Are designed through a collaborative effort between IT and sales staff.
- Integrate easily into existing work processes.

Leveraging Information for Estimating Account Potential

Several of the analyses shown as examples in this chapter include data on territory and account potential. Measuring potential has several benefits for a sales force. If salespeople know the potential of their customers and prospects, they can allocate their time more effectively. If sales managers know the market potential of each sales territory, they can better assess salespeople's performance. Measures of account and territory potential are also important for designing effective sales territories, for setting fair sales goals for salespeople, and for designing incentive compensation programs that pay for performance.

In many industries, obtaining objective and accurate account- and territory-level market potential data can be difficult. You may have to come up with creative approaches to develop surrogate measures of territory potential. The good news is that such measures can be found for virtually every industry. Figure 11-10 provides some examples of surrogate market potential measures that various companies have used. Potential data sources include the U.S. Census Bureau, industry trade associations, *Sales and Marketing* magazine's Buying Power Index, and data and research companies such as Cahners, Global Insight (formerly DRI-WEFA), and Dun & Bradstreet.

Industry	Surrogate Measure of Market Potential
Building materials	Number of households earning over $100K, housing starts.
Computer software and peripherals	Installed number of different types of computers, overall company revenue, and number of company locations.
Health and beauty aids sold in retail stores	Type of outlet (mass merchandiser, drugstore, grocery store, etc.), commodity sales volume in each store.
	Buying Power Index—census tract data on income, retail sales, and population.
Insurance	Number of employees.
Office equipment	Number of white-collar workers by industry.
Pharmaceuticals	Historical prescriptions written for a particular drug category in counties where pharmacy records are kept electronically.
	Physician office size, physician specialty, size of patient waiting area, and patient demographics in counties where electronic pharmacy records are not available.
Surgical instruments and supplies	Number of surgical procedures.

Figure 11-10. Surrogate measures of market potential for different industries

Should Salespeople Provide Estimates of Account Potential?

Often companies ask their sales force to provide estimates of account potential. Such data can be extremely valuable for account targeting and territory planning and alignment. However, if input about account potential provided by salespeople is used for goal setting, salespeople may develop a pessimistic view of the opportunity in their territory!

Salespeople Have Developed Outstanding Customer Databases

A large medical imaging company developed an exceptional database when it collected the type and manufacturer of installed equipment along with the date of acquisition for each hospital and imaging lab in the country. The salespeople provided the input for the database and used it for planning their calls, visiting prospects when their imaging equipment became dated.

Companies frequently find it useful to translate surrogate potential measures into potential revenue dollars, which makes the sales potential estimate more meaningful and actionable. Heuristic approaches (those that use commonsense rules rather than precise algorithms) accomplish this translation in a systematic and rational way. Two variations of a useful heuristic approach are described here.

Start by segmenting accounts based on such surrogate measures as industry and the number of employees. Then study the sales to accounts in each segment and develop a rule for estimating the level of sales that should be possible for each account. Consider the frequency distribution of sales at accounts in the market segment shown in Figure 11-11.

There are 100 accounts in the segment. The height of each bar shows how many of these accounts produce the sales levels identified on the horizontal axis. Here's one approach to estimating sales potential:

- Determine a certain percentile—for example, the 80th percentile of sales for the segment (that is, determine the level of sales such that

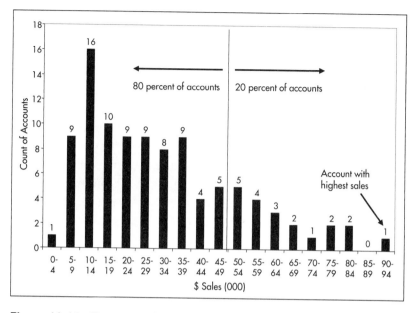

Figure 11-11. Frequency distribution of sales to accounts in one market segment

80 percent of the accounts in the segment have sales below this level). In the example, 80 percent of the accounts fall below $50,000 in sales.

- Use this level as a proxy for the sales potential of all accounts in the segment whose sales are lower than this level. In the example, any account with less than $50,000 in sales would have a potential of $50,000.

An alternative heuristic approach for translating surrogate potential data into revenue dollars is:

- For each segment, calculate the maximum sales that any account has achieved. In the example, maximum sales are $95,000.
- Define the sales increase possible in the other accounts as the difference between the account's current sales and a certain percentage, such as 50 percent, of the gap between current sales and the maximum. In the example, if an account has current sales of

$30,000, its potential is estimated as $30,000 + 0.5 × ($95,000 − $30,000) = $62,500.

The appropriate percentile (in the first approach) or percentage (in the second) to use for estimating potential depends on the life-cycle stage of the product or customer. In the growth stage, a higher percentile or percentage is appropriate. In the mature stage, a lower percentile or percentage is appropriate. Different heuristic approaches may be appropriate for different customers and prospects or for low-penetration and high-penetration accounts. Heuristic approaches are approximate, yet they can be extremely valuable to sales organizations that wish to develop meaningful estimates of account sales potential.

Regression Analysis Provides Insights About the Best Measures of Hospital Potential for a Medical Instruments Company

---

Sales leaders at a medical instruments company recognized that if the sales organization hoped to achieve its ambitious revenue growth goals, it would need to acquire many additional hospitals as customers. The company did business with approximately half of the hospitals in the United States, leaving more than 3,000 hospitals as prospects. With a limited budget for adding salespeople, the sales force would need to focus its attention on the subset of these prospects where sales effort was most likely to pay off.

An analysis to determine the potential of every hospital involved three main steps:

1. Merge the company's sales data with hospital profile data purchased from a third-party source to develop a combined database of hospital sales and potential. The third-party data included 32 pieces of profile data that sales leaders believed might predict each hospital's potential, including the number of admitted patients, the number of beds, the number of operating rooms, and the number of different types of surgical procedures performed. Consultation with the sales force helped to fill in some data for specific hospitals that was missing from the database.

2. Use the merged data for the 3,000-plus hospitals that were current customers to understand what profile characteristics are the best predictors of sales. A stepwise regression model was used to identify the most predictive profile characteristics, along with an appropriate weighting of those characteristics for projecting sales. The model that was chosen included three profile characteristics as the best predictors of sales. The mathematically derived model was vetted and refined through consultation with sales managers.

3. Develop an estimate of potential for each hospital (both customers and prospects), using the profile characteristics and weights determined in Step 2.

   Knowing the sales potential of every hospital account helped the sales force prioritize and target prospective new hospital accounts. It also helped the sales force identify current hospital customers where there was significant opportunity to grow additional business.

CHAPTER 12

How Sales Force Incentives Can Drive Results

Incentive compensation (IC) has a high impact on sales and a high cost for most sales organizations—and it is of high importance to salespeople. The right IC plan motivates a sales force to work hard and achieve challenging goals. It creates enthusiasm among the sales force collectively and energizes individual salespeople, providing a much-needed positive reinforcement for salespeople, who often work alone and face customer rejection as part of their job.

Incentives help sales leaders to set expectations for salespeople that reflect what is important to the company and to hold salespeople accountable for results. They are an important way in which many companies reinforce a sales-oriented culture so that high-performing achievers will want to join and stay with the company.

Yet the use of IC is a double-edged sword. Incentives create many challenges for sales leaders. Poorly designed incentives can encourage salespeople to focus on the wrong customers, products, or selling activities, or, even worse, to spend their time finding ways to manipulate the IC plan and maximize their personal earnings, rather than acting in the best interests of the company and their customers. Whenever pay includes a large incentive component, it may become difficult to control the sales force using levers other than money.

As a highly visible and quickly adjustable sales effectiveness driver, IC is often one of the first levers that sales leaders use to try to enhance sales effectiveness. But designing and managing an effective sales IC program is complex and challenging. Without foresight, as well as thoughtful planning and execution, it is easy to make serious errors for which there is little recourse. Designing a successful IC program requires blending just the right amount of financial analysis with the right amount of art and intuition about how salespeople will respond to the plan.

The Four Steps to Effective IC Plan Design and Implementation

The steps involved in designing and implementing an IC plan are shown in Figure 12-1.

Our discussion of these steps highlights key insights for creating an incentive plan that gets the desired results.

IC Assessment: Going Beyond "We Made Our Numbers, so the Plan Must Be Working"

Just how effective is your current IC plan? Answering this question is not easy. Understanding the effectiveness of an IC plan requires going beyond simplistic observations, such as "Our incentive costs were within budget" or "We made our numbers, so the plan must be working."

Does your plan really motivate your salespeople? Does it encourage them to spend their time in ways that help the company accomplish its objectives? Does the sales force understand the plan? Does the plan truly pay for performance? Is it fair?

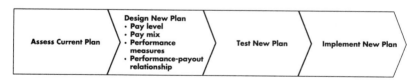

Figure 12-1. A process for designing and implementing an IC plan

How Motivating Is the IC Plan?

The right IC plan provides the motivation for high levels of effective sales force activity. Yet objectively measuring the impact of a plan on salespeople's motivation is difficult. Two metrics provide insight about how motivating an incentive plan is:

- Engagement Rate. What percentage of a sales force receives incentive pay? In sales forces where almost everyone earns some level of incentive pay, it is useful to look at the Meaningful Engagement Rate, or the percentage of the sales force that earns a motivating amount of incentive pay.

- Excitement Index. At what rate do salespeople earn their last incremental incentive dollar? A plan that pays at a higher rate creates more excitement than one that pays at a lower rate.

The data in Figure 12-2 explain how to calculate an incentive plan's Engagement Rate and Excitement Index.

The figure compares the engagement and excitement for two different incentive plans in order to show how motivating each plan might be for a particular sales force. Both plans link incentive pay to achievement of a territory sales goal. With Plan A, salespeople earn $500 for every percentage point attained over 60 percent of goal, and an additional $1,000 for every percentage point attained over 100 percent of goal. With Plan B, salespeople earn $1,000 for every percentage point attained over 80 percent of goal, and an additional $1,600 for every percentage point attained over 100 percent of goal. The Engagement Rate, Meaningful Engagement Rate, and Excitement Index for each plan are calculated based on the distribution of goal attainment across the sales force.

With Plan A, the Engagement Rate is 91 percent: All but 9 percent of the salespeople have achieved at least 60 percent of their goal and thus are earning incentive pay. With Plan B, the Engagement Rate is just 67 percent: 33 percent of the sales force has not yet achieved the 80 percent of goal needed to earn incentive pay. Sales leaders at this company defined the Meaningful Engagement Rate as the percentage of the sales force that was earning at least 75 percent of the target incentive of

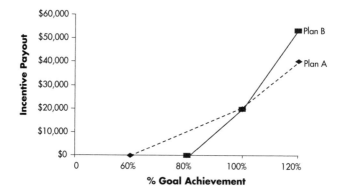

Figure 12-2. Engagement and excitement: a comparison of two IC plans

$20,000. With Plan A, the Meaningful Engagement Rate is 49 percent, while with Plan B, the Meaningful Engagement Rate is 38 percent. The Excitement Index for Plan A is $605, reflecting the average incremental reward for the last percentage of goal attained, calculated as follows: 30 percent of salespeople are earning the highest possible amount of $1,000 per percentage point of goal attained, 61 percent are earning $500 per percentage point, and the bottom 9 percent earn nothing; the $605 Excitement Index reflects the average earnings across all salespeople. Excitement is higher with Plan B: The average incremental reward for the last percentage point of goal attained is $850.

Sales leaders at this company need to trade off the importance of having high engagement and high excitement when choosing between

Plan A and Plan B. Plan A distributes money across more of the sales force—all salespeople with a reasonable workload are likely to make some incentive money. Plan B, on the other hand, creates more excitement for top performers who are willing to put forth exceptional effort to exceed their goal.

What Is the Benchmark for the Engagement Rate?

With a plan in which at least 30 percent of total target pay comes from incentives, at least 90 percent of the sales force should receive some IC payout. As the IC component increases, the Engagement Rate should also increase. In many transactional sales environments, companies seek 100 percent engagement by using commission plans that reward every transaction.

The distribution of payout across the sales force provides further insight into how motivating an incentive plan is. For example, how does the average actual payout compare to the target payout and to industry benchmarks? How much are the company's best performers making, and how much are the poorest performers earning? Figure 12-3 shows one such comparison. The data highlight a problem that occurs frequently in sales organizations. Even though the company's median pay is close to its target, the company paid out less than it intended to the top performers and more than it intended to the bottom performers. A

	Industry Benchmark Pay	Company Target Pay	Company Actual Pay	Company Actual as a % of Target Pay
75th percentile of performance (minimum pay for top 25% of company salespeople)	$143,000	$150,000	$129,476	86%
50th percentile of performance (median pay for company salespeople)	$110,000	$110,000	$114,309	104%
25th percentile of performance (maximum pay for bottom 25% of company salespeople)	$72,000	$67,000	$76,301	114%

Figure 12-3. Comparison of pay for top, middle, and bottom performers

plan that is supposed to motivate top performers by paying them more than the industry benchmarks is not achieving this desired objective.

Does the IC Plan Encourage Sales Force Activity That Aligns with Company Objectives?

In simple terms, an IC plan sends this message to the sales force: "Here is the payout formula. Now you figure out how to use your working time to make the most money." When many salespeople are trying to answer this question, it is not surprising that some of them will find ways to make money that the sales leaders did not envision. If there are, say, five products with different payout rates, salespeople are going to allocate their time to those five products in the way that they think will make them the most money.

So how does one look back at plan performance and deduce what the sales force was thinking? One way is to compare a plan's Engagement Rate and Excitement Index across different products, customer segments, or whatever measures the plan uses. Figure 12-4 shows a product-line analysis for one company. Salespeople at this company have sales goals for each of four major product lines (A, B, C, and D), and they earn a commission on sales above 75 percent of their product-line goal and an accelerated commission on sales above goal. The Engagement Rates and Excitement Indices are quite different across the four product lines. The data reveal a potentially serious problem for Product B, a new product line. More than half of the salespeople are not making any money selling Product B, and the Excitement Index for it is also quite low. Sales for this new line were difficult to predict, and in hindsight, the sales goals for Product B were too aggressive. Most salespeople felt that their Product B goal was unattainable and consequently focused more on other product lines that had more achievable goals.

	Product A	Product B	Product C	Product D
Engagement (% earning incentive pay)	89%	43%	60%	100%
Excitement (average commission rate)	4.2	1.5	2.0	7.9

Figure 12-4. Plan engagement and excitement by product line

This allowed them to begin earning commissions at the accelerated rate sooner. This flaw in the IC plan and goal-setting process hurt the company's sales of Product B, which was strategically the most important product in the portfolio.

The right IC plan encourages salespeople to act in ways that are aligned with company objectives. Since company goals and strategies change as markets evolve, new products are introduced, and other products mature, the IC plan needs to adapt accordingly. Figure 12-5 provides some examples of ways in which the IC plan can help achieve the desired alignment between sales force activity and company objectives.

Is the IC Plan Too Complex?

IC plan designers and sales leaders frequently praise the virtues of simple IC plans. Yet when they look at the plans that are in use at their company or at other companies that they are familiar with, they see that many plans are too complex.

In our experience, at least 40 percent of plans are too complex. Why? Even when plans start off simple, over time sales leaders add features to fix perceived flaws or to focus attention on specific short-term goals. So one basic rule of thumb is: Keeping plans simple requires having the discipline to dismantle some old features when new ones are added.

If company objectives are to . . .	In your incentive plan . . .
Build long-term customer relationships by providing excellent customer service.	Have a large salary component and avoid excessive short-term incentives that drive salespeople to focus on making immediate sales at the expense of providing the service needed for long-term success.
Stress profitability ahead of sales growth as product lines mature.	Pay incentives based on gross margin rather than on sales.
Successfully introduce a new product.	Reward attractively for early sales of the new product and avoid tying incentives to goal attainment if accurate forecasting is not possible.
Generate more new customers.	Reward the extra effort it takes to sell successfully to new customers by paying higher incentives for sales to new customers than for sales to current customers.

Figure 12-5. Some examples of ways to align an incentive plan with company objectives

Complexity Hinders an IC Plan's Impact

Software company Phoenix Technologies started out each year with an incentive plan consisting of three relatively simple components: a base salary, a quota-based commission structure, and an annual bonus. Yet each year the plan's complexity would grow significantly during the year. Whenever volume was down or there was a need to boost sales for a specific product line, management looked to the compensation plan for a quick fix. The product groups often competed for the time and attention of the sales force by adding special incentives to the pay plan. By the end of the fiscal year, the plan would have as many as 20 special incentives for six different product groups. It became so bulky and lacking in a singular purpose that the sales force lost its focus on any single metric included in the plan.

A salesperson from another company once told us, "Our IC plan is so confusing that when I get my monthly incentive check, I'm often not sure what I'm being paid for."

A Simpler IC Plan Improves Sales Force Focus

Sales leaders at one company suspected that the current IC plan was not eliciting the desired sales force behaviors because most of the sales force did not understand it. The plan was several pages long and included dozens of different commission rates and multiple bonuses for achieving various objectives and gates. A newly designed plan included just four possible commission rates, plus a bonus for competitive displacements. The new plan fit on a business card that was small enough to be placed in a salesperson's wallet. The new, simpler plan provided salespeople with a clear understanding of what was important to the company.

If understanding an IC plan requires too much energy, salespeople will either pay no attention to the plan or misinterpret its intent. In either case, the result can be that sales effort is allocated inappropriately.

Interviews with salespeople and sales managers will usually reveal any existing complexity issues. If they do not, here are a few useful tests for evaluating plan complexity:

- **The elevator ride test.** The average elevator ride lasts less than a minute. If a plan cannot be explained to a salesperson in an elevator ride, it needs to be simplified.

- **The four-measures test.** If the plan is tied to more than four key metrics, it needs to be simplified.

- **The business card test.** If the plan cannot be summarized on a business card, it needs to be simplified.

Does the IC Plan Pay for Performance?

A key goal of IC plans is to "pay for performance." A simple way to assess whether a plan achieves this goal is to compare average payouts for high, average, and low performers, as in the analysis in Figure 12-3. A more complex pay-for-performance analysis is shown in Figure 12-6; sales leaders at this company wanted to ensure that the IC plan was not biased against the company's high-performing salespeople. A statistically derived performance rating percentile for salespeople was plotted against the salespeople's incentive earnings for the last period. The

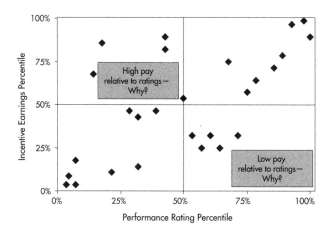

Figure 12-6. A metric for evaluating the extent to which an incentive plan pays for performance

performance rating percentile was based on analysis of territory sales performance relative to territory market potential; ratings can also be based on sales leaders' input and/or ratings from the company's performance-evaluation system.

The graph shows the extent to which the company's "winners" are being rewarded by the IC plan. Those in the "high pay relative to ratings" quadrant received above-average earnings despite below-average performance ratings. Similarly, those in the "low pay relative to ratings" quadrant received below-average earnings despite above-average performance ratings. There will always be a few salespeople who fall into the "high pay" and "low pay" quadrants temporarily as a result of explainable factors, such as unexpected market dynamics, poor goal setting, or characteristics of the salespeople themselves. However, having a large number of salespeople in these quadrants often indicates that there is a defect in the IC plan.

Is the IC Plan Fair?

This goal is difficult to achieve because so many potential sources of unfairness can affect sales forces. Differences among territories in sales potential, competition, and local conditions make it very difficult for an IC plan to be totally fair to all salespeople at all times. One can, however, try to discover and neutralize systematic biases toward or against salespeople or territories with predictable characteristics. For example, if the salespeople making the most money consistently have territories with particularly high (or low) historical market share, market potential, and/or sales growth, there may be a bias in the incentive plan.

Does the Territory Goal-Setting Process Create Biases in the IC Plan?

Companies that tie incentive pay to the attainment of a territory sales goal often introduce systematic biases into their IC plans through their goal-setting processes. A commonly used method of territory goal setting is to ask every salesperson to match what he sold last year and to grow sales by a projected national sales-growth percentage. This method, although simple, can make it hard for high-performing salespeople with historically high sales and high market share to earn good incentive money. Because differences in untapped market potential are not accounted for in the goal-setting process, salespeople who had high sales last year and who have already achieved high penetration within their territory are penalized with a large growth goal that will be difficult to achieve the following year. Territory goal-setting methods can be improved when the data measuring territory market potential are available so that each territory can be given a unique growth goal based on the amount of market potential that has not been realized.

Figure 12-7 shows an example of a bias test for one company's goal-based incentive plan. The test looks for IC payout biases across five different territory characteristics. For each of the five characteristics, territories were clustered into three groups—high, medium, and low. The median payout and payout range are shown for each cluster on each characteristic. A bias is discovered on one of the five characteristics: prior sales growth. Territories with low historical sales growth are systematically exceeding their goals, while those with historically high growth are consistently falling short of their goals. Upon further analysis, the company discovered that its territory goal-setting formula unfairly penalized territories with historically high sales growth and

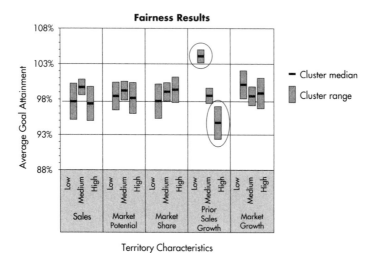

Figure 12-7. Fairness test: are there systematic biases in goal attainment?

implemented changes in the goal-setting formula to improve the fairness of the IC plan.

Designing a New Plan: Four Key Decisions for Designing an IC Plan

When designing an IC plan, sales leaders should consider four areas, shown in Figure 12-8, and should think about them based on several key factors.

Setting the Right Pay Level

It is a common story: Sales force turnover is high, and sales managers point to an inadequate pay level as the cause. At the same time, the company's finance department is concerned that sales force pay levels are too high. The decision on pay levels must answer the question, "What is the right average target pay for each sales job?" But there is another question that is just as important: "How should total pay vary across salespeople within each sales role?"

Setting Target Pay. There are wide differences in sales force pay levels across industries. Consider the different pay ranges for the two sales job postings shown in Figure 12-9.

The beer distributor's sales job pays $25,000 to $38,000, while the medical equipment manufacturer advertises the job at $80,000 to $150,000. The target pay matches the role, which matches the profile of the person and what the market pays for that type of person. The medical equipment salesperson plays a prominent role in driving sales

Decision	Description
Pay level	How much should salespeople be paid?
Salary-incentive mix	What proportion of sales force compensation should be variable pay and what proportion should be salary?
Performance measures	What measures should be used to determine the incentive component of sales force compensation?
Performance-payout relationships	How should the incentive payment vary with measured performance?

Figure 12-8. Four key sales IC plan design decisions

Beer Distributor	Medical Equipment Manufacturer
Pay range: **$25,000–38,000 (salary)**	Pay range: **$80,000–150,000 (commission-driven with base salary)**
Job Responsibilities Sell and merchandise beer to retail accounts in assigned territory: – Properly sell, merchandise, and service accounts. – Maintain good professional relationship with account decision makers and store personnel. – Complete paperwork on time. – Maintain route book and use sales history as a selling tool. – Respond to account complaints within 24 hours. – Pursue opportunities for shelf management and promotions. – Manage out-of-date/breakage to <$0.02 per case. – Secure primary position for displays at accounts. – Ensure that all price features are priced competitively with comparable brands. – Maintain current or seasonal themes within accounts. – Prepare special instructions needed by the merchandiser and driver. – Restock shelves, fill displays, and replenish the cold vaults for all products. **Qualifications** – Sales experience preferred. – At least 21 years of age. – Ability to manage multiple tasks and demonstrate solid business acumen and customer service. – Excellent problem-solving skills, creativity, team attitude, interpersonal and communication skills.	**Job Responsibilities** Sell high-tech medical equipment to physicians and hospital accounts in assigned territory: – Generate proposals, prepare sales quotes, and demonstrate equipment. – Maintain after-sale relationships. – Penetrate competitive accounts and communicate current market intelligence back to the business. – Provide leadership in market analysis and development and execution of strategies and action plans to drive sales. – Grow and maintain existing customer portfolio. – Prospect for new customers and business. – Achieve multiple territory sales targets. – Develop long-term customer relationships while identifying and capitalizing on opportunities that immediately satisfy customer needs. **Qualifications** – Sales experience including strategic selling, negotiation, high-end medical equipment sales, and selling to managed care/hospital organizations. – Willingness to travel 50%. – Bachelor's degree. – Demonstrated ability to work independently and with a team. – Ability to energize, develop, and build rapport at all levels within an organization. – Ability to analyze customer data and develop financially sound sales offers. – Strong communication and clear thinking skills with the ability to synthesize complex issues into simple messages.

Figure 12-9. Two sales job postings with different pay levels

results, with job responsibilities that include "generate proposals," "prospect for new customers," and "achieve multiple territory sales targets." Job responsibilities for the beer distribution position are service-oriented tasks such as "properly sell, merchandise, and service accounts," "respond to account complaints," and "restock shelves and fill displays."

The medical equipment sales job also requires more advanced skills and knowledge, including a bachelor's degree, advanced sales experience, and conceptual abilities like "synthesize complex issues into simple messages." Consequently, the company needs to pay more to attract people with the necessary qualifications. Industry norms and company budgets and culture also affect pay levels.

Some companies choose to lead their industry in total pay in order to attract the best possible candidates. At other companies, interesting work, a collegial environment, an effective management team, professional development, significant opportunity for advancement, and/or an appealing culture trump the higher pay offered by competitors.

Do Salespeople Need "Combat Pay"?

The U.S. military pays its members an extra, tax-free $225 a month if they are assigned to a combat zone. And companies frequently have to pay their salespeople more if a job is more difficult or if the company has difficulty attracting people. We have seen start-ups pay their salespeople 20 to 35 percent more than the industry norm and sometimes offer stock options in order to overcome the risks candidates may perceive in joining a start-up. On the other hand, companies with strong positive cultures can offer pay that is competitive within the industry and can attract top talent by providing non-pay benefits, such as a favorable working environment or significant opportunity for advancement.

Determining the Right Pay Variation. Significant differences in pay across a sales force are most appropriate when these differences are warranted by large variations in performance, which can be derived statistically. Figure 12-10 shows scatter plots of performance for two sales forces. Salespeople are plotted in terms of their territory market volume and this year's territory sales. Market volume is the best measure of territory potential for these companies. Companies that do not have accurate

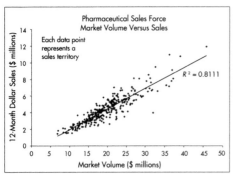
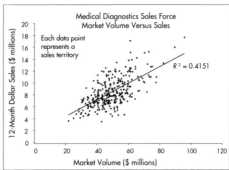

Figure 12-10. Performance scatter plots for two sales forces

territory market volume data may use other surrogate measures for territory potential (see Chapter 11).

A regression line on each graph shows the average sales expectation (or historical performance) for every level of market volume. The scatter of salespeople around the regression line shows the degree to which their performance varies from the expectation. The medical diagnostics sales force showed more variation in performance than the pharmaceutical sales force. Consequently, it is logical to expect greater pay variation across salespeople in the medical diagnostics sales force and less pay variation across salespeople in the pharmaceutical sales force. Plots like these help companies determine reasonable pay-variation distributions.

Watching for Escalating Pay. It's relatively easy to *increase* sales force pay. The only gripe is likely to be, "They have been underpaying me all along." But *cutting* pay is very difficult. One wealth-management company lost half its salespeople and assets to competitors when it tried to rein in the $1 million plus income of 25 percent of its salespeople. When faced with a pay decrease, some salespeople will leave because they are angry, not because they can make more money elsewhere. Consequently, pay-level decisions should always be made with an eye toward the future. Be sure to anticipate likely market and company strategy changes, and ensure that the appropriate pay level can be maintained.

When the Going Is Good, Is It Better to Share the Wealth and Pick Up the Pieces After the Crash, or Is It Preferable to Avoid the Crash?

In the early 1990s, a start-up firm developed a revolutionary new cardiac medical device. The firm's 50 salespeople were paid a base salary plus a commission on sales. In the first year after launch, the salespeople made $75,000 to $120,000. The sales force helped cardiologists across the country establish centers to perform an innovative procedure. As the use of the new device caught on, sales grew dramatically, and five years after launch, salespeople were earning an average of $650,000. Since the company was incredibly profitable and did not want to risk any decline in sales force morale, management decided that it should continue to "share the wealth" with the sales force. This led to some resentment among employees working in internal departments, such as marketing and research and development, who felt it was unfair for the sales force to be rewarded so generously. Then competitors entered the market, cutting into the company's market share and slowing sales growth. It was clear that, given the new market conditions, the company could no longer afford its high sales force costs, yet paying salespeople less would be very disruptive and unpopular. The firm's salespeople were in high demand by competitors, and many of them jumped ship to seek the next big payoff. According to a top executive at the firm, "A few years ago, I did not have time to rein in the pay plan. I was too busy walking around with a big smile on my face." In 2007 the entire industry averaged $250,000 target pay for a salesperson, which is high, but well below the stratospheric levels of the mid-1990s.

Determining the Appropriate Salary-Incentive Mix

In designing an IC plan, sales leaders need to decide on the proportion of a salesperson's pay that should be salary and the proportion that will be incentive pay based on performance. As with total pay, significant variation in the salary-incentive mix (or pay mix) exists across industries. Plans in some industries are 100 percent salary; in others, sales forces earn most or even all of their pay from incentives. Even within a given industry, differences can exist that reflect varying management philosophies and cultures.

What Mix Is Right? In the job postings in Figure 12-9, the beer distributor's sales job pays a fixed salary, while most of the pay for the medical equipment company salespeople comes from incentives (in the form of commissions) rather than salary. Several factors determine the right pay mix, and some of these factors explain the differences between the two jobs.

- The company's selling process and the role of the sales force. Having a large incentive component of pay works well for the medical equipment company because the job is highly focused on selling and the salesperson has considerable *causality*, or ability to influence results. Consequently, incentives are likely to motivate salespeople to work hard to produce results that lead to personal financial rewards. Salary-based compensation is more appropriate at the beer distribution company because the salespeople's primary role is to provide ongoing service and support (rather than selling), and because sales are affected by factors that the salesperson cannot control (such as brand name, advertising, and distribution). Generally, the IC component of sales force pay is larger for salespeople who sell to new (rather than repeat) customers. In addition, the length of the sales cycle influences the pay mix decision; long sales cycles are generally associated with a larger salary component.

- The measurability of company and customer results. Incentives cannot work if the measures on which they are based are unavailable or inaccurate. Measurability is usually accurate when a company ships products directly to customers. When intermediaries are involved in the distribution process, such as sales that go through distributors in the computer industry, the intermediary may not provide data on where the shipments go even though a manufacturer's salesperson assists in the sales process. This leads to poor measurability. If the sales organization cannot assign sales results to the individual salesperson, the company cannot pay based on results.

- Industry norms. Industry norms not only provide a good model of a pay mix that has worked well for other similar companies, but are also important for ensuring competitiveness in the market for salespeople. The medical equipment company needs to pay incentives that offer significant upside earnings opportunity in order to attract top performers.

- Company history, culture, and management philosophy. In the 1990s, a media company that owned many local newspapers had a pay mix for similar advertising sales jobs at the different papers that varied all the way from 100 percent salary at some papers to 100 percent incentives at others. The pay mix decision was a matter of history and culture. The strength of the sales force cultures that favored incentives and those that favored salary made it difficult to implement any other option.

These influencing factors must be considered jointly when sales leaders are deciding on the pay mix. The sales leaders in the companies profiled in Figure 12-11 evaluated each of the factors for their own situation. For the office supply sales force, which sells a broad line of office products to businesses, all factors favor a high-incentive environment; hence, 100 percent of the sales force's pay comes from a commission based on sales. For the animal lab systems sales force, which sells complex, customized water-filtration systems that require a long, consultative sales process and considerable engineering skill, three of the factors favor a low-incentive environment (with the fourth favoring incentives only slightly); hence, this company decided to pay its sales force entirely with salary.

For the newspaper sales force, which sells newspaper advertisements to businesses, the pay mix decision is the most difficult of the three. Historically, the sales force had been paid primarily by salary, a policy dating from a time when the newspaper had a virtual monopoly on advertising in its local market, the sales force sold to a captive audience, and decision making was in the hands of Pulitzer-seeking editors rather than financial people. In recent years, however, the number of media options has expanded, as magazines, radio, the Internet, and television have challenged and eroded newspaper readership and advertising. As a result, the newspaper's sales force has become much more important for bringing in top-line advertising revenues. Sales leaders need to develop a plan for changing the historical compensation system to one that is more consistent with current market conditions.

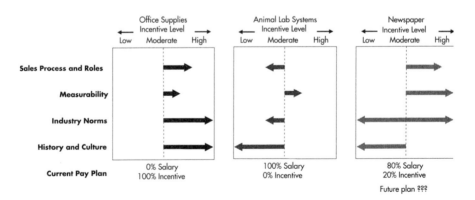

Figure 12-11. A comparison of factors that influence the pay mix for three sales forces

The Impact of Choosing the Wrong Mix. A salary-incentive mix that is incompatible with the sales environment creates dissonance within the organization that leads to undesirable consequences. Incompatibility can take many forms:

- A large incentive component with poor measurability or causality. The incentive plan is viewed as a lottery. Salespeople may receive incentive pay for outcomes that they have not created, while failing to get paid for some that they have created. The plan does not drive behavior. In fact, it will be demotivating if the sales force perceives it as unfair.
- A small incentive component with good measurability and causality. This incompatibility creates missed opportunity. Salespeople may go to sleep, since they make about the same amount of money regardless of how much they sell. The company misses out on the power of monetary incentives to motivate the sales force to achieve high levels of sales.
- A mismatch between incentives and culture. This type of mismatch typically occurs when a sales force needs to adapt to a changed world brought about by a transformation in customer buying processes or by new industry dynamics (as was the case for the newspaper advertising sales force). It also can happen when a new leader is brought in to "shake up" a culture that is perceived to value security for its people over performance. IC can be designed to conform to a desired culture, but it cannot be the primary force driving culture change. In our experience, salespeople who are comfortable with earning mostly salary like the security it brings and will bolt from a tense environment driven by high incentives. On the other hand, salespeople who relish the sales-focused, high-risk/high-reward mode of earning mostly incentive pay are unlikely to stay if the IC component is drastically reduced.

Hidden Salary: Why Increasing the Incentive Component of Total Pay Does Not Always Increase Sales Force Motivation

---

Incentives are designed to motivate sales success. Yet increasing the proportion of pay that salespeople earn through incentives rather than salary does not necessarily increase their motivation. Consider these two situations:

1. Salespeople at Company A earn target pay of $100,000, of which 50 percent comes from salary and 50 percent from incentives paid as a commission on total sales from the first dollar sold. Since most sales are repeat purchases from existing customers who have predictable usage and buying patterns, the company can project sales results at the territory level with great accuracy. Commission rates are set and territories are aligned so that each salesperson earns very close to the target incentive. Actual pay for the vast majority of salespeople varies from total target pay by less than 10 percent.

2. Salespeople at Company B earn target pay of $100,000, of which 75 percent comes from salary and 25 percent from a bonus earned when a territory sales goal is achieved. Salespeople also earn commissions on sales beyond goal. Territory goals are challenging "stretch" goals, designed to motivate the sales force to achieve peak performance. Approximately 70 percent of the sales force achieves the stretch goals and earns incentive pay; the bottom 30 percent who do not make goal earn only the base salary of $75,000. Only those who make the stretch goal can earn the target pay level or above.

Despite the greater proportion of sales force pay coming from incentives at Company A (50 percent) versus Company B (25 percent), Company A's incentive plan is not necessarily more motivating to its sales force. A good portion of the incentive pay earned at Company A is actually "hidden salary" because salespeople earn commissions on repeat sales that are likely to occur regardless of what the salespeople do. Incentive pay will motivate salespeople only if they have to put forth extra energy to earn it. It is quite possible that if a large proportion of the incentives earned at Company A are indeed hidden salary, then Company B's plan will be more motivating (even though it has a smaller incentive component) than Company A's plan.

Pay Mix Affects Motivation and Control of Sales Force Activities and Behaviors. The pay mix decision affects the importance of incentives (relative to the other sales force effectiveness drivers) for motivating and controlling sales force activity. An IC plan's impact on sales force behavior becomes more significant as the proportion of total compensation that is incentive increases. At the same time, the ability to use control mechanisms other than incentives, such as coaching by the sales manager and performance management, is diminished as the percentage of compensation derived from incentives increases.

At the animal lab systems company, where salespeople earn salary only (see Figure 12-11), the sales manager plays a critical role in inspiring and controlling the activities of the company's salespeople. The manager is intimately involved in the sales process, visiting customers with salespeople and helping to structure the best offering for each customer. He closely monitors how the salespeople manage their prospects through the CRM system and provides considerable direction to salespeople about how to allocate their time.

At the office supply company, where salespeople earn incentives only, the salespeople report to "working" sales managers who are themselves active salespeople (in fact, the managers are among the top sellers in the company). The managers spend very little time with the people who report to them; their managerial responsibilities are mostly administrative. The company motivates the sales force and controls how salespeople spend their time by adjusting product commission rates or by offering special bonuses for sales to different customer segments.

Many companies choose a pay mix with a moderate level of incentives (20 to 35 percent of total pay) that allows them to take advantage of the power of incentives while at the same time leveraging sales manager coaching and performance management to control and motivate the sales force effectively.

Selecting Performance Measures with Impact

A third important IC plan design decision is what measures should be used to determine the incentive component of compensation. The choices are many. The most frequently used metric is sales revenue. But other metrics can also be used to determine incentive pay, including units, gross margin, market share, customer satisfaction, and activity. Measures can be based on the absolute numbers achieved, growth over the previous year, the percentage of goal attained, or ranking versus peers. Measures can reflect aggregate performance or can be broken down by market segment, product, or channel.

Use Just a Few Measures. Plans based on just three or four measures drive sales activity most effectively. Using just a few measures makes an IC plan memorable and helps salespeople stay focused. Too many measures can lead to two problems. First, they can confuse salespeople and send mixed signals about what is important in the eyes of the company. Each plan feature gets so little weight that salespeople may ignore important priorities. Second, too many measures can blur the focus on company strategy; if salespeople have too many choices, they may find ways to be personally successful that do not align with the company strategy.

Multidivisional companies in which the divisions share a single sales force often experience problems with overly complex plans. When each division is intent on controlling its own metrics, the result can be a plan that has a complex and confusing array of measures and features.

Match the Measures to the Business Life Cycle. The measures on which the IC plan is based need to support company goals at each stage of the product life cycle. The measures should link company sales and marketing strategies with the goals and challenges of each life-cycle stage, as shown in Figure 12-12. Because forecasting new product sales is very difficult, goal-based incentive plans for newly launched products often end with one of two undesirable outcomes. If the forecast is too low, sales forces blow out their goals and are awash in IC cash. If the forecast is too high, an unmotivated sales force realizes that it cannot make money selling the new product and abandons it, making a bad situation even worse.

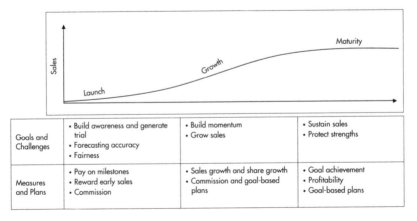

	Launch	Growth	Maturity
Goals and Challenges	• Build awareness and generate trial • Forecasting accuracy • Fairness	• Build momentum • Grow sales	• Sustain sales • Protect strengths
Measures and Plans	• Pay on milestones • Reward early sales • Commission	• Sales growth and share growth • Commission and goal-based plans	• Goal achievement • Profitability • Goal-based plans

Figure 12-12. IC plans and the product life cycle

Good IC plans for newly launched products reward early sales by paying a commission on all sales for at least a short time. As products grow and forecasting accuracy improves, sales momentum can be sustained and enhanced by paying salespeople for sales growth or for attaining challenging but realistic territory goals. Finally, as products mature, the company can maintain sales and protect its strengths by paying salespeople incentives for reaching the goals for their territory or for retaining profitable business.

Paying for Profitability Is Not as Simple as It Sounds. Profitability is the CEO's objective, and leaders are tempted to devolve this responsibility all the way down to the sales ranks. The board of one Global 50 company recently decided that all sales IC plans must be based on the profitability of sales. This laudable goal is easy to decree but difficult to implement successfully.

The Challenges of Paying Salespeople on Profitability

- When a lease-financing company changed its revenue-based IC plan to a profit-based plan, the territory-level profit calculations were so complex and difficult for the sales force to understand that the company switched back to the revenue-based plan after just one year; the value of simplicity outweighed the value of using the more strategic measure.

- A company in the rolled steel distribution business quickly realized that pricing, and hence profitability, were driven primarily by competition and global supply-and-demand forces, rather than by the salesperson. The company switched to an IC plan based on units instead of sales or profitability.

- A major computer manufacturer successfully made the transition to an IC plan that bases 40 percent of IC pay on a profit-based component, although the transition was more difficult than had been expected. The first year was a nightmare—unanticipated challenges erupted constantly. It took three months just to get the first sales and profitability reports produced. Then numerous factors—product sourcing decisions from different plants, exchange rates, supplier cost changes—worked their way through the system and into the IC calculations, affecting current payouts and even payout calculations for prior periods. The sales force was mystified, and the finance group was overwhelmed by questions and complaints. In the second year, adjustments were made to the plan to improve the situation. Standard costs were applied for the various product lines to protect the sales force from the vagaries of cost fluctuations during the year. Selling price continued to be used in the estimates of profitability. This approximate solution continues to be fine-tuned and is now working quite well in spite of the continuing assertion that salespeople have less control over profitability than they do over sales.

If the sales force does influence price, paying incentives on gross margin can be a good idea; but the company has to get the computations right—or at least stable and transparent—before using the measure in the IC plan. Another technique that companies have used to encourage salespeople to focus on profitability, in addition to sales, is to pay incentives based on sales revenue, but to vary the payout rate across products based on product margins.

Pay for Activities and the Quantity of Activities Will Go Up, but the Quality Will Go Down. Not many companies pay salespeople for activities such as the number of calls, demos, or proposals. However, tracking an activity can motivate an increase in the quantity of that activity but a decrease in its quality. Some companies fall into the trap of paying their salespeople to enter customer data into the CRM system. We see this most often at companies that have CRM systems that add little value to the salesperson or the sales process; these systems are destined to fail anyway, with or without incentives for data entry. We also find that paying for activities reinforces a "vending machine culture": getting something requires putting the money in and pushing a button.

As a general rule, smart sales leaders pay incentives on results only and use the performance management system to influence activities. On rare occasions, paying incentives on activity measures can work if it is done for short periods of time to encourage specific behaviors. For example, an executive search firm pays new salespeople incentives for

such activities as daily calls to potential job candidates and company visits, reinforcing the skills that new salespeople learn during training and
enhancing their confidence. Once a new salesperson learns the business
and begins to establish her referral network, her pay moves to the firm's
traditional straight commission plan.

Designing Effective Performance-Payout Relationships

A fourth important decision when designing a sales IC plan is how incentive payout should vary with measured performance. Some plans use
commissions; salespeople get paid a specified percentage of every sale.
Others pay salespeople a bonus if they achieve territory goals or quotas
or attain other specified performance thresholds or gates. It is also possible to combine commissions and bonuses in a single plan. Figure 12-13
shows examples of different performance-payout relationships.

Generally, commissions work best in sales environments with short
selling cycles in which the salesperson is expected to sell (rather than service) and has significant ability to influence short-term results. Commissions are most effective when performance measures are straightforward,
so that feedback is timely and incentive payouts can occur frequently. In
such environments, commissions can be highly motivating, as salespeople
can see a direct link between their efforts and their results and are
rewarded continually for their success. Bonus plans are usually preferred
over commission plans in situations with longer selling cycles and where
the link between sales force effort and results is less direct. Bonuses can be
an effective way to motivate salespeople to work hard over a longer
period of time, perhaps as part of a team, to achieve their goals.

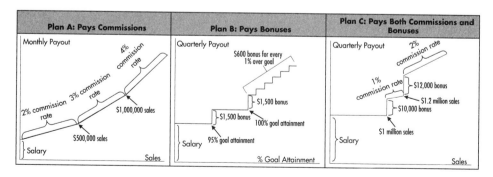

Figure 12-13. Examples of performance-payout relationships

**Start IC Payouts at Lower Performance Levels in More Volatile Environ-
ments.** In most bonus plans and in many commission plans, payout does
not begin at the first dollar of sales; instead, it begins at some threshold
of performance, as in Plan B and Plan C in Figure 12-13. There are two
reasons for this. First, in some environments, carryover sales—sales that
occur with little or no sales effort—are high. For example, if a manufacturer uses a supplier's packaging for a particular electronic product,
repeat sales of that packaging are driven by demand for the electronic
product and are likely to continue without sales effort. Incentives paid
on carryover sales are a hidden salary; salespeople do not have to put
forth extra energy to earn them. Setting a performance threshold for IC
payout that is above carryover sends a message to salespeople that they
have to work to earn their incentive pay.

The second reason to structure incentive payout to begin at a certain threshold of performance is that most companies that pay reasonable salaries expect a certain level of sales effort from salespeople. The
role of IC, then, is to motivate salespeople to work harder than this
minimal level.

Sales force engagement with an IC plan is affected by the performance level at which the incentive payout starts. Since incentives exert
the most motivation when they engage a large proportion of the sales
force, the point at which payouts begin should be set at a level such that
most salespeople can increase their earnings by working harder. In
moderate-incentive environments (20 to 35 percent incentive), payout
should start at a fraction of goal that ensures that at least 90 percent of
the sales force is engaged in the IC plan. In high-incentive environments
(over 50 percent incentive), payout should start at a lower performance
level so that sales force engagement is near 100 percent. At the same
time, the plan should provide high excitement for salespeople as they
work toward attaining the goal.

Market volatility also affects the point at which incentive payout
should begin. It is harder to set accurate sales goals in some markets
than it is in others. There are likely to be more salespeople performing
below goal in a new or uncertain market than in a stable and predictable
market. Consequently, incentive pay in volatile markets should begin at
a lower level of goal achievement and should rise more slowly than that
in markets in which there is high certainty. A salesperson might begin to

receive incentive pay at 90 or 95 percent of goal for an established product in a stable market, but at just 75 percent of goal for a product in an environment that is less predictable. Setting the goal lower ensures that more salespeople earn incentive money even if the goals for the product in the uncertain market turn out to be unrealistically high.

Monthly Goal Attainment Varies More than Annual Goal Attainment. Month-to-month variation in salespeople's performance is to be expected. Some salespeople make their goal by starting out strong and then coasting; others start slowly and end the year with a bang. The variation in goal achievement across salespeople is likely to decrease as the time frame for tracking gets longer. For example, in one sales force, the middle 90 percent of salespeople achieved between 60 and 140 percent of goal in the first quarter—a range that collapsed to 80 to 120 percent of goal by year end. Consequently, sales leaders need to consider the time frame for which incentives are paid when determining the right performance-payout relationship. When the time frame is short (a month), payout should begin at a lower level of goal achievement and rise more slowly. When the time frame is long (a year), payout can begin at a higher level of goal attainment and rise more quickly.

Salesperson Goal Attainment Varies More Than Sales District or Regional Goal Attainment. Often sales managers earn incentives based on district or regional goal attainment, which is dependent on the territory goal attainment of the salespeople they manage. Most sales managers have a mix of high-, average-, and weak-performing salespeople reporting to them. As the results achieved by salespeople with varied performance are tallied at the district or regional level, strong goal attainment in high-performing territories is offset by weak attainment in low-performing territories. Consequently, variation in goal achievement at the district or regional level is generally less than the variation at the territory level. Incentive plans for sales managers should acknowledge this fact. For managers, payout should begin at a higher level of goal achievement and should rise more quickly than it does for individual salespeople.

Make Payouts Steep at Predicted Levels of Performance. An IC plan can pay at the same rate for all sales, or the rate can vary through the use of accelerators and decelerators. Accelerators increase the payout rates as performance increases (in Plan A of Figure 12-13, the commission rate increases from 2 to 3 percent when salespeople hit $500,000 in sales and from 3 to 4 percent when they hit $1,000,000 in sales). Decelerators do the opposite; payout rates decrease once a goal or threshold is achieved. Accelerators can motivate a sales force to achieve high levels of sales and are an effective way to reward top performers. They can motivate salespeople to put out that extra burst of energy, particularly when they are used in the range of performance in which the sales force is likely to operate. For example, if most salespeople are likely to be between 95 percent and 110 percent of goal, placing an accelerator in this range can boost sales force performance to the next level. Accelerators can be costly if forecasting inaccuracies result in thresholds that are too easily achieved. Decelerators can be used in volatile markets to prevent the sales force from receiving unearned windfalls in the event of poor forecasting.

Do Not Use Caps. Caps are overused. An income cap on an incentive plan is always unpopular with a sales force but is sometimes demanded by finance: "If a salesperson gets a bluebird, why should he be paid for it?" The most significant disadvantage of caps is that they can dampen the motivation of top performers. Caps can be used to prevent the sales force from getting unearned windfalls in hard-to-forecast markets, but they seldom work well in high-incentive environments. Our experience shows that in most cases, the negative perception of caps among salespeople is a very significant downside; it is not worth the risk of demotivating top performers just to avoid paying too much in a few isolated cases. We have seen deal-level caps used successfully in circumstances in which salespeople occasionally have the opportunity to close very large deals. A deal-level cap (for example, one that prevents salespeople from earning more than three times their target incentive on a single deal) rewards the salesperson for closing a large sale while keeping her hungry to earn more. "Soft caps," in which the payout amount continues to increase at high levels of sales, but at a reduced rate, have also been used successfully to balance the desire to motivate top performers with the need for fiscal responsibility.

Aggregation Helps Underperforming Products. When a multiple-product plan has accelerators, sales leaders must choose whether to tie the accelerators to aggregate sales across all products or to sales of individual products. Figure 12-14 illustrates the implications of this choice. The first plan has separate accelerators for motivating goal achievement in Product Group A and Product Group B; the second plan has a single accelerator for total goal achievement (Product Group A plus Product Group B). The first plan costs the company $24,000 in payout for $1,050,000 in sales, while the second plan costs just $22,500 in payout for the same level of sales.

Salespeople are likely to prefer the first plan because it gives them greater flexibility. A salesperson can earn the accelerated commission rate by exceeding goal for either of the two product groups. If sales of both product groups are above goal or both are below goal, the two plan payouts are identical. However, when one of the product lines is underperforming, the first plan gives the sales force the option of focusing on the product line that is doing well in order to make more money. The impact of this flexibility multiplies as the number of products (or other independent plan components) increases. Salespeople have more ways to succeed and can pick and choose the easiest ways to earn money.

From a company perspective, the second plan has two significant advantages. First, it has a cost advantage whenever product performance is unbalanced (that is, whenever one product exceeds goal and the other does not). Second, the first plan may encourage the sales force to

Plan 1

Product Group	Goal ($000)	Rate to Goal	Rate Above Goal	Actual Sales	Payout
A	$500,000	2%	5%	$450,000	$9,000
B	$500,000	2%	5%	$600,000	$15,000
Total	$1,000,000			$1,050,000	$24,000

Plan 2

Product Group	Goal ($000)	Rate to Goal	Rate Above Goal	Actual Sales	Payout
All products	$1,000,000	2%	5%	$1,050,000	$22,500

Figure 12-14. Impact of aggregation

abandon an underselling product line; salespeople are likely to focus their energy on the product line that has already met its goal in order to make more money. The second plan is more likely to encourage the sales force to continue a balanced selling effort regardless of each product line's performance.

Team Incentives Have Limited Ability to Inspire Teamwork. In team selling environments, incentives based on team performance can play a small role in encouraging teamwork, although the impact of team incentives depends on the structure of the sales team. Consider two common team selling situations.

In the first situation, salespeople spend most of their time selling individually to their own customers. A team consists of salespeople who report to a common district, regional, or business unit sales manager. Members of the team are accountable for performance within their own territories, yet all members of the team are expected to work together to reach common district, regional, or business unit goals. With this type of loose team structure, it is best to tie most, if not all, of salespeople's incentive pay to their own individual territory performance. Sometimes companies will tie a small component of IC pay to the performance of the larger team (such as the district, region, or business unit) to encourage teamwork, sharing of best practices, and cross-selling. However, strong salespeople generally dislike this type of team incentive. They feel that they have limited ability to influence performance outside their own territory and that the team component unfairly hurts the strongest performers and benefits the weaker performers. Approaches other than incentives, such as group training sessions and district sales meetings, are usually more effective than monetary incentives at encouraging teamwork among salespeople on this type of selling team.

In the second type of team selling structure, multiple salespeople must collaborate to meet customer needs and create sales. For example, many sales forces in the computer industry have customer account managers (AMs) who manage relationships with major accounts. The AMs enlist the help of one or more product specialists as needed to design specific solutions. In team selling situations like this, using incentives to motivate performance is a challenging task. Since it is difficult to measure the contribution of each team member to the sales outcome, common metrics have to be used across the team, which can lead to a "free-rider" problem—a few nonperforming team members benefit from the actions of the productive members. Generally, the best sales compensation solution for this type of team selling situation is to have a larger salary component and a smaller incentive component. The incentive component can be allocated to team members based on the number of hours they work on an account, manager discretion, and/or peer ratings by other team members. Alternatively, some companies give all team members credit for an entire sale, and sales are double- and triple-counted (or more) for purposes of determining incentive pay. By keeping the incentive component small in this type of team selling situation, the company motivates salespeople to cooperate to meet customer needs and minimizes the productivity losses that occur when team members spend a lot of time worrying and complaining about how to allocate team incentives fairly.

Focus Spiffs on Strategic Outcomes. Spiffs and sales contests are powerful and relatively inexpensive ways to create incentives that focus sales force attention on specific short-term goals, improve morale, and recognize the efforts of top performers. However, such programs should be used with caution so that they do not divert sales force attention away from strategically important products, customers, and selling activities.

Spiffs Can Ensure Fair Compensation for Salespeople

The sales force of a computer server company was unmotivated because most salespeople were not making overly aggressive sales goals for a new product line. The company established a spiff that paid a supplemental 5 percent commission for sales of the new product during the last five months of the year. This incentive helped to ensure that salespeople would continue to sell this new product line and not "check out" for the rest of the year, saving their efforts for the following year when their goals might be more attainable. It also helped to ensure that the salespeople who worked hard were compensated fairly and were not unduly penalized for the company's goal-setting error.

Spiffs Can Distract the Sales Force and Are Costly to Administer

At one pharmaceutical company, individual product managers had the authority and the budget to introduce spiffs to the sales force without centralized sales force or marketing approval. At one point, there were 48 different spiffs and sales contests running at the same time, confusing the sales force and diverting attention away from the company's main strategic priorities.

Testing a New Plan: Making It Future-Proof

Every proposed new IC plan should be tested before it is launched. Failing to thoroughly evaluate and assess the potential impact of a new IC plan can have a variety of possible adverse consequences.

An Untested IC Plan Increases Cost and Reduces Sales

A company with an incentive plan that paid salespeople for achieving quota on multiple products introduced a new product. Sales leaders realized that they could not forecast sales of the new product well, and so rather than tying incentive payout for the new product to quota achievement, they paid a 10 percent commission on all new product sales. By the end of the first quarter, the 1,200-person sales force had blown out the sales of the new product, achieving 512 percent of goal. Unfortunately, this success came at the expense of existing product sales that accounted for more than 90 percent of company revenues; sales of these products were at just 94 percent of goal. Even though the total IC cost was 25 percent more than budgeted, total sales missed goal by 5 percent. The bottom line took a $47 million hit in just one quarter.

An Inadequately Tested IC Plan Contributes to Low Sales Force Motivation and Poor Performance

Salespeople at a consumer finance company earn commissions based on the loan volume they generate. Each salesperson has a territory goal, and commission payouts accelerate once he reaches 100 percent of his goal. While the sales force plays a very prominent role in creating the demand for loans, interest rates are also important. One year, interest rates went up unexpectedly, and as a result the demand for loans was well below expectation. Fewer than 10 percent of the salespeople made goal; hence, more than 90 percent of salespeople did not earn the accelerated commission rate. The sales force was extremely unhappy, feeling that it was being penalized for circumstances beyond its control. Salespeople became demotivated, which further depressed loan sales, and the company had one of its worst years in terms of achieving its sales goal.

Sales leaders can avoid unsatisfactory outcomes by testing the company's sales IC plans thoroughly before implementing them. Anticipating how the sales force might react to the plan would have unearthed the possible problem with the product launch example. One solution would have been to pay a 5 percent commission on the new product and another 5 percent on the new product if the total sales goal for the existing products was achieved. At the finance company, more thorough testing up front for the possibility of an interest-rate increase would have resulted in a plan that was fairer to the sales force. Not every contingency can be anticipated, but many can, and testing a potential plan makes it possible to avoid many adverse outcomes.

Run the Numbers but Do Not Assume That Forecasts Are Right On

Estimating the cost of an IC plan is more complex than simply multiplying target pay by the number of salespeople. National forecasts may be inaccurate, causing pay to be either significantly above or significantly below target. In addition, even when national forecasts are accurate, variation in performance across salespeople can cause average pay to deviate from target. With a progressive IC plan—one that pays salespeople at a higher rate after they achieve goal—actual compensation costs when national goal attainment is 100 percent can be significantly higher than target pay times the number of salespeople. This happens because the accelerators at goal cause the salespeople who are above goal to exceed the target pay by more than the shortfall from target pay for those who are below goal.

Plan testing involves not only predicting the cost of the plan, but also estimating engagement, excitement, and other important metrics. Sales leaders can make these predictions and estimates by integrating historical salesperson performance data with future sales forecasts and using these data to evaluate the payout implications of the new IC plan. The tools and metrics suggested for assessing current IC plans (described earlier in this chapter) are all relevant for evaluating proposed new plans before they are launched—including testing for a plan's motivational power by measuring expected engagement and excitement levels, and checking to ensure that the proposed plan pays for performance.

Testing also includes analyzing multiple what-if scenarios to ensure that a plan's consequences are understood for a range of possible future outcomes. For example, what happens if the national sales goal is too aggressive—will salespeople still make money and be reasonably motivated by the plan? What if the goals are achieved too easily—will plan costs get out of hand? A thorough risk analysis helps sales leaders gain a better understanding of the consequences of possible incentive plans so that they can build in the needed flexibility. Figure 12-15 shows plan testing results for one incentive plan.

Sensitivity analysis is also useful for fine-tuning plan features. For example, sensitivity testing may reveal that plan cost, engagement, or excitement can be improved by adjusting the point at which payout begins or by making slight changes in commission rates.

Assess the Impact of Plan Change on Individual Salespeople

When a change in plan structure may result in redistribution of income among salespeople, it is useful to perform a salesperson-by-salesperson analysis of the impact of the plan change on income. The analysis in Figure 12-16 shows which salespeople will be helped and which will be hurt by a proposed IC plan change. Those who are expected to lose a lot of money are a flight risk. If these are salespeople whom the company values, then either a transition strategy needs to be developed or the new plan needs to be reevaluated and changed to protect the earnings of these salespeople.

IC Plan Summary

	Products		
	Series A	Series X	Supplies
% Goal Threshold	80%	80%	80%
Pay per % of Goal to 100%	$100	$200	$250
Pay per % of Goal Over 100%	$300	$500	$600

Sensitivity of Plan Payout and Engagement to National Goal Attainment Level

	Assuming All Products Are at 100% of Goal	Assuming All Products Are at 95% of Goal	Assuming All Products Are at 105% of Goal
Total IC Payout	$4.13MM	$3.18MM	$5.17MM
Average Incentive	$20,638	$15,924	$25,842
80th Percentile	$37,800	$30,190	$45,420
Median	$15,100	$10,950	$20,300
20th Percentile	$3,740	$1,990	$5,600
Engagement Rate	91%	89%	94%
Series A Engagement	64%	60%	66%
Series X Engagement	80%	75%	86%
Supplies Engagement	85%	81%	91%

Figure 12-15. Plan testing results example

Implementing a New Plan: Making It Work
Communication Is Key

Implementing any major modification to a sales IC plan can be challenging. The adjustments in work processes suggested by the new plan and the direct effect of the plan change on sales force income are guaranteed to elicit emotion and controversy. A well-planned and carefully executed implementation process ensures that the organization has the understanding, motivation, and resources needed to make the change successfully, and that the sales force fully understands the features and benefits of the new plan. Individualized reports and tools are needed to help each salesperson understand how much incentive money she would earn with the new plan if she sold the same amount as last year, and how much she needs to sell in order to maintain or increase her current income level.

Communication with the sales force is critical during the initial roll-out of a new IC plan, but it continues to be important on an ongoing

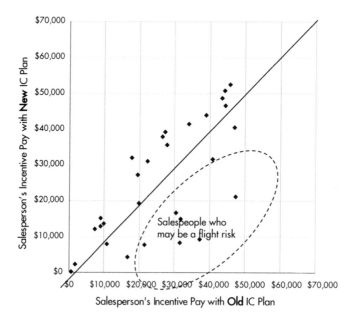

Figure 12-16. The impact of a proposed IC plan change on individual incentive pay

basis as well; constant reinforcement of the IC plan's message keeps sales force energy appropriately focused. A compensation and benefits vice president for a large financing company once told us, "Communication is the most underrated piece of comp design."

Major IC Changes Can Risk the Loss of Salespeople and Customers

Even with concerted efforts to "future-proof" incentive plans, changes in incentive plans are inevitable at some point for most sales forces, and with change comes the risk of losing salespeople and customers. Successful companies ensure that when changes are implemented, their best salespeople and customers are protected. This means understanding which salespeople and which customers are producing the most sales, understanding the impact of the change on those salespeople and customers, and developing appropriate transition strategies.

Transition strategies for top salespeople might include ensuring that they continue to be paid fairly, providing encouragement and recognition, involving them in the change process, and communicating with them to reduce their uncertainty. Transition processes for important customers might involve building multiple connections between the company and the customer (so that a single salesperson is not the customer's sole link to the company) and developing effective processes for moving customer relationships to a new salesperson, if necessary.

Insights for IC Success
Effective IC Plan Administration Provides Timely Feedback to the Sales Force and Sales Leaders

Well-designed IC plans succeed both because they are good and because they are administered well. The IC administrative systems are flexible, so that they can adapt to ongoing needs, and include feedback systems that provide relevant, clear, and timely performance information to salespeople and management. The system not only produces consistently accurate outputs for the payroll system, but also provides insights to the sales force and sales leaders.

Figure 12-17 shows a scorecard that one company uses to provide its salespeople with an accurate and timely picture of performance. Such scorecards can motivate salespeople to continue to work hard to achieve a goal or can help them discover where to make adjustments to improve their performance. If sales managers receive appropriate

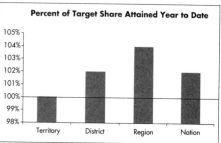

Salespeople at this company have quarterly market share targets. Graphically showing each salesperson his actual market share trends versus target share helps the salespeople see how they are doing. In addition, comparisons to others in the district, region, or nation, or comparisons to territories with similar characteristics, help salespeople compare their performance against others and see what levels of performance are possible.

Figure 12-17. Example of a performance scorecard for a salesperson

feedback on how their people are doing, they can coach them effectively to help improve their performance.

Effective IC plan administration also provides sales leaders with accurate and timely health reports on how the incentive plan is working, so that they can make needed changes quickly and keep the organization on track to achieve important goals. Health reports often include several of the analyses described earlier in this chapter: engagement and excitement estimates that show a plan's motivational impact, an evaluation of plan fairness, and an assessment of how well a plan is paying for performance.

Build Flexibility Into a Plan

Even though IC plans focus sales force attention on near-term results, the plans themselves have to take the future into account. An IC plan that works well in the current environment can fail in tomorrow's context. Incentive plans vary greatly in their flexibility, and plans that have limited ability to adapt to company and market change create considerable risk. For example, plans that pay a fixed commission on all sales often severely limit future management flexibility. If commission rates are fixed for a few years after a product is launched, salespeople begin to feel that they are entitled to that rate, even if their job becomes easier as more of their sales come from repeat buyers that require little sales effort.

Generally, incentive plans that link payout to goal achievement (rather than paying for all sales) have much greater flexibility because territory goals can be adjusted appropriately as circumstances change. An important part of any compensation plan review is anticipating likely market and company strategy changes and ensuring that the incentive plan either can continue to thrive or can be changed appropriately as needed. While some degree of stability in the incentive plan is usually desired, periodic plan changes in dynamic environments create an expectation of change among salespeople and allow salespeople to accept future plan changes more readily.

The Answer Is Often More than Incentives

While IC can be a powerful driver of sales results, sales leaders should see it as just one component of an effective sales management system. Figure 12-18 lists several sales effectiveness issues that are commonly

Perceived IC Problems	The Real Sales Effectiveness Issues	Non-IC Driver Solutions
The wrong salespeople seem to be making the money.	Good measures of success do not exist.	Invest in the development of better territory-level performance measures.
No one is making any money.	Products are not competitive or goals are too high.	Improve product forecasting so that sales force goals are more realistic.
Salespeople do not make money on targeted IC plan measures such as new account sales.	The sales force lacks needed capabilities.	Improve training and coaching, or perhaps redefine the hiring profile.
Some salespeople make lots of money; others make very little and turnover is high in the latter group.	There is large variation in territory opportunity.	Redesign sales territories.

Figure 12-18. Sales effectiveness issues that are frequently misdiagnosed as IC problems

misdiagnosed by sales leaders as IC plan problems, when in fact additional and sometimes better remedies exist within other sales effectiveness drivers.

Be cautious when trying to solve sales effectiveness problems by changing the IC plan; when sales leaders come to us for help with redesigning their IC plan, at least half of the time the primary source of the problem turns out to be something other than IC.

A Useful Reference

Sales IC is a complex topic, yet numerous frameworks and analytic approaches exist to help sales leaders get the most from this important sales effectiveness driver. A useful reference for anyone contemplating IC plan assessment and change is *The Complete Guide to Sales Force Incentive Compensation: How to Design and Implement Plans That Work,* by Zoltners, Sinha, and Lorimer (AMACOM, 2006).

CHAPTER **13**

Setting Fair and Realistic Goals to Motivate Your Sales Force

Effective Goals Motivate the Sales Force

Top athletes, successful businesspeople, and achievers in all fields use goals for motivation. People who have specific, challenging goals consistently outperform those who do not have goals and those who have only vague goals, such as, "I'll do my best." And organizations that are goal-focused are typically more successful in the long run than those that do not set goals. We estimate that over 90 percent of sales forces set goals for their salespeople, and most of them also link incentive pay to goal achievement.

It is hard to set territory-level goals that are fair, realistic, and motivational. Salespeople want easy-to-achieve goals that help them to earn a good income. Company leaders want aggressive goals that help the company achieve and even exceed its financial objectives. Customers want goals that encourage the company to meet their needs. It is challenging to find the right balance among these competing objectives, while at the same time dealing with the inherent uncertainty in markets. Yet setting the right goals for your salespeople is extremely important to sales success.

Goal setting is particularly critical for sales forces that earn a large portion of their income through incentives that are tied to goal attainment. If goals are set too low, the company will give the sales force incentive pay that is undeserved, salespeople will put forth less effort, and sales will suffer. If goals are set too high, sales force earnings will take a hit, salespeople will become disengaged, and sales will suffer. If goals are not allocated fairly across the sales force, the wrong salespeople will make the money, incentive pay costs will escalate, and sales force morale will suffer.

Effective goals can energize salespeople and organizations. Goals that are sufficiently challenging, yet attainable, drive sales force behavior and increase sales force motivation. Goals also:

- Communicate what is important and suggest an allocation of effort that reflects management's priorities.
- Help management evaluate sales performance.
- Provide a benchmark against which sales force activity and results can be measured, controlled, and rewarded.
- Provide a convenient way for management to recognize territory and personal differences when evaluating salespeople. Management can give each salesperson a different goal that takes into account the territory characteristics, such as growth potential; the competitive intensity of the market; and perhaps the salesperson's skills and experience as well.

The Cost of Poor Goal Setting

Goals that are too difficult, too easy, or not assigned fairly across the sales force have an adverse impact on sales force motivation, costs, and results.

Financial Dynamics of Goal Setting

Inappropriate goal setting costs companies money. Figure 13-1 shows how the level of challenge in a salesperson's goal has an impact on the top line (by influencing the salesperson's motivation, then effort, and then sales) and on the bottom line (by affecting his incentive pay). In this

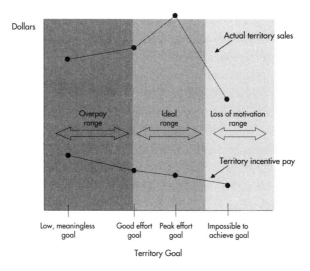

Figure 13-1. How the degree of goal challenge affects the top and bottom lines

example, the salesperson earns either a bonus or higher commissions for achieving a territory sales goal. If the goal is easy to achieve, he earns more incentive pay than if the goal is difficult to achieve. At the same time, the level of challenge inherent in the goal affects the salesperson's motivation, effort, and hence sales. If the goal is so easy to reach that it is virtually meaningless, he will put forth little extra effort, and the goal will be achieved with minimal work. Sales fall well short of what they could be if the goal were more challenging. The salesperson ends up in the "overpay range" and receives incentive pay that is inappropriately high for the amount of effort he expends and the sales he brings in.

The flip side is even more problematic. If the goal is so high that it is almost impossible to achieve, the salesperson becomes either discouraged or angry because the company is treating him unfairly; he may enter the "loss of motivation" range and even give up. The impact on sales can be devastating.

A salesperson's motivation, effort, and sales are highest when the goal is in the "ideal range"—at a level that is achievable, yet challenging enough to push him to attain peak performance.

Figure 13-1 also provides insight regarding the impact of goal setting on profitability. Profits are maximized when the goal is in the ideal range—sales are high and incentive pay costs are controlled. In the over-pay range, profitability is dampened by excessive incentive costs and less-than-peak sales levels. The lowest profitability occurs in the loss-of-motivation range—incentive costs are low, but the profit reductions resulting from the falloff in sales usually dwarf these cost "savings." A sales organization that has a large number of salespeople in the loss-of-motivation range may face serious long-term problems, especially if top-performing salespeople become disheartened and leave the company.

The Company Goal Is Too High: Unrealistic Aspirations Lead to Too Little Motivation

When 10 or 20 percent of salespeople miss their goal, there may be a problem with those salespeople. However, when the majority of the salespeople miss their goal, the problem is most likely to be with the overall goal.

Goals That Are Too High Discourage a Beverage Sales Force

A beverage bottler paid its sales force a base salary plus commissions on sales over a territory goal equal to last year's sales. The company encountered a period of flat or declining market potential in most areas, and it became difficult for salespeople to beat last year's numbers. Very few of them were earning commissions; consequently, sales force morale and motivation suffered, and sales force turnover increased. To improve the situation, the company revised its goal-setting process to create goals that were in line with the new market conditions. In addition, the incentive pay-out structure was changed so that commission payments started when 90 percent of the new goal was attained. The number of salespeople receiving incentive pay increased substantially, and sales force morale and retention improved.

If a company goal is overly optimistic, it's likely that territory sales goals will be too high across the board and that a large proportion of the sales force will be in the loss-of-motivation range. Consistently high territory sales goals are a common cause of low sales force morale.

Unfortunately, sales leaders may not have control over how challenging their sales goals are. Company sales forecasts may be driven by corporate expectations and handed down to the sales force from the executive suite. The goals that sales leaders feel are realistic and appropriate from a sales force motivation perspective may be lower than the goals that top management insists are necessary from a financial perspective. Sustaining sales force motivation when there is a substantial gap between what the sales force feels it can achieve and what top management demands is a daunting challenge.

Some leaders like to stretch their sales force. They believe that stretch goals are very motivating. The relationships in Figure 13-1 suggest the following goal-setting rule of thumb: Do not stretch beyond the peak-effort goal.

The Company Goal Is Too Low: Undemanding Targets Create Excessive Costs

When companies underestimate the success of their products and set company sales goals that are not challenging enough, territory sales goals will be too low across the sales force. Most salespeople will exceed their goals easily, and a large proportion of the sales force will be in the overpay range.

Goals that are too easily achieved not only cost the company money in the short term, but also have an undesirable impact on future sales force expectations. An occasional "bluebird" can be motivating, but when a sales force earns high incentive pay without high levels of effort, an entitlement culture can develop—and such a culture may be very hard to change. Salespeople expect the high pay for moderate work to continue, making it difficult for the company to set more challenging goals in the future without adversely affecting morale.

Goals That Are Too Easy Can Encourage Undesirable Sales Force Behaviors

---

A large industrial firm found that its best performers reached their sales goal by midyear and then basically quit working hard. As the year end approached, the sales force delayed closing additional deals in order to have them count toward meeting next year's goal.

Goals Are Not Allocated Fairly Among Salespeople

Sometimes sales leaders fail to allocate reasonable company goals appropriately across salespeople, giving some salespeople goals that are too easy to reach and giving others goals that are impossible to achieve. The result: The discontent of those salespeople who are in the loss-of-motivation range is exacerbated when they see that some of their peers in the overpay range are exceeding their goals easily without working hard. The combination of loss of motivation in some territories and incentive overpayment in others has a measurably negative impact on profitability.

A regional sales manager once told us, "When headquarters gives me a regional goal that I know will be hard to reach, I always give a disproportionately large share of that goal to my strongest performers. They are the ones that I can always rely on to deliver." However, when weak performers systematically get goals that are less challenging than the goals set for high performers, the company's best salespeople are not rewarded enough for their hard work and superior results. And strong performers are likely to observe that some poor performers are making more money because of their low goals. This imbalance in the allocation of goals sends the wrong message to salespeople and has a negative impact on morale.

Some companies set goals by assigning every territory an equal percentage of growth over last year's goal. This commonly used goal-setting formula is often unfair to the salespeople who sold the most last year. Top sellers are expected not only to protect their current sales base, but also to contribute a disproportionately large share of the sales increase in the current year. Top salespeople will lament, "I had a great year, and what do they do? They significantly raise my goal for next year." If top sellers have already captured a high share of their territories' market potential, it may be impossible for them to protect their current business and at the same time grow sales significantly. When they see that their goals are unachievable, they may reason, "I am not going to make my goal this year, so the best strategy is to hold back so that I can get a low goal next year." This results in goal oscillation—alternating high and low goals from year to year.

The data in Figure 13-2 show the bias inherent in a goal-setting methodology used at one company that asks each salesperson to grow sales by the same percentage over the previous year's sales. The significant negative correlation indicates that salespeople who had high sales last year are having a hard time making goals this year, while those who had low sales last year are more likely to make this year's goals.

Goal-setting methods can be biased against particular salespeople or territories, and objective statistical analyses like Figure 13-2 are very useful for revealing goal-setting problems. Whenever there is a significant correlation between goal attainment and a territory characteristic that does not reflect a salesperson's effort or skill, smart sales leaders suspect a potential goal-setting bias. The most common goal-setting biases are the result of such variables as territory size, geographic region, market segments served, market potential, past sales level, market share, past sales growth, and goal increase.

Effective goal-setting methods ensure that the right salespeople are rewarded. High performers consistently exceed their goals. Low performers do not; either they show improvement over time, or they leave the company.

Dealing with Challenging Goal-Setting Issues
How to Set an Accurate Company Goal

If the overall company goal is not accurate, it will be impossible to set good territory-level goals. Inaccurate national goals are sometimes the

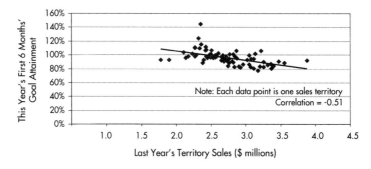

Figure 13-2. Goal-setting bias favors territories with low historical sales

result of poor forecasting of environmental or company events that unexpectedly increase or decrease demand. Quite often, however, company goals are inaccurate because they are based primarily on the expectations and aspirations of ambitious company leaders rather than on thoughtful analysis of trends, future influences, and events.

Growth is a visible and ingrained measure of company success, and the quest for growth can lead to national goals that are overly ambitious. Company leaders reason, "We exceeded our sales growth goal of 15 percent in each of the last three years, so let's continue our growth trend and set next year's goal at 20 percent above last year's sales." On the other hand, when success is measured in terms of goal attainment, sales leaders have an incentive to set goals that are too easily achieved, making the leaders appear successful when the goals are surpassed.

A familiar annual negotiating ritual at most companies involves executives trying to set higher goals while the sales organization argues for lower ones. But company goals that are driven by ambition rather than by analysis of market dynamics are often not accurate. Setting challenging yet achievable national goals requires investing in the best possible data and solid forecasting methods that take the market, the company, and environmental factors into account.

National goals are likely to be more reasonable when the goal-setting process includes input from both marketing and sales. People in marketing can estimate a product's potential based on historical sales and market trends, and experienced sales and marketing people can refine these forecasts.

One firm's marketing department improved its ability to set national goals significantly when it began using the structured analytical approach illustrated in Figure 13-3. First, it examined historical sales trends for key products and, assuming that the historical trends would continue, projected sales. Next, it took into account anticipated events that could affect next year's sales. An expected competitive launch would have a negative impact on sales, while a price increase, new product features, and an increase in the size of the sales force would have a positive impact. Management considered both quantitative and judgmental inputs when estimating the impact of these events on sales, and also factored in contingencies for events that were not part of the core forecast—for example, the possibility of price erosion or a second

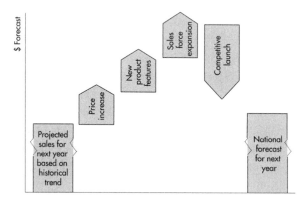

Figure 13-3. A structured approach to national forecasting that acknowledges contingencies

competitive launch—and their likely impact on sales. This structured approach to national goal setting increased the firm's accuracy in forecasting the success of various products and thus allowed the sales force to set more realistic territory-level goals.

In selling environments with long, multistep sales processes, salespeople and companies commonly track customer opportunities as they move through the sales cycle. For example, the company may know how many qualified leads salespeople are pursuing at a given point in time, and how many prospects have progressed through the needs identification, solution design, and deal closing stages. The data on the "sales pipeline" can be a key input for territory-level and national sales forecasting. A process for gathering bottom-up forecasts from the sales force can be structured objectively to help company leaders develop realistic forecasts and prevent salespeople from providing overly conservative forecasts that are too easy to exceed. Some companies have incentive plans that reward salespeople both for attaining their sales goals and for providing accurate forecasts of demand for their territories.

Company leaders who integrate top-down numbers, marketing forecasts, and sales force estimates into their goal-setting process increase their odds of creating attainable yet challenging national goals.

What to Do When Company Goals Are Too High

If it becomes evident partway into an incentive period that company goals are unachievable, management must balance the desire to remain committed to its goals ("We can't move the goalposts in the middle of the game") with the need to energize a demotivated sales force.

To a large extent, a company's culture determines whether it is acceptable for sales leaders to "re-goal" in the middle of an incentive period by reducing goals that are inappropriately high. Many companies want to maintain the integrity of the goal-setting process and therefore will keep the original goals intact, even when it is clear that they cannot be achieved. But it is important to keep the sales force motivated to prevent further sales shortfalls and the loss of top-performing salespeople. Spiffs and add-on incentive features are good ways to overcome the effects of overly aggressive goals.

If you want to create special incentive plan features to compensate for inappropriately high goals, determine the most reasonable goals using the latest data and use that information to design the supplemental or new element. For example, if the latest market trends and sales data suggest that reasonable goals would be at a level equal to 80 percent of actual goals, consider offering salespeople an added bonus for achieving 80 percent of goal. Ironically, re-goaling may actually increase the integrity of the process.

An Add-on Incentive Generates Sales Force Excitement When the Goal Is Out of Reach

---

Management at a financial company overestimated national demand for the firm's services and set sales force goals much too high. By the end of August, fewer than 10 percent of salespeople were on track to make goal. Management did not want to establish a precedent of reducing a company goal that was too challenging. However, it feared that many salespeople would "check out" for the rest of the year, saving their efforts for the following year, when goals might be more attainable. In order to generate some short-term excitement, management established a special incentive for the sales force covering the last trimester of sales. In addition, the incentive plan for the following year was revised so that modest commission acceleration kicked in when a salesperson attained 80 percent of goal, with additional acceleration once he achieved 100 percent of the goal. This revision helped to protect the sales force if it turned out that goals had once again been set too high.

What to Do When Company Goals Are Too Low

If it becomes evident partway through an incentive period that the company's initial forecast was too low and that salespeople will achieve territory-level goals too easily, the appropriate response depends on the length of the incentive period.

If the incentive period is fairly short (a quarter or less), it is usually best to absorb the temporary cost increase. The negative impact on morale that results from increasing goals in midstream is greater than the cost of paying the sales force a windfall gain. At the same time, it is important to carefully manage sales force expectations for the future. Start by communicating to salespeople that the gain is a windfall and should not be expected to continue in future incentive periods. Then implement more realistic goals for the next incentive period.

If the incentive period is longer (a year), the cost of paying the sales force a windfall gain over a long period of time may be very significant; in fact, many companies choose to increase sales force goals in midstream while managing the adverse effect on morale.

What to Do When It Is Hard to Tell What the Company Goal Should Be

Sometimes even the best data and the most respected forecasting techniques cannot overcome the uncertainty inherent in setting company goals. For example, goal setting for new products is always difficult, since historical sales data do not exist. And if the new product is the first of its kind, neither do data on the market or competitive sales. In such settings, the ability of a management team to set accurate company goals, let alone territory-level goals, is very limited. There are several ways to accommodate goal setting in highly unpredictable selling environments:

- Set goals with short time frames. If a goal turns out to be unrealistic, the sales force is affected only for a limited period of time, and the impact of the error is minimized.

- Set goals that reward a realistic range of performance rather than goals that focus attention on a single number. For example, define a "success" range of goal attainment that begins at 80 percent of the target sales level. With this approach, more salespeople will feel successful, even if the goal comes to be seen as unrealistically high.

- Use earnings caps or decelerators to ensure that the company will not have to pay out excessive unearned incentive money if company goals were set too low.

- Design IC payout curves that adjust so that sales force motivation stays high when company goals are too high and undeserved incentive payouts are minimized when company goals are too low. An individual's incentive payout might be linked both to her own territory performance relative to goal and to her goal attainment relative to the rest of the sales force. If she achieves 100 percent of her territory goal, she earns a target incentive amount if company goal attainment is also 100 percent. However, she earns more than the target incentive if company goal attainment is below 100 percent, and she earns less than the target incentive if company goal attainment is above 100 percent. Such plans help to manage sales force motivation and incentive compensation costs in unpredictable environments.

How to Ensure that Goals Are Allocated Fairly Across Territories

When allocating goals to territories, some sales organizations rely on input from sales managers and salespeople. Others rely on formulas (sometimes very complex ones) to set goals. The best allocation methods typically rely on a combination of data analysis and sales force input, with the relative importance of each being determined by the company's selling situation and the availability of data. When it is possible to use data-driven formulas as part of the goal-setting process, territory goals are generally more objective, explicit, and fair. Two formula-based approaches—the generalized maintenance plus adjusted growth method and the Performance Frontier method—consistently create good results. Both approaches require data on both historical territory-level sales and market potential. Ideas on how to obtain measures of territory-level market potential are discussed in Chapter 11.

Generalized Maintenance Plus Adjusted Growth. Figure 13-4 illustrates the generalized maintenance plus adjusted growth method of setting territory goals. Each salesperson's goal has two components: maintenance and growth.

Calculate individual territory goals using the following steps:

1. Calculate a maintenance goal for each territory by requiring that each salesperson retain a certain percentage of last year's sales. Companies often ask for 100 percent sales retention (as is the case in Figure 13-4), but a percentage greater than 100 percent may be appropriate for markets with rapid growth and/or high carryover, and a percentage of less than 100 percent may be used in markets with low carryover or sales declines. (The carryover concept is introduced in Chapter 4.)

2. Add up the maintenance goals across all the territories and subtract this number from the national goal. This is the national goal gap, which is typically a positive number, but which can be negative in a declining market.

3. Estimate the market potential of each territory. Estimates can be based on numerous factors, including competitors' sales, surrogate measures of account potential, account demographics, projected market growth, current customer penetration, and prospect lists.

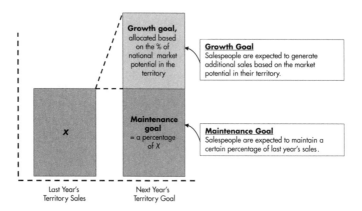

Figure 13-4. Generalized maintenance plus adjusted growth method of territory goal setting

The sum of all the territory market potentials equals the national market potential.

4. Allocate the goal gap across territories in proportion to each territory's share of the national market potential. This yields the growth goal for each salesperson. Using market potential to determine the growth component of goals encourages fairness in goal setting. The growth component will be a larger proportion of the total goal in a territory that has high market potential and a smaller proportion of the total goal in a territory that has low market potential.

Performance Frontier. The Performance Frontier approach to territory goal setting challenges all salespeople to strive to perform as well as the best performers in the sales force. (Chapter 2 introduced the Performance Frontier method.) This approach uses historical territory-level data to determine the level of performance that is possible for each territory. By controlling for territory differences (for example, in market potential, prior sales, or market share), the method isolates the variation in performance that results from a salesperson's efforts.

The Performance Frontier approach can consider multiple dimensions of territory differences, but it is most intuitive when it is viewed in two dimensions, as shown in Figure 13-5. This company enhances the maintenance plus adjusted growth method of territory goal setting by using Performance Frontier Analysis. Each salesperson is asked both to maintain last year's sales (a maintenance goal) and to grow sales (a growth goal). The analysis in Figure 13-5 is used to calculate the growth portion of goals. Territory market potential is thought to influence the amount of sales growth that is possible. The best-performing territories are those that have achieved the highest sales growth relative to their market potential. These top performers create a performance frontier that defines the best sales growth that has been attained by members of this sales force for every level of market potential. Salespeople in territories that fall below the performance frontier may not be performing up to their potential, as other salespeople with similar market potential have demonstrated that higher sales growth is possible.

Use Performance Frontier Analysis to give underperforming salespeople growth goals that challenge them to move closer to the frontier.

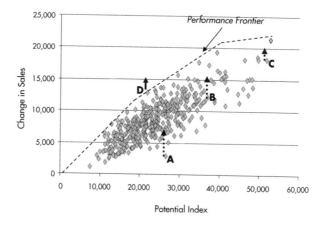

Figure 13-5. Performance Frontier Analysis—an example

For example, the tips of the three vertical dashed arrows in Figure 13-5 show the new growth goals for three underperforming territories: A, B, and C. Then, to compute the total goal for each territory, add the growth goals to the maintenance goals (equal to last year's territory sales).

Goals that are derived using the performance frontier challenge salespeople to move their territories closer to the frontier. The amount of improvement to be expected depends on the product and the market and on the degree to which management wants to challenge low performers. Note also that salespeople who are on the frontier can be given goals that challenge them to shift the entire frontier upward, as shown by the vertical solid arrow for territory D.

Choosing the Right Method. There are many possible goal-setting formulas and approaches. A reference suggesting several additional possibilities is *The Complete Guide to Sales Force Incentive Compensation: How to Design and Implement Plans That Work,* by Zoltners, Sinha, and Lorimer (AMACOM, 2006). When considering the type of formula or approach that will work best for you, take into account your company's selling situation, analytical capabilities, and data availability. When sales leaders are selecting a goal-setting approach, there is usually a trade-off between simplicity and accuracy. A complex formula that creates very realistic goals can be difficult and costly to implement and explain to the sales force. Sometimes a simpler process, although less exact, creates a better result because the sales force can understand and embrace the resulting goals more readily.

Insights for More Effective Goal Setting
A Good Goal-Allocation Methodology Cannot Fix the Problem of an Impossible Company Target

Even the most sophisticated goal-allocation formula cannot fix the problems created by a national forecast that is unrealistic. If the national goal is too aggressive, the best that an allocation formula can do is create territory goals that are consistently too large across the sales force. Similarly, if the company goal is too low, a good allocation formula simply creates territory goals that are uniformly too easily achieved. Companies that want the best territory goals need to invest both in developing good allocation formulas and in creating realistic national forecasts.

Goal Setting Is Improved When Estimates of Territory Potential Are Available

Sales leaders who fail to acknowledge differences in market potential from territory to territory can set unfair goals. This error, which is easy to fall into, is especially costly because it often punishes a company's top performers. Salespeople who achieve high sales and high levels of market penetration are "rewarded" with tougher goals every year, and at some point, achieving these goals becomes nearly impossible because so much of the territories' potential has already been captured. Building an analysis of territory market potential into your goal-setting process will give you a leg up in setting fair territory-level goals. In some industries, good measures of potential are readily available; in others, you may need to devise creative approaches to develop good surrogate measures. With resourcefulness and persistence, measures can be found for virtually every industry.

Allocate the National Goal Using a Successive Down-and-Up Yo-yo Process

In sales forces with multiple management levels, goals need to be assigned to all of the levels—regions, districts, and territories. A good way to accomplish this is to use a down-and-up "yo-yo" approach, which begins by allocating the national goal to all territories based on the most appropriate formula. When summed, the territory goals produce goals for the district, region, or any other managerial level.

The next phase incorporates sales force input. Top-level (say regional) goals are negotiated first. If regional managers feel that the formula has overlooked critical regional factors, they can suggest changes to their goals, which are subject to approval by headquarters. In addition, the new regional goals must sum to the national goal.

Once regional adjustments have been finalized, the goal-setting formula is reapplied to all the territories in each region, and new district goals are developed by summing up the new territory goals. The district managers in each region then negotiate to accommodate any critical overlooked district conditions. Changes are subject to the approval of regional managers, and the regional goal is maintained during the negotiations.

Finally, the formula is applied one last time to the territories in each district, and the district managers finalize territory goals. Many companies facilitate the adjustment and review process using Web-based systems that provide quick turnaround, ensure accuracy of adjustments, and provide an audit trail of all changes.

This back-and-forth approach provides the benefits of using a formula to suggest good territory-level goals, yet at the same time involves sales managers in the final goal-setting decisions and captures their local knowledge. In addition, when sales managers participate, they better understand how goals are set and can communicate this to their salespeople more knowledgeably, which in turn increases the sales force's commitment to the goals.

CHAPTER 14

Staying on Track Through Better Sales Force Performance Management

Performance management is the control system of the sales organization. If this important sales effectiveness driver is neglected, salespeople can veer off course quickly. Consider the following salespeople and situations.

- James does well one-on-one with customers, but he is hesitant to utilize other people from his company—product specialists, manufacturing, R&D, or telesales—because he would thus lose power with his customers. His performance is good with simple accounts and very erratic with complex accounts.

- Susan had a great streak in the stock market and is now independently wealthy. Intense and successful in the past, she is now biding her time until retirement—her sales job has become a sideline.

- Donna has personal problems. She is distracted, intensely preoccupied with those issues, and not focused on the job.

- Sam shows exceptional results, but he does whatever it takes to make the sale, at times going beyond the company's ethical guidelines.

- Antonio had a reasonable territory until a huge customer decided to no longer purchase locally. His quarterly goals have not been adjusted in response to this change in buying behavior. As a result, he has missed his goals for two successive quarters.

In each of these situations, customers may not be getting the right level of attention, and sales are less than what they could be. However, all of these situations can be addressed with the right performance management system. If James has trouble with complex accounts, he needs coaching and training, and he may benefit from observing the sales approach of a colleague who is successful with such accounts. Susan, for whom the sales job has become a sideline, and Sam, who has lapses of professional ethics, need to be dealt with firmly—put on probation, or even terminated. Donna may need professional counseling for her personal problems. Finally, if Antonio has lost a major customer in his territory, the company needs to either improve his opportunity or reset his goals.

Along with a company's culture, its performance management system is what ensures that salespeople, who work largely unsupervised, continue to do what they are supposed to do. When the performance management system is working effectively, salespeople's behaviors and activities stay aligned with evolving company goals and strategies.

Figure 14-1 shows how performance management drives effectiveness within the Sales System by influencing salespeople and their activities. Coaching and guidance from sales managers help salespeople upgrade their capabilities, and direction and feedback from the company

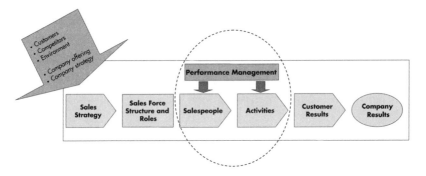

Figure 14-1. The role of performance management in the sales system

help them channel their actions to high-value activities. Through its influence on salespeople and their activities, a strong performance management process is a key driver of customer and company results.

The Performance Management Process

Through the performance management process, sales leaders effect changes in salespeople and their activities that sustain or enhance their performance. Change typically occurs through a formal, active, and directive series of prescribed steps, shown in overview in Figure 14-2. *Goals* lead to *plans*, which result in *actions*. *Measurement* is used to *evaluate* how well the goals are being met, how good the plans are, and the quantity and quality of sales activities. The evaluation leads to supportive or corrective *consequences*, and also to the establishment of new goals, reflecting the reality that performance management is a continuous process.

Performance Management Steps

Effective sales managers pay attention to key steps in the performance management process, as shown in Figure 14-2.

Set Goals and Expectations. The performance management process begins with the establishment of goals and expectations for salespeople. Goals can focus on:

- Capability development (for example, "Improve consultative selling skills")
- Activity ("Make a minimum of six calls per day")
- Results ("Achieve territory sales targets")

Figure 14-2. The performance management process

Goals can be established by the salesperson, by the manager, or by the salesperson and the manager working together. Chapter 13 explains how to set goals that will motivate the sales force.

Make Plans. Once goals have been established, sales managers and salespeople need to develop plans for achieving these goals. Some plans are customer-centered, focusing on how to implement the sales strategy and including the customers the salesperson will visit, the products he will emphasize, and the selling activities that will drive sales success. Other plans center on the salesperson and focus on personal development strategies for increasing an individual's skills and knowledge. Like goals, plans can be established by the salesperson, by the manager, or by the salesperson and the manager working together.

Take Actions. Through their actions, salespeople carry out the customer-centered and salesperson-centered plans. At some companies, managers control sales force actions closely. At others, salespeople have considerable leeway in carrying out the actions they think are best, with the company holding them accountable for results.

Measure Sales Force Performance. Measurement assists with the evaluation of sales force performance. Almost all organizations measure such company results as sales and profits. Companies can also measure upstream components of the sales system (see Figure 14-1), including customer results (for example, customer satisfaction scores or repeat sales rates), sales force activity (number of calls or time spent with strategic accounts), and salesperson capabilities (salespeople's product knowledge or selling skills).

Evaluate Achievement of Goals and Expectations. In evaluating performance, smart sales managers look at results, opportunity, and effort measures to determine whether plans and actions were successful in achieving goals and meeting expectations. Such evaluation forms the basis for constructive feedback to salespeople and for determining consequences (ways to correct weaknesses and reward for success). Evaluation also leads sales managers to work with their salespeople to establish new goals and expectations as they start a new performance management cycle.

Implement Consequences. Consequences that can enhance performance are a critical component of the performance management process. They can range from a reward and a revised goal for top performers to an improvement plan, probation, or termination for salespeople who did not perform up to expectations. Sales managers play a key role in implementing appropriate rewards and corrective consequences.

The Critical Role of Sales Managers in Performance Management

Throughout the performance management process, the sales manager is a key link between the company and the salesperson. It is the sales manager who works with the salesperson annually (or more frequently) to set goals and develop a plan for meeting those goals, and who then provides the salesperson with regular coaching and guidance.

At many companies, sales managers are expected to spend a prescribed amount of time with each salesperson—perhaps two half-days a month. In most performance management systems, the sales manager meets with a salesperson semiannually or quarterly for a formal performance review, and the two meet once a year for a performance review in which they agree on goals and plans for the upcoming year. Figure 14-3 shows how ongoing communication between managers and salespeople is an important part of the performance management process.

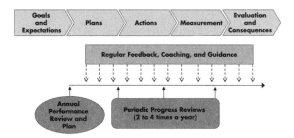

Figure 14-3. The critical role of managers in the performance management process

Control or Empower? The role of sales managers in the performance management process depends largely on the philosophy that sales leaders choose for managing the sales organization. Most philosophies fall into one of two contrasting categories, empowerment and control, although companies can also choose an approach that falls between these two approaches.

With an *empowerment* approach, the sales force is evaluated on the results it achieves for the company—sales, profits, or market share. Salespeople have a great deal of latitude in determining their goals and creating plans to achieve those goals. While the company may provide information to help salespeople improve their performance, each salesperson is empowered to do what she thinks will best lead to her achieving her goals. Sales force pay is closely tied to the results that salespeople achieve and typically has a large incentive component. Empowerment is part of the company culture.

With the *control* approach, the company is more extensively involved in monitoring and influencing salespeople's capabilities and activities. The skill and knowledge of the sales force are closely controlled through company hiring and training programs. The company provides guidelines for how salespeople should spend their time, and these guidelines are reinforced as sales managers coach salespeople. Often a customer relationship management (CRM) system tracks sales force effort. Salespeople typically earn a majority of their pay through salary. Control is part of the company culture.

Figure 14-4 shows how the roles of sales managers and salespeople differ depending on which model dominates in managing sales force performance.

If an empowerment model is to succeed, sales results must be able to be measured accurately at the salesperson level, so that salespeople can be held accountable for their performance. If measuring results accurately is not possible, then sales managers should seek to influence performance either by controlling the activities and capabilities of individual salespeople or by creating a culture that encourages success even in the absence of individual accountability. Even when a company has a good ability to measure results, company culture plays a large role in determining whether an empowerment or a control approach to sales force performance management is most appropriate.

	Control Model	**Empowerment Model**
Goals and Plans	• Activity goals are emphasized, in addition to results goals. • The company and the manager set goals for salespeople and suggest plans for achieving them, with input from the salespeople.	• Results goals are emphasized. There are no activity goals. • Salespeople have major input in setting their goals and developing plans for achieving them, with additional input from the company and the manager.
Actions	• Salespeople's actions are closely monitored. Managers often accompany salespeople on customer visits. • Sales activity may be tracked through a CRM system.	• Salespeople carry out actions largely unsupervised. • Sales activity is not tracked. Salespeople are managed by the results that they achieve.
Measurement, Evaluation, and Consequences	• Emphasis is on measuring and evaluating activity in addition to results. • Consequences are based on achievement of activity and personal development goals in addition to results.	• Emphasis is on measuring and evaluating results. Activity is not measured. • Consequences are based on achievement of results.

Figure 14-4. A comparison of a control and an empowerment model of performance management

Frameworks for Evaluating Performance

Most companies provide some type of framework for sales managers to use when evaluating salespeople. Frameworks encourage consistency of evaluation and consequences across the sales force. Three types of evaluation frameworks—a classification system, a competency model, and a ranking system—are popular.

Classification Systems Can Enhance Performance Management. Figure 14-5 shows how one company evaluated and classified salespeople in order to determine the appropriate consequences for individuals. Part of the classification was based on the sales manager's qualitative assessment of the salesperson's skills and attitude, while the other part was based on quantitative data measuring territory sales growth and goal attainment. Salespeople who met their sales goals and had a "success attitude" were the ones that the company wanted most to keep; it recognized and rewarded these A and B players for their efforts. Those who did not make their financial objectives and also lacked the skills and attitude needed for success (the D players) were put on a performance watch, with an eye to possibly terminating them. The C players in the middle—those who missed their financial objectives but had the

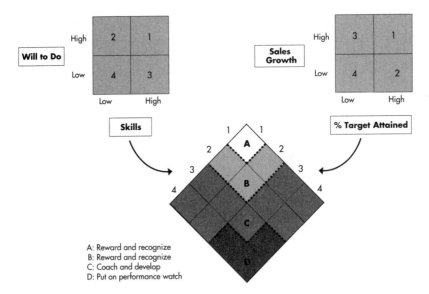

A: Reward and recognize
B: Reward and recognize
C: Coach and develop
D: Put on performance watch

Figure 14-5. Classifying salespeople for performance management

right attitude, those who made their financial objectives despite a poor attitude, and those whose high skills and strong growth gave them potential for success—were placed in a development and coaching program to help them become more successful.

Classification systems like the one shown in Figure 14-5 help sales managers match performance management plans to different situations. The company can take various steps—providing new opportunities, special recognition, professional development, and good pay—to try to retain the company's A and B players. It can focus its development efforts on the C players and place D players in the probation pool. Too often, growing companies are so focused on recruiting new salespeople that they fail to give enough attention to retaining A and B players, and at the same time allow D players to stay around for too long. When overall sales performance is strong, sales leaders may feel little pressure to change. But failing to identify D players while losing many A and B players creates a significant drain on sales effectiveness and sows the seeds for future trouble.

Competency Models Can Guide Performance Management. Competency models define the skills, knowledge, and capabilities needed to be successful in a particular sales role. A competency model provides a blueprint for managing performance, as well as for recruiting salespeople and creating sales force learning and development programs. Figure 14-6 shows a competency model used by one sales organization.

The top half of Figure 14-6 shows that in this organization, four competencies—product and market knowledge, sales process, planning and territory management, and relationship management—are important for sales success. The number and type of competencies included in the model depend on the nature and complexity of the work, and on the culture and values of the organization.

The top half of the figure also lists specific sales force behaviors that define three levels of achievement for each competency. The bottom half of the figure shows how the company uses the competency model to guide the performance management process. For each position

Competencies Needed for Sales Success

	Basic	Experienced	Advanced
Product and Market Knowledge	Has basic understanding of products and their benefits, competitive offerings, and customer needs.	Is able to identify sales opportunities and developing customer and market issues.	Actively uses customer and competitor information to adapt sales strategy.
Sales Process	Listens and probes to identify needs, communicates benefits, handles objections, and is able to use appropriate closing techniques.	Has high energy and is able to negotiate and sell to more than one buyer using customized sales materials and presentations.	Confidently handles complex sales and negotiation processes and is able to respond to unanticipated situations.
Planning and Territory Management	Is a self-starter; customizes and implements the marketing plan; meets call rates; tracks progress to goals.	Has a customer-specific account plan with goals and planned activities; clearly knows the advances sought at each customer interaction.	Is able to bring varied company resources to complex situations; has a long-term view of customers and how to grow them.
Relationship Management	Builds a good working relationship and instinctively has a positive attitude; is adept at getting repeat business.	Builds long-term cooperative relationships with key customers; coordinates internal resources to bring the best to each customer.	Anticipates evolving customer needs; is viewed by customers as an advisor; has peer group respect and propagates ideas.

Competency Expectation by Position and Supervisor and Self-Assessment of Current Competency for One Salesperson

	Below Standard	Basic	Experienced	Advanced
Product and Market Knowledge				
Sales Process				
Planning and Territory Management				
Relationship Management				

- ▬ Expected range for account managers
- ▬ Expected range for senior account managers
- ◇ Supervisor assessment
- ● Self-assessment

Figure 14-6. An example of how a competency model guides performance management in one sales organization

(account manager and senior account manager), there is an expected range of achievement on each competency. As part of an annual performance review, salespeople evaluate their own achievement on each competency, while their managers also evaluate them. The grid helps guide the discussion between the manager and the salesperson during the review, with the discussion centering on deficiencies in needed competencies and linking them to recommended learning and development opportunities that should help the salesperson improve.

Should You Publish Rankings of Salespeople? As part of the performance management process, many companies rank all their salespeople on certain criteria—sales, sales growth, quota achievement, or market share, for example. When we ask sales leaders who attend our executive-level courses if such forced rankings should be published for the entire sales force to see, a lively debate usually ensues. Some sales leaders believe adamantly in making ranked lists available to the entire sales force, while others feel that it is best to tell each salesperson his rank, but to publish only the top of the list. Still others use rankings to determine promotions and sales awards, but keep all rankings confidential.

Most advocates of publishing forced rankings of the entire sales force are firm believers in the motivational power of their approach. We hear comments like:

- "Salespeople like competition. It's what motivates them. Ranking drives the competitive juices. Look at sports—everyone knows where each team stands."
- "Salespeople will work harder because they want to move up. We once had a salesperson who moved from number 73 to number 56 to number 23 to number 3 in just three years."
- "The ranking identifies the top talent and helps us differentiate between excellent, average, and poor performers."
- "We don't have to deliver the bad news. The people at the bottom get embarrassed and leave."

However, sales leaders should use caution in publishing forced ranking of all salespeople, for several reasons.

- Since by definition there will be winners and losers, a forced ranking system can generate a lot of internally focused competition. In order for one person to move up in the rankings, another person has to move down. Salespeople may become more concerned with how they compare to their peers than they are with serving customers and beating their competitors. An "every man for himself" attitude can develop, and salespeople may be less likely to help one another out, share information, and collaborate with one another. They may forget that the competition is out there in the marketplace, not within the company.

- Forced ranking tells a sizable fraction of the salespeople that they are "losers," since many salespeople will not feel successful unless they are ranked at or near the top. Do this simple test: Ask yourself what rank you would need to attain to feel personally successful. Most people in sales will say that they need to be at least in the top 25 percent (if not higher). Consequently, a published forced ranking is likely to make a large fraction of the sales force feel unsuccessful in a very visible way. The ranking risks alienating the "middle" performers (75th to 25th percentile)—a large group that is likely to be important to company success.

- Forced ranking runs counter to the supportive culture that many sales forces want to create, particularly if published rankings are used as a substitute for ongoing performance feedback from managers. Published rankings can make employees feel undervalued and afraid to take risks for fear that a mistake might place their name on the "wall of shame" or make them a victim of "rank and yank."

- Rankings can be demotivating when there are only small performance differences between salespeople across a large range of rankings. Say that quota achievement for the top 20 salespeople ranges from 120 percent down to 118 percent. The perceived difference between the salesperson ranked number one and the salesperson ranked number 20 exaggerates a very small actual difference in performance.

- Published forced rankings can diminish the importance of sales managers in the performance management process. Weak managers can allow rankings to deliver the bad news to underperforming salespeople, instead of summoning the managerial courage to have honest and frank discussions with those salespeople that can help them improve.

These downsides to forced ranking are generally much less significant when companies rank-order salespeople but publish only the list of top performers, asking managers to share personal ranking information with the individuals who report to them. When managers relay ranking information face to face, they can work with individuals to develop strategies for improving their rankings. At the same time, the published list publicly acknowledges the outstanding performance of top-ranked salespeople, who are perhaps also rewarded with an award trip or "President's Club" membership. Those in the elite group become a model for the rest of the sales force, with others aspiring to become part of the select group.

If sales leaders feel strongly that forced rankings of the entire sales force should be published, the downsides of doing so can be managed in two ways. First, if the company keeps the time period for the ranking short, salespeople can recover quickly from a low ranking. Second, when the ranking is done using multiple criteria, salespeople have many ways to win. One company publishes monthly rankings of its salespeople on the following five measures:

- Total sales favors the large sales territory.
- Sales growth favors the small sales territory.
- Market share rewards the best performance relative to the competition.
- Market share growth favors the salesperson who is able to grow share in a territory that is underpenetrated.
- Varying monthly measures (such as individual product growth or new product sales) focus attention on specific short-term priorities.

Using a variety of measures makes it possible to highlight the success of salespeople with different strengths and different types of territories.

Forced rankings, whether published or not, should always be based on clearly articulated objective criteria and should be contemplated only when the measures used as the basis for the ranking are accurate and fair to all salespeople. For example, if sales potential is not equally distributed across sales territories, a ranking based on sales will favor salespeople whose territories have more potential. The ranking will not reflect true performance and will be demotivating to many salespeople (see the section "Effective Performance Management Systems Reward the Salesperson—Not the Territory"). A forced ranking based on unfair or inaccurate measures can make a satisfactory employee appear to be underperforming or can make an average performer appear excellent.

Legal Issues with Forced Ranking Systems

Forced ranking systems have triggered several employee lawsuits against companies, including Ford, Microsoft, and Conoco. Employees at these companies claimed that ranking had a discriminatory impact on their employment. At Ford, employees alleged that the ranking system intentionally discriminated based on age and gender and was being used to weed out older white male employees. At Microsoft, employees made similar allegations of prejudice against African Americans and women, while the Conoco lawsuit alleged that the company's forced ranking process discriminated against U.S. citizens. Any forced ranking system must be carefully designed and continuously monitored to ensure that it is legally defensible against claims of discrimination.

Performance Management Insights
The Best Sales Managers Learn From Their Salespeople
Through the Performance Management Process
Sales managers are a vital part of the performance management process. Good first-line sales managers spend time with the salespeople they manage. Likewise, higher-level managers within the sales organization spend time with first-line managers, and so on up through the sales ranks.

Spending time with their subordinates helps managers develop a strong understanding of performance. Given the inherent independence of the sales job and the natural variation in the situations and opportunities facing salespeople, an involved manager will see many different scenarios play out. One salesperson performs better than another. Sales to seemingly similar customers are different. Sales in one territory exceed expectations, while sales in another territory are below expectations. Sales to existing customers are developing well, but the conversion of new accounts is lagging. As managers work with individual salespeople to help them improve, they are constantly observing what salespeople do right. Over time, an astute manager develops a menu of behaviors that drive sales success and, through ongoing interactions with salespeople, propagates these behaviors across the sales force.

The Power of Performance Management Is Enhanced Through Alignment with Learning and Development Programs

Blended learning approaches leverage a variety of educational methods and are best for helping salespeople learn and develop. Blended learning involves formal training (for example, classroom training and e-learning) that is reinforced by sales managers through the performance management process. When sales managers visit customers with salespeople, they can reinforce the knowledge and skills that were learned in the classroom. The immediate and specific feedback that managers give salespeople as they coach them builds a salesperson's confidence by reinforcing his individual strengths. At the same time, coaching encourages improvement through guidance tailored to an individual's needs and the obstacles that he faces. When sales managers use coaching to reinforce formal training programs, salespeople learn more quickly, the change lasts longer, and a culture of continuous learning and growth is encouraged.

Effective Performance Management Systems Reward the Salesperson—Not the Territory

An effective performance management system recognizes the reality that outstanding sales results are frequently the result of exceptionally high opportunity, not exceptional effort or ability on the part of the salesperson. Consider two top sellers for a newspaper advertising sales force:

- Mary (ranked number one in sales) has a territory made up of 50 fast-growing information technology companies. She happened to be in the office when a marketing executive for a global electronics firm called to place a first-time order—30 pages of advertising to launch a new product. The order made Mary's year. Although she did very little to generate the sale, her windfall gain skyrocketed her to the top of the sales rankings.

- Joe (ranked number two) is a veteran salesperson who over the years has developed a very lucrative territory. He handles more large accounts than any other salesperson at the company. He spends most of his time on the phone taking orders from loyal customers. He keeps busy making these easy sales and does not feel that he needs to go out and prospect for new business.

Too often, companies underestimate the importance of differences in opportunity when they evaluate the performance of their salespeople. If Mary and Joe are recognized and rewarded by their company for their "outstanding" sales performance, morale among other salespeople who feel that they worked harder but had fewer sales because of poorer account assignments is likely to suffer. It is likely that Mary and Joe are being recognized only because they had superior opportunity.

Across companies and industries, territory potential is usually a better predictor of territory sales than any characteristic of the salesperson, including experience, ability, and effort. Territories with high market potential often have high sales regardless of sales force effort. This reality is evident in the sales district performance data shown in Figure 14-7, in which eight salespeople are ranked on sales, the primary performance measure used historically at this company. Recently, the company invested in developing a territory market potential index that reflects the purchasing potential of accounts in each territory. Adding these data to the analysis significantly changed the conclusions about performance. The top seller, Everett, has the highest market potential index in the district; perhaps potential rather than effort explains his high sales (he is ranked only sixth on the number of calls). Harper, who is ranked only fourth in sales, has the lowest market potential index in the district; she has to work hard (she is ranked second on calls) to get her sales. By dividing sales by the market potential index for every salesperson (potential adjusted sales), it is possible to see who is selling the most

	Calls (Rank)	Sales ($000) (Rank)	Sales $/Call (Rank)	Market Potential Index (Rank)	Potential Adjusted Sales ($000) (Rank)
Everett	1,176 (6)	2,208 (1)	1,878 (1)	1.25 (1)	1,768 (4)
Brown	1,418 (4)	1,920 (2)	1,354 (3)	1.23 (2)	1,566 (5)
Donahue	1,544 (3)	1,800 (3)	1,166 (5)	0.94 (6)	1,914 (3)
Harper	1,601 (2)	1,560 (4)	974 (6)	0.42 (8)	3,758 (1)
Franklin	1,129 (7)	1,464 (5)	1,297 (4)	1.19 (4)	1,227 (6)
Good	987 (8)	1,344 (6)	1,362 (2)	0.70 (7)	1,918 (2)
Carlson	1,271 (5)	1,056 (7)	831 (7)	1.08 (5)	977 (7)
Anderson	1,722 (1)	744 (8)	432 (8)	1.20 (3)	622 (8)

Figure 14-7. Performance by salesperson for one sales district (ranked on sales)

relative to potential. These data can be used as a surrogate measure of territory market share. The new data suggest that Harper, not Everett, is perhaps the strongest performer in the district.

If territory-level potential data are not available, companies will need to be creative in developing surrogates for potential. The numerous sources of data that are useful for this purpose include the U.S. Census Bureau, industry trade associations, and data and research companies.

PART 3

Addressing Common and Challenging Sales Management Issues

CHAPTER 15

Preventing Sales Force Complacency

The Silent Killer of Sales Effectiveness

I n a sales force that suffers from complacency, salespeople do not work at their true capacity. As a result, customers are underserved, and the company sacrifices sales, profits, and market share.

Battling the Silent Killer of Sales Effectiveness

Some sales organizations tolerate complacency, while others do not even notice it. And spotting it is not always simple. Two examples show how complacency is a serious issue for a sales force.

Complacency Is Systemic to a Distribution Company's Business Model

For many years, a U.S. distribution company has maintained the same structure and compensation plan for its sales force. Salespeople cover accounts in broad geographic areas. Once a salesperson sells to an account, it is permanently assigned to that salesperson. Salespeople earn a small salary, but most of their income comes from commissions that they earn on sales to their accounts, starting with the first dollar sold. Most of the company's veteran salespeople have amassed very lucrative territories that comprise many accounts; they earn generous commissions on the considerable book of business they have either inherited or built in their early years.

For the company, the downside of this sales force structure and compensation plan is that many of the experienced salespeople seem content to live off their earnings from existing customers and are unwilling to work hard to increase sales in an increasingly competitive market. Their account lists are so large that some 85 percent of the customers in veterans' territories do not receive any attention over the course of a year. At the same time, fewer than 50 percent of new salespeople stay for even one year. While the company gives new salespeople a few small accounts to help them get started, they are largely expected to develop their own book of business, and it typically takes them several years to develop enough business to earn a satisfactory income. Since the guaranteed salary level that the company offers is quite low, it has become difficult for the company to recruit and hire new salespeople. Year-end revenues are predicted to be several percentage points below goal, and sales costs are running high. Turnover is contributing to the high costs, and sales leaders speculate that complacency among the veteran salespeople is compromising the top line. Management feels that the time has come to make some changes.

Systemic complacency at the distribution company has several characteristics:

- Territories for established salespeople (sometimes called "Fat Cats") have more opportunity than it is possible for even the most motivated salesperson to serve.

- Many established salespeople have decided not to work very hard.

- Established salespeople can earn a great income (several hundred thousand dollars a year) with a modest amount of effort.

- Too many customers in established territories are underserved.

- The company is leaving money on the table because of inadequate account coverage.

- The salespeople who put forth only a small amount of effort to service their large book of business are sales force heroes; new people aspire to become like them.

Complacency Is Tolerated *by a Food Broker*

A food broker has a sales force that sells to and stocks products in super-markets, convenience stores, and other retail outlets. The broker carries a wide product line that includes many popular brands. A newly appointed sales manager for the food broker describes her frustration with several salespeople she has inherited who seem satisfied with the mediocre results they are achieving.

- "Sonny has been in his territory for two years. He seems unwilling to really work hard. He has concentrated on opening the larger accounts, without too much success. This is definitely one of our more serious problems."

- "Owen has been successful investing in real estate and seems to be losing interest in the company. His real estate investments apparently provide enough income to insulate him from financial pressures. He has been a decent performer for at least 20 years, but the sales job is not his number one priority anymore."

- "Ernie is a solid performer who refuses to sell based on our marketing programs or to push our most profitable products. He has been with us and in the same territory for 15 years. He has a classic sales personality, but he is a bit lazy."

The food broker suffers from what we call "tolerated complacency," which is characterized by several factors that exist simultaneously:

- Many salespeople are easily satisfied. Even though their efforts and their results are substandard, they are content with their income and their performance.

- Sales managers accept the complacency and allow it to continue.

- Sales leaders tolerate the complacency and the mediocre performance.

- The environment is friendly. The broker carries many popular brands that are easy to sell, and the company can survive and even succeed despite endemic complacency.

Complacent people are often experienced employees who know how to work the system. They have strong relationships with some important customers, and they can be very efficient in the way they use their time. They have strong friendships with their manager and other sales leaders. Their sales results can even look quite good.

Complacent salespeople with "customer power" are the most problematic. A highly paid veteran salesperson who controls important customer relationships may hold the company hostage, making demands or fighting changes that threaten his earning power. In such situations, making changes to eradicate complacency becomes risky because it can lead to sales force turnover and the loss of customers.

The Consequences of Complacency

Sales force complacency can lead to a considerable loss of opportunity for a company. In addition to its negative effect on customer coverage, excessive complacency can destroy an otherwise healthy sales force culture.

The Complacency Gap

Complacency can cost your company money because it leads to inadequate customer coverage and therefore lower sales. Complacent salespeople choose the easy route, typically exerting only modest effort and focusing on their existing book of business and friendly customers. As a result, they may neglect strategically important customers who are difficult and/or unfamiliar.

Figure 15-1 illustrates what happens to sales in a territory over time when the salesperson becomes complacent. A complacent salesperson will not fully take advantage of the opportunity that could be realized by a highly motivated salesperson. Territory sales flatten out, and the company forfeits more and more sales opportunities as the "complacency gap" widens. In a typical sales force, a complacent salesperson who is working at two-thirds capacity forfeits 20 percent of territory profits on an ongoing basis.

A Culture Breaker

Complacency also robs a sales organization of vitality because complacent salespeople affect the morale of others. In a sales force with several complacent members, the hardworking and highly motivated salespeople will tend to wonder:

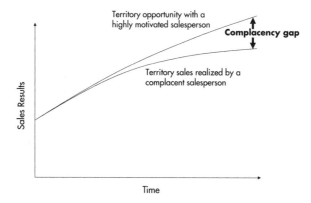

Figure 15-1. The complacency gap

- "Why are my easygoing colleagues so satisfied?"
- "Why are they earning so much money without working very hard?"

When the behavior of complacent salespeople is viewed as acceptable by others in a sales force or, even worse, when complacent salespeople are celebrated as heroes, the sales force culture is seriously at risk. A sales force culture that tolerates complacency will not produce sustained excellence and high performance.

Complacency and the Career Life Cycle

A complacency gap can start to form at any time in a salesperson's career, and it can occur very quickly if the wrong person is hired. Luckily, in the case of a hiring mistake, quick action by the company can prevent a long-term problem. Complacency that starts to take hold within the ranks of veteran salespeople presents an entirely different problem, one that is much harder to solve. It may take several years to diagnose such complacency, and there may be very little that the company can do to remedy the situation without disrupting customer relationships and risking a significant loss of business.

Detecting Complacency

Complacency is reflected in activities and attitudes that can be hard to observe and measure. Vigilant managers are constantly looking for the first signs of it among the people they manage—a slippage in the quantity or intensity of a salesperson's effort, slackening responsiveness to customers, avoidance of difficult accounts, a loss of "edge" in dealing with issues, and, eventually, plateauing results.

Complacency is complex and multifaceted, but performance dashboards like the one shown in Figure 15-2 can aid sales managers in detecting complacency in its earliest stages so that they can correct it before it gets out of hand. The dashboard indicates that salesperson G is showing signs of complacency. His solid revenue performance and high commission earnings may be due to the large market potential in his territory when in fact he has captured a relatively small share of that potential. The small number of new accounts he has opened and his below-average retention of existing accounts are also signs of possible complacency.

Addressing Complacency

Motivating a complacent sales force is a significant management challenge. If complacency is allowed to become part of the sales culture, it usually cannot be eliminated quickly without disrupting the sales organization. When sales are highly dependent on customers' relationships with specific salespeople, such disruption can create a significant loss of sales.

District A   Print | Help | Log Out

Salesperson	Revenue YTD	Market Potential	Market Share	New Accounts	% of Revenue Retained with Existing Accounts	Commission $ Earned YTD
Salesperson A	$3.88M	$14.20M	27.3%	18	117%	$194,062
Salesperson B	$3.78M	$10.22M	37.0%	19	108%	$189,156
Salesperson C	$3.34M	$8.48M	39.4%	15	94%	$167,117
Salesperson D	$3.08M	$7.38M	41.7%	20	85%	$154,206
Salesperson E	$5.30M	$19.68M	26.9%	13	82%	$267,005
Salesperson F	$2.30M	$6.96M	33.0%	9	93%	$116,085
Salesperson G	$4.86M	$18.72M	26.0%	1	90%	$243,190
Salesperson H	$3.64M	$11.46M	31.8%	4	98%	$182,002
Average	$3.77M	$12.14M	31.1%	12	97%	$189,103

Figure 15-2. Example of a performance dashboard that helps a sales manager detect complacency

Addressing complacency requires discovering its root causes and developing solutions that address them. There are two types of complacency:

- Tolerated complacency. Sales managers and leaders have allowed complacency on the part of individual salespeople for too long. The food broker sales organization described earlier in the chapter was afflicted with tolerated complacency.
- Systemic complacency. This type of complacency is a side effect of the business model. The distribution company described earlier in the chapter was plagued by systemic complacency.

Different approaches are appropriate for addressing the causes of each type of sales force complacency. These approaches are described here, along with some possible remedies.

Tolerated Complacency: When Sales Managers and Sales Leaders Allow Complacency to Develop and Linger

When sales managers and sales leaders tolerate complacency among salespeople, an increasing number of salespeople become satisfied with mediocre results. Eventually, complacency becomes part of the sales force culture.

How Tolerated Complacency Takes Root. As Figure 15-3 shows, tolerated complacency starts within individual salespeople. It is fostered by the actions (or inactions) of first-line sales managers and is accepted by sales leaders. Factors external to the sales force also contribute to the complacency, as a favorable environment can allow the company to survive and even thrive despite sales force complacency.

Complacency originates within the salesperson. Complacent salespeople will make statements like these:

- "I've been in this job for a long time. I've reached a comfortable income level, and I'm tired of working hard. The company owes me."

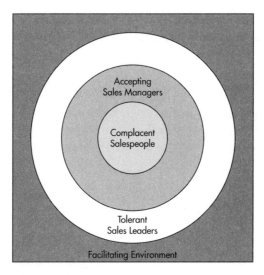

Figure 15-3. How tolerated complacency takes root

- "Success in sales is no longer a top priority for me. I'm focusing more on outside interests."
- "Selling for this company is a lot harder than I expected. Our products aren't that well received by customers, and I face rejection every day. Sometimes I just want to do whatever is easiest."
- "The company's products and services have substantial competitive advantage. I'm able to back off the work and still make goal—the offering 'sells itself'!"
- "I'm not advancing in my career as quickly as I'd hoped."

First-line sales managers accept complacency. Complacency in salespeople cannot survive unless sales managers accept it and let it live. First-line sales managers are often in the best position to detect complacency quickly and take steps to correct it. But that is not an easy challenge, for several reasons.

- Complacency is not easy to document.
- Complacent veteran salespeople probably generate reasonable levels of sales.

- Salespeople are likely to argue if their manager suggests that they have grown complacent.
- Salespeople may leave if they are confronted about their work style.

At many companies, sales managers are not well prepared to deal with complacency effectively. However, when managers lack proof of complacency and also lack the skills and confidence needed to deal with complacent individuals, the number of complacent salespeople usually grows over time, and sales opportunity is lost. And when there are a large number of complacent salespeople in a sales district, it is quite likely that a weak or inadequately prepared first-line sales manager is not dealing with the issue.

Sales leaders tolerate complacency. Sales leaders enable complacency among sales managers and salespeople by making inappropriate choices in the design and implementation of the sales effectiveness drivers. Complacency is likely to be a problem if, for example:

- The recruiting process does not screen for traits like self-motivation, competitiveness, hard work, and accomplishment.
- Rewards are not commensurate with performance—for example, they are too generous to salespeople whose success is due to their high-potential sales territory or to their hard work in prior years, rather than to their hard work this year.
- Sales goals either are not challenging enough or are perceived as impossible to achieve.
- Performance management systems do not provide adequate feedback to salespeople, or complacent salespeople routinely receive positive feedback from their managers.
- There are too few career options for salespeople, or the job is boring and provides little opportunity for new learning.

If the sales effectiveness drivers are not designed and implemented appropriately, complacency is likely to fester and become ingrained in the sales culture.

Sales Goals That Are Too Easily Achieved Can Lead to Complacency

A top-performing salesperson at a global services provider sold enough to reach his annual goal only five months into the year. His performance far exceeded that of his peers—at that point, the next best salesperson was only 10 percent above his year-to-date goal. Even though commission rates increased for any sales above goal, the top-performing salesperson lost the competitive momentum to be number one after reaching his goal and went into autopilot mode for the rest of the year. In the end, he finished the year in second place and lost the company reward trip to the salesperson who had been chasing him all year.

A facilitating environment contributes to complacency. Certain sales environments are more likely to lead to complacency. For example, at companies whose strong products enjoy considerable competitive advantage, selling can be very easy. If companies in favorable situations have generous reward structures, a culture of overconfidence and complacency can easily take hold. Such a culture can be deadly if competition increases, making the sales job more difficult. As one sales leader confided, "Last year, the fish were jumping into our boat. This year, competition has increased and we have to learn how to fish." As salespeople must work harder to make sales, the increased competition puts pressure on margins, making it impossible for the company to maintain a generous reward structure yet remain profitable.

Complacency Among the Elite

Many great sports coaches have observed that it is often tougher to keep a winning team on top than it is to transform a mediocre team into a champion. The same can be said for a sales force—salespeople who have recently achieved success can easily lose the edge that brought them that success in the first place.

Solutions for Addressing Tolerated Complacency. Complacency solutions fall squarely on the sales management and leadership teams. Diagnosing complacency and discovering possible solutions starts with increasing the awareness of complacency. Then, as Figure 15-4 shows, sales leaders can address complacency by identifying its focal point (the salesperson or the sales manager), asking the right questions to identify the probable root causes, and forging links to remedies based on the sales effectiveness drivers.

If the focal point of complacency is within individual salespeople, then the solutions depend on the reasons why those salespeople are underinvested in their jobs. Solutions can range across a wide spectrum of sales effectiveness drivers, including recruiting, performance management, goal setting, and territory alignment.

If the focal point of complacency is tolerant sales managers, sales leaders can employ several sales effectiveness driver solutions. To deal with complacent salespeople effectively, sales managers need to be supported with the right metrics, usually ones that measure activity. Sales

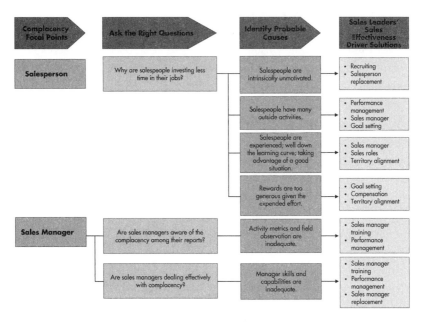

Figure 15-4. Addressing salesperson- and sales manager–centered complacency issues

managers, who should be on the lookout for complacency during every field visit, need training and support to maintain the courage required to confront complacent salespeople, even when they may be friends and/or have reasonable territory sales.

The sales manager should give the complacent salesperson a realistic picture of her performance. Performance Frontier Analysis (introduced in Chapter 2 and described in detail later in this chapter) is useful for painting this picture in a data-intensive and scientific way; it shows a complacent salesperson that others in the sales force with similar territory opportunity are outperforming him. A manager who is not successful at dealing with complacency among his people may need to be replaced.

Sales Leaders' Tolerance of Rogue Behavior From Sales Managers Demotivates the Sales Force

To encourage continued sales growth, a distributor of safety products designed a new incentive compensation plan to align sales goals with corporate objectives. While the design of the new quota-based plan was solid, implementation fell short. Regional managers had too much autonomy in setting quotas for salespeople; a few managers who did not buy into the new plan gave some salespeople "slam dunk" quotas and gave others "grandfather" timelines that exempted them from the new system. Initially, sales leaders allowed this behavior, which was demotivating to the entire sales organization and led to complacency among the favored salespeople. In the end, though, the leaders made the difficult decision to replace the noncompliant managers.

Selecting the right talent for a sales organization is a big part of complacency management. Selecting the right sales managers is especially critical—complacent salespeople usually have complacent managers. Compensation and territory design are two other sales effectiveness drivers that can be significant complacency busters. Reward systems that adjust for territory differences and that pay for performance can have a big impact on eliminating complacency.

Territory expectations need to reflect territory opportunity, and good goal setting can help tremendously. If your salespeople are aware of what their territories are capable of accomplishing, they are in a better position to acknowledge their complacency and reverse it. Effective goal setting also allows salespeople to be paid fairly for their performance. And you may need to revise a compensation plan that is too generous to a complacent salesperson. Sales territories need to provide appropriate opportunity for everyone to succeed, and it is easy for average people to hide in attractive territories.

Two pay and reward conditions may lead to complacency:

- **Not enough incentive pay.** The best mix of salary and incentive pay varies from organization to organization. If your sales force has a very prominent role in creating sales, and if sales results can be measured accurately, then you have considerable opportunity to motivate salespeople and drive higher sales by paying largely through performance-based incentives. If salespeople in such environments earn too much of their pay through salary, they may go to sleep; they will earn a good salary regardless of how much they sell, and the company misses out on the power of incentives to drive peak sales force performance.

- **Incentive pay and recognition that are based on inappropriate criteria.** Incentive plans that pay commissions based on total sales may motivate new salespeople, but for veteran salespeople, they merely reward them for their existing book of business, especially in environments in which many of this year's sales are the result of sales effort in prior years. Plans that pay on growth or goal attainment are more likely to motivate proactive selling, particularly by salespeople with large, lucrative territories. The criteria for recognitions such as President's Club should also reflect true performance in order to discourage complacent behavior.

Chapter 12 suggests approaches for evaluating and redesigning compensation and reward systems and for overcoming obstacles to implementing changes in an incentive compensation plan.

Using Recognition to Reengage Successful but Complacent Salespeople

At Northwestern Mutual Life Insurance Company, early signs of complacency often emerge when salespeople have been with the company for 12 to 15 years. These experienced salespeople have mastered the skills of the job, have built their book of business, are earning a good income, and often start to feel that they do not have to work all that hard. Sales leaders have discovered that for salespeople at this career stage, using ribbons and recognition is more effective at motivating extra effort than offering additional money. Frequent introductions of new products also help to keep veteran salespeople motivated to continually expand their business within their existing client base.

Sales leaders who want to eliminate complacency may also consider publishing a rank ordering of their salespeople on critical measures. A complacent salesperson may wake up when he sees his ranking. The advantages and disadvantages of publishing forced rankings are discussed further in Chapter 14. You should contemplate publishing rankings only when the measures used as the basis for the rankings are accurate and fair to all salespeople. For example, if sales potential is not equally distributed across sales territories, a ranking based on sales will favor salespeople with territories that have larger potential. Fat Cats usually have fat territories.

Systemic Complacency: When Complacency Is a Side Effect of the Business Model

Several industries have established aggressive, high-commission sales force cultures based on an "eat what you kill" philosophy—the person who makes the initial sale to a customer is responsible for servicing that customer indefinitely. Salespeople receive a large financial benefit from each initial "kill" because they earn commissions on repeat sales to every customer they bring on board. This model, used by the industrial distribution company cited at the start of this chapter, is common in such industries as insurance, office products, financial products (like mortgages), and many distributor businesses. Product lines in these businesses tend to be undifferentiated compared to those of competitors. Consequently, the sales force has a pronounced effect on sales. The business model in these sales organizations is compatible with complacency.

How Systemic Complacency Takes Root. Systemic complacency tends to evolve when a company hires many entry-level salespeople, pays them a small salary with a commission structure that rewards sales or gross margin, and assigns them a few accounts or prospects to help them get started. The company expects to see many of the new salespeople depart when they discover that it is difficult to build a book of business and earn a good living, but a few diligent newbies work especially hard and build a book of business, with their earnings accelerating as their established customers generate more and more repeat sales. Eventually, they too no longer have to work very hard because their book of business carries them. New people aspire to become like these successful veterans and are willing to spend many hours early in their careers to achieve this coveted elite status.

Figure 15-5 describes what happens to a salesperson's effort and income over time in companies that subscribe to this model. As sales effort declines, income continues to increase, although not as quickly as it would if the salesperson were fully engaged.

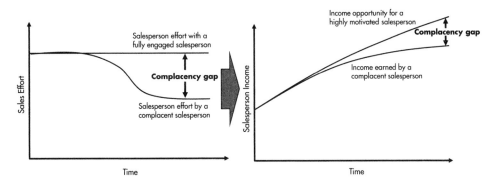

Figure 15-5. The effort/income trade-off for salespeople over time in an environment in which complacency is a side effect of the business model

This model works well in some respects. New salespeople are attracted to the job and are motivated to work hard so that someday they can become like the veterans. Through their hard work, they bring in new customers who generate a stream of revenues for the company. Particularly in cases where salespeople are independent agents whose pay is entirely commission-based, the company can take on many new salespeople at minimal cost, since salespeople are paid only if they generate sales. This model has been particularly successful during the growth stage of markets as companies seek to increase sales by expanding their sales organizations.

But when markets mature and sales growth slows, the complacency that can result from this type of business model becomes visible and problematic. Since complacency is very difficult to address once it has become embedded in the culture, the most successful companies will anticipate this outcome and will begin to change their business model before it is too late.

The model has at least two shortcomings:

- The costs of hiring new salespeople and bringing them on board every year can be significant, as turnover among new salespeople is usually quite high. One insurance company had to replace 60 percent of a 60,000-person sales force every year.

- Veteran high-earning salespeople can make a lot of money without working hard. Figure 15-6 describes how customers, salespeople, and the company are affected when an experienced salesperson has cultivated a territory with so many customers that she cannot adequately cover them.

Constituent	Wants and Needs	Result
Customer	Wants/needs more products and services	Needs not met
Salesperson	Does not want to exert more effort	Needs met
Company	Wants to sell more to existing customers; wants to find new customers	Needs not met

Figure 15-6. Systemic complacency: what happens when a veteran salesperson cultivates a territory that cannot be covered adequately

Solutions for Addressing Systemic Complacency. Sales leaders who are dealing with complacency that is perpetuated by the business model face the dilemma highlighted in Figure 15-7. On the one hand, complacent salespeople are not fully meeting their customers' needs, and the company is losing some sales opportunity. On the other hand, these same salespeople may leave and take their best customers with them if they feel threatened by any change. The sales leadership needs to weigh these two risks. Complacency solutions vary depending on which risk is the most pronounced.

Take action when the customer/company risk is high. If your company feels an urgent need to improve its revenues and strengthen its relationships with customers, you need to take action. In order to address systemic complacency, you need to acknowledge three dynamics that occur simultaneously in this type of business model:

1. The incentive plan pays salespeople for all the sales or profit they generate.

2. Sales territories have unequal potential, making it easier for salespeople in large territories to make money.

3. High customer retention is the norm, and thus it is easier for salespeople who have built up a large customer base to make money.

Veteran salespeople with big territories do not have enough time to meet the needs of all their customers adequately or to develop attractive new business. At the same time, they are reluctant to part with any accounts for fear of losing income and companywide recognition.

The most promising remedy for systemic complacency involves two key actions—realignment and remotivation. Chapter 6 points out

Figure 15-7. The business model complacency dilemma

the advantages of making sure that in all sales territories, workloads are well matched to the capacities of salespeople. However, realigning accounts serviced by overloaded salespeople is not easy. Some strategies that companies have used with at least partial success include:

- For a short period of time, allow the veteran salesperson to continue earning a share of the variable pay on sales to accounts as they are moved to a new salesperson.
- Allow salespeople to "sell back" some of their accounts to the company so that those accounts can be assigned to a new salesperson. This way, experienced salespeople are at least partly repaid for their past efforts through a one-time payment.
- Limit the number of active accounts a salesperson can have at any one time.

The company can alter the incentive plan to remotivate veteran salespeople, paying them based on goal attainment rather than paying an uncapped incentive on all sales from the first dollar sold. Changing the metrics that determine incentive pay can also help discourage complacent sales force behavior. Measuring such dimensions as growth over last year or new business development can refocus a pay plan so that it pays for *current* performance.

On occasion, companies change their sales force structure to deal with complacency. By redefining sales jobs and redistributing responsibilities, companies can help ensure that important customers, products, or selling activities are not ignored by complacent salespeople. For example, if salespeople are not spending enough time hunting for new customers, some companies have established a "hunter" sales force to focus specifically on new business development. Likewise, if salespeople are overlooking certain products or markets, companies can set up specialty sales forces to focus solely on those products or markets. Some companies encourage their large-volume salespeople to recruit dedicated junior salespeople to take on their administrative burden and handle small accounts. Note that these solutions do not solve the basic problem—complacency—and should be implemented cautiously. Chapter 5 discusses the advantages and disadvantages of specialized sales structures, and ways to manage the stresses that they cause.

Eliminating Sales Force Complacency Creates Considerable Disruption
for an Investment Firm

A new leadership team at a financial services firm faced a serious sales force complacency challenge. The firm sold investment products to high-net-worth individuals. All sales force earnings came from commissions on investments sold. The firm had an "eat what you kill" philosophy; every client remained indefinitely with the salesperson who made the initial sale. The compensation system was designed to motivate salespeople to be good hunters and to generate large volumes of business. Many of the firm's top-selling salespeople had built large client bases and could earn considerable sums of money from easy repeat sales to loyal clients without needing to expend a lot of effort. At the same time, business would slip through the cracks because these veterans had more clients than they could service adequately. Salespeople who had established a strong book of business earned well over $1 million a year while working only 30 hours a week. These "super salespeople" were regarded as heroes by the rest of the sales force. New salespeople entering the sales force wanted to be just like them. Yet the firm was leaving millions of dollars on the table, as many clients were being neglected.

The firm's new leadership team felt strongly that the sales force was overpaid. It restructured the sales organization, assigning small teams of salespeople to important clients, and thus reducing the power of individual salespeople to control client relationships. In addition, the leaders established a new team-based incentive compensation plan with substantially lower commission rates. Unfortunately, the company implemented these changes poorly, and the new structure and pay plan were not readily embraced by the sales force. A number of veteran salespeople quit, taking business with them. But despite the short-term setback, after several years the company regained its market share and was better positioned for the future with a more highly motivated and customer-focused sales force.

Evolve when the risk of defection by salespeople is high. In situations where salespeople have a great deal of power over relationships with customers, sudden, quick change is not always a viable option; the negative impact on the sales force, customers, and the company is often too great. To ensure the company's long-term success, it may be better to reengineer the sales force slowly as salespeople leave the company and new people are hired. Changes that can be implemented gradually and that will begin discouraging complacency include:

- Reassigning overlooked accounts to new salespeople.
- Slowly changing the incentive plan by incorporating or increasing the weight given to metrics that reflect recent performance, such as growth over last year.
- Establishing performance metrics that adjust for territory opportunity, perhaps publishing rankings on these metrics for everyone to see.

Taking steps like these to eliminate complacency will take time, but they will help avoid major disruption of customer relationships, significant sales force turnover, and considerable short-term loss of business.

A balancing act at the distribution company. The distribution company described at the start of the chapter was in the middle of the risk fulcrum (Figure 15-7). Sales leaders felt an urgent need to improve revenues and strengthen relationships with customers, yet they risked salespeople leaving and taking customers with them. The company took action by implementing several of our recommendations focused on structure, compensation, and alignment, incorporating some of the changes right away and phasing others in gradually to avoid significant sales force turnover and short-term sales loss.

Eradicating Sales Force Complacency

The good news is that while eliminating sales force complacency is never easy, there are several insights that can help sales leaders deal with complacency effectively, regardless of whether the complacency is tolerated or systemic.

Prevention Beats Reaction

What is the best remedy for sales force complacency? Preventing it from occurring in the first place. Long before complacency becomes an issue, the best sales leaders ask, "What steps can we take today to ensure that complacency does not harm our sales organization five years from now?" An ounce of prevention goes a long way toward ensuring sustained levels of sales force motivation for many years to come.

Sales leaders should look to the sales culture as the best lever for preventing complacency. Sales forces with cultures that embrace continuous change and in which salespeople are constantly challenged are unlikely to become complacent. Constant improvement and adaptation of the sales effectiveness drivers encourage a culture of change and keep a sales force challenged and motivated:

- Definers. Regular changes in customer assignments, added selling responsibilities, new product introductions, new promotional programs, reassignment to different managers, clearly defined career paths, and occasional special assignments are just a few of the ways in which you can continually adjust the definer sales effectiveness drivers to keep salespeople motivated.

- Shapers. Ongoing training initiatives encourage salespeople to always learn and grow in their jobs. Ongoing feedback and appreciation and regular career planning meetings with managers keep salespeople motivated and focused on their future with the company.

- Exciters. Sales leaders who change incentive compensation programs as markets and company strategies evolve ensure that sales force energy stays aligned appropriately with company goals. Pay based on goal attainment, sales or margin growth, and new business development keeps salespeople focused on capturing all of the opportunity in their territories.

- Controllers. A key element in preventing sales force complacency is having the right metrics to detect and measure complacency. Continuous investment in the development of good performance metrics and better goal-setting methodologies helps companies ensure that sales managers keep on top of complacency.

Salespeople who face constant challenge in their jobs and who come to expect and embrace change have little opportunity to become complacent.

Providing Opportunities Helps Avoid Complacency

The Society of Human Resource Management has named CXtec, a value-added reseller of networking equipment, one of the Best Small & Medium Companies to Work For in America. The company's ability to retain experienced workers is a key component of this selection. CXtec strives to provide salespeople with a variety of opportunities so that they are continuously learning and growing. For example, seasoned salespeople mentor and train new employees, lead weekly roundtables to discuss online training classes, are allowed to have flexible work schedules, and are encouraged to participate in company-funded charitable work.

First-line sales managers play a critical role in preventing complacency. An assessment of the quality of sales managers, along with investments to improve sales manager selection and development, is likely to have high impact in any effort to prevent sales force complacency.

Investments in Sales Manager Development Can Prevent Complacency

A salesperson's dissatisfaction with her manager is often a cause of complacency. Some companies have addressed this type of situation by implementing 360-degree evaluations of sales managers, including input from superiors, peers, and subordinates:

- Abbott Laboratories had its 500 diagnostic division salespeople evaluate their sales managers, and this input was given substantial consideration during manager performance reviews.

- Before a sales manager attends sales management classes at GE, his reports and peers are asked to fill out a survey about his skills and effectiveness. The manager's strengths and weaknesses are identified, and his performance is compared to that of his peers. At the training session, each sales manager creates a personal, confidential development plan focusing on areas for improvement.

Events Can Trigger Complacency Cleanup

Sometimes an event occurs—a merger, a new strategy, a new product launch, an environmental shift, a missed financial goal—that sets up the conditions for a major sales force change, including a complacency-busting shakeup. Nothing focuses attention as sharply as a sales organization not making its financial goals. The distribution company described at the start of this chapter was operating well below its financial targets. In general, sales leadership can take advantage of any number of events to shake up the complacency of a sales force and restart the organization on a different path.

Be Prepared for Denial

To combat complacency, sales leaders frequently must redefine salespeople's understanding of what levels of activity and results are acceptable. As a first step, sales managers may need to prove to complacent salespeople that a problem in fact exists. Complacent people will argue that they are not complacent. "I am managing my territory as well as I can" and "All my accounts are getting my attention" are typical responses.

Good performance metrics that measure a salesperson's results relative to territory opportunity are an effective way to show salespeople that in fact their performance is not what it should be. Clever analytics can be used to show complacent salespeople that they have a performance problem. For example, Figure 15-8 shows how Performance Frontier Analysis can be used to estimate a "complacency gap" for salespeople who are performing below the frontier. The gap for territory 130 is highlighted in the analysis. This analysis, which demonstrates clearly that others in the sales force are outperforming the salesperson in territory 130, will be useful when the sales manager begins a dialogue with that salesperson. Key performance indicators (KPIs) that focus on activities may provide an explanation for the complacency gap. The most effective sales managers are willing to state and restate the complacency gap message to underperforming salespeople. Individual stretch sales and activity goals can reinforce the message.

Change Will Not Be Easy

Changes made to reduce complacency affect the sales force. When people are asked to do more for possibly less pay, they will not be pleased.

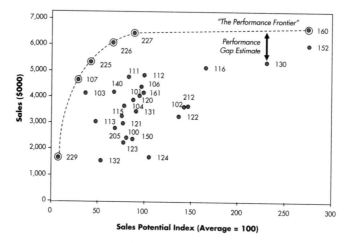

Figure 15-8. A complacency gap estimate using performance frontier analysis

After all, they have worked hard, and they feel entitled to their current pay level. Sales managers may need to alter the way they manage or be removed. They too may not be happy about the change. Consequently, some customer relationships will be disrupted and company results will be affected in the short term.

Yet despite the possibility of a temporary setback, in many cases change is necessary in order to ensure continuing customer and company success. Particularly when customer loyalty to the company and its products is significant, it is worth taking the risk in order to strengthen your company's competitive position for the future.

CHAPTER 16

Adapting a Sales Strategy to Meet New Challenges

Evolving Sales Strategies

A company's sales strategy defines which customers and prospects the company sells to (and, by implication, which it does not sell to), what the value proposition is, and how the selling is done. Successful sales strategies are never stagnant; they evolve constantly as external and internal pressures create the need to build the most effective connection between companies and their customers.

In this chapter, we discuss how to recognize the events that precipitate the need to change your sales strategy and how to put the change into operation. To illustrate the process of changing a sales strategy, we introduce two case studies here and return to them later in the chapter.

United Airlines Responds to New Industry Realities
Salespeople at United Airlines build and manage contractual partnerships between United and corporate travel departments and travel agencies. This sales force's mission is to capture a disproportionate share of high-profit travel (largely business travel) for United. For many years,

United's sales success was driven primarily by price and by personal relationships between its salespeople and their customers. In the early 2000s, however, a number of events—including the declines in air travel following September 11, 2001, high fuel prices, and inflexible labor agreements—created significant financial challenges for United and the entire airline industry.

To help the company succeed in a more demanding environment, United's leadership team reshaped the company's sales strategy. It embraced a value-based selling approach that focused on the total business value that United creates for customers. Instead of relying on price and personal relationships alone to drive sales, salespeople began to work closely with corporate and travel agent customers to understand their needs and tailor a customer-specific mix of offerings that created business value well beyond best-price alternatives.

Figure 16-1 summarizes how United's sales strategy changed to enable the company to succeed in the new environment. Later in this chapter, we'll lay out the process United used to accomplish this change.

Novartis Pharmaceuticals Strives to Enhance Sales Effectiveness

The Novartis Group is a leading multinational manufacturer of pharmaceutical products. The company employs a large number of salespeople who educate physicians on patient profiles and the benefits and side effects of the company's drugs for treating different patients and diseases.

Novartis is engaged in an ongoing effort to continuously enhance its global sales effectiveness. Every year, the company conducts an

	Old Sales Strategy	New Sales Strategy
Which customers to sell to?	Travel agents and corporate travel departments.	Continue to focus on the same audience, with a slight shift in emphasis toward corporate travel departments.
What is the value proposition?	United has a good selection of routes at competitive prices.	United provides services and support programs that enhance business value beyond best-price alternatives.
How is selling accomplished?	Loosely defined sales process. Discussions between salespeople and customers focus on routes and price, and on nurturing friendships.	Well-defined sales process (see Figure 16–12) that adds consistency and discipline to customer interactions and focuses customers on the total business value that United delivers.

Figure 16-1. Sales strategy change as United Airlines responds to a new, more challenging environment

effectiveness review to identify ways to enhance sales. After the review, the company leadership establishes an improvement plan, executes it, and measures the resulting progress. Several enhancements that Novartis has made as part of this process have involved adjustments in the company's sales strategy.

Figure 16-2 summarizes how a sales force effectiveness review for Novartis Pharmaceuticals in the United States affected the sales strategy and helped drive growth. Again, later in the chapter we'll provide more detail about these reviews and the process that Novartis used to accomplish changes in its sales strategy.

The Forces of Change

Sales strategies quickly become dated as customer needs and buying processes evolve, the competitive landscape or economic outlook changes, and/or companies launch new strategies, enter new markets, or introduce new products. Even in the absence of significant external and company events, the best companies continually fine-tune their sales strategies as they strive to constantly improve and become more competitive.

How to Know When a Sales Strategy Upgrade Is Needed

Very often, major events trigger changes in sales strategy. Frequently those events originate outside the company. For United Airlines, a number of external events created pressure on the industry, forcing the

	Old Sales Strategy	New Sales Strategy
Which customers to sell to?	Physicians who write prescriptions for the types of drugs that Novartis sells.	Strategically concentrate effort on the top 35 percent of prescribing physicians.
What is the value proposition?	Message that sells benefits and reduces the perceived risk of using the company's drugs.	Tailored message that moves physicians incrementally along the path to adopting Novartis products.
How is selling accomplished?	Gain access, understand physician needs, deliver value proposition, and remind physician of value.	Changes to the specific activities emphasized at each step of the selling process enabled a more effective delivery of the tailored value proposition.

Figure 16-2. Sales strategy change as Novartis Pharmaceuticals in the United States strives to enhance sales effectiveness

company to reevaluate its sales strategy. In 1999, Shell Energy responded to government deregulation of the natural gas industry in the state of Georgia (see Chapter 2) by developing a much more proactive sales strategy aimed at acquiring major corporate customers in the face of competition. Other external events that frequently create a need to change sales strategies include:

- Increased competitive intensity that creates pressure on companies and salespeople to find new ways to differentiate their offerings
- Customer consolidation
- Economic cycles

Hearing Aids Manufacturer Responds to Change in the Sales Channel

For years, salespeople at a hearing aids manufacturer sold a broad line of hearing aids to audiologists, ear-nose-and-throat (ENT) physicians, and other hearing specialists, who would recommend and sell the right devices to their patients. To be successful, salespeople had to convince practitioners that the manufacturer's devices were medically superior to those of its competitors. Then, in the late 1990s, a new purchasing channel shook up the market. Rather than purchasing hearing aids directly from the manufacturer, many practitioners were joining group purchasing organizations that bought in large volume and consequently got better pricing than individual practitioners could. The new market structure required a change in the manufacturer's sales strategy. To be successful, salespeople had to do more than sell to individual practitioners based on medical facts. A new *market segment*—buyers at the group purchasing organizations—had become important in the sales strategy. These buyers required a new *value proposition:* They had to be sold on business criteria—price, distribution, service, and overall value—in addition to product features. In turn, the manufacturer established a new *sales process* for group purchasers that involved assessing their business needs, developing a value offering, negotiating contracts, and continually reinforcing business value.

Events originating within a company can also provide the impetus for sales strategy change. Any time a sales organization launches a significant new product or enters into a new market, sales strategy is affected. In the late 1990s, Kinko's made a strategic decision to seek out larger corporate customers (see Chapter 2) in addition to the business travelers, college students, and employees of small businesses who had traditionally used the company's service centers. This required Kinko's salespeople to contact a new type of customer with a different value proposition and sales process.

Company acquisitions and sales force mergers are other classic examples of company events that usually lead to a redefinition of sales strategy.

Overhauling Sales Strategy Following the Hewlett-Packard–Compaq Computer Acquisition

The 2002 acquisition of Compaq Computer by Hewlett-Packard (HP) created a need for a substantial sales strategy change that affected all of the combined company's more than 6,000 salespeople. HP and Compaq had been rivals for years, selling against each other at the same accounts, and now these two large sales organizations with broad product portfolios, different compensation plans, and very dissimilar cultures had to be integrated. Over a period of six months, an integration team worked to create a single combined sales organization aligned around a new sales strategy and culture. The new, larger combined sales organization allowed HP to reach more customers and prospects. Because of its broader product and service offering, the new company's value propositions became more powerful, and delivering these more powerful value propositions required more complex selling processes. Implementation of the new sales strategy required adjustments to almost every sales effectiveness driver. Extensive planning, good communication, and swift implementation helped HP implement major sales strategy revisions without losing many customers following the acquisition.

While major events are obvious triggers for sales strategy change, other, more subtle signals can also indicate that a company's sales strategy needs to be upgraded. As we described earlier, sales leaders at

Novartis engage in an ongoing hunt for such signals in order to ensure that they are constantly fine-tuning their sales strategy to be the best that it can be.

The Sales System framework shown in Figure 16-3 provides a structure for diagnosing emerging sales strategy issues. By working backward through the framework, you can identify signals of potential sales strategy concern and trace their causes upstream to determine what adjustments you might need to make.

The framework (working from right to left) suggests the following series of diagnostic questions that you can ask:

- Are our *company results* below expectation? Is the company losing sales, or is growth less than expected? If so, perhaps changes in which customers and prospects our sales force sells to, what value it sells, or how the selling is done can improve our results.

- What do our *customers* say? Trouble is looming if customers are not responding well to our salespeople or if customer satisfaction is waning. Is our sales force calling on the right customers and prospects? Are the value propositions on target with our customers' needs? Do our customers find our selling process to be effective and efficient?

- What *activities* do our salespeople engage in? Is their selling process made up of activities that add the most value and produce the best possible results? If the best-performing salespeople engage in different sales activities from average performers, then perhaps adopting the methods of top performers can improve our sales strategy.

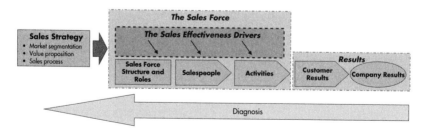

Figure 16-3. Diagnosis: Do we need to change the sales strategy?

- What do our *salespeople* and sales managers say? If their feedback indicates that our current value propositions and sales process are not working well with customers, perhaps our sales strategy needs to be reexamined.

- Do we have appropriate sales force *roles and structure* in place? Does our current structure encourage salespeople to spend time with the right types of customers and prospects? Do sales roles allow salespeople to embrace and implement a value-added selling process?

If a careful diagnosis suggests that your company might benefit from a sales strategy upgrade, a well-planned and proactive process will ensure the successful implementation of a change in your sales strategy.

Implementing a Sales Strategy Upgrade

Whether a change in sales strategy is prompted by specific external or internal events or by a company's desire to improve its effectiveness, implementing a sales strategy change involves two main steps, shown in Figure 16-4 within the context of the Sales System.

First, implementing a sales strategy change requires defining what changes in the company's market segments, value proposition, and selling process are needed.

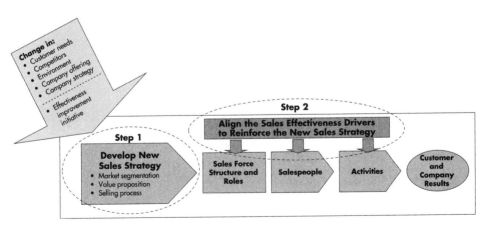

Figure 16-4. Two steps for implementing a sales strategy upgrade

Second, implementing a sales strategy change involves getting the sales organization to execute the new selling process effectively—that is, to perform the activities noted in Figure 16-4 correctly. Since performing activities well depends on salespeople's skills and abilities, and also on the sales force structure and the definition of its roles, any change in the selling process is likely to require changes to the sales effectiveness drivers that affect these dimensions. A sales strategy is most potent when every sales effectiveness driver supports and reinforces that strategy.

Step 1: Developing a New Sales Strategy When Faced with Challenges

Chapter 3 shares ideas for developing a sales strategy that maximizes effectiveness and helps companies outperform their competitors. Here we share ideas for rethinking sales strategy in the context of a changing environment or as part of an initiative to improve effectiveness.

A Process for Identifying Needed Sales Strategy Changes. When you have identified a need to change your sales strategy, the questions laid out in Figure 16-5 can help you identify what changes are required.

Sales strategy starts with a definition of who your customer is, so

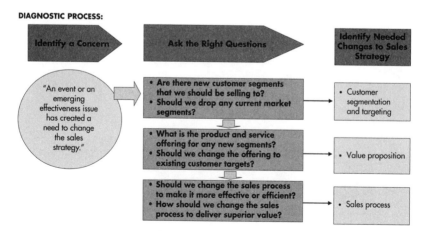

Figure 16-5. Identifying how to change sales strategy in response to events or emerging effectiveness issues

that you can then determine what it is that the customer values and figure out what the best sales process is for delivering that value.

There's a natural hierarchy among the questions that helps you identify how to change a sales strategy:

1. The change starts with an evaluation of customer segmentation and targeting strategies. If your sales force needs to target different types of customers and prospects, then typically you must formulate a new value proposition and develop a sales process for the new audience. The emergence of a new market channel required the hearing aids manufacturer to develop a revised value proposition and sales process tailored to the needs of a different type of customer.

2. Next, a sales strategy change requires reevaluation of the value proposition. Even if the audience your company reaches remains the same, if the value proposition changes, then your sales process is likely to change. At United Airlines, delivering a new value proposition to a largely unchanged group of target customers required considerable change in the sales process.

3. Finally, changing the sales strategy requires you to take a fresh look at the sales process. Even when the same customers are targeted and the value proposition is largely unchanged, a company can sometimes evolve its sales processes to achieve higher impact. For example, Novartis identified how changes in the specific activities emphasized during each step of the sales process could make for a more effective delivery of its value proposition. Figure 16-6 shows a set of questions that another company used to continuously improve

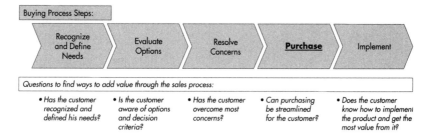

Figure 16-6. How one company identified opportunities to add value through the sales process

its sales process. The questions look at each step of the customer's buying process and help the selling company find ways to increase the effectiveness of its sales process by sharing expertise or information that can help buyers make the right purchasing decision.

Developing a New Sales Strategy When the Company Faces Commodification or Slowing Growth. When faced with the challenge of sustaining and improving success in markets that are experiencing increasing competition or slowing growth, many companies adopt a "consultative" sales approach to help them maintain sales, profits, and market share in the more challenging environment. These companies invest in training their sales forces in consultative selling approaches, but the most successful implementations of consultative selling require more than training—they start with a look at how the various elements of the sales strategy need to change in order to fully embrace an effective yet efficient consultative selling model.

A process like the one shown in Figure 16-5 can guide a successful sales strategy change—one that derives the most value from a consultative selling model:

- Start with customer segmentation and targeting. Understand your different customer segments and what those customers need and value. The framework in Figure 16-7 uses two dimensions—customer need for a product versus a solution, and a customer's level of expertise—to segment customers in order to understand what they value and what sales processes will be most effective with them.

- Next, determine what your different customer segments value so that you can develop the most effective value proposition for each segment. In the Figure 16-7 framework, a customer who needs a product that he knows a lot about probably values an easy and inexpensive purchasing process. A customer who wants a solution to an unfamiliar problem, on the other hand, will probably value advice and consulting throughout the purchase process. Your value propositions will be most effective when they are tailored to the specific needs of each of your customer segments.

- Finally, design a sales process that delivers value effectively and effi-

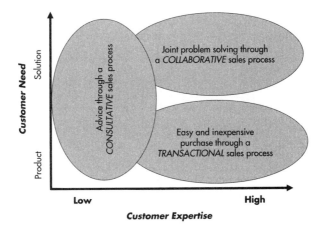

Figure 16-7. The role of customer expertise and needs in determining the value proposition and sales process

ciently to each of your market segments. As the example in Figure 16-7 shows, not every customer is likely to value a consultative sales process. Customer expertise and needs determine what type of sales process—transactional, consultative, or collaborative—is likely to be valued most by each of your customer segments.

Step 2: Implementing Sales Strategy Change by Aligning the Sales Effectiveness Drivers

Once a new sales strategy is developed, the next step is to implement it, which requires getting salespeople to change their activities and their behaviors so that the new selling process is carried out effectively. The Sales System framework provides an approach for implementing a sales strategy change.

Figure 16-8 shows a series of questions that helps in identifying the sales effectiveness driver changes needed to support and reinforce a new sales strategy. Once the needed changes have been identified, you will need to examine your sales force structure and roles, assess the skills and capabilities of your sales force, and finally, look at any needed enhancements that will encourage sales force activities that align with the new strategy.

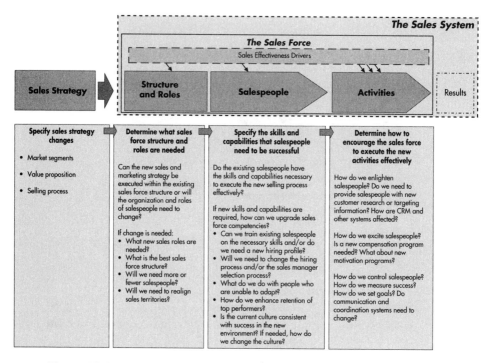

Figure 16-8. A process for implementing sales strategy change

Case Study Examples: Sales Strategy Change Across a Spectrum

Some sales strategy changes are very significant and involve a major overhaul of a company's market segments, value propositions, and selling processes. Other changes are more moderate, and still others are incremental. The scope of the sales strategy change determines the extent to which the sales effectiveness drivers will need to be adjusted.

Figure 16-9 shows a continuum of sales strategy change. The sections that follow describe the situations that United Airlines and Novartis faced and the solutions they implemented.

Refining the Sales Strategy to Accelerate Sales Growth at Novartis Pharmaceuticals. Even incremental changes in a sales strategy require careful attention to the sales effectiveness drivers. Pharmaceutical

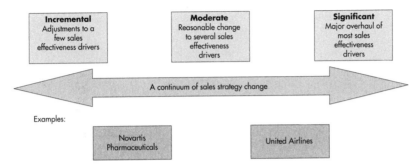

Figure 16-9. Two examples that span the spectrum of sales strategy change

manufacturer Novartis uses a structured process to continuously enhance its global sales effectiveness. An annual sales force effectiveness review helps the company identify ways to constantly improve the performance of its sales organization. Often this involves adjusting the company's sales strategy.

Figure 16-10 summarizes how sales strategy adjustments that came out of two sales effectiveness reviews at Novartis Pharmaceuticals in the United States were implemented using the sales strategy change framework (see Figure 16-8).

Example 1: Sales strategy enhancements and sales effectiveness driver changes that focus effort on high-value physicians. One of the first initiatives identified through the sales force effectiveness review process was an effectiveness-enhancing sales strategy adjustment for Novartis Pharmaceuticals in the United States. A 2001 analysis revealed that salespeople's time was scattered among a large number of physicians, many of whom did not write many prescriptions for the company's classes of drugs. Identifying the physicians the sales force should target resulted in a significant improvement in sales effectiveness. Novartis altered its sales activity to strategically concentrate on approximately the top 35 percent of physicians who wrote the most prescriptions for the company's classes of drugs.

Implementation of the new sales strategy required some adjustments to the sales effectiveness drivers.

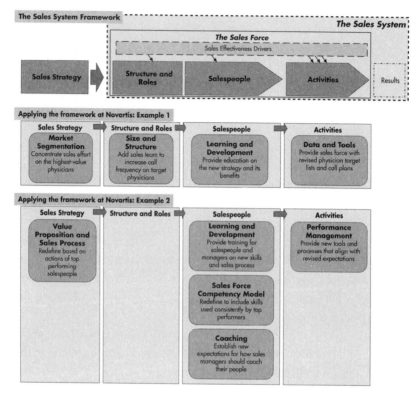

Figure 16-10. Changing the sales strategy at Novartis by aligning the sales effectiveness drivers

- **Structure and roles.** The addition of a new sales team helped the sales force increase the frequency of calls on the highest-value physicians.
- **Salespeople.** Training programs taught salespeople which physicians they should target and communicated the benefits of executing the new sales strategy.
- **Activities.** Marketing personnel provided targeting data and tools to allow the sales team to effectively retarget physicians across the sales force.

Following implementation of the initiative, the company experienced a significant acceleration in sales, which it attributed to the strategic shift in sales effort.

Example 2: Sales strategy enhancements and sales effectiveness driver changes that propagate value propositions and selling processes used by top performers. In another initiative that came out of the sales force effectiveness review process at Novartis, sales leaders observed high-performing salespeople (identified using Performance Frontier Analysis, described in Chapter 2) on typical sales calls in order to identify how they interacted with physicians. Average performers were observed on calls as well, and their behavior was contrasted with that of the high performers. Interviews with district sales managers and physicians provided further input for determining what sales force behaviors were most successful in educating physicians regarding the value of Novartis products. Novartis identified a set of success principles differentiating top-performing salespeople and used them to improve the sales process for the entire sales force.

Sales leaders focused on specific behaviors that could improve every step of the sales process and move physicians incrementally along the path to regularly prescribing Novartis products, including:

- Emulating the relationship-building activities used by top performers to improve their access to physicians
- Using the call preparation, probing, and listening techniques used consistently by top performers to better understand customers and their needs
- Adopting the approaches utilized by top performers to adapt communication strategies to physician and patient needs so as to deliver the company's value proposition more effectively
- Emulating the communication techniques and relationship-building activities used by top performers to strongly reinforce value

Implementing the sales strategy change required several adjustments to the sales effectiveness drivers in order to align sales force systems and programs with the new selling model, reinforce the desired behaviors, and set new expectations for salespeople and managers.

- **Salespeople.** The sales force success principles were incorporated into a selling skills training program for the sales organization called Performance Frontier—The Next Generation in Sales Excellence.

After the initial phase of training, "mini-training" refresher modules reinforced specific elements of the training and helped drive high adoption of the new selling model by the entire sales force. Sales managers also received new leadership training. A team composed of sales, human resources, and training and development leaders created a new sales force competency model and established hiring guidelines and coaching expectations for managers that were aligned around the new competency model.

- Activities. A new coaching tool and field coaching report were rolled out to aid managers in more effectively evaluating salespeople within the new selling model. The company also realigned the performance management processes to reflect the new sales approach and selling competencies.

The new selling approach was linked to a more favorable perception of Novartis salespeople among physicians and better sales results, and the success of the program in the United States led Novartis to adapt the new training approach for use with its sales organizations in other countries. In addition, Novartis has used Performance Frontier Analysis to identify success behaviors for roles outside the sales organization. Annual sales force effectiveness reviews at Novartis continue to reveal new opportunities for sales strategy improvements.

Aligning the Sales Effectiveness Drivers to Effect a Major Sales Strategy Change at United Airlines. Earlier in this chapter, we described how United transformed its sales strategy to embrace a value-based selling approach that focused customers on the total business value that United creates.

Figure 16-11 summarizes the process of transforming the sales strategy at United Airlines using the sales strategy change framework (see Figure 16-8).

"Value-based selling is simple in concept: Win and grow customers through product, service, and program offerings whose total value relative to price exceeds that of alternatives. But the reality has proven more difficult. Transforming from deeply engrained behaviors such as friendship, product features, and

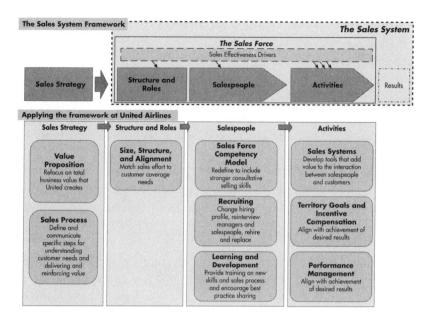

Figure 16-11. Changing the sales strategy at United Airlines by aligning the sales effectiveness drivers

price-based selling to value-based selling requires dramatic shifts in sales culture, strategy, operations, skills, and execution. A comprehensive and purposefully orchestrated approach to capability building is required to achieve excellence in value-based selling."

Mike Moorman,
Managing Principal, ZS Associates, Chicago

The new United Airlines sales strategy. United's new sales strategy was formulated based on extensive customer research with more than 1,200 corporations and travel agencies. This research revealed that many customer segments placed significant value on factors other than a low-price ticket and a good network of routes. Many customers were looking for what United terms "valued consultative travel management support." These customer insights shaped the development of the new sales strategy.

Instead of relying on price and personal relationships alone to drive sales, United's new strategy required salespeople to work closely with corporate and travel agent customers to understand their needs and show them how United could tailor a customer-specific mix of airline routes and seats, consultative services, travel management and support programs, and comfort and productivity for business travelers that created business value well beyond best-price alternatives. The new sales strategy included a new value proposition and a new sales process for delivering that value to customers.

Figure 16-12 summarizes the key steps in the new sales process.

Aligning the sales effectiveness drivers around the new sales strategy at United. Multiple adjustments in the sales effectiveness drivers were needed to bring the sales organization into alignment with the new sales strategy.

- Structure and roles. Since the new sales strategy required different selling activities, United reevaluated the size and structure of its sales force in light of the revised customer workload. The company developed a new sales structure that matched the number of global, national, key, and field account managers to the opportunity, and redesigned field sales territories to ensure that sales effort was allocated effectively in terms of market potential. The new structure included a telesales group that encouraged efficient support of selected small and medium-size accounts.

- Salespeople. To make the new sales strategy a success, United needed to effect changes in its salespeople and their skills. The company developed a new sales force competency model that outlined the skills and capabilities needed for success in executing the new sales strategy. In addition to traditional sales and relationship-building

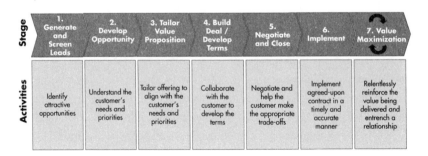

Figure 16-12. Key steps in the sales process at United Airlines

skills, the new model called for salespeople who could work closely with customers to understand their business needs and demonstrate how United could meet those needs. Sales leaders implemented several changes in sales effectiveness drivers to align the sales organization around the new competency model. A revised sales force hiring profile was developed, based on the new competency model. The change in hiring profile required United sales leaders to make some difficult personnel decisions. The entire sales force had to reinterview for jobs, and approximately 30 percent of the people who did not have the capability or desire to adapt to the new selling model were replaced. Once the new sales force was selected, all salespeople received training in the new sales process and the consultative selling skills they would need in order to be successful at executing the process. Sales managers received additional training in how to effectively coach salespeople in the new process. Sales leaders also established mechanisms to encourage sharing of best practices across the organization.

- Activities. United implemented several changes to the sales effectiveness drivers to ensure that the sales force effectively carried out the activities needed for successful implementation of the new strategy. Sales leaders developed systems to assist in the interaction between salespeople and their customers. A suite of sales technology products—designed to help salespeople demonstrate to customers the value that United offers—permitted a more structured, menu-based discussion that helped salespeople better understand the unique needs and priorities of customers so that solutions could be tailored to best align with those needs. The technology also helped reinforce the total business value of solutions. Sales leaders introduced territory goals, based on measures and outcomes on which salespeople could have an impact. The goals reflected territory opportunity and were designed to motivate profitable share growth, not just revenue. Sales contests recognized and rewarded the salespeople who attained the highest percentage of goal. Sales dashboards created transparency concerning territory performance and goal achievement. Revamped performance management systems encouraged sales force behaviors that aligned with the new sales strategy and that would drive the desired results.

What Actions Were the Most Important in Achieving the United Sales Strategy Transformation?

Jeff Foland, senior vice president of worldwide sales for United Airlines, identifies the following actions as key contributors to the successful implementation of United's new sales strategy:

- "We anchored everything around deep customer insights gained from unprecedented industry research."

- "We developed and institutionalized a more effective and structured sales process, providing us with a common language around how we sell and a structure around our training and tools."

- "We were very explicit about what success looks like for account management and what good first-line sales management and coaching means."

- "We introduced discipline to call planning fundamentals and institutionalized and recognized good performance by creating heroes and holding them up for the organization to see."

Results at United. The new sales strategy had positive results for United's sales force, its customers, and the company. Sales force feedback was very positive. Salespeople stated that the transformed culture was more strategic, professional, and aggressive and that customers seemed pleased with the new approach. Comments from customers include, "This is the most professional sales process I've seen" and "This is more thorough work than anything I've seen from an airline and is tailored specifically around our needs and priorities."

Following implementation of the new sales strategy, United established contractual relationships with many high-priority new accounts and renewed contractual relationships with many high-priority existing accounts. Company leaders felt that the new sales strategy made substantial performance contributions worldwide as fuel prices soared past $100 a barrel. As fuel costs continue to rise, further challenges lie ahead for United and the rest of the airline industry.

CHAPTER 17

Allocating Sales Resources to Maximize Results

The sales force is the company's sales resource allocation engine—the ways in which salespeople distribute their efforts across customers, products, and selling activities has considerable impact on sales and profits. And dissatisfaction with the way salespeople spend their time occurs even in sales organizations with sound sales strategies, effective organizational structures, and salespeople who have strong skills and capabilities. Small but demanding customers; marginally profitable, nonstrategic products; internal meetings with questionable sales benefit—these are just a few examples of the many time traps and time wasters that can reduce the effectiveness of a good sales force.

Sales leaders frequently share their frustrations with us about how sales force attention often gets diverted.

- "My salespeople don't spend enough time with the valuable but challenging customers."
- "New business development is lagging. The salespeople spend too much time with friends and family."

- "Strategic products aren't getting enough sales force support. Salespeople prefer to sell what's fun and easy."
- "Our new products are being ignored."
- "My salespeople don't spend enough time with customers because they have too much administrative work."
- "The best salespeople are always asked to participate on internal task forces and projects at headquarters—when are they supposed to see their customers?"

Some companies have cultures of empowerment in which salespeople are evaluated on their results and are free to spend their time in whatever ways they think best. Other companies exercise greater control, with managers giving salespeople specific directions on how to spend their time. Yet even in cultures where sales leaders desire high levels of control and are confident that they know how salespeople should spend their time, salespeople often work alone and unsupervised, and individual salespeople ultimately decide which work activities they will perform. Such choices typically result from a combination of many factors, including what the salesperson enjoys doing, what his customers are pushing for or against, and what his managers and the company direct him to do through training, coaching, performance management, and the incentive compensation plan.

Whatever their origin, errors in sales force time allocation are common. More important, they are costly for any sales organization.

The Outcomes

Misallocation of sales resources is reflected in the activities and behaviors of salespeople. Figure 17-1 lays out some of the many choices salespeople have about how to spend their work time. They must decide how their time with customers should be spent—which accounts they will call on, which products they will sell, and which selling activities they will engage in. In addition, they must decide how much time to spend on non-customer-focused activities that the company mandates—internal meetings, training, and administration.

Effort allocation mistakes fall into two categories:

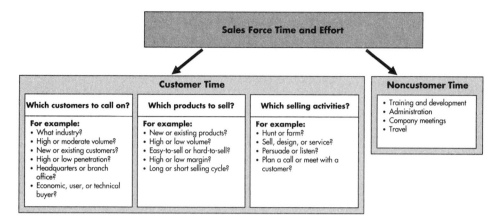

Figure 17-1. The sales force: a resource allocation engine

- Misallocation of time spent with customers. Salespeople may spend too much time with less valuable customers and/or too much time selling unprofitable or nonstrategic products. Also, they may engage in selling activities that are not very effective at creating customer relationships and sales.

- Too much time spent in activities other than selling to customers. The company may ask salespeople to attend meetings, participate in training sessions, help with internal projects, feed data into complex CRM systems, or engage in other activities that do little to drive sales results.

Each of these sales force time traps reduces the effectiveness of a sales organization. Smart sales leaders know that diagnosing allocation problems is an important step in bringing sales force effort into proper alignment with their sales strategy.

Assessing the Time That Salespeople Spend with Customers

Are Important Customers Getting Enough Attention? Many sales forces spend too much time with easy and familiar accounts ("friends and family," as they are sometimes called), time that could be more productively spent with more important customers. Take the case of a computer and office supply company that sells a broad line of products over the telephone to small and medium-size businesses. Salespeople's earnings come entirely from commissions on sales. When a salesperson sells a new account, it becomes part of her ongoing responsibility, and she is expected to maintain the customer relationship and generate repeat business. Veteran salespeople typically have developed very lucrative customer lists over the years. Many of them no longer need to make outbound calls, since they can live comfortably by taking orders from loyal customers. But the market is becoming increasingly competitive, and the company feels that it is leaving money on the table because many high-potential customers are not getting enough proactive attention.

Salespeople often spend more time than they should with low-potential accounts. For example, a pharmaceuticals company has a large sales force that calls on physicians. Salespeople are asked to focus their effort on the top 30 percent of physicians (Segments A and B), who write 90 percent of the prescriptions for the classes of drugs that the company sells. Figure 17-2 compares ideal calls (how the sales force should spend its time in order to maximize profitability) with actual calls. The results are dramatic: This sales force is wasting close to half its time calling on physician segments that are not profitable. The data illustrate the familiar 80-20 rule (80 percent of sales come from 20 percent of customers)

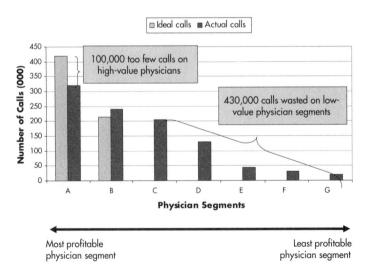

Figure 17-2. Example of misallocation of effort across customers

and also reflect the less-well-known corollary to that rule: The high investment that most companies make in the bottom 30 percent of customers cuts profits in half.

Demanding Customers Are Not Always Important Customers

Salespeople at a financing company spent a lot of time assisting small but demanding broker customers. These brokers, who generated very little revenue for the financing company, kept asking for help in developing their own businesses, and the financing company's salespeople found it hard to say no. As a result, they had very little time left to increase their business with the more profitable large brokers.

Are Important Products Getting Enough Sales Effort? When salespeople sell several products, they must choose the products to emphasize with each customer, and they often decide to focus on the products that they find familiar, easy, or fun to sell. At other times, salespeople are influenced by sales contests and incentives that product managers put in place to boost short-term sales of specific products. Sometimes the products that get too little attention from the sales force may have strategic importance or may provide significant profit opportunity for the company.

The data in Figure 17-3 show the profit impact of allocating sales resources across a broad product line at a medical supply company. The

Product Line	Current Effort Allocation, Salesperson Full-Time Equivalents (S-FTE)	Incremental Return for an Additional S-FTE
A	18	$164,381
B	9	$ 69,245
C	10	$385,696
D	31	$270,206
E	23	$198,068

Figure 17-3. Projected incremental return on additional sales effort for five product lines at a medical supply company

company wanted to estimate the relationship between sales force effort and sales for five product lines. The data show the current number of salesperson full-time equivalents (S-FTE) allocated to each product line and the estimated multiyear incremental return (loss) if one additional S-FTE were added to (removed from) each product line. Profits are maximized when incremental returns on sales force effort are equal across all products; yet the ratio of the largest incremental return ($386,000 for Product C) to the smallest incremental return ($69,000 for Product B) was 5.6, which indicates a serious misallocation of selling effort across products. A shift of just one S-FTE of effort from Product B to Product C would increase return by $317,000. Return could be increased still further if effort allocation were optimized across the entire product line.

The critical issue of sales effort allocation to products arises every time new products are launched. It is a tough balancing act to find the right mix of effort allocation across existing and new products. New products need attention and focus if they are to succeed, but if they consume too much sales force time, sales of existing products will suffer.

Is the Sales Force Engaged in the Highest-Impact Sales Activities? Even if your sales force targets the right customers and products, it can fall into the trap of spending time on wasteful activities that add little value or that should be done by someone else.

Figure 17-4 shows how a sales force that sells newspaper advertising spent its time, according to a survey of the company's salespeople. The sales force was engaged in active selling only about 35 percent of the time. Approximately 40 percent of its time was spent servicing accounts, including several activities that could be performed more efficiently by sales assistants, who were paid less than the salespeople. When lower-cost sales assistants took over these servicing duties, the salespeople had more time to spend on higher-impact selling activities.

Assessing the Value of Time Spent on Activities Other Than Selling to the Customer

Time spent on planning, training, travel, and other activities besides selling to customers should help make salespeople's time with customers more valuable. But this does not always happen. When noncustomer

	Type of Activity		Activity	Percent of Time
Customer Time	Selling	34.6%	1. Active selling to advertisers (face-to-face or phone)	22.8%
			2. Active selling to nonadvertisers (face-to-face or phone)	10.7%
			3. Entertaining advertisers and nonadvertisers	1.1%
	Servicing	40.8%	4. Developing presentations and proposals	4.6%
			5. Account planning	4.4%
			6. Account maintenance and customer service	8.5%
			7. Insertion orders	8.4%
			8. Creative and layout work	4.9%
			9. Dealing with production problems	4.0%
			10. Dealing with credit, billing, and collection problems	6.0%
Noncustomer Time	Administration	16.8%	11. Meetings	3.0%
			12. Paperwork and administration	7.6%
			13. Training	2.0%
			14. Travel (to/from accounts)	4.2%
	Other	7.8%	15. Other	7.8%
	Total			100.0%

Figure 17-4. How salespeople in a newspaper advertising sales force spent their time

time does not add value, it can significantly reduce salesperson effectiveness. Some familiar time traps include the following.

Too Many Meetings. Sales leaders at a company in Australia discovered that members of the sales force spent 40 workdays (17.5 percent of their available time) in internal sales meetings: 16 days in training, 8 days in quarterly district planning meetings, 4 days in a national sales meeting, 7 days in meetings with the product marketing groups, and 5 days in other ad hoc meetings. Overnight, the company cut the number of internal meeting days in half and increased the time the sales force spent with customers by almost 9 percent.

Too Much Administration. Many salespeople spend too much time doing things that have little direct sales impact. The paperwork trap of 20 years ago has become the technology trap of today—salespeople spend countless hours answering and sending internal e-mails, dealing with requests and directives from multiple marketing managers, and/or feeding data into awkward CRM systems that create few benefits relative to the amount of time they consume. A district sales manager for a company in Spain told us, "The most important part of my job is to protect the salespeople that I manage from all the requests from headquarters."

Lack of Headquarters Support. When salespeople do not receive adequate support from headquarters, they spend too much time solving problems that others should be addressing, such as dealing with production, distribution, or service issues. Salespeople can spend hours preparing sales materials or proposals that could have been adapted from boilerplates prepared much more efficiently by personnel at headquarters.

Shadow Accounting. When the system for administering sales incentive compensation is unreliable or inconsistent, salespeople can spend a lot of time tracking and checking their sales numbers to verify that they have attained their goals or qualified for an incentive payout. One financial services firm estimated that its salespeople spent 10 percent of their time chasing invoices, verifying pay calculations, and lobbying management for incentive payout corrections.

Too Much Travel. When sales territories are not geographically compact and travel is inefficient, salespeople can spend too much time traveling and too little time in front of customers. Insufficient planning and organization can also lead to haphazard travel schedules, inefficient use of time, or situations in which salespeople make time-consuming trips to accomplish something that could have been done over the telephone.

The Behaviors

Salespeople use a variety of decision rules when choosing whom to call on, what to sell, and which activities to perform. While all of the following decision rules have merit in some situations, they often lead to an allocation of sales resources that does not serve the company well.

Do Everything

Sell Everything That's in the Bag. One company's sales plan called for each of its 100 salespeople to sell all of its 37 products. The result: Each product received an almost equal allocation of the sales force's time. An analysis showed that profits could be dramatically improved if the sales force focused on just 8 of the 37 products.

Sell to Everyone in the Territory. A salesperson who sells to small and medium-size businesses (for example, a seller of office supplies or employee insurance programs) typically has many thousands of prospects in her territory. A typical pharmaceutical salesperson has 400 physicians in his territory. In these selling organizations, the 80-20 rule almost always applies—a large percentage of the company' sales come from a small percentage of the company's accounts. In such situations, salespeople can easily make the error of allocating their time too uniformly across customers with very different sales potential.

Do What Is Best for Me

Do What Makes Me the Most Money. If a large portion of sales force pay comes from incentives, a poorly designed compensation plan can lead salespeople to engage in activities that maximize their earnings, sometimes sacrificing what is best for the business or for customers.

Do What Is Easy, Comfortable, and Fun. Salespeople often shy away from difficult accounts and spend too much time calling on "friends and family." Similarly, when salespeople sell a broad product line, they have many ways to be successful and may choose to sell only the products they know best. Maintaining a good relationship with a tough buyer at a major account creates another set of challenges that some salespeople may choose to avoid.

Do What Others Ask Me to Do

Do What the Customer Wants. Customer focus is a dominant theme; salespeople are told to "put the customer first," and they may be evaluated and paid based on customer satisfaction measures. Yet a salesperson who always does what the customer wants is likely to spend too much time with demanding, low-potential customers, time that could be better spent with higher-potential customers.

Do What My Manager Wants. Often sales managers and the company are not aware of the best strategies for allocating effort. They may lack the proper information or focus on the wrong metrics. Some sales forces manage salespeople based on the number of calls they make.

Consequently, in order to make challenging call targets, salespeople may choose to make several easy but not very productive calls on friendly customers, rather than making more difficult calls on prospects that are likely to produce a high return. An inappropriate metric can get in the way of good effort allocation.

Do What the Data Suggest Is Best

Focus Effort Where Past Sales Have Been Highest. There is logic to a decision rule that aligns effort to sales; such a rule encourages salespeople to protect their revenue base. However, since the rule ignores account potential or the sensitivity of sales to effort, salespeople who allocate all their effort to accounts where they have had past success may perhaps miss out on significant opportunities at high-potential accounts that have not yet been penetrated.

Focus Effort Where Potential Is Highest. Allocating effort based on future account potential can also be a flawed strategy. Matching effort to potential can encourage salespeople to go after big prospects where there is a low likelihood of success. If high-potential customers and market segments are not responsive to selling effort, efforts to sell them may be wasted.

What Can Be Done to Improve Sales Resource Allocation?

Make sure that the decision rules your salespeople use to allocate their effort create the best possible outcomes for your customers and for your company. The process of redirecting work to the highest-impact customers, products, and sales activities involves two main steps. The first is to assess how your salespeople currently spend their time and identify improvements that need to be made. The second step is to effect this change by adjusting the sales effectiveness drivers so that they align with the desired effort allocation strategy.

Assess How Salespeople Currently Spend Their Time

Sales force time can be tracked in varying degrees of detail. Some salespeople perform a consistent set of activities across their customer base or follow a well-defined, multistep sales process. If that's the case in your company, you can track the frequency, duration, and content of cus-tomer meetings through a CRM system. If your sales process is not tracked through a computerized system, then you can ask your sales-people to keep detailed time logs for a specified period or send an observer on a random set of sales calls to assess how salespeople spend their time. You can then summarize these data across the sales force and analyze them to find out how much time your salespeople are spending on various products, customers, and markets, or sales activities.

If your salespeople are engaging in a consultative sales process, the activities required for them to prepare for, execute, and follow up on sales calls vary a great deal. You'll need to observe your salespeople and solicit input from them to understand how their time is spent and to identify time-consuming activities that perhaps could be performed more efficiently in another way.

The newspaper advertising sales force that is the subject of Figure 17-4 used a consultative sales process that involved a mix of selling, servicing, and administration. Sales managers developed time estimates by first observing salespeople to determine the different types of activi-ties that they performed and then administering questionnaires that asked the salespeople to indicate how much time they spent on each of the various activities. Sales manager interviews and focus groups can also be used to gauge how time is spent.

Browning-Ferris Industries Asks Salespeople to Keep Diaries of Activity

---

Waste collection company Browning-Ferris Industries (BFI) conducted time-profiling studies to assess the efficiency of its sales force. Over a six-week period, salespeople kept daily diaries of their activities. The company discovered that salespeople were spending as much as 50 percent of their time on activities such as administration and travel. To increase efficiency, the company established an internal telesales force to take over some lower-value-added tasks, including selling to small accounts and service-related activities. Efficiency increased, and the company was able to cut its sales force from 1,600 to 1,250 people.

Assessments of how sales forces spend their time often reveal that too much time is being spent on noncritical selling activities. In many companies, planning meetings, training sessions, and reporting requirements whittle down the number of days that salespeople spend in the field. This is especially a problem in large, multiproduct organizations in which uncoordinated demands by headquarters staff can burden salespeople with non-value-adding tasks. A zero-based accounting of where the days and hours go and a reexamination of what is truly valuable can add considerably to sales force capacity. One company appointed a "czar of STUFF" whose job was to police and rationalize the communication between headquarters personnel and salespeople.

Seek to Change Sales Effort Allocation by Adjusting the Sales Effectiveness Drivers

To redirect sales effort to the right customers, products, and activities, use the sales effectiveness drivers.

A Framework: The Drivers of Sales Effort Allocation. Figure 17-5 provides a framework for how the sales effectiveness drivers influence deployment of effort. While much of the sales force activity is affected by factors such as customers, competitors, and product quality, the decisions that sales leaders make can have an equally big impact on how salespeople spend their time. Sales effort allocation is influenced by:

- The roles and responsibilities that sales leaders give salespeople, which are defined by the structure of the sales force and its size, and by territory alignments (the *definers*)

- The skills, capabilities, and confidence of salespeople, which are influenced by the quality of the people who are hired and the way they are trained and coached (the *shapers*)

- The guidance that salespeople receive from the company through the information, training, and coaching they receive to help them do their jobs (the *enlighteners*)

- Salespeople's motivation, which sales leaders can affect through incentives, motivation programs, and strong leadership (the *exciters*)

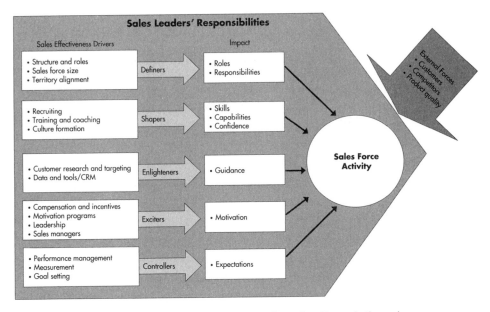

Figure 17-5. Influencing sales resource allocation through the sales effectiveness drivers

- Sales leaders' expectations, reflected in the way they evaluate and manage salespeople (the *controllers*)

You can influence the deployment of sales effort by adjusting the sales effectiveness drivers to create the desired impact.

Using the Framework to Address Sales Effort Allocation Challenges. You can discover solutions to any sales effort allocation challenge through a diagnostic process guided by the Figure 17-5 framework. Consider one very common allocation challenge:

"Salespeople are not devoting enough time to developing new business."

How do you respond to this challenge? Start by identifying its underlying causes, which typically originate in one or more of five "impact" categories:

- Roles and responsibilities. Salespeople do not have the time or the bandwidth to develop new business.

- Skills, capabilities, and confidence. Salespeople are not very good at developing new business.

- Guidance. Salespeople do not know which prospects to call on or what to say to them.

- Motivation. Calling on prospects is hard, and salespeople would rather do something else.

- Expectations. Salespeople do not realize that new business development is an important priority.

The process of diagnosing a concern and identifying possible solutions involves working backward through the linkages in the Figure 17-5 framework. The diagnostic process illustrated in Figure 17-6 flips the Figure 17-5 linkages from right to left to show how a step-by-step diagnosis leads to identification of probable causes and, ultimately, solutions.

The diagnosis begins with the activity concern: "Salespeople are not devoting enough time to new business development." Through a series of questions, we can identify the probable causes of the concern, which link to remedial sales effectiveness drivers. You can adapt the questions used to diagnose this particular activity concern to address any sales resource allocation challenge.

In Figure 17-6, the questions are sequenced so that those that are asked first link to the sales effectiveness drivers that are easiest to change. For example, a sales organization can generally make adjustments to performance management processes, goals, and prospect lists fairly quickly and without significant disruption. The questions near the bottom of Figure 17-6 lead to sales effectiveness drivers that are more challenging to change—the hiring program and the size and the structure of the sales force. Because these drivers determine who will be included in the sales force and the assignment of customer responsibility, changing them is generally more disruptive, is harder to implement, and will take longer to have an impact.

Some companies have considerable success in effecting change by leveraging the easier-to-change sales effectiveness drivers. Others have

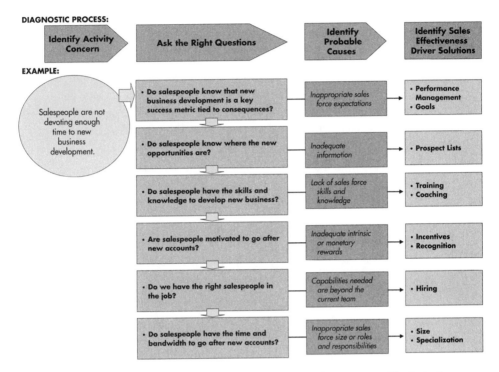

Figure 17-6. A process for diagnosing sales activity concerns illustrated with an example

to rely on the harder-to-change drivers to create an effective solution. Often solutions require adjustments to multiple drivers.

Formalizing the Sales Process Can Increase Sales Force Time Spent on Important Activities

At times, sales leaders observe their salespeople engaging in a range of activities that suits their own style and interests. Salespeople may spend time doing what works for them—comfortable customers, familiar products and services—resulting in insufficient customer-value selling. When the sales process is highly variable across salespeople and sales leaders desire greater control over effort allocation, they can bring greater structure and discipline to the sales process by formalizing it, and perhaps even rethinking the sales strategy—market segmentation, value proposition development, and sales process definition (see Chapter 3). If the current sales force activity diverges significantly from the desired sales process, then perhaps a major overhaul of the company's sales strategy is in order (see Chapter 16). If, on the other hand, the formalization requires only a moderate change, then a series of questions like the ones in Figure 17-6 can help sales leaders identify which sales effectiveness driver solutions will be most effective at formalizing and implementing the company's desired sales process. The benefits of efforts to formalize sales processes are primarily realized by the 60 percent of salespeople in the middle tier of performance. The highest performers typically resist such sales process formalization initiatives.

The Questions and Potential Solutions. Companies we have worked with have used the diagnostic process shown in Figure 17-6 to reveal many sales effectiveness driver solutions for addressing sales effort misallocation across customers, products, and selling activities. In this section, we provide examples of general solutions organized around the probable causes of the misallocation. Because the diagnostic questions asked here are more general than the questions posed in Figure 17-6, they apply to any sales resource allocation challenge. As in the Figure 17-6 example, the sequencing of the questions is important.

Do salespeople have appropriate expectations? Salespeople are likely to misallocate their time if they are unclear about what is expected of them. For example, if salespeople do not know that the company wants them to spend significant time selling a new strategic product or developing business with new rather than existing customers, they are likely to create their own decision rules to determine how to spend their time, and these rules can be misaligned with company expectations. When sales effort misallocation is the result of poorly communicated expectations, the solutions lie in the performance management system and the goal-setting process. Some possible remedies include:

- Communicating with the sales force clearly: "Here is what we want you to do," or "Here are the results we expect you to achieve for each customer, market segment, or product." One way to do this is to provide salespeople with goals that encourage the desired behaviors—for example, sales goals for specific products or customers—rather than providing a single aggregate goal. Goal attainment can then be used to motivate the desired behaviors.

- Measuring how salespeople are spending their time, tracking their sales, and providing them with ongoing feedback on these metrics. Remember: "What gets measured gets done."

- Incorporating activity and results metrics into the performance management process, having sales managers review the metrics with salespeople regularly, and using these metrics as criteria for coaching and performance evaluation.

Goals Help to Communicate Sales Activity Expectations to New Salespeople

At a small executive search firm, new salespeople are given goals for three important activities that the company believes drive sales success: daily calls to potential job candidates, company visits, and "balls in the air," or leads that could convert to sales. These activity goals help new salespeople understand what is expected of them and what they need to do if they are to be successful in the long run. The desired activities are emphasized in the training of new salespeople, are reinforced through coaching by the sales manager, and are tracked and reported on weekly. New salespeople even earn small bonuses on top of their salary for meeting their activity goals. These activity goals help new salespeople make the best possible use of their time while they are learning the business and establishing their referral networks. After several months, successful salespeople have mastered the behaviors necessary for success and are empowered to work more independently. Their activities are no longer tracked, and they make the transition to the firm's traditional sales compensation plan, which pays commissions exclusively.

Do salespeople have the information they need to do their jobs? Sometimes salespeople know what the company wants them to do, but do not have the information they need to make it happen. The company says, "Develop business with new customers," but salespeople are not sure how to go about identifying good prospects. The company says, "Demonstrate the new product in competitive accounts," but salespeople do not know where the vulnerable competitive accounts are and are not sure how to perform demonstrations that highlight the company's competitive advantages. When the sales force is not spending time on the right activities because it lacks guidance about what to do, the answer is to provide the needed information. Some possible remedies include:

- Investing in the development of customer databases that contain relevant, up-to-date information to enhance salespeople's customer knowledge
- Providing salespeople with easy-to-use tools that make information actionable and help salespeople do their jobs better
- Showing salespeople how the right effort allocation makes them more effective and enables them to increase their personal earnings

---

Identifying the Best New Prospects for Salespeople Increases New Business Development

---

Salespeople at a not-for-profit organization had historically received little direction from management about which prospective business customers they should contact to obtain sponsorship revenues. Each salesperson was given a list that included thousands of prospective sponsors. Salespeople had to rely on their own experience and intuition to decide which prospects to call on. In an effort to increase sponsorship revenues, the company conducted a study to determine the value and the cost of calling on prospective sponsors in different market segments. The segments were defined by industry and business size. The study was based on primary market research, analysis of company historical data, and the gathering of structured sales management input on the growth potential of different segments, the cost of calling on the segments, and the likelihood of success. The study suggested that some segments had a very high expected return on the investment in sales coverage, while others had a low or even a negative expected return. When sales leaders shared these results with salespeople, their sales efforts became much more focused on the types of prospects that were most likely to become sponsors. The time the salespeople spent prospecting increased, and revenues from new sponsors rose as well.

Sharing information with salespeople regarding which customers to spend time with and which products to emphasize can have a measurable impact on sales. Figure 17-7 shows the analysis that one company used to educate its salespeople about how they could use their time more effectively to earn more incentive pay. The company analyzed data from the previous year to formulate a plan that reflected the profit-maximizing allocation of sales effort across customers and products. Management tracked salespeople's activities over the course of a year to see how closely they followed the recommended plan, and also tracked their performance.

The left side of Figure 17-7 shows the benefits of following the suggested call plan. Salespeople who followed the plan (that is, who allocated their time across customers and products the way the company suggested) had greater success in attaining their goals than those who

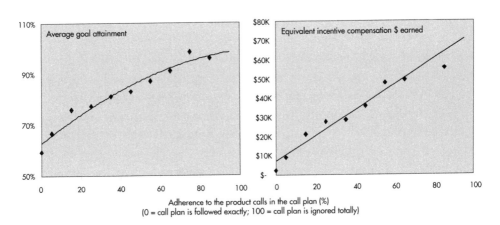

♦ = Groups of salespeople organized by how closely they follow the company-suggested call plan.

Salespeople who adhere to the company-suggested call plan have higher average goal attainment and earn more money.

Figure 17-7. The value of effective sales force effort allocation and the impact on incentive compensation

did not adhere to the plan. The right side of Figure 17-7 shows sales-people how much more incentive money they could make if they followed the suggested call plan. The company provided this information to every salesperson and empowered the sales force to make the right decisions about how to allocate their time.

Do salespeople have the skills and knowledge needed to be successful? Even if salespeople know what the company wants them to do and have the information necessary to make well-informed decisions, they still may lack the skills they need if they are to be successful. While some of the characteristics needed for sales success are inherent in the candidate (such as energy level and intellect), much of the required knowledge and many sales skills can be developed through training and coaching. If salespeople are avoiding important customers, products, or activities because they lack customer knowledge, product knowledge, or specific sales skills (such as how to negotiate effectively or how to close a sale), or because they lack confidence, then the remedy for the problem is coaching and training.

Improved New Product Training Increases Distributor Support of New Products

---

In the mid-1990s, sales leaders at computer disk drive manufacturer Seagate Technology Inc. observed that the company's distributors were often reluctant to sell Seagate's new products. The considerable amount of time it took the distributor's salespeople to get comfortable with these new products meant lost opportunity for Seagate and kept the company from enjoying the competitive advantage of being first to market. Seagate provided product training to distributors' salespeople, but it focused mostly on how the products were designed rather than on how to sell them effectively. While the training was adequate for the best and most experienced salespeople, who could wade through the technical detail and pick out the most usable information, it left the average salesperson overwhelmed and unsure of where to start with customers. To improve the effectiveness of its training and get all distributor salespeople comfortable selling new products more quickly, Seagate redesigned its training approach and focused on communicating what salespeople needed to know to sell the value of the Seagate products. Topics such as "Why people buy the product," "The best way to find and qualify buyers," and "How can I differentiate the product from competitive options?" replaced a good deal of the technical detail that had formerly been covered in training sessions. As a result, distributor salespeople became skilled at selling new Seagate products and provided stronger support for new product launches.

Are salespeople motivated to do what the company wants? Motivation pushes salespeople to act. Salespeople need to be motivated to do what the company wants them to do, whether that means selling a new product, developing new accounts, or entering data into a CRM system. Salespeople are motivated when they perceive that value results from their efforts—whether that value is career success, recognition of achievement, personal satisfaction, monetary rewards, or all of the above. When important sales tasks are not getting done because salespeople are not motivated to do them, some possible remedies include:

- Changing the incentive plan so that greater rewards are tied to the desired behavior
- Aligning the criteria for nonmonetary recognitions, like membership in the President's Club, to the desired sales activities
- Publicly recognizing those who are successful at the desired activities and celebrating their success
- Demonstrating to the sales force how a failure to grow business leads to lost market share, insufficient word of mouth among customers, and less long-term income for salespeople

Companies often leverage their incentive plans to direct sales effort to strategically important products and customers. For example:

- When a medical instruments manufacturer wanted its sales force to spend more time trying to displace competitive accounts, it offered a bonus for every competitive instrument displacement, encouraging salespeople to spend more time with important competitive accounts and helping the company increase its market share.

- When shipping and logistics company Federal Express wanted to encourage its salespeople to spend more time on three strategically important product lines, it gave salespeople goals for each of the three lines and provided them with weekly updates on their progress toward the goals. Salespeople earned certain bonuses and commissions if all three goals were achieved. The new incentive plan helped to ensure that the three key product lines got the majority of the sales force's attention.

Do we have the right salespeople in the job? While some of the skills and knowledge of effective salespeople can be developed through training and coaching, other capabilities needed for success are inherent in the person and therefore need to be screened for in the recruiting process. Training and coaching have limited ability to affect such traits as self-motivation, intellectual flexibility, and the will to win. In technical sales roles, education and aptitude may also be traits that a company has to hire for. When misallocation occurs because people with the wrong capabilities are in the job, sales leaders must address the challenge through better recruiting and retention of high performers. Remedies include:

- Changing the hiring profile to reflect the capabilities needed for success, and changing the recruiting process to screen candidates for those capabilities
- Evaluating current salespeople and encouraging those who lack the capabilities necessary for success to seek other jobs
- Changing the sales culture so that salespeople with the right characteristics and capabilities will want to join and stay with the company

---

A Hiring Profile That Emphasizes Sales Ability Over Industry Experience
Increases Sales Force Focus on the Activities
That Create the Most Sales

In the mid-1990s, sales leaders at E. B. Bradley Company, a distributor of construction and woodworking supplies, realized that the company's practice of hiring salespeople with strong industry knowledge, rather than sales background and desire, was no longer working well. The company's sales force was made up of experienced construction people, many of whom were former clients. Salespeople could talk about the technical details of tools and woods, but many of them were not very good at identifying whom to call on, following up on leads, understanding customers' business needs, and overcoming setbacks. Some salespeople spent considerable time talking shop with other Bradley salespeople rather than meeting with customers and prospects. Salespeople focused on the activities that they enjoyed and were good at, rather than on what was needed to drive business success in a sluggish economy.

The company changed its hiring strategy. Rather than looking for industry experience, the company began to hire salespeople who knew how to sell and liked to sell, and then educated them about the industry. At the same time, systems for generating leads were improved, and salespeople were made more accountable for results. Some of the existing salespeople bought into the new system, and those who did not moved on to other opportunities. The changes led to a considerable improvement in sales growth.

Do salespeople have the time and the bandwidth to do what the company asks? Effective sales effort allocation requires having enough salespeople with the capacity to do the work. For example, if salespeople are already working considerable overtime to meet the needs of their current customers, a directive to "spend more time developing new accounts" is likely to be ignored. At the same time, effective sales effort allocation requires job definitions that contain reasonable responsibilities. If salespeople are asked to take on many diverse duties that require dissimilar skills and abilities (for example, selling a broad and complex product line to many different types of customers with varied needs), they may become overwhelmed and be unable to master the skills needed to do their job effectively. They will probably choose to focus on the subset of customers, products, or activities with which they are most comfortable and successful, and these will not necessarily be the ones that are most important to the company. When sales resources are misallocated because salespeople are too busy or do not have the capacity to carry out all of their responsibilities, then the possible remedies include:

- Adding salespeople
- Realigning sales territories so that the workload is more equitably distributed across the sales force, leading to higher sales without increased sales force headcount
- Restructuring the sales force so that salespeople have more specialized responsibilities and can be more effective with the customers, products, and sales activities that matter the most
- Moving some low-value sales activities to lower-cost channels, freeing salespeople's time for the most important customers, products, and activities

Many companies use sales force specialization to ensure that important customers or prospects receive sufficient sales effort. For example:

- Usually there is a small number of "key" accounts that have significant strategic importance to a company. The company can ensure that these accounts get focused sales force attention by assigning them to dedicated global or strategic account managers or teams designed to serve their special needs. The company controls the amount of sales force effort allocated to each key account by changing the size of the dedicated selling team. The roles of different salespeople on the team (for example, the number of general account managers or product specialists) influence how sales effort gets allocated to different buying influencers, selling activities, or product lines.
- Some companies ensure that effort is appropriately allocated to new customer development by organizing their sales forces in a hunter/farmer structure. "Hunter" salespeople specialize in finding business at new accounts. Once a sale is made, a "farmer" salesperson takes over to cultivate and grow the relationship with the account and generate repeat business. Companies that operate with these two sales roles can balance a desire for continued focus on new business development with the need to serve existing customers well. The best hunters are not slowed down by time-consuming service activities as they bring in more accounts, while the farmers ensure that the needs of existing customers are met.

Sales force specialization can also help to control effort allocation across products. Whenever new products are launched, effort allocation issues are likely to arise. When a new product is added to the portfolio of an existing sales force, the sales time devoted to the new product is taken away from established products. The sales force may lack the time and expertise to sell both the new and the older products effectively. Once again, changes to the *definer* drivers are usually required to allocate sales force time to selling new products. For example:

- CIBA Vision had a single sales force selling contact lenses and lens-care solutions to eye-care practitioners. In 2003 the company launched several new products, but the existing sales force did not have the capacity to manage these products on top of the numerous product lines it was already selling. The company increased the number of salespeople by more than 30 percent and split the sales force, creating a dedicated sales force for contact lenses and a second dedicated sales force for lens-care solutions. The new structure ensured adequate focus on both product lines and allowed salespeople to develop greater expertise so that they could be more effective with customers.

- An industrial products supplier changes the distribution channel for its products as they mature. For new products, customers need a company salesperson who can answer technical questions. Later, after customers have been using the product for a while, they want a convenient way to purchase the product and do not need as much face-to-face contact. At that point, the product is turned over to a less-expensive, lower-touch channel, such as a distributor or the company's telesales group, freeing up sales force time for newer and more strategically important offerings.

By utilizing such less-expensive selling channels as telesales, sales assistants, and low-cost distribution partners, companies can become more efficient at covering certain types of customers and at the same time direct more sales effort to the most important customers. Less-expensive sales channels can be used as either a substitute for or a supplement to the existing sales force effort. While these channels are not as effective as face-to-face selling, the benefits of cost reduction often more than compensate for any lost sales. For example:

- A consumer products firm decided to focus its field sales force efforts in densely populated areas, while using telesales to cover small, remotely located accounts. The field sales force was able to reach customers who contributed more than 80 percent of the company's total sales volume by covering just 25 percent of the U.S. geography. With less travel time, the field sales force could spend more time with important customers and prospects. The sales benefit was far greater than the small sales loss that occurred at remotely located accounts that were reassigned from field sales to telesales.

- The newspaper advertising sales force, whose activities are shown in Figure 17-4, hired sales assistants to take over many of the non-selling tasks related to servicing existing accounts, such as checking advertisements, dealing with production problems, handling billing and collections, and completing paperwork. As a result, salespeople were freed up to spend more time selling. Since the sales assistants were paid less than the salespeople, cost efficiency improved dramatically.

- At Oracle, inside and outside salespeople are matched up in teams that work together to meet customer needs and achieve territory sales goals. Some of the inside salespeople who are assigned to teams that cover U.S. customers are located in India. The inside team members handle many of the administrative selling duties and also do telephone prospecting, online product demonstrations, and other selling tasks that can be handled remotely, freeing up more of the higher-paid salespeople's time for face-to-face selling activities.

Most Sales Resource Allocation Challenges Have Multiple Sales Effectiveness Driver Solutions. When sales leaders at one company wanted the sales force to spend more time developing new accounts, they adjusted the sales incentive plan so that sales to new accounts paid double the commission rate of sales to existing accounts. Sales leaders hoped that the higher commissions would motivate salespeople to develop more new business. To the sales leaders' surprise, however, the incentive plan adjustment had very little impact on sales force behavior; new business development hardly increased, yet costs went up because the company had to pay double commissions on new business that would probably have been sold even if the commission rate had not been doubled. When asked why they were not devoting more time to new business development, salespeople had a variety of different responses:

- "I don't know who the good prospects are in my territory. It would take me so long to figure out whom to call on and how to make contact that it's just not worth my time."
- "I can barely keep up with the service demands of my current customers. I don't need more customers to worry about."
- "I like working with my current customers. Seeking out new customers is hard work and involves a lot of rejection. I just don't enjoy it."
- "I know the needs of my current customers, and I feel confident that I can sell them anything. I'm not sure that I have the knowledge I need to be effective with new customers."

These responses revealed that salespeople were avoiding new business development for a variety of reasons; motivation was only one piece of the puzzle. A complete diagnosis uncovered many possible causes of the problem. An effective solution required adjustments to multiple sales effectiveness drivers, including:

- Improving the prospect information provided to the sales force
- Adding service representatives who could assist with after-sale support
- Enhancing training for salespeople on how to be effective with new customers

Retaining Successful Salespeople

Salesperson turnover averages around 15 percent per year in the United States, but it can vary widely across industries and companies. A modest amount of turnover is normal and even healthy—poor performers leave and new people bring in fresh ideas, approaches, abilities, and attitudes that keep the sales force from becoming stagnant. But too much turnover is costly for a company.

Differences in turnover across industries are in large part due to different expectations of different sales jobs, the types of people attracted to those jobs, and the compensation for the job. Yet within any given industry, turnover can vary considerably from company to company.

Figure 18-1 shows the range and distribution of voluntary sales force turnover across 35 pharmaceutical companies. Sales force turnover is generally lower in this industry than in many others; median turnover in 2007 was about 10 percent. However, turnover varies quite a bit across companies. At the nine companies with the lowest turnover (the 25th percentile), voluntary turnover averages just 6 percent, while at the nine companies with the highest turnover (the 75th percentile), it averages more than 20 percent. The difference between a sales force

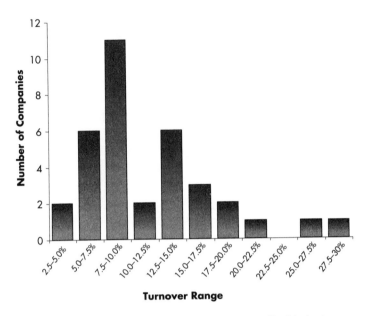

Figure 18-1. Turnover distribution in the pharmaceutical industry (Source: 2007 IPR Study by ZS Associates)

turnover of 20 percent and one of 6 percent is quite significant in terms of the costs incurred and the revenues lost when good salespeople leave a company.

Turnover Costs

Sales force turnover is expensive, as it affects both costs and revenues. Consider the financial impact of sales force turnover on two sales organizations:

- A medical rehabilitation services company discovered that attrition of underperforming first-year salespeople was a significant financial drain. Each departure cost three to four times the person's annual salary: The company lost its investment in recruiting and training the person, and because of the salesperson's poor job performance, it also lost both revenues and the company goodwill needed to maintain future sales opportunities.

- Salt River Project, a Phoenix public utility company, estimated that it would take several years for the company to recover from the loss of a 20-year veteran salesperson, one of ten people who were responsible for trading and negotiating sales of energy to be used up to a year in the future. A fast-paced work environment required extensive industry and company knowledge, making it extremely difficult to find a new salesperson and train him to be fully effective.

Sales force turnover creates several direct costs:

- Departure costs, including the costs of administrative functions related to termination and possible severance pay
- Internal recruiting costs, including identifying a strong applicant pool for replacements, screening résumés, interviewing and testing candidates, and convincing those who are chosen to join the company
- External recruiting costs, including fees paid to headhunters or employment agencies and costs to advertise jobs or post positions online
- On-boarding costs, including the new hire's travel and moving expenses and other preemployment administrative expenses
- Training and ramp-up costs, including the cost of both formal training and of coaching by managers and mentoring by colleagues to help the new salesperson get up to speed

While companies usually recognize the direct costs associated with sales force turnover, they frequently overlook the loss of opportunity for revenue. As Figure 18-2 shows, turnover creates a possible loss of sales over what can be an extended period. Sales erosion begins when a salesperson begins to think about leaving her position and "checks out" before she actually leaves. Once she departs, the lack of customer coverage while the territory is vacant creates further erosion. When the position is finally filled, the new salesperson goes through a ramp-up period, during which he is usually less than fully productive while he learns the job. And for each sale lost during the withdrawal, vacancy, and hiring/orientation periods, future carryover sales are lost as well.

Managing turnover takes considerable energy and time. During the withdrawal period, sales managers have to deal with salespeople who

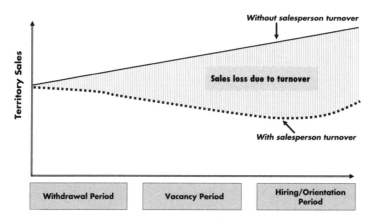

Figure 18-2. Sales loss due to turnover

have checked out, either convincing star salespeople who are courting competitive offers to stay or advising salespeople who are not doing well about other opportunities. During the vacancy period, managers must ensure that key customers are covered, either by doing it them-selves or by arranging for coverage by another salesperson. At the same time, managers must devote a significant amount of time to finding, screening, and attracting strong candidates. During the hiring and orien-tation period, managers are likely to be extensively involved in helping new hires learn the job and become acquainted with the customers in their territory. When sales force turnover is excessive, these activities can consume so much time that managers have little time left to coach, motivate, lead, manage, and reward the rest of their sales team.

Turnover Dynamics

The causes of sales force turnover can originate both outside and inside your sales organization. While a certain amount of sales force turnover is inevitable in any organization, you can successfully minimize undesir-able turnover of strong current and up-and-coming performers.

A Model of the Influences on Sales Force Turnover

As Figure 18-3 shows, some influences on sales force turnover are outside of your sales organization's control, originating instead in the industry,

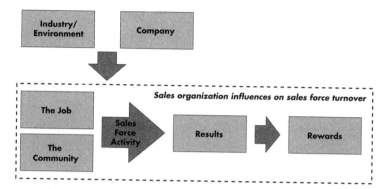

Figure 18-3. Influences on sales force turnover

the environment, the company, or some combination of those areas. Other influences come from within your sales organization itself.

Understanding the dynamics of sales force turnover begins with examining the reasons that salespeople like or dislike their jobs.

Industry/Environment Influences on Sales Force Turnover. One salesperson reports, "I like working for my company because it is a leader in a strong and growing industry." Another, who has just resigned from an established company to join a start-up, explains, "The start-up company targeted our company's sales force for recruiting. It has stronger products and offered me stock options, so I am leaving for a better opportunity."

The growth outlook and reputation of the industry, the availability of other job opportunities, and industry competitiveness play a key role in determining whether salespeople stay in their jobs. Poaching of salespeople by the competition is common in high-growth industries where the demand for experienced salespeople exceeds the supply, as well as in competitive industries where products lack differentiation and customer relationships matter so much that salespeople who are close to important customers are highly sought after.

The demands that customers place on salespeople also affect turnover—difficult customers create stress for salespeople and encourage turnover.

Company Influences on Sales Force Turnover. One satisfied salesperson states, "I like working for my company because it has good products and a clear plan for the future." Another, who is considering leaving her job, says, "The company is facing some tough competition, yet top management puts constant pressure on the sales force to deliver without giving us the support we need if we are to be successful." A company with high-quality products, strong brands, and a good reputation will generally have lower turnover than one with less competitive products, weak brands, and/or a poor reputation. Company leadership and culture also affect sales force retention; salespeople like to work for companies with supportive cultures and strong leaders.

Sales Organization Influences on Sales Force Turnover. Within a sales organization, several key dimensions—the job, the community, results, and rewards—influence sales force turnover.

The job. One salesperson says, "I like what I do. It's an exciting job, and I learn something new every day." Another, who has just been through a major reorganization, complains, "I don't like my new job responsibilities. I enjoyed working with my existing customers, and now I have to spend most of my time prospecting for new business." Salespeople who find their work interesting and satisfying, and who are learning and growing in their jobs, are more likely to stay with the company than those who dislike their work or are not developing new skills and knowledge. The amount of autonomy that salespeople are given also influences turnover. Experienced salespeople who are tightly controlled by their managers are more likely to leave their jobs than those who are empowered to make decisions on their own.

The community. One satisfied salesperson reports, "My job has a great working atmosphere. My manager is responsive to my needs, and I have many dedicated and motivated colleagues." Another, who is looking for a new job, explains, "My manager is ineffective. His micromanaging creates animosity among the salespeople." Good colleagues, supportive first-line sales managers, and strong sales leadership can all result in lower sales force turnover. Surveys show that a salesperson's relationship with her immediate supervisor is a key factor in turnover and retention in many sales organizations.

Results. One salesperson tells us, "I am good at my job. As long as I keep producing, my manager gives me a lot of autonomy." Another, who is unhappy, explains, "I missed my goal again this month. I don't think the goal was fair, and my manager will be calling soon, demanding an explanation." Results are driven by the sales force's activities but are also influenced by various industry, environmental, and company factors. Salespeople who feel successful are more likely to stay in their jobs than those who do not.

Rewards. One salesperson says, "My pay is better than in most of the industry. The commission structure is fair, and there is recognition for strong performance." Another, who has just left his job, states, "The sales force incentive plan was basically a lottery. The people who worked the hardest were rarely the ones who made the most money." Turnover in a sales organization is lower when salespeople view the rewards they receive as desirable and equitable.

The Challenge of Implementing Change to Affect Sales Force Turnover.

The reasons behind the turnover in your sales force will affect the degree of difficulty you will face as you strive to reduce turnover and increase sales effectiveness. External factors, such as industry growth or uncompetitive products, should be triggers for your significant and immediate attention. Even though such external triggers are largely outside your control, acknowledging them and taking appropriate action can limit their impact on turnover.

When turnover is the result of factors internal to the sales organization, such as work that has become uninteresting or a sales management team whose skills have atrophied, the need for change can be less obvious and reducing turnover more difficult. The most effective sales leaders are committed to constantly making improvements so that issues within the sales organization's jobs, community, results, and rewards are addressed before they escalate into major problems that are difficult to fix.

Types of Turnover

Understanding the different types of turnover will help you gain insights for dealing with it.

- Systemic or controllable turnover. Turnover that is systemic is an inevitable part of doing business. Turnover that is controllable can be influenced by the decisions and actions of sales leaders.

- Desirable or undesirable turnover. Not all turnover is bad. Turnover is good when low performers with little potential for future success leave the company. Turnover is undesirable when the company loses strong performers or those with high potential.

Systemic or Controllable Turnover. *Systemic* sales force turnover is influenced by the industry/environment component in Figure 18-3 and is part of a company's business model. Some industries, like pharmaceuticals, have low systemic turnover because of the type of people who are attracted to a pharmaceutical selling job (career-oriented professionals, often with an interest in medicine), the role that pharmaceutical salespeople play (educating physicians and other health-care professionals while selling), and the way in which salespeople in the pharmaceutical industry are paid (typically, 75 percent of their pay comes from salary).

Other industries have much higher systemic turnover. For example, in the insurance industry, only 11 percent of sales agents stay in their jobs for four or more years. Turnover of new insurance agents is high because agents are expected to develop their own base of customers, and most, if not all, of their earnings come from commissions on sales. Successful agents who have built up a base of lucrative, loyal customers can earn a lot of money, but newer agents often struggle to earn a decent living in their early years. Many new agents are not cut out for the demands of the job and leave the industry, usually within their first or second year.

A traditional insurance sales model has more systemic turnover than a traditional pharmaceutical sales model. Differences in systemic turnover reflect differences in industry business models and environments. Unless you are prepared to make major changes to your business model, you will have to accept a certain amount of systemic turnover.

Controllable turnover occurs within all business models and is influenced by the company and sales organization components of Figure 18-3. Within every business model, there is a range of turnover across companies (see Figure 18-1). Controlling this type of turnover requires discovering and addressing its causes. Controllable turnover can occur for many reasons, including salespeople's dissatisfaction with some combination of the company, the community of people they work with, the job they do, the success they feel, and/or the rewards they receive for doing their job.

With any business model, controllable turnover can be highly variable. Companies in growing industries with good products, highly supportive cultures, strong first-line sales managers, interesting sales jobs, and above-average rewards will generally have less controllable sales force turnover than companies with the opposite characteristics.

Desirable or Undesirable Turnover. In two companies in the same industry, approximately 15 percent of the sales force turns over every year, which is about the industry average. Sales leaders at the first company are concerned because the company has recently lost many high-performing salespeople, and they suspect that these people are leaving because they are not motivated, challenged, or rewarded enough for their performance. At the second company, sales leaders are pleased with the 15 percent turnover. The majority of the salespeople who leave the organization are weak performers with little potential for future success. Sales leaders attribute this desirable turnover to an effective performance management system and a strong first-line sales management team.

It is desirable that low performers with little potential for future success leave the company. Turnover is undesirable only when strong or high-potential performers leave.

How to Manage Turnover

The process of managing sales force turnover effectively has three elements:

1. Measuring and understanding the turnover dynamics that currently exist

2. Leveraging the sales effectiveness drivers to minimize undesirable, controllable turnover within the sales force

3. Leveraging the sales effectiveness drivers to reduce the impact of turnover on sales performance

Measuring and Understanding Turnover Dynamics

Turnover statistics are most meaningful and actionable when they are broken down by:

- Turnover that is systemic or controllable
- Turnover that is desirable or undesirable

Measuring Systemic and Controllable Turnover. You can track your sales force turnover, benchmarking every year against company historical norms and/or industry averages. And you can assess systemic sales force turnover by looking at turnover among the best companies in your industry (or in industries with similar selling models).

Figure 18-1 shows an example of this type of data for the pharmaceutical industry. The best pharmaceutical companies (say the top 25 percent) have voluntary turnover of approximately 6 percent. These data provide evidence to pharmaceutical companies with turnover above 6 percent that it is possible to reduce their turnover to this level, as other companies have demonstrated that this level of turnover is achievable.

You can estimate your level of controllable turnover by subtracting the turnover rate achieved by the best companies in the industry from your company's current turnover rate. External surveys that you can use for benchmarking sales force turnover data are available in many industries.

Measuring Desirable and Undesirable Turnover. In order to measure desirable and undesirable turnover, you need to categorize turnover statistics according to the performance of your salespeople. You can measure that performance in a number of different ways, using metrics such as sales, market share, and goal attainment. Data analysis techniques, such as the Performance Frontier approach described in Chapter 2, are also useful for assessing salespeople's performance.

Management ratings of salespeople that take their longer-term potential for success into account are another way to measure performance. Management ratings are particularly relevant for newer salespeople who currently may not be generating high sales, but who have the potential to be successful as their experience grows. Effective sales organizations hold on to salespeople who are successful now or will be successful in the future.

You can gain further insight into sales force turnover by examining the reasons that high- and low-performing salespeople leave your company. Figure 18-4 shows a turnover analysis for one company's sales force. The most often stated reason for departure among salespeople who left the company voluntarily is a lack of respectful treatment, followed by lack of recognition, pay, and advancement opportunities. However, note that the reasons for departure vary depending on whether the departing salespeople are in the top or the bottom half of the rankings. It is mostly lower performers who leave because of inadequate pay and recognition. The higher performers are more likely to leave because of lack of advancement opportunities and respectful treatment.

You can use several techniques to uncover the reasons why salespeople leave your company. Exit interviews with departing salespeople provide insight but may not be completely reliable. If your company's personnel conduct the interviews, salespeople may be reluctant to reveal the true reasons for their departure for fear that candid feedback might taint their employment record. Departing employees may be more honest in exit interviews with a third party who provides anonymous feedback to the company. It is important to screen departure feedback for

Primary Reason for Departure	% of Sales Force	% of Salespeople in Upper Half of Ratings	% of Salespeople in Lower Half of Ratings
Respectful treatment	23%	52%	48%
Recognition	21%	26%	74%
Pay	20%	27%	73%
Advancement opportunities	13%	70%	30%
Interesting and challenging work	10%	45%	55%
Quality of life	9%	40%	60%
Other	4%	50%	50%
Overall	100%	42%	58%

Figure 18-4. Analysis of turnover showing stated reasons for departure

biases, which sometimes come into play when salespeople who leave in anger speak with emotion and externalize the reasons for their exit.

You can also conduct ongoing sales force surveys to identify issues that are of concern to the salespeople and to assess sales force morale. As salespeople leave, these surveys provide a history of their attitudes, which may be more candid than feedback obtained during exit interviews. You can also use sales force surveys to link attitudes to tenure, helping to identify issues that are of concern specifically to new or experienced salespeople.

Reducing Controllable Turnover

You can reduce controllable turnover by discovering its causes and addressing them, using the sales effectiveness drivers. The sales effectiveness framework (see Chapters 1 and 2) guides the diagnostic process.

Turnover Solutions Depend on Performance. If you want to address the reasons for turnover, start by looking at the performance level of the salespeople who leave your company. Strategies and solutions will vary, depending upon whether the company is losing:

- Poor performers with low potential who are unlikely to ever succeed
- Poor performers who have high potential for future success
- Current good performers

Figure 18-5 shows strategies for reducing turnover and identifies the sales effectiveness drivers that can provide the best solutions. The number of checkmarks represents the importance of a sales effectiveness driver for each performance category.

Sales Managers Have a Big Role in Managing Turnover. First-line sales managers play a key role in managing sales force turnover, regardless of the level of performance of those who are leaving. Just as the salesperson is the company for many customers, the sales manager is the company for many salespeople. As Figure 18-5 shows, sales managers are important implementers of most of the suggested sales effectiveness

	Poor Performers with Low Potential	Poor Performers with High Potential	Good Performers
Strategy for reducing turnover	Have fewer of them in the sales force	Develop their skills, protect their compensation, and give them roles that enable success	Appreciate, reward, and recognize their success
Possible Sales Effectiveness Driver Solutions			
Roles; responsibilities; territory alignment*		√√√	
Career advancement*			√√√
Culture*			√
Recruiting*	√√√		
Development*; coaching*		√√√	
Compensation; goal setting*		√√√	√√√
Recognition*			√√√
Performance management*; early detection*; metrics	√√√	√	
Positive feedback*; appreciation*		√√	√√√

* Sales managers play a key role in implementing these sales effectiveness drivers.

Figure 18-5. Strategies for reducing turnover and possible sales effectiveness driver solutions for companies losing salespeople at different performance levels

driver solutions. Sales managers implement the performance management processes that deal with poor performers, and are in the best position to provide positive feedback and appreciation to those who are successful. Sales managers often play a key role in goal setting and in recognizing salespeople with strong performance and good potential. Sales managers shape the skills and capabilities of the sales force through their role in recruiting, coaching, and developing the people who report to them. Sales managers also influence the roles and responsibilities of their reports by aligning territories so that everyone has a chance to succeed. Investing in the development of a strong sales management team is critical for successful turnover management.

When the Company Is Losing Many Poor Performers with Low Potential for Future Success. Turnover is desirable when the departing salespeople are not succeeding or when they lack the potential for success. The turnover that occurs among this group of salespeople is the result of poor hiring.

When a sales force has too many low-performing, low-potential salespeople leaving, you need to ask the two key questions in Figure 18-6, which also shows the sales effectiveness drivers that link probable causes with solutions.

Improving retention when turnover is due to poor performance is usually a two-part process. First, you should invest in developing better performance management systems or in enhancing the skills of the sales managers who are responsible for implementing those systems. Strong performance management processes will allow you to identify performance issues quickly and to dismiss weak performers as soon as it is evident that they will not succeed. In the short term, this increases desirable turnover but creates more openings that need to be filled.

The second part of reducing turnover resulting from nonperformance involves improving the recruiting process and enhancing the recruiting skills of sales managers, which helps to ensure that the salespeople who fill the open slots have the capabilities required for success. When recruitment is done well, salespeople who will not be successful are not hired in the first place, which reduces turnover in the long term because the sales force has fewer nonperformers.

Many companies have had considerable success in reducing sales force turnover by investing in their recruiting processes so that salespeople who are likely to become turnover statistics are not hired. Consider the following examples.

- Industrial valves and controls distributor Valquip Corporation cut its sales force turnover in half when it began using a psychological test to screen candidates for sales positions. Questionnaires were

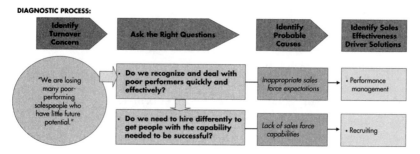

Figure 18-6. Diagnosis when too many poor-performing salespeople with little future potential are leaving

used to assess behavior in four areas: drive/dominance, interpersonal skills, steadiness (rate of activity), and compliance with rules and regulations. When the test was administered to the company's top salespeople, a consistent profile emerged: Almost all of the successful salespeople had very high levels of drive and strong interpersonal skills. The company began hiring only those candidates whose psychological profile matched the success profile.

- The turnover rate for salespeople at automotive dealerships is quite high; the average salesperson in this industry stays in the job for only three to four months. One dealership group wanted to reduce its turnover rate, which was running at over 50 percent per year. The majority of those leaving were poor hires who left the job within the first 90 days because of low performance. The dealership group reduced turnover considerably by raising managers' awareness of the importance of recruiting and by creating a more diligent hiring process that included thorough background checks. In addition, requests for transfers between dealerships were scrutinized closely to ensure that it was not easy for one dealership to simply transfer a "problem hire" to another.

- The vice president of sales at RTI, a computer equipment manufacturer, discourages turnover by hiring only people that he is highly confident can succeed and by creating an open and honest work environment for his team. He makes sure that candidates clearly understand the responsibilities and expectations of the job. For example, he required one candidate to spend several days watching production at the company to be sure that he fully understood some of the challenges the company faced.

When the Company Is Losing Poor Performers Who Have High Potential for Future Success. Some companies lose many relatively new salespeople who, despite having a lot of talent, are unable to reach a threshold of success quickly. This "build a book or leave" situation is found in industries like office products and insurance, where customer offerings are mostly commodities and salespeople's earnings come primarily from commissions. There is high turnover among recent sales force hires because the difficulty of building a book of business makes it hard for most inexperienced salespeople to be successful immediately. While some of the salespeople who leave are not cut out for the job (and consequently are examples of desirable turnover), many could be successful and make a decent living if they were given the necessary guidance, support, encouragement, and opportunity.

Sometimes talented new salespeople inherit weak territories. Placing good people in weak territories is a surefire way of creating undesirable turnover—when good people see little chance of success, they look for better opportunities.

Ask four questions if many low-performing but high-potential salespeople are leaving your sales force. Figure 18-7 shows how these questions can help you understand the probable causes for the turnover and find solutions.

To reduce turnover of salespeople who are not performing well but have long-term potential for success, let salespeople know that they can succeed and then leverage the sales effectiveness drivers that will help them be successful. Low-performing/high-potential salespeople may benefit from additional coaching and training. They may need a good opportunity to shine, perhaps with an assignment that is designed to build their confidence and develop their skills. Finally, salespeople in this situation may require compensation that allows them to survive until they can become fully successful.

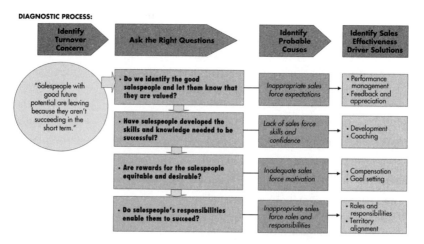

Figure 18-7. Diagnosis when salespeople with good future potential are leaving because they cannot succeed in the short term

An Example: New insurance salespeople leave because they cannot reach a threshold of success. An insurance firm's sales force sells companies a range of supplemental insurance policies to be included in employee benefits packages. Company leaders believe that growth of the sales force is the best driver of company growth. A large recruiting effort takes in thousands of entry-level salespeople every year. At the same time, leaders expect high turnover among new salespeople, as many of them discover quickly that they are unsuited for a job that pays entirely on commission and that requires a strong entrepreneurial spirit. In fact, the company relies on the business that new salespeople generate in their first weeks on the job as they leverage their contacts with friends and family; the income stream of premiums that these customers generate often outlasts the tenure of the salesperson making the initial sale. In addition, high sales force turnover allows the company to sustain a promotion hierarchy that rewards strong performers.

Even though the insurance company relies on sales force turnover as part of its business model, company leaders are concerned that their controllable turnover has become excessive and is costing the company money. The investment in recruiting and training new salespeople is not paying off because too few of those salespeople stay long enough to produce significant results.

Figure 18-8 shows that first-year sales production is closely related to sales force retention. Practically all of the salespeople who sold nothing in their first year left the company within the year. Of the salespeople who sold more than $100,000 in their first year, almost all stayed with the company for a year, and the majority still remained after three years.

The data suggest that at this insurance company, early success is important for sales force retention. Consequently, sales leaders at this company have launched an effort to improve the early success of new recruits by enhancing several sales effectiveness drivers:

- *Learning and development* programs for new salespeople improve their mastery of the skills needed for early sales success.
- Increased emphasis on sales manager *coaching* of new salespeople helps new recruits reap the benefits of their manager's experience.

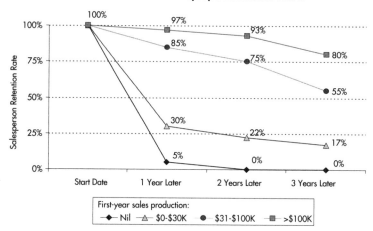

Figure 18-8. Three-year retention of sales force recruits based on first-year sales production at an insurance company

- Sales managers are encouraged to give new salespeople a few decent *account assignments* to start, and to work with them at these accounts while coaching them on effective sales approaches.

A Technology Company Helps New Salespeople Succeed Early

A global technology company has identified a milestone required for sales associates to remain in their positions: They must make their first sale within 90 days. Early training and rewards focus on accomplishing this single task. For example, basic sales classes focus on easy-to-sell, quick-turnover products. Training on more advanced products happens only after several months of success in the job.

A Direct-Marketing Firm Reduces New Salesperson Turnover by Establishing New Pay Metrics for First-Line Sales Managers

Analysis of turnover statistics for a direct-marketing company revealed that many talented new salespeople were leaving the firm within the first six months. Through exit interviews, the company learned that lack of training and attention from first-line district sales managers was the leading cause of the turnover. The primary responsibility of those sales managers was to train and guide new salespeople, but they also retained some selling responsibility, and a substantial portion of their incentive pay and recognition was based on their own sales performance. Thus, sales managers' rewards did not align well with their expected job responsibilities.

The company responded by implementing a new district sales manager reward program that placed less emphasis on individual sales and more on new performance metrics reflecting other important responsibilities. For example, metrics such as achievement of sales goals by new employees and year-to-year district revenue growth were added to the managers' incentive pay formula. This change reduced new salesperson turnover and ultimately helped drive sales growth.

When the Company Is Losing Good Performers. Salespeople's success is visible to customers and to competitors. Good salespeople are in high demand in the job market, and sales organizations are constantly challenged to retain their strong performers. When a sales force is losing many of its strong salespeople, turnover is a significant management concern. Diagnosing the causes for that concern involves asking three questions that link to remedial sales effectiveness driver solutions, as shown in Figure 18-9.

The best strategy for dealing with the loss of top performers is to do a better job of appreciating, recognizing, and rewarding the success of salespeople that the company does not want to lose. Enhancements to sales effectiveness drivers such as incentive and recognition programs, new career opportunities, and a positive sales culture help to keep top performers motivated and happy.

When successful salespeople are poached by competitors. In high-technology industries, product innovation can induce top salespeople to pursue opportunities to sell for companies with hot new technologies. A "buy the mercenaries when the going is good" situation develops— companies with new technologies expand their sales forces by poaching the forces of competitive companies in order to drive the success

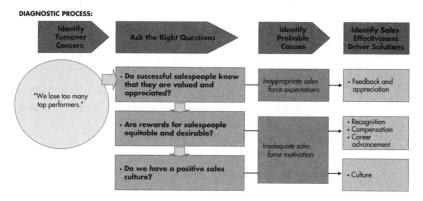

Figure 18-9. Diagnosis when too many high-performing salespeople are leaving

of new products. The companies that are the victims of this kind of poaching have employed different strategies to successfully hold on to good salespeople.

- During the late 1990s, the Internet boom made it very difficult for established Silicon Valley companies to hold on to their best employees, including their salespeople. Top employees were lured by start-ups offering stock options that could be worth millions of dollars someday, making it very difficult for established companies to compete in the war for talent. To attract and retain the best and brightest people, companies began offering their employees significant perks. For example, in 1997, software maker Novell had some of the ugliest offices in Silicon Valley—salespeople were embarrassed to bring their customers there. The company invested $130 million in the development of a new campus, complete with tennis, volleyball, and basketball courts; a restaurant; a gym; and an espresso bar. Some of the best restaurants and gyms in Silicon Valley are not open to the public; they are offered as perks to employees of companies like Novell, Lucent Technologies, Oracle, and Sun Microsystems.

- Sometimes legal action is required to keep salespeople from defecting to competitors. In 1997, retailer Montgomery Ward got a temporary restraining order to keep Sears, Roebuck and Company from recruiting Ward's managers while it underwent bankruptcy-law proceedings. Employment contracts with noncompete agreements can also help protect employers against people leaving and going to a direct competitor, although the legality and enforceability of such agreements varies by state.

- Financial services firm Plante & Moran limits its annual staff turnover to half the industry average through a "re-recruiting" program that is part of the firm's daily activities and culture. The idea behind re-recruiting is that managers envision what they would do if a valued staff member were to tell them that she was leaving, but they do not wait for such an announcement to be made before taking action; they take it now. Managers are expected to continually re-recruit members of their teams by scheduling frequent one-on-one meetings and making staff members feel important and valued. Managers attend re-recruiting workshops where they share ideas for consistent and proactive communication with their staff. Staff members have buddies who can offer advice and more experienced mentors who can provide career coaching and planning. A strong performance management system is also an important element of the firm's re-recruiting program.

When change creates uncertainty for successful salespeople. Companies are especially vulnerable to losing top salespeople during periods of change. For example, mergers and acquisitions often bring uncertainty that causes top performers to question their future with the company and to look for other opportunities. Headhunters and competitors' recruiters often target good performers at companies that are affected by mergers. At the same time, the merging companies want to send a message of consistency and stability to their customers, making it especially important for them to focus on the retention of top performers.

When Canadian company London Life Insurance bought the Canadian operations of Prudential in 1996, the company made a great effort to retain Prudential's force of 850-plus salespeople. The company flew Prudential's salespeople to its headquarters immediately following the announcement of the acquisition. For two days, its executives welcomed the new salespeople to the organization and addressed their major points of uncertainty, including which products they would sell, whom they would work for, where they would work, and how they would be paid. Ultimately, 92 percent of Prudential's salespeople signed new contracts with London Life. By predicting the acquired salespeople's concerns and addressing them quickly, London Life successfully allayed those concerns and blocked the threat of turnover.

Working to Reduce the Impact of Turnover

A certain amount of turnover is inevitable in any sales organization. Consequently, you can enhance the effectiveness of your sales force by working to reduce the impact that turnover has on your organization. Figure 18-10 shows four ways in which you can reduce sales loss attributed to sales force turnover:

1. Minimize the sales loss that occurs during the withdrawal period.
2. Reduce the period of time that a territory is vacant.
3. Minimize the sales loss that occurs during the vacancy period.
4. Enhance the performance of replacement salespeople.

Minimizing the Sales Loss During the Withdrawal Period. You can minimize sales losses during the withdrawal period by detecting the possibility of a salesperson leaving as early as possible. If you can identify an

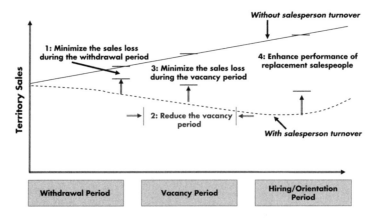

Figure 18-10. Reducing the sales loss due to turnover

impending departure before the salesperson has made a final decision to leave, there may be a chance of preempting the departure by discovering and addressing the reasons for her dissatisfaction. If you cannot preempt the resignation, then you can employ strategies to provide temporary coverage of important customers (see "Minimizing the Sales Loss During the Vacancy Period") before the salesperson actually leaves.

Early-Warning Systems Predict Attrition of Indian Call Center Agents

As a means of increasing profits, many U.S. and European companies have outsourced their call centers to firms in India that employ large numbers of low-cost, English-speaking, technically talented people. Business process outsourcing (BPO) has become an important factor in the Indian economy, and continued strong growth of the industry is expected. With attrition rates for call center agents at Indian BPO companies averaging between 30 and 60 percent, managing turnover has become a significant challenge. Several companies use early-warning systems that track employee behavior and predict the likelihood of resignations. Companies will track as many as 50 different triggers they have identified as signs of impending departure, including fluctuating productivity, increased absenteeism, a drop in call quality, and increased off-phone time. When "at-risk" employees are identified, HR meets with them to work out solutions tailored to their situations; these might include job rotation, job enhancement, relocation, team-building exercises, and greater control over the work schedule. And sometimes managers decide that the job and the employee are not well matched. Companies have also invested in better training of managers, since agents with more effective managers have higher job satisfaction and therefore stay on the job longer. The investments that BPO companies have made to reduce turnover have paid off; companies have attributed turnover reductions of up to 25 percent to these efforts.

Reducing the Vacancy Period. A 1,000-person sales force with 20 percent turnover can expect to lose 200 people a year. When a company can anticipate such a large number of likely vacancies, it can work to reduce the vacancy period by:

- Having a "bench" of newly hired and trained recruits ready at all times to fill vacancies

- Organizing the recruiting process so that several candidates are close to the "offer" stage at all times

If your sales force is large and includes sales jobs that require a significant amount of training before the salesperson can be effective, consider establishing a bench of recruits. The bench consists of current employees who are in training or serving in apprenticeship positions while waiting for a sales position to become available, and thus are ready to jump into a sales job quickly when needed. Maintaining a bench allows you to fill vacant territories with trained salespeople quickly. If the training needs are modest or if the extra cost of maintaining a bench is deemed too high, having a pool of job candidates who are close to the offer stage can help cut the time required to fill sales positions. As we note in Chapter 7, continuous recruiting is a best practice.

Minimizing the Sales Loss During the Vacancy Period. Your company can lose sales during a vacancy period when customers in open territories are not covered and their needs go unmet. Uncovered customers may become frustrated by a lack of attention. When the sales cycle is long or when salespeople need in-depth customer knowledge to be effective, even the best customers may reason that perhaps the time is right to consider competitive offerings. Prospective sales to accounts that are already evaluating competitive offerings are especially vulnerable. In relationship-based selling environments, departing salespeople will often leverage their customer relationships as they seek jobs with competitors, promising to "bring their customers with them" to the new job. Consequently, these customers are particularly vulnerable during the vacancy and into the hiring/orientation period.

To help minimize sales loss during the vacancy period, provide temporary coverage of major customers by a manager or by another salesperson. Give priority to the customers that the company cannot afford to lose—and the ones that competitors may be most interested in poaching. Temporary coverage is usually not as effective as permanent coverage, since the person filling in probably has incomplete knowledge of the customers and may not have sufficient time or motivation to do the job fully. Financial incentives can help to encourage strong temporary coverage of accounts (for example, the person providing coverage earns incentives for sales to these accounts during the vacancy period). Companywide incentives, as opposed to individual ones, also reinforce a "help each other" culture. It also may be necessary to reduce the temporary person's regular job duties in order to make time for the added responsibility.

In relationship-based selling environments, where there is a risk that departing salespeople will take customers with them to competitors, smart companies take action to minimize customer defection well before turnover is imminent. In such environments, it is essential to create connections between customers and the company that will outlive the connections between customers and individual salespeople.

You can establish multiple value-adding connections in many ways. For example, sales managers can be involved in important deals with long sales cycles and can accompany salespeople to meetings with customers where a more strategic perspective will be valued. In addition, sales specialists who know the technical details of a product or who understand the intricacies of financing can add value for customers, while at the same time strengthening the relationship between the company and the customer. Linkages outside the sales force—for example, to a strong customer service organization or technical support group—can also help to cement customer relationships and ensure that they outlast a specific salesperson's tenure.

When a salesperson's customer knowledge is a significant source of competitive advantage, it is important to have systems and processes in place that facilitate a successful transition of customer responsibilities when sales force turnover occurs. Many companies use CRM systems to capture information about key customers and/or to track the sales pipeline, making successful transitions more likely. You can also enhance the relationship transition by having the departing salesperson meet with the person who will take over his accounts (either temporarily or permanently) to share information about customer needs. If possible, the departing salesperson can even introduce the new person to each customer to encourage customer confidence in the transition.

Enhancing the Performance of Replacement Salespeople. A sustained focus on the sales effectiveness drivers helps new salespeople become productive quickly. Strong employee on-boarding programs allow new salespeople to absorb the culture rapidly, learn the products and the customers, establish good relationships with their managers, and become fully engaged in their jobs. Investment in learning and development programs can help new salespeople get off to a fast and productive start. Sales managers also play a critical role in facilitating a quick and successful transition of new salespeople into their jobs.

Sales force turnover is one of the most challenging issues that your sales organization has to face. High turnover creates unnecessary costs, results in missed sales opportunities, and diverts sales management attention. In order to be proactive in preventing undesirable turnover at your organization, you must first understand who is leaving (high or low performers) and the reasons behind their departure. This important information provides insights that can help you leverage the sales effectiveness drivers to improve retention of your successful salespeople.

CHAPTER 19

Achieving Better Sales and Marketing Alignment

Sales and marketing are a major customer-facing force for every company. Together, these organizations pursue a common objective: to create customer value and intimacy in order to drive company revenue growth. Typically, marketing has the responsibility for developing product and customer segment strategies, while sales implements those strategies by taking responsibility for the customer. This division of work and the tension created by the dependence of sales and marketing on each other can be healthy. Sales pushes marketing to develop strategies that address customer needs and get customers to buy. Marketing pushes sales to implement the marketing plan effectively. By keeping an eye on each other, sales and marketing work together to drive company excellence and success.

When the sales and marketing teams work together effectively:

- Marketing develops creative customer segment strategies using input from sales, and salespeople find that the strategies are in tune with customer needs.

- Marketing uses customer research to anticipate the evolution of customer needs and to help the company succeed in the long term. Salespeople take care of customers and achieve company revenue goals.

- Salespeople find that the marketing collateral, such as brochures and product configuration tools, makes the selling process easier.

- Marketing appropriately qualifies the leads it generates so that the salespeople can focus their attention on productive prospects.

- There is a healthy tension between the salespeople's need to discount the price in order to close sales and the need for the company to be disciplined about its pricing strategy.

- Sales pushes marketing to excel; marketing pushes sales to be its best.

The Sales and Marketing Thought Worlds

The different thought worlds of sellers and marketers can be a source of strength, but they can also be a significant impediment to sales effectiveness. Differences in perspectives, job responsibilities, and the skills needed for success in sales and marketing can lead to conflict. Despite their shared objectives, sales and marketing people often do not work well together. Sometimes sales and marketing people find fault with each other and engage in harmful finger pointing. Figure 19-1 lists some observations of sales and marketing leaders.

The vice president of sales and marketing at one company said, "My heart is in sales, but my head is in marketing."

As the observations of sales and marketing leaders reveal, the different points of view of sales and marketing people can be a significant source of tension. While a moderate amount of tension is healthy and constructive, a significant disconnect between the two major customer-facing organizations creates an effectiveness drain. However, when these two sometimes opposing, yet at the same time complementary,

Marketing says . . .	Sales says . . .
• "Marketing people work long, hard hours, but salespeople make more money."	• "Sales makes the money for the company; marketing just spends it."
• "On the hierarchy of business, marketing people see themselves as higher up."	• "To the customer, salespeople are the company. What can be more important?"
• "Marketing hires talented people who develop detailed, thoughtful strategies and plans based on the best available data and customer input. Yet most salespeople won't even take the time to understand the marketing plan." • "Marketing develops strategies and plans and sales is the implementation arm of marketing. Salespeople are paid agents of marketing."	• "Marketers are locked in the ivory tower and don't have a clue about what customers really want." • "Marketing created a warehouse full of brochures that salespeople don't use because the materials don't address the realities of what actual customers are concerned about." • "Marketing operates at a national level with specific product orientations. They are not familiar with regional and account differences. Sales knows customers better than marketing."
• "Marketing is more reflective; sales is more reactive."	• "Sales likes to get it done and move on. Marketing is more analytical." • "Marketing is more bureaucratic than sales. Marketing is too internally focused."
• "Salespeople are driven by specific accounts, volume shipments, and price discounts. They are just interested in the deepest deal that moves the most volume, regardless of the impact on profitability."	• "The sales force will lose significant business if it accepts the marketing price."
• "Marketing develops good leads at trade shows, but sales doesn't follow up. Salespeople spend all their time servicing familiar accounts."	• "The lead quality has been steadily declining. The last lead I got was for a business that shut down two years ago."

Figure 19-1. The different thought worlds of sales and marketing

teams are aligned successfully, they can create a unified and powerful customer-facing force.

A Sales and Marketing Framework: A Need for Specialization and Communication

Creating a successful customer-facing organization requires a lot of work. The diversity of this work leads to a need for specialization within the sales and marketing teams, and this creates a need for communication and coordination among team members. Developing customer segment strategies, product positioning, account management, personal selling, distributor management, installation, after-sale service, and merchandising support are just a few examples of the day-to-day activities that companies must accomplish in order to create customer value and intimacy effectively. This wide range of activities requires a diverse set of skills and capabilities. It is unlikely that one person will be good at all of them.

Some of the work required to maintain a successful customer-facing organization is very tactical in nature. Customers and prospects have a variety of day-to-day needs that must be met. If a prospect has a question about a proposal or if a customer wants to place a repeat order, the organization needs to respond quickly and effectively.

Other work required if the company is to be successful is strategic in nature. Sales and marketing leaders must develop strategies to ensure the long-term success of the organization. The organization needs to understand who its customers are, how they value the company's offering, what advantages that offering has over those of competitors, and how customer needs and competitive offerings are likely to evolve. Market research, competitive analysis, market segmentation, product positioning, and branding are a few examples of the type of work that is required to ensure strong customer relationships in the long run.

Successful organizations bridge the gap between long-term strategies and day-to-day interactions with customers. Salespeople need guidance regarding which customers and prospects are most attractive and require attention, which products and services should be emphasized, and what the most effective value proposition is for different customers. Prices need to be established, promotions need to be designed, sales collateral and selling tools need to be produced, and sales forecasts must be developed. Successful customer relationships can be created and sustained only when sales and marketing accomplish all of these different activities successfully.

Excessive Bandwidth Requires Specialization and Communication

One significant factor in the challenge of meeting customer needs is the bandwidth that is required. The range of skills, knowledge, and capabilities needed to manage day-to-day interactions with customers, develop market strategies and plans, and at the same time carry out all the activities that bridge the gap between strategy and tactics is much greater than the capacity of any single individual. Hence, there is a need for separate and specialized sales and marketing roles.

At the same time, because sales and marketing share the common objective of driving revenue growth by building and sustaining customer value and intimacy, there is a clear need for coordination and communication between the two. When sales and marketing work together effectively—with a tension that is healthy rather than destructive—they create considerable value for both customers and the company.

The Need to Specialize When High Bandwidth Is Required

The sales force at a global financial services company was unhappy with the marketing brochures and other sales collateral that the company's product management team provided. Many salespeople felt that marketing's materials did not address important customer issues, and therefore they rarely used the materials with customers. Marketing was not responsive to the concerns of the sales force, so a group of sales managers took things into their own hands and initiated a project to develop their own collateral materials within the sales organization. When the sales force started using these materials, the reaction from customers was not positive. The salespeople had neither the creative skills nor the necessary time and resources to develop high-impact marketing materials. The initiative failed to produce any usable results.

Figure 19-2 shows a representative division of work between sales and marketing and illustrates the need for effective coordination and communication. Marketing takes primary responsibility for executing the "upstream" marketing activities, which occur well ahead of any sales interactions with customers. Marketing is also responsible for ensuring that the necessary information created by this work flows to sales.

Sales takes primary responsibility for performing the sales activities that occur "downstream" in the customer connection process, where the day-to-day interactions with customers and prospects take place.

Figure 19-2. How work is typically divided between sales and marketing

Sales is also responsible for ensuring that the feedback obtained through this work flows back to marketing. The downstream marketing activities in the intersection of the two circles usually require joint decision making and cooperation between sales and marketing. These activities are performed effectively only through a synchronized effort.

How Sales and Marketing Leaders View the Roles of Sales and Marketing

More than 80 sales and marketing leaders attended an October 2007 Summit for Sales Executives at the Kellogg School of Management that focused on strategies for integrating sales and marketing. Prior to attending the program, the attendees were asked to complete a short questionnaire that included two open-ended questions. The responses reflected a very focused view of the role of sales and a very diffuse view of the role of marketing.

What Is the Role of Marketing at Your Company?		What Is the Role of Sales at Your Company?
• Advertising	• Market development	• Customer management
• Analytic support	• Messaging	• Achieve sales plan
• Awareness creation	• New products	
• Brand plan	• Positioning	
• Branding	• Presale collateral, tools, events, and aids	
• Competitive intelligence		
• Creative execution	• Pricing	
	• Promotions	
• Customer satisfaction	• Segmentation	
• Direct response marketing	• Value proposition	
• Lead generation		

Specialization Creates Different Points of View and Thought Worlds

Upstream marketing activities require very different skills and perspectives from sales activities. Figure 19-3 illustrates three important dimensions of difference between the marketing and sales mindsets.

Customer Success Versus Product or Brand Success. Salespeople are responsible for success with a set of customers. They decide which products, services, and sales activities to focus on, based on individual customer needs. Most marketing people, such as brand and product managers, are responsible for the success of a specific product or brand. They are charged with increasing the value of that product or brand in the eyes of many customers. When they look at customer data, they

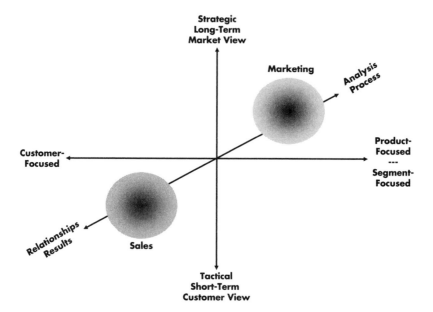

Figure 19-3. A three-dimensional view of the sales and marketing mindsets

usually deal with aggregations of customers in order to develop a more general understanding of customer segment needs.

Relationships and Results Versus Analysis and Process. The nature of sales jobs generally requires salespeople to be people-oriented. Success in sales is driven by a salesperson's ability to build relationships with customers that will help create customer value and thus drive sales results. Marketing jobs require greater analytical capability and success in applying processes for gathering and analyzing data in order to derive a "big picture" view of customer segments and products.

Short-Term Customer Tactics Versus Long-Term Market Strategies. The sales force is expected to help the company achieve its short-term financial goals. Sales force recognition and reward structures are tied to the achievement of annual, quarterly, or even monthly sales goals. Marketing people, on the other hand, are charged with building a long-term competitive advantage and brand. The impact of marketing projects and decisions is longer term and is sometimes not evident for many years.

The Clash of the Two Revenue Drivers

The different points of view and thought worlds of marketers and sales-people often create tensions. These tensions tend to arise when there are conflicts in work processes; these arise when one group (either sales or marketing) believes it needs to perform certain activities in order to accomplish its objectives, and at the same time the other group per-ceives that these activities will negatively affect its own efforts and jeop-ardize its ability to achieve its objectives. For example, marketing generates leads for the sales force. Sales finds these leads to be less than ideal, while marketing feels that its leads are excellent and that the sales force is dropping the ball by not pursuing them adequately.

Tensions can also arise when work processes are harmonious, but either sales or marketing perceives unfairness in the work required or the rewards received. For example, sales may feel that the most difficult work is converting leads into sales and that marketing gets too much credit for simply coming up with a list of prospects; at the same time, marketing feels that generating the leads required considerable creative thought and insight and that salespeople earn disproportionate kudos and rewards for simply closing a sale. Consider some typical examples of sales and marketing tensions shown in Figure 19-4.

Since there are numerous potential sources of tension, there are also considerable opportunities for your company to increase its sales effectiveness by building a strong, positive working relationship between your sales and marketing organizations.

Achieving Better Sales and Marketing Alignment

There are a number of ways to improve sales and marketing integration and alignment. Figure 19-5 shows four categories of solutions: culture solutions, people solutions, structure solutions, and process/system solutions.

Striving for the Ideal Sales and Marketing Organization

Some solutions for aligning sales and marketing organizations require continuous emphasis, while others are more contextual and depend upon the situation. Culture and people solutions are continuous-emphasis mechanisms. Organizations should always strive to build a

Tension	Industry	Marketing View	Sales View
Lead generation, customer targeting, and resource allocation	Vision products	Marketing has done extensive research to identify the best criteria for predicting which customers and prospects have the greatest profit potential. It wants sales to use the criteria to target better, so that less time is wasted with accounts that are unlikely to generate strong incremental future revenues.	Sales argues that while marketing's criteria may look good on paper, they do not work in practice. Many of the leads that marketing generates are not that good. Many of the accounts that sales spends time with have been customers for years and represent the core of the business.
Customer messaging	Chemical	Marketing wants to develop memorable, high-impact messages that convey a consistent company image that appeals to a broad audience. It wants more time, more research, and more budget to ensure that the message is the best it can be.	Sales wants straightforward messages that differentiate the company from competitors and are focused on specific high-priority accounts. It wants the messages right away and does not mind if they are only 80 percent done.
Pricing	Office products	Marketing has established a price based on thorough analysis of the value that customers derive from the company's products as well as analysis of competitive pricing. Marketing argues that sales should hold the price—this will increase profitability and help to maintain the brand's premium image.	Sales feels that the price is too high and routinely lobbies for deeper customer discounts. Sales argues that the company will lose sales if discounts are not offered, and that discounting is necessary to build long-term customer relationships.
Long-term or short-term focus	Automobile dealer	Marketing wants sales to emphasize new models that it believes will be important to the company's future. Marketing is successful when brands are successful over the long term.	Sales wants to emphasize the models that customers want today. By devoting sales time to currently popular models, the sales force is more likely to achieve quarterly goals. Sales is successful when short-term financial goals are met.

Figure 19-4. Examples of tensions between sales and marketing

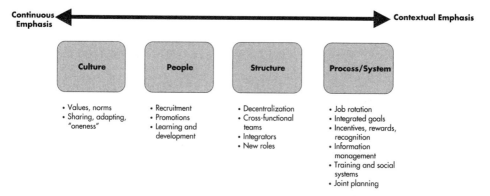

Figure 19-5. Solutions for improving sales and marketing alignment

culture of trust, respect, and teamwork. They should also always be on the lookout for cooperative and supportive employees when they recruit or promote *people* into sales and marketing management and leadership positions. This does not mean that all the people in sales and marketing should be alike. The diversity of the work to be done requires that the sales and marketing team be composed of individuals with a wide range of skills and capabilities. Yet to function effectively, team members must be empathetic and capable of working effectively with others who bring different skills and capabilities to the table.

Structure and *process/system* mechanisms for aligning sales and marketing depend on the context—what is required in one situation may not be appropriate in another. Addressing the most difficult sales and marketing alignment tensions will typically require some type of process/system solution, in addition to having the right people and the right culture. Structure solutions may also be required in some cases.

Bearing Headquarters Company: Using Business Processes to Increase the Role of Marketing in a Sales-Driven Organization

---

Bearing Headquarters Company (BHQ) is a large midwestern distributor of hundreds of bearings and power transmission parts from major manufacturers. Like most distribution companies, BHQ was originally a highly sales-driven company, its success largely determined by the personal relationships that salespeople had with their customers, most of whom were primary metals manufacturers. In 2002, BHQ lost one of its top five customers when National Steel Corp. filed for bankruptcy and was ultimately acquired by U.S. Steel. The loss awakened BHQ's leaders to the fact that increased attention to marketing was needed to help BHQ become less reliant on a small number of customers in a single market segment.

In 2003, BHQ implemented a business process solution called the Market Share Initiative (MSI) that increased the role of marketing in helping the sales organization strategically grow revenues. The objective of MSI was to create a more diverse customer base by increasing sales in nontraditional industries in which BHQ already had some experience. The initiative resulted in a change in the company's sales strategy that was implemented using the process outlined in Chapter 16:

1. *Determine the new sales strategy.* The MSI initiative began by determining new market segments on which BHQ should focus its efforts. It identified power generation, glass manufacturing, pharmaceuticals,

package handling, and machine tools as viable target industries that were within BHQ's geographic reach. Using data obtained from Dun & Bradstreet, the company identified key target accounts in each geographic region. Marketing built information packets that outlined the needs of customers in the new target markets and suggested the products, value proposition, and sales process that were appropriate for each segment.

2. *Align the sales effectiveness drivers to support the new sales strategy.* The company shared information packets about each market with its approximately 100 outside salespeople, allowing them to get up to speed quickly. Marketing provided salespeople with customized PowerPoint presentations to guide their discussions with customers in each market segment. Management also developed processes for maintaining accountability—salespeople were required to report back to their managers on the progress they had made in contacting prospects.

The MSI program generated double-digit sales gains in the five new major market segments in each of the first four years following its launch.

Improvements in sales and marketing alignment can be quick or episodic. If sales and marketing are at loggerheads and have a dysfunctional relationship, then quick change is required. Sometimes a change in sales and marketing leadership is the best solution. The new leader may need to attack the dysfunctional organization on all fronts by implementing solutions in all four categories.

Alternatively, if the sales and marketing interface is basically sound, but there are areas that could be improved, then episodic change is required to resolve tensions. Companies accomplish such change by identifying specific sales and marketing tensions and then developing strategies from the set of solutions given in Figure 19-5.

Sales–Marketing Alignment Solutions at a Medical Technology Company

We asked the vice president of sales and marketing for a global medical technology company how she encouraged the company's sales and marketing departments to work together effectively. She identified several key success drivers that cut across all four categories of solutions. First and foremost, a cooperative corporate *culture* was essential for encouraging a successful relationship between the two departments. This culture was encouraged by developing *people* on the sales and marketing teams through appropriate training and by providing opportunities for cross-fertilization of ideas between sales and marketing. *Structure* solutions were part of this effort: The company frequently used cross-functional teams and coordinating groups or committees made up of both sales and marketing people to address important issues. Finally, decision *processes* such as town hall meetings and *systems* enablers such as the company intranet provided opportunities for exchange of ideas and for addressing differences in sales and marketing perspectives.

There are many choices of solutions for enhancing sales and marketing alignment. In this section, we discuss some of the more common options, which we describe along a continuum that runs from "continuous emphasis" to "contextual emphasis."

Culture Solutions

Chapter 9 points out that winning cultures embrace appropriate values and choices, create a strong consensus, and encourage participants to live those values with intensity. An effective sales–marketing culture requires values and choices that promote harmony and healthy tension.

Harmonious choices involve sharing, adapting, and "oneness." Healthy tension comes from appreciating the diverse marketing and sales expertise that each side brings to the table. Strong leaders help to foster consensus and intensity by demonstrating their commitment to integration of the entire organization. Some ways to do this include:

- Communicating the preferred culture choices to the sales and marketing groups continually. Use heroes, legends, myths, and parables to communicate these choices, since stories are remembered better than concepts.

- Rewarding appropriate behaviors constantly. Because of the differences between the sales and marketing thought worlds, intrinsic rewards (like appreciation and recognition) are most effective.
- Celebrating the heroes who consistently make appropriate culture choices.
- "Walking the talk"—ensuring that actions and words are compatible.
- Discouraging organizational politics.

Eastern Transport Used Meetings to Create a Culture of Sharing Between Sales and Marketing

Eastern Transport Corporation, a Canadian shipping and logistics company, worked hard to create a culture of sharing and collaboration between sales and marketing. "Sales meetings" always included all members of the company's marketing department. This set the tone that the departments were linked and should be viewed as one organization. The company also sponsored monthly lunches for groups of sales and marketing people. These informal meetings encouraged a constant exchange of ideas and discussion of issues that affected the organization.

People Solutions

Effective sales–marketing integration requires having people in sales and marketing positions who are open-minded team players and who understand that working together is important for customer and company success. Communication skills are critical for ensuring smooth flows of information between sales and marketing. Collaboration and teamwork skills are important, particularly when there are many downstream marketing activities that require joint decision making and cooperation between sales and marketing. Sometimes sales and marketing people will need the skills to design and/or participate in process solutions that resolve tensions and enhance the alignment of sales and marketing.

Effective recruiting and development programs for the sales and marketing teams ensure that people with the right attitudes and capabilities are hired and promoted, and that they develop the skills and knowledge necessary for working effectively with one another. When necessary, companies can incorporate sales–marketing cooperation in job descriptions or in key performance indicators (KPIs) that are part of the performance management process for both sales and marketing people.

Intel Provides Marketing and Sales Rotations for New Hires

Intel, the world's largest semiconductor supplier, believes that college graduates who are seeking a career in sales or marketing benefit by spending time working in both departments of the company. Select technical graduates participate in Intel's Sales and Marketing Rotation Program (SMRP). Program participants spend a year working in a technical marketing position, followed by a year focused on account responsibilities. Participants quickly gain an understanding of Intel's products and services and its business models. At the end of the program, SMRP participants are placed in either a technical marketing or a technical sales position.

Lucent Technologies: Using Training to Align Sales and Marketing

Historically, Lucent Technologies was a product-focused telecommunications company. As one marketing director stated, "If you have a product, you have a solution looking for a problem." In 2003, Lucent set out to broaden the company's product offerings and to develop the company's professional services arm. Doing so required Lucent to change its selling model to improve understanding of the customer's problems so that the best overall solution for the customer (products and services) could be developed. Success with the new selling model required a more effective alignment of the sales and marketing organizations. A common sales–marketing training platform helped to achieve this alignment. Lucent's salespeople were trained in consultative selling techniques, while marketing people attended classes to learn how to create consultative-oriented materials to support the sales team. The sales and marketing organizations began working together more closely to develop customer solutions. Preliminary results of the effort were positive for Lucent, yet further changes were to come, as in 2006, when Lucent merged with Alcatel SA of France, to form Alcatel-Lucent.

Structure Solutions

Structure solutions for improving sales and marketing alignment can involve establishing joint sales and marketing leadership, creating cross-functional teams, and designing sales and marketing integrator roles.

Joint Sales and Marketing Leadership. In some companies, sales and marketing organizations operate independently, with each reporting to its own leader; the two come together only at the highest levels within the company, such as the CEO or COO level. Since the CEO or COO has diverse responsibilities, sales and marketing alignment can easily be overlooked in this structure. Silos can emerge, with a resulting climate of tension and internal competitiveness.

One way to improve the relationship between sales and marketing is to have the leaders of the two report in at a lower level—say, to a single vice president of sales and marketing, who reports to the CEO or COO. In such a structure, the vice president of sales and marketing is accountable for making sure that sales and marketing are on the same page.

Cross-Functional Teams. Cross-functional teams composed of people from both sales and marketing can help improve the alignment of the two. These teams can have joint responsibility for specific issues, such as incentive compensation, market segmentation, product positioning, or customer messaging. When they work together, sellers and marketers often develop empathy for one another and create better outcomes for the company because the design process incorporates a wider range of views.

Team members grow as they develop a more complete understanding of the entire sales and marketing organization. When they make decisions jointly, team members feel a sense of ownership of their decisions and become stronger champions of those decisions.

Sales and Marketing People Team Up at a Software Company to Develop More Effective Sales Collateral

When software company Mozart Systems was challenged by an aggressive new competitor, the company's marketing people and salespeople collaborated to create powerful sales collateral that would allow the company to compete more effectively. The marketing manager in charge of the project recognized that extensive involvement of the sales force in developing the collateral would ensure a result that was targeted to issues that resonated with customers, and at the same time would be enthusiastically embraced by salespeople. Marketing and sales agreed that a competitive white paper would be an effective vehicle for communication with customers. To start the process of developing the white paper, salespeople shared with marketing what they had learned about the competitor from customers. Marketing complemented this knowledge with its own research into the competitor's products. Marketing wrote an initial draft of the paper, which went through a structured evaluation process in which comments were collected from sales, the comments were discussed in joint sales–marketing meetings, and the paper was revised accordingly. The result was a powerful piece of sales collateral that the sales force was very comfortable using and that had high impact with customers.

Integrating Sales and Marketing Roles. Companies can improve the integration of sales and marketing by assigning people to roles that facilitate alignment. Some companies create an integrator role that gives a person or a team responsibility for improving the interaction between the two. Some integrators help to facilitate communications from salespeople to marketers and vice versa, but do not have the authority to affect the way in which work is done. Other integrators are given responsibility for specific joint sales–marketing projects, such as the development of sales forecasts or the design of a new customer targeting approach. Many companies have established downstream marketing roles—for example, field market managers have responsibility for performing downstream marketing activities in a specific sales region or for a particular market segment.

Siebel Creates an Organizational Structure That Supports Sales and Marketing Alignment

Siebel Systems Inc. (acquired by Oracle Corporation in 2005) is a software company that develops and sells CRM applications. The company realized that marketing and sales were inseparable and designed its sales and marketing organizations with this in mind. Siebel's marketing organization had Corporate Marketing and Field Marketing teams. Corporate Marketing was responsible for product branding, trade shows, and public relations. Field Marketing was responsible for generating product demand and leads. Field Marketing people were located in the field and worked directly with the local sales organization to design and implement programs, ensuring that the field-focused marketing programs were delivering the results desired by the sales force. Marketing people and salespeople were able to work together to develop, implement, evaluate, and modify programs.

Process/System Solutions

Process/system solutions for aligning sales and marketing define business *processes* that specify the goals, steps, and participants required to address specific sales and marketing issues. Defining processes clarifies responsibilities and specifies the communication flows between sales and marketing that need to occur if the company is to make good decisions and design the best possible customer solutions.

Well-defined business processes encourage cooperation and effective communication between sales and marketing, which result in better decisions. Figure 19-6 shows the process that a business-to-business (B2B) company uses to create alignment between sales and marketing as the company continuously refines its sales strategy in response to ongoing changes in customer needs. Marketing takes the lead role in some of the activities, while sales takes the lead role in others. The

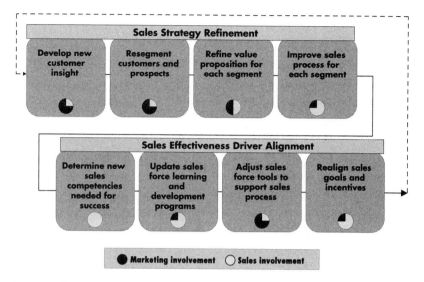

Figure 19-6. An example of how a B2B company continually revised its sales strategy through a business process that required a joint effort between sales and marketing

cooperation of sales and marketing people throughout the process is a key element of the successful implementation of ongoing sales strategy changes.

Sales and Marketing Processes Align Around the Customer

A pharmaceutical company encourages an effective sales–marketing alignment by defining a common goal for sales and marketing: to satisfy the customer. One week every year is designated as "customer week," during which all marketing people are required to accompany salespeople on customer visits. By aligning the sales and marketing organizations around the company's sales process, the company ensures that the two departments operate from a common framework and use a common language.

Information systems support the sales and marketing processes, making them more efficient and effective. Some such systems are:

- CRM systems that manage customer databases and strengthen sales processes
- Tools for product configuration, customer solution development, and pricing
- Knowledge management systems that facilitate the sharing of insights (see Chapter 8)
- Living documents that are continuously updated for sales and marketing projects

At the center of customer relationship coordination in many companies are CRM systems, which include a variety of components, such as tools for managing the sales pipeline, software that helps salespeople configure products for customers, and performance dashboards that show salespeople how they can improve. CRM systems ensure an integrated view of company-customer interactions, so that if multiple salespeople or marketers interact with a customer, no one in the company is blindsided by what someone else may have said, done, or promised.

D. A. Stuart's Technology-Driven Process Improves Communication Between Sales and Marketing

---

D. A. Stuart, a worldwide leader in the production of lubricants for the metalworking industry, developed a process to provide salespeople with easy access to the most recent company marketing information. A company intranet keeps the D. A. Stuart sales force up to date. Details about marketing activities—the updating of collateral, the mailing of promotional materials to specific customers or prospects, modifications to the firm's web site, the uncovering of useful competitive information—are posted on the intranet, which salespeople can access from anywhere, making the most recent marketing information readily accessible. Both marketing personnel and salespeople benefit from this process. Marketing sees its work communicated to the sales force immediately so that it can be put to use. Salespeople are never surprised by marketing activities and can leverage that work as appropriate.

Should Reward Systems Be Used to Align Sales and Marketing? Some companies use incentives to try to get sales and marketing to work together effectively. These companies tie rewards and recognition for sales and marketing team members to achievement on common performance metrics. The rationale behind this approach is that metrics and rewards drive action. Using metrics such as customer satisfaction and company financial success provides incentives for sales and marketing to work together to achieve results on these dimensions. Despite the apparent logic of this rationale, there are several reasons why incentive solutions should not be used as a primary mechanism for aligning sales and marketing.

- Sales and marketing jobs are different in terms of the activities they require, the intermediate outcomes they seek, and their time frames. Both jobs are necessary, and people should be rewarded for doing their jobs and for the results they achieve. However, it is difficult to define good, common, measurable metrics on which both sales and marketing have a direct impact.

- Some aspects of sales and marketing jobs are easier to measure than others. Placing emphasis on the measurable dimensions that only the sales force can affect, for example, may underemphasize the important work that is done by marketing, and vice versa.

- Sales and marketing people are usually paid differently. Salespeople often earn considerable variable pay, which rewards short-term sales. Marketing people typically earn a salary and an annual bonus that reflects company performance and the achievement of annual job objectives.

- A little tension between sales and marketing is healthy. If rewards for the two teams are completely aligned, this commonality may jeopardize the beneficial tension. Both sales and marketing need to focus on what they need to accomplish individually.

Sales and marketing reward systems should not clash, but neither should they be the basis for alignment. Better than incentives for aligning sales and marketing are the right people embracing the right culture with appropriate controls through structure and company processes and systems.

Addressing Sales and Marketing Tensions: Two Examples

Here, we share two examples of how companies have used structure and process/system solutions to address specific sales and marketing alignment challenges.

Improving Lead Generation, Customer and Prospect Selection, and Resource Allocation

Deciding which customers and prospects the sales force should spend time with is an important sales effectiveness issue and a common source of conflict between sales and marketing. Recall the disagreement that existed at the vision products company mentioned earlier in this chapter:

Marketing View	Sales View
Marketing has done extensive research to identify the best criteria for predicting which customers and prospects have the greatest profit potential. It wants sales to use these criteria to target better, so that less time is wasted with accounts that are unlikely to generate strong incremental future revenues.	Sales argues that while marketing's criteria may look good on paper, they do not work in practice. Many of the leads that marketing generates are just not that good. Many of the accounts that sales spends time with have been customers for years and represent the core of the business.

Figure 19-7 shows a simplified version of the process that one company uses to align sales and marketing for more effective lead generation. Marketing is responsible for managing leads from multiple sources, for qualifying them with the help of telesales personnel, and for passing qualified leads on to the field sales force. Field salespeople contact qualified prospects and are responsible for converting leads and

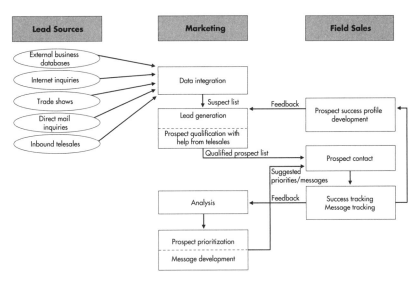

Figure 19-7. The roles of sales and marketing in the lead generation process at one company

tracking success. A cross-functional team composed of sales and marketing people facilitates the capture of data on the quality of leads, the effectiveness of marketing's suggested messages, and the reliability of the prospect success profiles. Marketing analyzes the data, updates the business rules for qualifying and prioritizing prospects, and enhances the recommended messages appropriately. A clearly delineated process helps this company's sales and marketing departments to work together to convert leads and to continuously improve the lead generation process.

Improving Lead Generation at Siebel Systems

A leader in the enterprise CRM market, Siebel Systems focused its initial marketing efforts on branding and on educating prospective customers. As the market matured, Siebel became more systematic in its process for generating demand, seeking to expand the sales pipeline and to close more deals. To that end, Siebel established a specific role for transferring leads from marketing to sales. After experimenting with outsourcing this responsibility, Siebel decided to keep it in-house in order to tightly control the quality of the people and the process. The company charged its Sales Development organization with qualifying prospects, gathering and validating account and contact information, and creating opportunities for the field sales organization, using both inbound responses generated by marketing campaigns and outbound outreach efforts to targeted accounts. Well-defined processes for generating leads and handing those leads off to sales made this model successful at Siebel. This success was enhanced by:

Unified goals and measurement. The company defined goals and measured against them. There were goals for the size of the pipeline (three times the size of sales targets for the next quarter), the number of leads that should be generated by marketing campaigns, the cost per opportunity, the number of accurate and relevant senior contacts acquired and maintained at the top 2,000 major accounts worldwide, and the number of new accounts penetrated in each region.

Defined criteria for qualifying leads. While Sales Development people did not use guided scripts, they did use well-defined criteria for qualifying prospects.

Follow-up and feedback. New leads qualified by Sales Development had to be followed up by sales within ten business days. At that point, sales could either accept ownership of the lead or reject it. For any lead it rejected, sales needed to provide feedback based on a standard set of rejection criteria, which helped marketing analyze the results of its lead generation activities relative to its goals.

Tools that enable transfer of ownership of leads from marketing to sales and that provide built-in performance measurements. Siebel used its own CRM system to manage the lead generation process. Dashboards provided real-time measurement of key operational metrics (such as response rates for the various marketing programs and lead follow-up time) and financial metrics (such as the cost to generate and realize an opportunity).

Establishing the Right Price

Pricing is a critical issue that requires collaboration between sales and marketing. Recall the disagreement that existed at the office products company mentioned earlier in this chapter:

Marketing View	Sales View
Marketing has established a price, based on thorough analysis of the value that customers derive from the company's products, as well as analysis of competitive pricing. Marketing argues that sales should hold this price—this will increase profitability and help to maintain the brand's premium image.	Sales feels that the price is too high and routinely lobbies for deeper customer discounts. Sales argues that the company will lose sales if discounts are not offered, and that discounting is necessary to build long-term customer relationships.

Figure 19-8 shows the process one company uses to establish and implement the right pricing strategy for different customer segments. Marketing is responsible for developing a pricing strategy based on a historical and prospective assessment of customers, competitors, and business value. Salespeople, who are responsible for implementing the pricing strategy with their customers, have some leeway to provide discounts up to a certain level, which depends on the customer segment and the customer's situation. Larger discounts require the approval of sales managers, and even larger discounts require marketing's approval. Sales managers act as a key link between salespeople and marketing, helping to ensure that pricing strategies stay aligned with customer needs. A clearly delineated process helps this company's sales and marketing departments to work together to implement a pricing strategy that balances the need for good margins with a desire not to lose sales to competitors.

Achieving Better Sales and Marketing Alignment in Two Common Business Environments

Sales-Driven Organizations

Many business-to-business companies have historically been highly sales-driven. Personal selling and account management are a major focus of sales-driven organizations. Sales success is attributed largely to differentiated products, to the personal relationships that salespeople

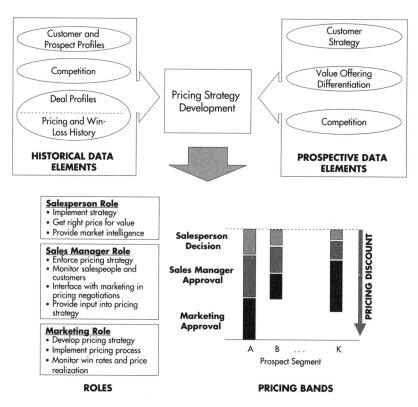

Figure 19-8. The role of salespeople, sales managers, and marketing in the pricing process at one company

have with customers, and to the value that the sales force delivers to customers. Examples of sales-driven companies include many technology, medical, insurance, and distribution companies, and direct sales organizations such as Avon. Marketing at sales-driven companies is seen as a sales support function and focuses primarily on downstream marketing activities that directly support the sales force. There is less focus on upstream marketing activities, such as understanding customer needs, market segmentation, and branding.

Sales and Marketing Roles at Medline

Medline is a large manufacturer and distributor of medical supplies to hospitals, nursing homes, and home-health-care agencies. The company has over 700 salespeople who sell more than 100,000 medical products and services. The company's marketing team is organized by product group, each with its own product manager. Since the product line is so diverse, the sales force counts on the product managers to supply it with up-to-date product information. The product managers, who have goals that they need to achieve, attempt to get the sales force's attention through promotional materials and deals. "Sales runs the show," says one product manager. "I spend 25 percent of my time in the field helping salespeople be successful with my products. I help out with big deals because I can bring product expertise. I succeed when the sales force succeeds."

Poster Seen in the Marketing Department of a Sales-Driven Company in Spain

The job of sales is to take care of the customer. The job of marketing is to take care of sales.

Many sales-driven companies are now seeking a competitive advantage by bolstering their upstream marketing capabilities. For example, GE's "Commercial Excellence" commitment (see Chapter 20) is helping the formerly sales-driven company achieve greater organic revenue growth through increased emphasis on upstream marketing activities in the customer connection process. Sales and marketing leaders from many companies have attended educational programs designed around marketing concepts hosted by top business schools, such as the Kellogg School of Management. A goal of these programs is to help companies become more marketing-focused.

Creating balance between sales and marketing in sales-driven organizations requires an increased role for marketing. It is not easy to make such a transition, as sales has to cede some of its power to marketing. In a sales-driven company, marketing and sales both see the role of marketing as being to support sales. In a balanced company, there are clear, separate responsibilities for sales and marketing as well as joint ones. Both process and structure solutions are frequently needed to facilitate the transition of a sales-driven company to a more balanced, sales–marketing-driven company.

Product- and Sales-Driven IBM Becomes More Market-Driven

Once the dominant player in the computer industry, IBM lost a record $5 billion in 1992, as the company continued to rely on mainframes while the market was moving into more disaggregated computing. A new CEO from outside the company, Louis Gerstner, arrived on April Fool's Day in 1993 and was faced with an existing plan to break up the company into its product divisions. After spending time with key customers to understand their evolving needs, Gerstner abandoned the plan to break up the company, recognizing that IBM's product and process breadth could bring value to customers who were struggling to tie together disparate systems across multiple functions, countries, and suppliers. Periodic restructurings of IBM's sales and marketing organizations have moved IBM along the path from being a product- and sales-driven company to becoming a market-driven company. Recurring themes include:

- Know the customer's business, and then differentiate IBM from the competition by providing total solutions, not simply selling products. IBM Global Services—a group that provides consulting, custom programming, and systems integration services and that accounted for 40 percent of 2007 revenues—is a focal point of IBM's total solutions value proposition.

- Segment customers and potential customers more finely, and deliver messages, proposals, and information targeted to meet their specific needs.

- Consider the sales–marketing function as a process, similar to manufacturing. Map this process to uncover wasted steps, and exploit technology to make people more productive.

   IBM's current success is credited to this focus on customer needs and solutions.

Sales-Driven Financial Services Company Establishes a New Marketing Role to Improve Customer Focus

---

The sales force at a financial services company sold dozens of different investment products to individuals. The company's product managers competed for the sales force's time by running sales campaigns for specific investment products. Salespeople received so many details from product managers about the various sales campaigns that they became overwhelmed with information. To help the sales force sift through the information and make good decisions about which products to offer customers, the company created several market segment manager positions to complement the efforts of product managers. Market segment managers were responsible for recommending the best product offerings for specific market segments, such as families with young children or people nearing retirement. Segment managers helped salespeople find the best offerings for their customers, and also freed up more of their time for selling.

Multitier Markets

Sales and marketing collaboration becomes critical in multitier distribution markets. For example, many consumer goods markets are multitiered. Procter & Gamble sells its consumer packaged goods through food, drug, and mass merchandise retailers (the customer), but the ultimate end user is someone in a household (the consumer). Similarly, GE sells appliances through retail stores such as Home Depot (the customer) to the ultimate user of the product (a consumer). Sellers of group insurance face an even more complex multitier distribution system. Salespeople at insurance provider Trustmark, for example, work both with insurance brokers (a first type of customer), who assemble quotes from multiple insurance providers for companies, and also directly with companies (a second type of customer), who ultimately offer the insurance to their employees (the consumer). In multitier distribution markets, companies usually use their sales forces as the primary influence on customers (push strategy), while relying on marketing as the primary influence on consumers (pull strategy). It is especially important that sales and marketing collaborate to ensure that their efforts are not pushing and pulling in opposite directions.

As the power of retailers in consumer goods markets has increased (with large retailers such as Wal-Mart now controlling a substantial share of the business), the need for effective coordination of sales and marketing activities in these multitier distribution markets has also increased. Before the growth of large retail chains, sales and marketing at consumer goods manufacturers operated largely independently. Marketing focused on generating demand among consumers by developing brands and creating compelling product positioning and competitive differentiation in consumers' eyes. Sales activities focused on establishing partnerships with the retail trade to gain shelf space and promotional support for products, largely by convincing retailers that the company's marketing efforts were driving demand among consumers. Sales needed to know what marketing was up to so that it could convince retailers that consumers would buy the products, but the coordination required was basically a handoff of information.

Today, marketing efforts focus not only on consumers, but also on the large retailers that control a substantial share of the business. Developing and executing these retailer-focused marketing programs (see the Oral-B example) requires sales and marketing to work together much more closely to deliver value to retailers and to ensure that the experience of consumers at the retailer's site encourages them to buy.

Oral B: Focusing on Sales in a Marketing-Driven Organization

Oral-B Laboratories (which became part of Procter & Gamble in 2006) relied on alignment between sales and marketing when it launched a new toothbrush line in 1998. Marketers not only developed consumer-focused marketing programs, such as in-store displays and a $30 million advertising campaign, but also invested in crafting a two-part message for the key accounts group to use with retailers. The first part of the message focused on why consumers would want to buy the toothbrush—a traditional consumer sales pitch. The second part focused on how this high-margin, high-repeat-purchase product could benefit the retailer's bottom line. Sales and marketing had to work closely together to create the right value proposition and deliver it to retailers effectively. Today most consumer packaged goods firms have marketing programs aimed at major retailers that require substantial coordination between sales and marketing.

Structure solutions have helped companies in multitier distribution systems enhance their sales and marketing coordination. Figure 19-9 shows a potential structure for the sales and marketing organization in these types of companies. Field sales has primary responsibility for generating demand among customers, while consumer marketing has this responsibility for consumers. Strategic marketing oversees upstream marketing efforts that guide the activities of both of these groups. Field marketing supports field sales with downstream marketing activities, such as effective customer messaging and sales support tools.

Some Final Insights
Improving Sales and Marketing Alignment Starts with Identifying Sources of Tension

Solving any type of sales and marketing tension requires determining the root cause of the stresses. For example, suppose that sales and marketing disagree about which customers and prospects the sales force should spend its time with. This tension can come about because marketing does not do its job well, because sales activities are not carried out effectively, because the joint processes and systems are not working,

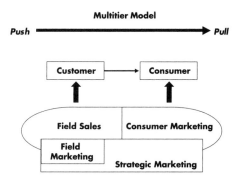

Figure 19-9. A potential structure solution for achieving sales–marketing alignment in a multitier distribution system

and/or because the information flows between sales and marketing are inadequate. Often more than one source contributes to the tension. Figure 19-10 illustrates how you can use the diagram in Figure 19-2 to develop questions that can uncover the root of a sales and marketing misalignment so that you can develop solutions.

Specialize for Bandwidth and Coordinate for Specialization

Complex markets, complex channels, and/or product complexity can place varied and extensive demands on the sales and marketing functions. Achieving customer value and intimacy requires high bandwidth, which is best handled through specialization. Specialization into sales and marketing roles improves effectiveness and drives success. High specialization, in turn, creates a need for coordination, since the two diverse groups function better when they collaborate to move together in the best direction.

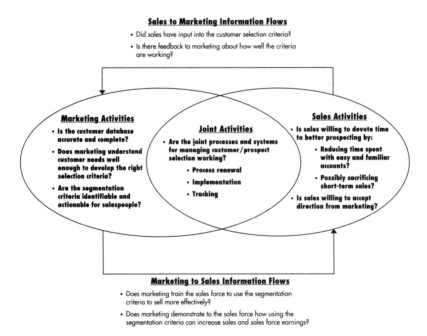

Figure 19-10. Identifying the source of a customer/prospect selection conflict between sales and marketing

Figure 9-11 shows the consequences of inappropriate specialization relative to bandwidth, and also the undesired consequences of inadequate coordination between sales and marketing.

Conditions in Which Sales–Marketing Alignment Is Essential

An effective alignment of sales and marketing can enhance effectiveness in any organization, but some situations make alignment particularly important. There are several examples of conditions where strong sales and marketing alignment can provide you with a competitive advantage:

- Considerable uncertainty in the environment makes it difficult to predict how your customer's needs are likely to evolve.

- Your company's business is concentrated among a few large customers, so that a single customer's decision to take its business elsewhere has a major impact on your company's performance.

- High competitive intensity makes it particularly important for your company to deliver superior value to your customers.

- You frequently have a need to launch new products and services in the market.

Bandwidth	Specialization	Coordination	Consequence
High	Low		This is ineffective because individuals lack sufficient skill to accomplish all the work required.
Low	High		Specialists do not have enough to do. Costs increase. Too much coordination leads to inefficiency.
High	High	Low	Information is not shared. There is competition for resources. There are independent or conflicting goals. Turf battles are likely.

Figure 19-11. The consequences of inappropriate specialization or insufficient coordination between sales and marketing

CHAPTER 20

The GE Story: Improving Sales Force Effectiveness Across Businesses

n the opening chapter of this book, we suggest that practically every company has the opportunity to improve the effectiveness of its sales force. Improvement is possible when:

- Companies respond effectively to *events* originating outside the Sales System. They react to opportunities and concerns brought about by changes in customer needs, competitors, the environment, and company strategies. They take timely and appropriate steps to realize opportunities and correct concerns, putting them in a better position to grow faster than their competitors.

- Companies constantly look for ways to make their sales organizations better, even when no event that requires change has occurred. They engage in ongoing *effectiveness hunts*, seeking constant improvement within the Sales System.

Many companies with large sales forces have initiated cross-divisional and worldwide programs to enhance their effectiveness. While these initiatives have not been uniformly successful, many of the successes have had a dramatic bottom-line impact.

GE is an excellent example of a company that has had considerable success in implementing a cross-organizational initiative aimed at enhancing the global effectiveness of its sales forces. Drawing on two of GE's traditional strengths—a process orientation and an ability to develop and implement management ideas—the company has made substantial investments in enhancing global sales force effectiveness, beginning in 2006. Just two years later, benefits from this investment had already been realized in all six of GE's major businesses and on six continents.

In this chapter, we describe why GE decided to invest in sales force effectiveness, how it is executing a successful plan for making global effectiveness improvements, and the impact that these improvements have had on GE's business.

> "That business continually seeks ways to get closer to customers and markets is not new, nor is it easy. At GE, we recognize that developing the best sales and marketing teams is a critical and ongoing process. Our efforts are focused on giving commercial teams the strategic frameworks and how-to tools that help them better target customer potential and align incentives. Our commercial excellence programs have to be easily translated, repeated, and scaled to be successful, especially in a company the size and dimensions of GE."
>
> Beth Comstock,
> Chief Marketing Officer, March 2008

Why GE Is Investing in Sales Force Effectiveness
GE's History of Innovation
GE is a diversified technology, media, and financial services company focused on solving some of the world's toughest problems. With products and services ranging from aircraft engines, power generation, water processing, and security technology to medical imaging, business and consumer financing, media content, and industrial products, GE serves customers in more than 100 countries and employs more than 300,000 people worldwide.

GE's financial results demonstrate the company's ability to deliver. Between 2003 and 2007, GE generated double-digit earnings and revenue growth ($173 billion in revenues and $22.5 billion of earnings in 2007). In 2007, GE achieved organic growth of two to three times GDP growth for the third consecutive year.

GE traces its beginnings back to Thomas A. Edison, who established Edison Electric Light Company in 1878. In 1892, a merger of Edison General Electric Company and Thomson-Houston Electric Company created General Electric Company. Known for its long history of technological innovation, GE today employs more than 35,000 technologists, approximately 3,000 of whom work in the company's global research center, which is dedicated to developing innovative technology for all of GE's businesses. In 2007 alone, GE research resulted in approximately 1,000 new patents.

In addition to its rich history of engineering excellence, GE has long taken management innovation seriously. As early as the 1970s under the leadership of CEO Reginald H. Jones, GE was developing innovative management ideas, such as the GE business strength–industry attractiveness matrix. Under the leadership of Jack Welch, CEO and chairman of GE from 1981 through 2001, GE saw great growth and expansion. Welch's no-nonsense leadership style gave him a reputation for being hard but also fair when making business decisions. Welch streamlined operations, acquired new businesses, and ensured that each GE business was one of the best in its field. He pushed GE business leaders to make their units more productive, eradicate inefficiency, and dismantle bureaucracy. Under Welch's leadership, GE's revenues grew dramatically. At the same time, GE was transformed into a process-driven organization with strict bottom-line discipline, making it one of the most valuable companies in the world.

A Commitment to Growth Brings a Need for Commercial Excellence

In September 2001, Jeffrey Immelt succeeded Welch as chairman and CEO of GE. In a world stunned by the events of September 11, 2001, Immelt's challenge was to take the fine-tuned productivity machine that GE had become and continue moving it forward. He set ambitious goals for sustaining organic growth, with the aim of growing existing

GE businesses organically two to three times faster than the increase in world GDP. Achieving this would require GE to develop a more global, diverse, and customer-driven culture.

Immelt's plan had six components (see "Growth as a Process" in Figure 20-1), one of which was a commitment to "commercial excellence." Achieving commercial excellence required putting talented sales and marketing leadership in place and developing a world-class sales and marketing organization. Building on GE's strength as a process-driven organization, the company set out to create consistent processes and methodologies for sales and marketing decision making that would enable the company to draw new revenue streams from existing businesses.

"For 22 years I sat around this company saying if we could ever be as good at growth as we were at operations, what an incredible company this would be. If we could ever add to the process discipline, financial rigor, the strong-willed leadership team, the leadership engine, if we could ever be as good with customers and with marketing and with innovation as we are

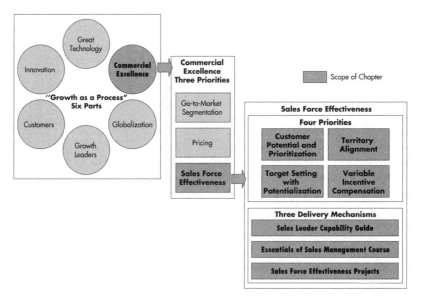

Figure 20-1. The role of sales force effectiveness in GE's plan to achieve organic growth

with grinding numbers and processes and controllership and risk management, there's nothing stopping this company."

Jeff Immelt,
CEO, September 2004

A look around at the various GE businesses led to an interesting insight. Those that had been most successful at driving organic growth over the previous several years were those that had been effective at utilizing data, analyses, processes, and tools to help with sales force decision making. Consequently, GE's commitment to commercial excellence would require bringing a more scientific approach to sales and marketing decision making and applying that approach more consistently across businesses.

Analysis Helps GE's U.S. Equipment Financing Unit Find New Customers

---

GE's U.S. Equipment Financing organization is an excellent example of a GE business that had been successful at creating organic growth by applying a more scientific approach to sales and marketing decision making. Under the direction of president Mike Pilot, the business implemented a data-driven methodology for segmenting customers. After compiling a database of all available customer and potential customer data, Mike's group used regression analysis to identify the six criteria that are the best predictors of customer potential. Prospects were assigned a potential value based on these six criteria. This analysis gave salespeople a focus on 10,000 new high-priority prospective customers. Targeting these customers helped the division sell $300 million in new business (10 percent organic growth) in 2005 in a market that was once believed to be maturing.

Bringing Science to Sales and Marketing

By the start of 2006, several pieces for building consensus around a unified mission of commercial excellence at GE were in place. According to Kevin Decker, director of commercial excellence, GE had:

- Strong leadership from CEO Jeff Immelt, who had a vision and the conviction to make it a reality.
- A definite need that was felt by many GE businesses. Several businesses were looking for help in revamping their variable sales incentive compensation plans and identifying customer potential in their markets.
- Several leading academics and consultants who were available to advise and work with GE sales and marketing leaders.
- An organization rooted in science and process, with the operational resources to make the mission of commercial excellence a reality.

With the hiring of Dan Henson as chief marketing officer in January 2006, the final piece needed to get GE's commercial excellence initiative up and running was in place. Dan believed that technical depth and focus were needed to create the discipline and rigor required for success, and he chose three initial areas of focus (see "Commercial Excellence— Three Priorities" in Figure 20-1). He appointed a global director at the corporate level to oversee each of the three areas: go-to-market segmentation, pricing, and sales force effectiveness (SFE).

The three directors were charged with bringing commercial excellence to their respective areas. They would do it by:

- Developing a consistent set of frameworks, models, capabilities, and best practices to be used by all GE businesses
- Propagating best practices across the GE portfolio of businesses through training and education
- Serving as a resource for GE businesses by providing wisdom, experience, and project team members who could help businesses execute the frameworks
- Continually improving the frameworks, models, and approaches in order to ensure ongoing progress in global commercial excellence

A Focus on Sales Force Effectiveness Improvement

To implement the sales force effectiveness component of the commercial excellence vision (see "Sales Force Effectiveness" in Figure 20-1), the company appointed Kevin Decker as director of commercial excellence, with responsibility for global sales force effectiveness. Kevin had spent the previous seven years in the finance leadership track at GE, which provided excellent preparation for the process rigor, critical thinking, and leadership that his new role would require. Kevin's team had an ambitious mission: to develop and continually enhance frameworks and best practices for improving sales force effectiveness while propagating the ideas across all the GE businesses and providing resources to help the businesses turn the ideas into reality.

> "We're constantly revising our methods using Sales Force Effectiveness to further the company's 'Growth as a Process' strategy. By combining corporatewide frameworks with our experience working with individual GE businesses, we're able to blend high-level planning with on-the-ground execution."

> Kevin Decker,
> Director of Commercial Excellence, March 2008

The rest of this chapter focuses on how this global sales force effectiveness initiative has been implemented at GE and the impact it has had on the business in its first two years.

Sales Force Effectiveness Implementation Plan

To provide focus for GE's global sales force effectiveness (SFE) effort, a framework was established defining four SFE priorities and three delivery mechanisms that could make them live (see "Sales Force Effectiveness" in Figure 20-1):

- Four sales force effectiveness priorities. Customer potential and prioritization, territory alignment, target setting, and variable incentive compensation were selected as initial priorities that could benefit from a centralized resource and could have a big impact on GE's businesses.
- Three delivery mechanisms. The company developed a Sales Leader Capability Guide, a course in Essentials of Sales Management, and plans for executing projects in the four SFE priority areas

to encourage the effectiveness ideas to take root in the businesses and to ensure that the ideas were implemented to produce tangible business results.

An implementation plan was built around the philosophy that effective change management requires methodical rigor. By providing carefully thought-out frameworks with steps broken down into executable pieces, along with the necessary resources and support, the global SFE initiative allows GE businesses to embrace the new approaches and put them to work quickly to start enhancing sales force effectiveness.

Four Sales Force Effectiveness Priorities

The four SFE areas selected as initial priorities for GE go hand in hand, as one area flows logically into the next. The goals of each SFE priority are summarized in Figure 20-2.

For each of the four SFE priorities, GE has established frameworks, tools, and best practices to be used as a guide by all GE businesses. These approaches have been synthesized from what the best businesses had been doing already, as well as from the approaches suggested by leading academics and consultants from outside GE. The approaches, documented in best practices manuals, are continually enhanced and improved as new learning takes place. In the first two

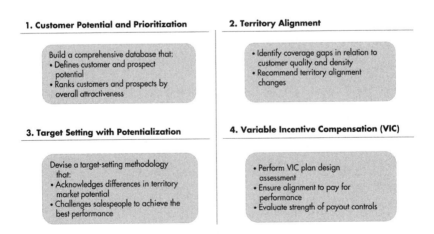

Figure 20-2. Goals of the four SFE priorities at GE

years of the initiative, more than 50 people within GE contributed to refining the frameworks as a result of their learning on projects.

Customer Potential and Prioritization. A logical first step for enhancing sales force effectiveness is to understand market potential—the backbone of GE's four SFE areas. If salespeople know the potential of their customers and prospects, they can allocate their time more effectively. Market potential is also necessary for designing good sales territories, setting fair sales targets, and designing variable incentive compensation programs that pay for performance.

Customer potential and prioritization requires building a comprehensive database that defines customer and prospect potential and then ranking customers and prospects according to their overall attractiveness to the company. The GE framework for achieving this includes three main steps:

1. Establishing a customer database. Creating a clean customer database can be a considerable challenge, especially when numerous internal and external data sources need to be matched up and verified. Thorough and disciplined processes facilitate successful completion of this step.

2. Calculating customer potential. Algorithms and proxies can be established for assigning a potential dollar value to every customer and prospect, based on account profile information. The link between account profiles (for example, account size and industry) and potential can be based on managerial input and/or on analytics. Several GE businesses have used regression techniques to determine which profile characteristics are the strongest drivers of account potential.

3. Prioritizing the customers and prospects. The profile characteristics that drive sales success make up a list of key measurable attributes of customers and prospects that determine their potential to GE. Salespeople who understand these attributes can be more strategic in how they allocate their time, ensuring an appropriate focus on those customers and prospects with whom there is a high likelihood of sales success.

We present approaches for developing measures of customer potential in Chapter 11 of this book.

Territory Alignment. Territory alignment has an impact on a sales organization's performance by influencing the efficiency of customer coverage and by affecting salespeople's opportunity to create sales. The goal of territory alignment at GE is to identify coverage gaps by comparing customer workload, potential, and density across territories and to recommend territory alignment changes that can enhance sales force effectiveness. The GE framework for accomplishing territory alignment includes three main steps:

1. Evaluating account quality. Customer potential is an important measure of account quality, and therefore is a critical input into the territory alignment process.
2. Evaluating account density. GE integrates mapping tools with account potential data to assist in this evaluation.
3. Deploying effectively and efficiently. Using the mapping and evaluation tools, changes in territory alignments can be easily evaluated and implemented.

We discuss approaches for designing sales territories that match sales effort to market opportunity in Chapter 6.

Target Setting with Potentialization. Territory sales or profit targets that acknowledge differences in territory potential help a sales organization to better identify performance variation across salespeople and create variable incentive compensation plans that pay for performance. The goal of target setting with potentialization at GE is to determine territory sales targets based on the best-performing salespeople in each market size category. The GE framework for accomplishing this includes three main steps:

1. Building the frontier curve analysis. In several chapters of this book, beginning in Chapter 2, we describe the Performance Frontier approach for identifying top-performing salespeople. The frontier

curve shows the sales or profit performance that is possible for every level of territory market potential.

2. **Setting targets based on the frontier.** Territory targets should challenge all salespeople to improve their performance by moving toward the performance level achieved by the best performers in the company—those who are on the performance frontier.

3. **Determining reduction factors.** Some targets may need to be adjusted downward as a result of individual territory circumstances that justify performance below the frontier level. For example, a target might be reduced for a new salesperson or for a salesperson in a territory that is affected by unfavorable local conditions.

We present approaches for setting fair, realistic, and motivational sales force goals and targets, including the Performance Frontier approach used by GE, in Chapter 13 of this book.

Variable Incentive Compensation. Variable incentive compensation plans that pay for performance and create a clear linkage between activity and income are likely to motivate the highest levels of sales force effort. The SFE initiative aimed at variable incentive compensation at GE involves performing an assessment of the variable incentive compensation plan design to ensure that the plan pays for performance, evaluating the strength of payout controls, and building a communication plan for implementing successful plan changes. The GE framework includes several guiding principles for plan design:

- Plans should motivate high levels of sales force achievement by linking payouts to challenging goals or hurdles, by using accelerators to motivate peak performance beyond the hurdles, and by removing systemic caps, leaving deal caps only when necessary.
- Plans should align with business goals and strategies.
- Plans should include no more than three or four metrics to keep sales force attention focused on what is most important.
- Plans should include a metric that reflects profitability.

We present approaches for using the power of variable incentive compensation to drive results in Chapter 12.

Three Sales Force Effectiveness Delivery Mechanisms

To ensure that the frameworks, tools, and best practices developed for each of the four SFE priority areas took root within GE and became well engrained into the sales culture, company leaders developed delivery mechanisms to propagate the ideas to the GE businesses. They selected three delivery mechanisms—a Sales Leader Capability Guide, a course in Essentials of Sales Management, and plans for executing projects in the four SFE priority areas—as the focus of the first phase of the effort. These delivery mechanisms helped to ensure that the global SFE initiative produced tangible results for GE businesses.

Sales Leader Capability Guide. The Sales Leader Capability Guide describes what GE expects its 5,800-plus sales managers to do. It identifies and defines the capabilities that are necessary to be successful as a GE sales manager, across the portfolio of businesses.

Before GE introduced the guide, its businesses did not have a consistent approach to managing the performance of sales managers. Every business had its own set of criteria, and many businesses had only loosely defined performance management processes. The guide provides a standard framework for communicating the capabilities necessary for GE sales managers to be successful, for identifying the strengths and weaknesses of sales managers, and for locating appropriate sales manager development opportunities.

Figure 20-3 shows the 31 sales manager capabilities that the guide defines, organized into three main categories: tools and technical skills, process skills, and leadership skills. Notice that the four SFE priority areas match the tools and technical skills that sales managers need in order to manage their teams successfully.

To develop the guide, Kevin Decker and his corporate sales force effectiveness team worked with sales human resources leaders from a wide range of GE businesses. The guide was vetted through interviews and focus groups with over 100 senior sales leaders from across the portfolio of GE businesses and through input from senior company officers.

Sales Leader Capability Guide

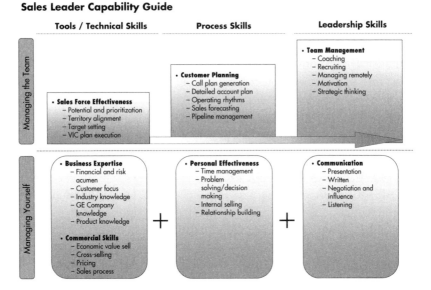

Figure 20-3. The organization of GE's Sales Leader Capability Guide

The guide includes an online assessment tool that allows an individual sales manager and that person's own manager to assess strengths and gaps in the various sales management capabilities. A consistent five-point rating scale, with clear definitions of what is expected at each capability level, helps to guide an objective and consistent performance management process. Capabilities are linked online to a number of learning opportunities, including applicable articles, white papers, books, seminars, internal and external courses, video clips, and Webinars. All sales managers have access to this information and are encouraged to utilize these learning tools to enhance their development.

> "I can start to use the guide immediately for my branch managers. It enables very specific identification of development needs and helps in feedback discussions."
>
> A GE Money Sales Leader

Education: Essentials of Sales Management. Another delivery mechanism used to propagate sales force effectiveness throughout GE is sales management training. The company makes available a course titled Essentials of Sales Management and encourages all GE sales managers to take it, with the intent of exposing new managers to the course as quickly as possible. The course teaches managers ways in which to execute the most critical of the capabilities included in the Sales Leader Capability Guide. The training provides a strong foundation for successful sales management that is heavily rooted in improving sales force effectiveness.

Before the global SFE initiative, GE did not have a corporate-sponsored or consistent sales manager training course. While some businesses provided training for sales managers, that training was mostly focused on effective coaching techniques; education on how to implement data-driven processes with analytical rigor to improve sales force effectiveness was not widely available within GE.

The corporate sales force effectiveness team designed the course and delivers it. Its three-day agenda, shown in Figure 20-4, incorporates best practices in sales management training, identified by looking across GE businesses as well as at outside training and education programs. The first day of the class is devoted to the four priority SFE areas and includes many of the concepts described in earlier chapters of this book. Implementation frameworks for each area are discussed, and examples of successful projects from within GE are provided. The first

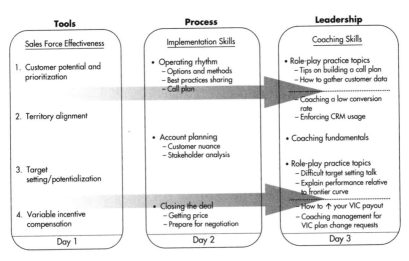

Figure 20-4. Agenda for GE Essentials of Sales Management course

day culminates with a case study that allows managers to try their hand at analyzing and revamping a sales force using the GE sales force effectiveness framework.

The second day of the training focuses on how to manage sales processes successfully for improved customer relationships and higher sales and profits. The final day addresses sales management leadership skills, including how to coach salespeople effectively and help them use the sales force effectiveness tools.

This course has been very positively received by GE sales managers across geographies and businesses.

> "The course has helped me think critically about business potential and people in a more positive and productive way. It has also helped me learn to coach my people to grow to the furthest extent possible."
>
> A GE Water Sales Leader

The Essentials of Sales Management course works together with the Sales Leader Capability Guide to improve and enhance the capabilities of GE's sales management and leadership team. These delivery mechanisms are excellent examples of the sales management and development support tools that are described in Chapter 10 of this book.

Sales Force Effectiveness Projects. The final sales force effectiveness delivery mechanism is the execution of projects within GE businesses. Projects focus on the four priority SFE areas: customer potential and prioritization, territory alignment, target setting with potentialization, and variable incentive compensation. Through these projects, information that is communicated through the training course and in the Sales Leader Capability Guide is applied tactically in the businesses, typically creating significant tangible gains in sales force effectiveness.

Sales force effectiveness is so important to GE that completing a project in this area has become a requirement for graduation from the company's prestigious Experienced Commercial Leadership Program (ECLP), a rotation-based management training program for future GE marketing, sales, and business leaders. A typical SFE project team includes not only people from the business conducting the project, but also one or more ECLP candidates, who bring analytical and business skills to the table. Having a pool of several hundred ECLP candidates greatly expands GE's capacity to complete SFE projects. The corporate sales force effectiveness team mentors, guides, and shares companywide frameworks, tools, and best practices with the SFE project teams.

All SFE projects have a predefined set of criteria that must be achieved if a project is to be considered successful. Projects are guided by consistent frameworks that include well-defined steps, processes, and ways to gauge success. The top leaders within each business give these projects high levels of visibility and support.

Next, we describe three projects from GE's Commercial Finance business. Similar projects have been executed throughout GE worldwide and in most of GE's major businesses, including Infrastructure, Industrial, Healthcare, NBC Universal, and Consumer Finance.

Improving customer targeting and territory alignment for GE Healthcare Financial Services: Vendor and Practice Solutions team. GE Healthcare Financial Services provides capital, financial solutions, and related services for the global health-care market. The Vendor and Practice Solutions team partners with non-GE manufacturers and distributors of dental, medical, optical, and veterinary equipment (called "vendor partners") to provide financing solutions for the vendor partners' customers. The GE sales force has approximately 60 field salespeople in the United States who work directly with vendor partners' sales reps, training them in how to sell GE financing, providing financing expertise, and helping them close specific deals with their customers. An inside sales team supplements the efforts of the field salespeople.

With a goal of increasing market penetration, the sales organization conducted a sales force effectiveness project under the leadership of Dean DeStazio, sales force effectiveness manager for GE Healthcare Financial Services. The project focused on one of GE's two large dental equipment vendor partners. The project's aim was to better understand market potential at the vendor partner's customer level so that the market potential of each of the vendor partner's sales reps could be evaluated. This would allow the GE sales team to be more strategic about which vendor partner sales reps it spent time with, and would also help the sales organization better align sales territories with market potential.

The project had two main phases:

- **Customer potential and prioritization.** A customer database was created, incorporating information obtained from the vendor partner on equipment sales and installations with dentists, market demographics (such as population density and number of dental practices), and GE's own sales data showing GE-funded volume. The database permitted a better evaluation of the potential of each vendor sales rep, allowing GE salespeople to see opportunities to grow their business and to identify more effective ways to spend their time. The data also helped GE identify ways to utilize inside salespeople to serve lower-potential vendor sales reps.

- **Territory alignment.** The customer potential and prioritization data were integrated with additional market demographic data and mapping tools to allow GE to evaluate territory alignments and identify coverage gaps in terms of customer quality and density. Based on this analysis, two territories were collapsed in areas where market potential was low and customers could be served more efficiently by other GE salespeople.

This project not only helped the GE Vendor and Practice Solutions team improve market penetration, but also helped the vendor partner gain a better understanding of its customers and market potential—a clear example of GE bringing commercial excellence to its customers.

Improving variable incentive compensation within GE Capital Solutions. GE Capital Solutions provides the financing that enables customers to acquire fixed assets, ranging from copiers to aircraft. With leases and loans varying in dollar volume from $10,000 to $50 million, its customers range in size from small businesses to Fortune 100 companies and span a wide variety of geographies and industries. The sales organization includes nearly 2,000 salespeople and sales managers in a variety of different roles across eight major P&L businesses.

To align with growth objectives, senior management decided that the Capital Solutions sales organization needed to be more consistent in how it measured and paid salespeople. Under the leadership of Linda Fiore, commercial excellence leader for GE Capital Solutions, and

Michael Pindell, initiatives leader for GE Capital Solutions, the organization conducted a sales force effectiveness project focused on creating variable incentive compensation plans that were more consistent across businesses. At the onset of the project, there were 165 different variable incentive compensation plans within GE Capital Solutions, and many of these plans were complex and lengthy.

The project began with the formation of a cross-functional core team that included experts from HR, Finance, Quality, and Sales. The core team worked with GE's corporate audit staff to analyze all of the existing compensation plans. The analysis helped to identify necessary overriding principles for all of Capital Solutions' incentive plans, including consistency, simplification and transparency, support with management tools, and metrics tied to targets. These principles were discussed with P&L leaders, and the guidelines shown in Figure 20-5 were agreed upon.

The guidelines were provided to all of the businesses, and each was asked to revise its variable incentive compensation plans in accordance with the new framework. Businesses presented their updated plans to Pindell's team, payout analysis was performed, and plans were revised as appropriate and approved by senior management.

The project resulted in a reduction in the number of plans from 165 to 68 and achieved approximately 90 percent compliance with the newly developed guidelines. The variable incentive compensation plans used within the GE Capital Solutions sales organization are now more focused on pay for performance and profitability.

Variable Incentive Compensation Plan Guidelines—GE Capital Solutions

- No more than 4 plan measures
- 1 measure must be profitability
- Minimum weight of 20% on any measure
- No discretionary payments
- Cross-selling incentives must be included
- Fixed pay should be decoupled from variable pay
- Variable pay hurdle rate should be less than 100% to engage participants
- Pay mix should be the same across business units for similar positions

Figure 20-5. Variable incentive compensation plan design guidelines for GE Capital Solutions

Improving customer potential and prioritization within GE Trailer Fleet Services. GE Commercial Finance, Trailer Fleet Services leases over-the-road trailers (as well as providing related fleet services) to trucking, retail, and manufacturing companies. GE's sales force has approximately 130 salespeople in the United States, Canada, and Mexico. Salespeople focus on either national or mid-market accounts and are responsible for both finding new customers and increasing business with existing customers.

In an effort to increase GE's visibility in the market and increase its market share, the sales organization conducted a sales force effectiveness project under the leadership of Yvan Giroud, sales operations leader, Trailer and Equipment Services, and Aileen Sheppard, an ECLP candidate. The ultimate goal of the project was to drive revenue growth by finding more GE customers, as well as by increasing the breadth of the offering to existing customers. Through this project, GE hoped to define customer and prospect potential so that the attractiveness of different accounts could be ranked and GE's sales efforts could be focused effectively.

The project was organized into several steps:

1. The business built a data warehouse that included customer data from several internal databases as well as data from external sources such as Dun & Bradstreet. The warehouse included profile data and historical GE sales information for more than 50,000 customers and prospects.

2. To make the data meaningful and actionable, the project team performed extensive analysis aimed at determining the best predictors of customer potential. Regression models were used to measure the relationship between 15 different customer profile variables and current GE sales. Based on the analysis, seven variables in three categories—fleet size and composition, company size, and industry—were identified as the best predictors of customer potential.

3. The team used input from the sales force to enhance and improve the results of the quantitative models. This input was particularly critical for assessing behavioral characteristics of customers, such as the likelihood of an account's pursuing leasing as an alternative to ownership.

The data helped GE to identify many new leads that were shared with the sales force through the business's lead generation system, resulting in a 33 percent increase in qualified leads after one year. The data and additional analysis were also used to redeploy several sales territories for increased efficiency and effectiveness. The effectiveness enhancements resulting from the redeployment allowed the business to grow sales productivity by 7 percent in one year and give back a budgeted $2 million for additional headcount, as business leaders were confident that the improvements would allow the sales organization to meet its growth goals without adding people.

Blending Models and Sales Force Input

While models and analytics are an important contributor to sales force effectiveness improvement at GE, communication and idea exchange between stakeholders throughout the change management process is equally important for a successful implementation. Trish Anderson, commercial excellence leader for GE Commercial Finance, says, "The model is only one part of the process. Collaboration with the sales team is essential. Salespeople's experiences contribute heavily to identifying the highest-priority customers."

How GE's Corporate Initiative Benefits GE Businesses

Just two years into the project, GE's cross-organizational initiative to enhance global sales force effectiveness has had many benefits for GE's businesses. Business leaders describe the many advantages of having global corporate support for SFE, including:

- **Strategic frameworks.** The comprehensive strategic framework developed by the corporate SFE team suggests a compelling and logical order for addressing issues and linking decisions back to business strategies.
- **Corporate voice.** Having corporate support behind SFE projects engages business leaders and facilitates decision making.

- **Experience.** Corporate SFE team members have broad exposure and are skilled at applying the frameworks and tools, enabling them to mentor and guide projects effectively.

- **Resources and tools.** The corporate SFE team has developed proven approaches and tools that individual GE businesses do not have the time or resources to develop.

- **Best practices sharing.** The corporate SFE team can identify and share best practices across businesses worldwide, offering a unique and valuable perspective for enhancing sales force effectiveness across the portfolio.

GE's global sales force effectiveness initiative has succeeded for many reasons. The company has backed up its promise to increase sales force effectiveness by committing the resources needed to make the

Issue	What to Do	What to Avoid
Objectives	Focus on a specific goal, such as enhancing a particular product's sales performance or improving a small set of sales effectiveness drivers, such as targeting and incentives.	Avoid trying to improve too many sales effectiveness drivers without a clear business objective. With too many initiatives, there is no focus, and the expertise needed to succeed is difficult to assemble.
Scope	Is it a sales force issue? Sometimes the significant payoff lies in coordinating sales with other departments, such as marketing. If trying to enhance product success, look across company functions. If trying to enhance a specific sales effectiveness driver such as hiring, focus within a function.	Avoid a scope that is not linked to the business goal. Business goals come first; scope and process can only follow, not lead.
People resources	Use local and global experts from within or outside the company. With internal resources, plan a career path so that expertise does not exit just as it is developed. With external help, either plan for a burst of effort, or forge a partnership with a clear working relationship.	Avoid using resources, internal or external, that bring energy but little expertise. Smart people without relevant experience frequently come up with an intuitive, but wrong answer. Use wise people to guide smart ones.
Measures and dashboards	Use relevant and useful measures at all levels. Match the granularity of the information on the dashboard to the person who sees it, and who can act on the information.	Avoid comparative measures that have no cross-division or cross-country comparison value, such as sales per rep or percent of incentive at risk. Also avoid too much granularity on global dashboards, as they only invite headquarters people to second-guess division or country actions and initiatives.
Forcing versus facilitating	Empower division or country organizations to seek the best ideas from other divisions or countries, and provide mechanisms to disseminate good ideas.	Do not enforce adherence to productivity enhancement rules across divisions or countries. No single answer fits all situations, and only solutions that a division or country believes in will be implemented with success.
Cross-divisional and multicountry forums	Use regional or global forums on difficult but focused issues of broad interest, such as how to launch new products while growing current products.	Avoid broad forums on broad issues. These lead to complaints of low value, and significant distraction from productive activities. Process-heavy and outcome-light initiatives drain organizational energy and motivation.
Sales effectiveness czar	Done well, this is a success factor. Treat divisions and countries as customers, and create an environment where they want your assistance.	Done poorly, this can be a key cause of disaster. Do not act as if division and country personnel are resources that you control.
Global sales effectiveness initiatives	Begin with great care and learn from others' successes and failures.	Do not jump in with untested preconceptions. Over 70 percent of such initiatives are value-draining and not value-adding, and a majority of them peter out as well.

Figure 20-6. What to do and what to avoid with cross-organizational sales force effectiveness initiatives

promise a reality. Under the leadership of Kevin Decker, the company has developed the capabilities and established the frameworks necessary to bring the needed rigor to the SFE enhancement process. Delivery mechanisms are in place, allowing GE businesses around the world to link successfully with the best practices and resources of the corporate SFE team. Sales force effectiveness is an important element of GE's commitment to commercial excellence and its quest for continued organic growth.

Authors' Advisory

The authors have participated in global and cross-country sales force effectiveness initiatives with many companies. Figure 20-6 shares the insights of our observations about what works well and what does not work when implementing cross-organizational sales force effectiveness initiatives.

Index

477